GOOD

REASONING

MATTERS!

GOOD
REASONING
MATTERS!

A CONSTRUCTIVE
APPROACH TO
CRITICAL THINKING

Second Edition

Leo Groarke
Christopher Tindale
Linda Fisher

TORONTO
NEW YORK
OXFORD
OXFORD UNIVERSITY PRESS

Oxford University Press
70 Wynford Drive, Don Mills, Ontario M3C 1J9

Oxford New York
Athens Auckland Bangkok Bombay
Calcutta Cape Town Dar es Salaam Delhi
Florence Hong Kong Istanbul Karachi
Kuala Lumpur Madras Madrid Melbourne
Mexico City Nairobi Paris Singapore
Taipei Tokyo Toronto

and associated companies in
Berlin Ibadan

Oxford is a trademark of Oxford University Press

Canadian Cataloguing in Publication Data

Groarke, Leo
Good reasoning matters! : a constructive approach to critical thinking

2nd ed.
First ed. written by J. Frederick Little, Leo Groarke and
Christopher Tindale.
Includes index.
ISBN 0–19–541225–7

1. Reasoning.   I. Tindale, Christopher W. (Christopher William).
II. Fisher, Linda, 1956–   .   III. Little, J. Frederick. Good reasoning
matters.   IV. Title.

BC177.L58   1996   168   C96–932004–3

Cover Design: Max Gabriel Izod

2 3 4 – 00 99 98

This book is printed on permanent (acid-free) paper ∞.

Printed in Canada

CONTENTS

Acknowledgements   xi
Introduction   xiii
    A Note to the Student   xiii
    A Note to the Instructor   xiv

1   Reading Between the Lines   1
   1.   Informative Language   1
   2.   Reading Between the Lines   3
      Exercise 1A   4
   3.   Biases and Vested Interest   4
   4.   Biased Reasoning   4
      Exercise 1B   9
   5.   Slanting by Omission and Distortion   9
   6.   Two Kinds of Propaganda   13
      Exercise 1C   15
   7.   Summary   7
      Major Exercise 1M   16

2   Looking for an Argument   17
   1.   Identifying Arguments   18
   2.   Definitions   19
   Exercise 2A   20

3. Distinguishing Arguments and Non-Arguments   21
    Exercise 2B   33
4. Diagramming Arguments   33
    Exercise 2C   39
    Exercise 2D   39
    Major Exercise 2M   40

3 *Choosing Your Words*   43
    1. Using Words Precisely   44
    2. Vagueness and Ambiguity   45
        Exercise 3A   49
    3. Formulating Definitions   49
        Exercise 3B   55
    4. Expressing Your Intended Meaning   57
    5. Looking Ahead   59
        Major Exercise 3M   59

4 *Building Arguments*   61
    1. Abbreviated Arguments   62
        Exercise 4A   71
    2. Constructing Good Arguments   74
        Exercise 4B   78
        Exercise 4C   78
        Exercise 4D   79
        Major Exercise 4M   79

5 *Evaluating Arguments*   83
    1. Good Arguments   84
    2. Valid and Invalid Arguments   89
    3. Forms of Argument   93
    4. The Laws of Thought   95
        Major Exercise 5M   98

6 *Classifying Arguments*   101
    1. Categorical Statements   102
        Exercise 6A   106
    2. Immediate Inferences   107
        Exercise 6B   110
    3. Categorical Syllogisms   111
        Exercise 6C   114
    4. Testing Validity by Diagrams   115
        Major Exercise 6M   126

7 *Testing Syllogistic Arguments*   130
   1.   Schematization   130
   2.   Distribution   131
   3.   Rules of Validity   132
   4.   Applying the Rules   133
   5.   Procedural Points   135
      Major Exercise 7M   137

8 *Some Ifs, Ands, and Buts*   140
   1.   Simple and Complex Propositions   140
      Exercise 8A   146
   2.   Translation in More Detail   147
      Exercise 8B   151
   3.   Valid Propositional Arguments   152
   4.   Constructing Simple Proofs   164
      Exercise 8C   166
      Major Exercise 8M   169

9 *Dilemmas and Reductios*   173
   1.   Conditional Introduction   174
   2.   *Reductio Ad Absurdum* Arguments   176
   3.   Dilemma   179
   4.   Answering a Dilemma   181
   5.   De Morgan's Laws   183
   6.   Summary: Rules of Inference   184
      Major Exercise 9M   185

10 *Assessing the Basics*   192
   1.   Ordinary Reasoning and Probability   193
   2.   Acceptability   195
      Exercise 10A   208
   3.   Relevance   209
   4.   Contextual Relevance   213
      Exercise 10B   216
   5.   Sufficiency   217
      Exercise 10C   220
   6.   Applying the Criteria   222
      Major Exercise 10M   225

11 *Forms of Reasoning*   229
   1.   Generalizations   230
      Exercise 11A   237
   2.   Causal Reasoning   238

3. Slippery Slope Arguments 246
   Exercise 11B 249
4. Arguments from Analogy 250
5. Appeals to Precedent 255
   Exercise 11C 257
   Major Exercise 11M 258

12 **Further Forms** 263
1. Two-Wrongs Reasoning 263
2. Two-Wrongs Reasoning by Analogy 267
   Exercise 12A 269
3. *Pro Homine* and *Ad Hominem* Reasoning 270
4. Guilt by Association 280
   Exercise 12B 282
5. Appeals to Ignorance 284
   Exercise 12C 286
6. Other Cases 287
   Exercise 12D 288
   Major Exercise 12M 289

13 **Essaying an Argument** 295
1. The Good Evaluative Critique 296
   Exercise 13A 299
2. The Good Argumentative Essay 301
   Exercise 13B 306
3. A Student's Paper 306
4. Critique 307
5. Revision 313
6. Conclusion 316
   Major Exercise 13M 316

Exercise Answers 317
Index 359

Dedicated to the memory of J. Frederick Little

ACKNOWLEDGEMENTS

The authors would like to thank everyone who contributed to the completion of this book. We are grateful to Zailig Pollock and Noranne Flower for technical assistance, and to Hans V. Hansen for a very careful report on our initial manuscript. We would also like to thank John Burbidge and Leslie Burkholder for valuable comments on a number of the ideas in the book. John's insights were particularly helpful in preparing Chapter 10. We would also like to thank Carolyn Morrison for preparing the illustrations for this edition.

We have benefited from many different texts over the years. Noteworthy among these are Ralph Johnson and Tony Blair's *Logical Self-Defense*, Trudy Govier's *A Practical Study of Argument*, and Jim Freeman's *Thinking Logically*. We are also indebted to insightful reviews of the first edition, and to the wealth of literature that continues to be produced in the areas of critical thinking, informal logic, rhetoric, and argumentation studies.

Janet George. Extract from Janet George 'Saboteurs—the Real Animals', *Manchester Guardian Weekly*, 28 Feb. 1993, p. 24. Copyright The Guardian. Reprinted by permission of The Guardian.

Eleanor MacLean. Extract from *Between the Lines: How to Detect Bias and Propaganda in the News and Everyday Life*, Eleanor MacLean, Montreal: Black Rose Books, 1981. Reprinted by permission of Black Rose Books

Scott Piatkowski. Extract from Scott Piatkowski, 'Scorched earth tactics', *Waterloo Chronicle*, 3 April 1996, reprinted by permission of Scott Piatkowski. (Scott can be contacted at (519) 579-7717 or by e-mail at activist@ionline.net. Visit his website at http://www.ionline.net/~activist)

Daniel D. Polsby. Extract from Daniel D. Polsby, 'The False Promise of Gun Control', is reprinted by permission of the author.

The Sporting News. Extracts from *The Sporting News*, 24 July 1995, are reprinted by permission of The Sporting News.

Geoffrey R. Stone. Extract from Geoffrey R. Stone 'Repeating Past Mistakes', *Society* 24, 5, 1987. Copyright © 1987 by Transaction Publishers; all rights reserved. Reprinted by permission of Transaction Publishers.

Albert Schweitzer. Extract from *The Psychiatric Study of Jews* by Albert Schweitzer, pages 71–2, 1948, reprinted by permission of Beacon Press, Boston.

Cartoon 'Perhaps it would gee-up better if we let it touch earth' is from Sir David Low, *Europe Since Versailles: A History in One Hundred Cartoons with a Narrative Text*, p. 18 (Garland Publishing, 1972). Used by permission of Garland Publishing.

INTRODUCTION

A NOTE TO THE STUDENT

At the millennium, crucial debates rage across the globe. What is the United Nations' role in regional conflicts? Who should provide aid to countries devastated by war and natural disasters? Should Americans receive universal medicare? What is the status of paramilitary groups in North America? Should Quebec seek independence? Should Australia become a republic?

Most of us are confused by such debates. How are we to decide who is right? Authorities on both sides of the issues, professing the best interests of all concerned, defend completely opposite positions.

We must take an interest in a wide range of reasoning concerning all aspects of our lives if we have any concern for what is happening around us. You are probably aware of the avalanche of claims and appeals directed our way by advertisers, special interest groups, televangelists, school recruiters, charities, and software manufacturers. We are on the receiving end of an enormous amount of argumentation demanding our acceptance or support. But most of us are poorly equipped to handle all of this and have difficulty responding with reasoned arguments. It is not that we do not have skills to deal with the reasoning of others. The problem is that in most of us these skills are not sufficiently developed.

This book is designed to help you improve your reasoning skills. You use these skills in all aspects of your life, and more attention to them should help you sort out the claims directed at you and leave you better able to reach your own conclusions about topics that concern you. It is our hope that you will become proficient not only at assessing the arguments you encounter, but also at constructing arguments of your own. These things are particularly important in a democracy, the success of which requires that all of us make significant decisions about social and economic issues that determine public policy. It is at least arguable that the focus on personality in many of our elections reflects a widespread failure to assess the arguments of the various candidates.

In developing your reasoning skills you should expect to work. Many people think they are good at reasoning because they like to argue and defend a position until the opposition is fatigued. But there is more to reasoning than that. We need to recognize what counts as a good reason for a claim, when a point is relevant and when it is not, when our conclusion follows from the evidence we offer, when we have enough evidence, and when the evidence we provide should prove acceptable to a reasonable audience. The key to success is not memorizing principles, but practising their application.

The study of good reasoning may also prompt us to ask why we reason the way we do. How did we come to hold the beliefs we hold? What does attention to aspects of reasoning tell us about ourselves? What social and environmental factors make up the perspectives of various audiences? What is it like to hold a position quite different from our own? Thinking about such questions will provide insight into notions of objectivity and fairness, notions crucial for reasonable behaviour in the contemporary world.

In working through the exercises as you read the book, keep in mind that reasoning is not cut and dried and that many issues, views, and arguments are open to differing interpretations. As we present examples and analyse them, we make a great effort to be fair and consider all relevant points of view. We do the same when we compose the answers to selected (starred) exercises, which are located at the back of the book. It is still possible that you will disagree with some of our analyses and decisions. When this happens, discuss your point of view with your instructor or another student. In doing so, you will begin putting into practice the principles presented in this text.

A NOTE TO THE INSTRUCTOR

Continued innovations in the fields of critical thinking and informal logic reinforce our belief that a range of texts is vital to the development of one of the most significant disciplines to emerge in the last few decades. Our approach is one among many of value, but one that offers important features that improve on others. We have taught with texts that offer all the major contemporary perspectives and continue to keep abreast of what is happening in the field. Judging by our experience, this text offers an account of features of everyday reasoning that still tend to be overlooked.

Our book continues to be distinctive in three ways. First—and we regard this as foremost—we emphasize the construction of arguments and not merely the analysis of other people's reasoning. Expecting people to argue well because they can analyse arguments is a hit-and-miss affair. We therefore stress the components of good reasoning. Given a solid introduction to good reasoning, students will have an easier time recognizing the counterfeits and will know why they are wrong and unacceptable.

The second distinctive feature follows from the first. One popular approach to the teaching of critical thinking and informal logic stresses fallacies. There is some value in this approach, and we continue to benefit from its insights. But we believe that this approach is unnecessarily negative and have found that it can produce a jaded attitude in some students, who come to feel that logic is simply a tool for finding fault with arguments and arguers.

With a growing number of commentators (Brinton, Govier, Walton, Woods, and Wreen), we share the belief that many arguments traditionally treated as fallacies can be classified as good forms of argument if they are properly constructed (by 'form of argument' we mean 'pattern of reasoning', not the narrower notion of form that characterizes formal logic). The *ad hominem* is a good example. According to the account still usually adopted in logic texts, its name is taken to be synonymous with a bad move in reasoning. But informed opinion has questioned this, and it is widely recognized that *ad hominem* arguments can be legitimate if they are correctly constructed. We think that this is not sufficiently emphasized in the fallacy approach, which may tend to encourage the dismissal of an *ad hominem* as soon as it is identified rather than the careful weighing of the reasoning in each case.

The counter side of many traditional fallacies is a legitimate form of argument, that is, an identifiable set of conditions and structure common to all arguments of that type. Our approach places emphasis on these good argument forms, and we give the conditions for their construction in each case. We treat as fallacious those arguments that violate the conditions governing the legitimate form. Analysing arguments in this way takes time and thought and avoids the hasty application of a label.

A third feature that characterizes our text is a recognition of the importance of rhetorical considerations. The work of Perelman has been particularly influential in pointing to this need, but insights into the role that rhetoric plays in informal reasoning have also been made by such writers as Wenzel, Crosswhite, Yoos, and Brinton. The chief concept we have adopted is that of audience. Readers familiar with Perelman's work will recognize the important role that the notion of the 'universal audience' plays in many of our discussions. We believe the failure of traditional logicians to recognize the importance of audiences in assessing the acceptability or truth of premises can no longer be countenanced if we are to deal effectively with reasoning in ordinary contexts.

One issue we have had to face is the question as to how we should handle the deductive/inductive distinction. This distinction has been seriously challenged in the literature. Some informal logicians have dropped these terms from their discussions, while others have retained them and expanded induction to include 'conductive' arguments (Govier). After considering the alternatives, we chose not to give the deductive/inductive distinction a pivotal role in the structure of the text, at the same time stressing the differences between what are commonly referred to as 'inductive' and 'deductive' reasoning.

That people do use arguments with premises that validly entail their conclusions justifies our including formal logic in our approach to reasoning. While familiar with the controversy surrounding the use of formal logic to teach ordinary reasoning, we are convinced that the basic principles of formal logic are present in much everyday reasoning and should not be ignored. Our emphasis on forms of argument rather than fallacies is a natural continuation of the valid forms of simple arguments introduced in prior chapters. In this manner our approach blends the two types of reasoning.

In the second edition, we have again adopted a structure that will allow instructors to decide how much or how little formal reasoning they cover. Syllogistic logic is introduced in Chapter 6. Its complexities are treated in Chapter 7. Instructors can omit these without disrupting the flow of the text. Propositional logic is introduced in Chapter 8 and then treated in more detail in Chapter 9. Again, one could teach a course without covering one or both these chapters.

Generally, the structure of the text is cumulative. Skills taught in earlier chapters are required in later chapters, and exercises are arranged in increasing complexity. Exercises grouped at the end of each major section of a chapter are intended to cultivate the skills discussed in that section, and at the end of each chapter is a 'major' exercise requiring the application of the material in it and preceding chapters.

In preparing the second edition, we have paid attention to research in critical thinking and informal logic since the book first appeared. Many chapters have benefited from the insights of that research. In revising the text, we have also tried to make it more accessible for a variety of college and university students. To this end, we have broken chapters into shorter units, added boxes to highlight core concepts, added more exercises, and adopted suggestions made by users of the first edition. These changes have involved considerable rewriting and reorganization. But users of the first edition will recognize the same basic approach to critical thinking, with the same focus on good reasoning and aspects of audience. They will also find the same topics and reasoning forms treated, though sometimes in different places in the text.

Over 150 new examples have been introduced in the body of the text and in the exercises, updating many of the issues we use to introduce critical thinking skills. As students and instructors requested, we have added a section containing selected sample answers for most exercise sets (starred questions are answered at the back of the book). In many cases, the nature of the material means that these answers are not definitive but represent reasonable possibilities. We encourage users to suggest alternatives and challenge our analyses.

This project has developed without the guiding presence of Fred Little, the loss of whom was keenly felt in 1990. His leadership, voice, and logical acumen were principal factors in making the first edition of *Good Reasoning Matters!* the success it was. For the second edition Groarke has been responsible for rewriting Chapters 1, 2, 3, 4, 5, 8, and 9. Tindale has been responsible for rewriting Chapters 6, 7, 10, 12, and 13 and for editing the manuscript. Joining the project for the second edition is Linda Fisher, who has rewritten Chapter 11 and reviewed the manuscript with a keen eye for miscues and awkwardness. She also prepared the index.

READING

BETWEEN

THE LINES

This is a book about reasoning. Because reasoning depends on our ability to understand spoken and written language, we will prepare the way by discussing:

- ◆ different uses of language;
- ◆ directly and indirectly informative language;
- ◆ bias and vested interest;
- ◆ slanting by omission and distortion; and
- ◆ two kinds of propaganda.

A good reasoner must learn to 'read between the lines', not in the sense that one should discard what is actually read or heard, but in the sense that its full significance must be recognized. This frequently extends beyond the actual words employed. Because reasoning takes place—at least in the most common and obvious cases—in the context of reading, listening, or speaking, we need to begin our account of reasoning by saying something about these more basic skills.

1. INFORMATIVE LANGUAGE

Our first point is a very simple one: language is used in many different ways. In our roles as parents, children, students, teachers, business persons, scientists, politicians, poets, and labourers we do many different things with words. When we reason, we use language 'informatively', to make claims and draw conclusions. In the process we commit ourselves to moral, historical, scientific, and speculative claims. The following are examples.

> The earth is saucer-shaped.
> We should have laws against euthanasia.
> Ernest Hemingway committed suicide.
> In ancient times, Aesop's fables were not regarded as children's reading.
> The world will end in the year 2001.

Claims like these may be true or false and generally accepted or controversial. In the context of reasoning it is particularly important to note that a claim may be accepted by one group of people (one audience) but not another. In the present context it is enough to note that claims express a belief or assert what we think is or is not the case.

Though reasoning is founded on the informative use of language, it would be a great mistake to think that language is always used informatively. Often, language is used in ways other than to make claims so as to draw conclusions—to ask questions, to vent or express emotions, to give commands or directions, or to enhance rituals and ceremonies. These are important uses of language and much of value might be said about them, but they are of secondary importance in the present context. In this book—and in logic more generally—we are primarily interested in the informative use of language and how the claims it conveys function in the context of reasoning.

One might distinguish between 'directly' and 'indirectly' informative language. In both cases, language sets out a claim, a thesis, a proposition, or a belief. In many cases, reasons are given in support of it. In directly informative language, the thesis is made explicit. In indirectly informative discourse it is not stated directly and explicitly. In view of this, we need to be alert to modes of literary expression that are not directly and explicitly, but indirectly and implicitly, informative.

Poetry provides many examples of indirectly informative language. Often a poet muses simply to express moods, to amuse, or to create a pleasurable feeling. But the poet may also use artistry to express and communicate insights that are difficult, perhaps impossible, to capture in straightforward informative assertions. In view of this the poet is allowed liberties denied to the essayist in his or her use of words. Poets juxtapose words and deliberately use expressions with multiple meanings and emotive associations, irony, paradox, contradiction, myth, and parable. They are allowed the linguistic irregularities of 'poetic licence'—which are a poet's stock in trade.

Many great works of literature, religion, and philosophy employ poetic techniques. Some have even argued that the principles of contemporary physics do not abide by the laws of directly informative language and that they must be conveyed with paradox and metaphor. According to Plato, the most profound truths of philosophy cannot be attained by the discursive intellect and require mystical insight that ultimately transcends it. Pascal, Kierkegaard, Beauvoir, and Sartre are widely regarded as great thinkers, but Pascal relied on paradoxes and contradictions, Kierkegaard on parables and verbal portraits, Sartre on novels and dramas, and Beauvoir on imaginative metaphors. The place of myth and metaphor in our lives is highlighted in the literature of Eastern and Western religious traditions. Zen koans purposely pose questions that are unanswerable so long as we remain attached to our ordinary conceptual framework and the directly informative discourse on which it is modelled.

Few texts about critical thinking say anything about the 'indirectly' informative use of language featured in these contexts. Nor shall we pursue it at length. That being said, we consider it important that you realize that this use of language is often profoundly, if indirectly, informative. We do not want you to think that all discourse is directly informative discourse or that this is the only discourse of value for study. Having made this point, we proceed next to the ins and outs of the directly informative discourse that is the focus of this book.

2. Reading Between the Lines

Perceptive readers and listeners already know that there is a correlation between language functions and the sentence types discussed by grammarians. Normally we use declarative sentences to communicate information directly, questions to ask for information, exclamations to express emotions, and imperatives to issue commands.

But not always. When the instructor announces to the class that 'Logic exercises submitted after the due date will be given a zero grade', this declarative sentence fulfils an imperative function. It is equivalent to saying 'Submit your exercises on time!' Likewise, we may ask for information without employing a question. The imperative 'Help me, please' followed by the declarative 'I don't know which bus to take to Dayton Centre' functions as an interrogative that is equivalent to the question, 'Which bus goes to Dayton Centre?' And the question 'How could anybody in his or her right mind believe that the Holocaust never happened?' is not a request for an answer. Rather, it functions as a rhetorical device which communicates the claim that 'No one in his or her right mind could believe that the Holocaust never happened.'

Because sentence structures do not necessarily correspond to an author's intended meaning, you must learn 'to read between the lines' to ascertain what the author intended to accomplish. Similarly, when you set about writing or presenting what you have to say, you must be clear about your objective and use language in a way that makes it relatively easy for your readers or listeners to understand your objective. Are you, for instance, trying to elicit from government officials a statement of their positions on some contentious issue? Or are you participating in a ritual or ceremony? Or are you trying to motivate your readers to do something that you think must be done?

Once you have established your objective, try to use language in a way that can establish it appropriately. In some cases, indirectly informative language may serve your purposes best—a parable or a quotation from a poem may be the best way to communicate what you want to say. In other cases, direct questions may be the best way to elicit some answers that you want. In the cases we want to deal with, your goal will be the use of directly informative language in a way that allows you to reason to—and convince others of—particular conclusions. In view of this, we need to proceed by noting some of the problems that frequently attend this use of language.

EXERCISE 1A

Read the following passage and answer the questions about it.

Can anyone still believe tuberculosis (TB) is a disease of the past? According to a recent report from the World Health Organization, 'the TB epidemic is growing larger and more dangerous every year.' Failure on the part of Western nations to act immediately will have disastrous consequences for us all. New strains of the disease have appeared and these resist treatment with common TB drugs. There is an uproar about mad cow disease but everyone is complacent about TB. Does that make any sense?

1. What is the author's principal point?
2. What role do the two questions play in communicating the author's point?
3. Does the author believe the fight against TB is hopeless?
4. Does the World Health Organization say that a failure to act immediately will have disastrous consequences?
5. What implicit claims are being made about mad cow disease?

3. BIASES AND VESTED INTEREST

In using directly informative language, and in reading or listening to other people, it is important to keep in mind that one's commitments inevitably influence and sometimes distort one's choice of words. Here again, a discerning listener or reader can read between the lines to determine an author's point of view. In doing so, he or she is detecting 'biases' that inform the claims in question.

A bias occurs whenever some situation or issue is interpreted in a way that unreasonably favours a particular point of view. In dealing with the facts of a particular situation a good reasoner lets the facts 'speak for themselves'. This means that she remains open to what the facts themselves reveal. A biased reasoner approaches the facts quite differently, emphasizing aspects that favour a particular perspective (usually, but not always, her own) and mini-mizing, ignoring, or dismissing aspects that invite other kinds of conclusions.

In some sense, bias is inevitable. Each of us has likes and dislikes, loves, loyalties, and commitments. We cannot turn them off at will, and it is there-fore inevitable that they colour our perceptions and our accounts of particu-lar issues and situations. The way they invite a biased view of particular incidents and issues is well illustrated in a classic psychological study by Hastorf and Cantril ('They Saw a Game: A Case Study').* Intrigued by opposing reactions by different fans to a rough and controversial Princeton-Dartmouth football game, they set out to determine the effects of loyalties on perceptions of the game.

In the course of their study, they showed the same film of the game to a sample of undergraduates and alumni from each school, asking them to record 'mild' and 'flagrant' infractions of the rules as they watched the film. The responses of the two groups were remarkably inconsistent. Princeton students and alumni saw a game that was 'rough and dirty' because of Dartmouth's play. In contrast, Dartmouth students who watched the same film 'saw both teams make about the same number of infractions. And they saw their own team make only half the number of infractions the Princeton students saw them make.' A group of Dartmouth alumni who could not see any of Dartmouth's alleged infractions concluded that they had been sent an incomplete film, noting the 'considerable cutting of important parts' of the film, and asked that a new complete version be delivered immediately.

Hastorf and Cantril conclude that the loyalties of the different groups made them 'see' different games and approvingly quote an account of boxing by the New York sports columnist Red Smith, who once wrote that 'after any fight that doesn't end in a clean knockout, there always are at least a few hoots when the decision is announced. A guy from, say, Billy Graham's neighbour-hood goes to see Billy fight and he watches Graham all the time. He sees all the punches Billy throws, and hardly any of the punches Billy catches.' The problem here is a bias that creates an impression that is not warranted by the facts themselves. As many parents know, such biases are endemic in organized youth sports, where families find it difficult to see past their attachments to particular players on a team.

But it is not only sports that give rise to the effects of bias. Inevitably, bias affects the way we look at a host of issues and concerns. The danger of bias is particularly strong in any situation in which we have 'vested interests', i.e., in which we will personally benefit from looking at things in a particular way. In the most obvious cases, the benefit will be monetary. Celebrities endorsing commercial products are being paid and cannot, therefore, act as objective

---

*Albert H. Hastorf and Hadley Cantril, 'They Saw A Game', in Richard E. Young, Alton L. Becker, and Kenneth L. Pike, eds, *Rhetoric: Discovery & Change* (New York: Harcourt, Brace & World, 1970), pp. 31–9.

judges. They have something—money—to gain from holding a particular view and this can easily distort their judgement. It is easy to think of many similar cases. If I hold shares in a particular company, I may be sceptical of charges that it has been violating worker safety codes or environmental laws in a way that would cost the company financially.

In other cases, vested interests may be more subtle. One may benefit from a particular interpretation of events in all kinds of indirect ways—by increasing the prestige of the university at which one studied, by vindicating a stand one has already taken, by protecting the image of a political party with which one is associated, or by some other way of promoting policies or beliefs in keeping with one's personal loyalties and commitments (see Box 1.1).

Box 1.1 A Comment on Bias

The following American cartoon from 1913, drawn by Art Young and entitled 'The Freedom of the Press', attacked newspaper corruption. It so angered the Associated Press that it took legal action, suing the publisher and the artist for libel. It would be hard to miss the biting satire: the newspaper owner and staff are portrayed as the occupants of a house of prostitution. The madam is the newspaper owner and the client is a hefty advertiser with a large wallet who is identified as 'Railroads—Mining—Dept. Stores, etc.' The suggestion is that newspaper reporting is inherently biased because newspapers are willing to say whatever large advertisers demand. In making this charge, Young recognizes two sets of vested interest—those of the advertisers who don't wish to be criticized, and those of the newspapers, who benefit financially from pleasing their advertisers. In spite of their anger, the libel suit was eventually dropped by the complainants.

THE FREEDOM OF THE PRESS

Having warned you about bias and vested interest, we must note that not all cases of bias are cases of vested interest, and not all cases of vested interest produce bias. Sometimes an account of a situation or an issue is not biased because of the author's viewpoint but because of biases that affect material it relies on. One may, for example, base one's account of an issue or a situation on a biased newspaper report and in the process unintentionally transmit the bias it includes. In another situation, someone who has a vested interested may set it aside and objectively report 'the facts'. The latter is an admirable accomplishment we will all do well to emulate.

4. BIASED REASONING

It is important to recognize biases—both our own and those of others—in the context of logic and reasoning because bias frequently distorts reasoning, suggesting and promoting conclusions that are unwarranted. A good example is the following, which has been adapted from an actual letter written to a university newspaper by a student after an incident in a student pub ('Fed Hall') in which her boyfriend was, she claims, set up and assaulted by a 'punk-rocker'. The letter appeared under the headline 'My Larry was obviously set up'.

To the editor:
After a recent incident at Fed Hall, I feel that it is necessary to bar punk-rockers from the premises. They have no class and should be kept from entering a class establishment. During Friday night my boyfriend, Larry, and his friends were in the washroom talking when they noticed a punker come in. He had a blond mohican-style haircut, army boots, and a leather jacket with inch high spikes on the shoulders. It was obvious he was only there to cause trouble. Larry asked him what his problem was and who he was trying to impress, but the punker wouldn't answer and gave my boyfriend a dirty look. Then after several attempts at finding out whether he was there to fight, the punker became violently deranged and they had to hold him from attacking them. When Larry tried to grab hold of him, the punk punched him several times in the face and kicked his friend in the kidney area. Larry was obviously set up.

Larry ended up in the hospital that night with a badly broken nose and several stitches under his lip. We went to the police and they said nothing could be done because the punker was outnumbered and that it sounded like Larry had been at fault for harassing the punker into fighting.

I know that Larry and his friends would not start a fight.

If someone is reading this to you, punker, it is only fair to warn you that if my boyfriend ever sees you again at Fed Hall or the Turret, he and his friends will make you pay dearly for this. I can only hope, for your sake, that you have the temporary intelligence to stay away from there for good.

The most remarkable aspect of the bias in this argument is the author's inability to detect it, for even her own biased account suggests that Larry was *not* set up, but that he and his friends harassed the punk-rocker into fighting (as the police suggested). The contradiction in her position is most obvious when she says that Larry and his friends would not start a fight, yet she goes on to threaten the punk-rocker with what sounds like physical assault.

In one sense, this example is, despite its extreme nature, characteristic of instances of bias, for it is especially difficult to recognize our own biases. They are so much a part of us that we frequently do not see them, and we assume that we are simply seeing things 'as they are'. We must struggle against our own biases if we hope to see things from an objective point of view.

That bias and vested interest can be impediments to reasoning is clear from cases where conflicting biases make it almost impossible to determine what is true or false. Consider, for example, a sensational case of alleged child abuse that was brought to light in 1992: after notifying a radio station of her intentions, a Manitoba woman robbed a bank at gunpoint and then took the money to the Manitoba Justice Minister, declaring, 'Here's some money to help my abusive husband get into a treatment program.'

One of the central issues in the debate that followed this incident was whether or not her husband, Ambrose, was guilty of child abuse. Here is a list of some of the charges and countercharges that characterized the case:

Charge:
Ambrose, in his affidavit, states that Mary Ann admitted to his lawyer that she fabricated the abuse charge. Mary Ann admitted this in her second affidavit.

The Countercharge:
Mary Ann claimed she was under a great deal of pressure to say whatever Ambrose wanted.

Charge:
An independent witness swore in an affidavit that Mary Ann told him the accusation was false.

The Countercharge:
Mary Ann accused the witness of lying.

Charge:
Mary Ann and her supporters made much of the point that Ambrose pleaded guilty to a charge of abuse.

The Countercharge:
Ambrose says that she promised to reconcile with him if he pleaded guilty, and Mary Ann admitted in court to threatening to keep the child away if he didn't plead guilty.

This is only a small part of the case in question and it would be impossible to get to the bottom of it here. Indeed, in such cases it may be impossible to establish what is true and false. The problem is exacerbated by the fact that we are faced with the conflicting testimony of two individuals with competing vested interests and, probably, two opposingly biased points of view.

Complicated cases of this sort are beyond the scope of an introductory text but we may still make some general remarks about the techniques typically employed when bias distorts a report or an argument. Learning about these techniques of 'slanting' helps you detect biased writing and presentations and, even more importantly, teaches you how to avoid bias in your own presentations.

EXERCISE 1B

For each of the following, identify any vested interests and discuss any possible biases.

1. [Former President Ronald Reagan] I want to be fair. Unemployment is 9.8 per cent. When we took office it was 7.4 per cent. Okay, I'll take blame for 2.4 per cent of the unemployment.
2. [From a real estate advertisement] $159,900. This all brick triplex is easy to rent and a pleasure to own. It is located near schools, bus stops, Rockway Golf Course, and the Conestoga Parkway. It's a real money maker and now is a great time to buy.
3. [University professor responding to the complaint that university professors are the most difficult shoppers] Of course we are. That's because we're grossly underpaid. We have to haggle.
4. [From an advertisement] BALDING: AS SEEN ON OPRAH AND GERALDO. An investment that Never Stops Growing. The truth about transplants: There is no alternative to your own growing hair. Call: 416 555-6063. CHAMBERS HAIR INSTITUTE.
5. [Letter to the *Toronto Sun*, 1 Apr. 1996, concerning police violence in a controversial strike] It was okay for the union goons to harass citizens crossing the picket lines to the point of tears or even a scuffle or skirmish, but as soon as the shoe was on the other foot they wimped out and cried police brutality.

5. SLANTING BY OMISSION AND DISTORTION

There are two principal means by which authors with biases typically slant their descriptions of particular situations. The first is by 'omission'. Anyone who presents a situation or an argument must select particular facts and issues to report and emphasize. This is unavoidable given that time and space are limited, but it means that other facts and issues must be summarized or left out entirely. In view of this, it is relatively easy for an author, for example, to report those facts and details that favour the impression he or she wants to create, deftly avoiding any mention of those that suggest an alternative conclusion. The author thus writes or speaks 'nothing but the truth' but fails to give 'the whole truth', leaving out aspects of the situation that may raise doubts or favour a contradictory point of view.

The following is the opening of a newspaper article in the *Halifax Chronicle-Herald.*

No Viable Energy Alternative to Nuclear Power, Churchmen Told
Sackville (Special)—Two professors from the University of New Brunswick in Saint John told United Churchmen here Saturday that there is no viable alternative to nuclear energy if Canadians wish to maintain their present lifestyle.

The rest of the article expands on this opening remark. The newspaper neglected to point out that there were in fact three professors who spoke. The third offered a critique of nuclear energy and the positions of the other two professors (all the professors had been given each other's remarks ahead of time). By omitting this important fact, the newspaper article slants the story in favour of the pro-nuclear position. It may be the correct position, but good reasoning would show this through a consideration of the opposing arguments, rather than implying that none exists by omitting mention of them.

Omission is a particular problem in television news, which relies on short, memorable copy with accompanying audio-visual summaries. Two minutes is a long news story, but it is difficult to fit all the relevant aspects of a complex issue into such a short span of time. Some critics therefore argue that TV news by its very nature distorts issues and events, primarily by stressing highly charged pieces of information that grab our attention and by not allowing the necessary—albeit boring—details that an informed report requires. Whatever one thinks of this, an awareness of the possibility of slanting by omission will help us to analyse and assess arguments and reports on television, in newspapers and magazines, and in conversation.

A second way of slanting is by 'distortion'. It occurs when one exaggerates or colours the facts that are reported in order to enhance the impression one desires. Without overtly falsifying facts, a newspaper reporter and editor can, for example, twist these facts by substituting terms with suggestive overtones for objectively descriptive ones; by adding apparently innocuous but insinuating phrases; or by using to advantage the size of headline type, the length of an article and its location with respect to the section of the paper, the page of the section, the column on the page, and the kinds of illustration that accompany it.

Distortion can be very subtle because it is easy to use descriptions that lean one way or another. The old adage that 'a half empty glass is half full' illustrates that the same fact can be cast in a positive or negative light. An extreme example of slanting by distortion is provided by the following newspaper headlines announcing the journey of Napoleon across France on his return from Elba (9–22 March 1815; this example is given in Eleanor MacLean, *Between the Lines: Detecting Bias and Propaganda*). In each case, the headline reports that Napoleon is in such and such a place, but colours this report in a way that sends more extreme messages that change according to the bias (and the vested interest) of the newspaper.

9 March
THE ANTHROPOPHAGUS [the monster who eats people] HAS QUITTED HIS DEN

10 March
THE CORSICAN HAS LADED AT CAPE JUAN

11 March
THE TIGER HAS ARRIVED AT CAP

12 March
THE MONSTER SLEPT AT GRENOBLE

13 March
THE TYRANT HAS PASSED THROUGH LYONS

14 March
THE USURPER IS DIRECTING HIS STEPS TOWARDS DIJON

18 March
BONAPARTE IS ONLY SIXTY LEAGUES FROM THE CAPITAL
He has been fortunate to escape his pursuers

19 March
BONAPARTE IS ADVANCING WITH RAPID STEPS, BUT HE WILL NEVER ENTER PARIS

20 March
NAPOLEON WILL, TOMORROW, BE UNDER OUR RAMPARTS

21 March
THE EMPEROR IS AT FONTAINEBLEAU

22 March
HIS IMPERIAL AND ROYAL MAJESTY
arrived yesterday evening at the Tuileries amid the joyful acclamations of his devoted and faithful subjects

Though these headlines never explicitly say that Napoleon is good, bad, loved, feared, hated, admired, or despised, their choice of words clearly implies a variety of claims in this regard and distorts the 'news'.

Whenever an individual or group has a point of view, product, or cause to promote, slanting is a likely possibility—even when that individual is you or a group to which you belong. Slanting is thus found not only in newspaper reports but in strategic analyses, feasibility studies, union and management reports on working conditions, committee reports, and political platforms. The key characteristic of slanting is the use of omission and distortion to create a bias that insinuates a particular interpretation of the facts or the issue discussed or reported. A good reasoner recognizes that a different 'slant on the issue' is a possibility.

In your own reasoning and reporting, you should be aware of the danger of bias and slanting and try to avoid them. If you want to go beyond objective reporting and express your feelings or opinions concerning the facts, be above board in doing so. If your intention is to inform, you should avoid the problems such influences can create by avoiding emotionally charged modes of expression. Be explicit about what you are doing and try to ensure that any opinions or feelings you express are justified by an unbiased view of the issue or situation you discuss. Some emotive uses are appropriate—it is, after all, reasonable to feel strongly about some things—but you must be cautious of linguistic excess and determine what constitutes an appropriate use of language in a given situation. Consider how emotive you need to be to secure the attention of your audience and modify this in light of how unemotive you must be in using reason to convince your audience.

Assuming you follow this advice, slanting should not be a major problem in your own discourse, though you still must decide whether other people's writing and speaking are reasonably objective. How can you detect instances of slanting? Often you will be aware of it only when letters to the editor appear, written by people who are offended by a distorted report and want to correct the impression made in an original article. Fortunately, this is not the only way to detect slanting. In many cases, the very manoeuvres used in slanting can alert you to the possibility of its presence. As you read, you should be able to identify at least some of the facts, including the primary fact, reported. Once you do so, you can ask yourself if the account is slanted. In the student letter complaining about the punk-rocker, for example, the facts show through and the letter in this way allows us to recognize its own bias.

As you read, you should be asking yourself: Is this discourse promoting a particular point of view regarding the facts? Does it seem to be assessing the facts and issues in a particular way? What is to be made of the way some details are emphasized and others treated as inconsequential or of secondary importance? Is there another way to 'juggle the facts' to create a quite different impression?

Symptoms of slanting are the use of inflammatory terms where neutral ones would have sufficed, sensational words that precipitate startling mental pictures, unnecessary phrases filled with innuendo, and suggestions that are implied but never explicitly stated. If terminology like this jumps out at you, try to compare the article you are reading with another report about the same facts and look carefully for omissions and counterbalancing features. Studying two reports of the same event—especially reports from sources with opposing commitments and loyalties—is a very useful way to arrive at a more accurate understanding of what you are being asked to believe. Considering your own views from opposing points of view will help you detect and eliminate the effects of bias on your own writing and presentations. In view of the possibility of bias and slanting in your own and other people's arguments, don't be too hasty in your conclusions and bear in mind that a particular argument may be slanted in ways that you have not yet detected.

6. Two Kinds of Propaganda

The word 'propaganda' is sometimes used in a general sense, to refer to any deliberate spreading of information intended to help or harm a cause. The *Oxford English Dictionary* thus defines propaganda as 'any association, systematic scheme, or concerted movement for the propagation of a particular doctrine or practice'. In this general sense, speeches and articles written to defend or promote particular beliefs are propaganda. Governments, corporations, political parties, and private organizations spend millions of dollars on propaganda of this sort—to convince us to vote a particular way, to build support for free trade, to raise questions about abortion, and so on. To the extent that such material is argued carefully and fairly, it deserves a hearing and should not be immediately dismissed.

In other cases, the word 'propaganda' is used to refer to advocacy characterized by extreme bias. Propaganda in this sense is characterized by selective and distorted reporting. Propagandists of this sort typically go even further, arguing in dubious ways to accomplish their objective. Self-serving analogies, shifts of meaning in the use of key terms in the course of an argument, unstated controversial premises, an aura of knowledgeability created through name-dropping and pseudo-technical jargon—these and other sophistries are the propagandist's stock in trade. Ironically, the propagandist's use of obviously ideological language and obvious omissions and distortions often make the arguments unconvincing, because he or she so obviously is not interested in looking at matters from an objective point of view.

Sometimes the use of the word 'propaganda' vacillates between the general and the pejorative sense, though the latter tends to prevail in ordinary language. The word itself was highlighted in a 1987 Washington decision to designate as propaganda the Academy Award-winning documentary film *If You Love This Planet*, produced by Canada's National Film Board. The film depicts the horrendous medical effects of nuclear conflict, tracing them from the obliteration of life at the point of detonation through the delayed but death-dealing consequences of radiation fallout at further distances. An internationally reputed medical authority from Harvard University provides an explicit commentary against a visual background of mushrooming nuclear explosions and footage depicting the effects of radiation.

The following is a summary of the contents of a newspaper report (*The Globe and Mail*, 30 Apr. 1987) on the American government's decision to classify the film as propaganda.

> Classifying the film as 'propaganda' means that it is deemed as reflecting adversely on US foreign policy and must be registered under the Foreign Agents Registration Act (FARA) which requires that a disclaimer precede each screening of the film labelling it as political propaganda not approved by the US Government. Distributors of the film must file a report with the Department of Justice listing organizations that will be showing it, the size of the audiences at the screenings and, if requested, the names of the people in attendance. When a California exhibitor challenged the 'propaganda' classification under FARA as in conflict with the First Amendment right to free speech, a District Court judge ruled in the exhibitor's favour on the grounds that 'to characterize a particular expression of political ideas as "propaganda" is to denigrate those ideas'.

> That decision was ultimately overturned by the US Supreme Court. Though all of the Justices agreed that the term 'propaganda' is widely perceived as having a negative connotation, the majority ruled that the term is a neutral one in law, and that the Government's labelling of the film as 'propaganda' does not affect freedom of expression. While acknowledging that there is a 'risk that a partially informed audience might believe that a film that must be registered with the Department of Justice is suspect', the Justices concluded that 'there is no evidence that this suspicion—to the degree it exists—has the effect of government censorship.'

We might wonder whether the Supreme Court justices involved in this decision were party to the propaganda—in the pejorative sense—of those who wanted to undermine concern about the effects of a 'nuclear exchange'. For though they did not classify *If You Love This Planet* as propaganda in the sense of being dishonest, deceptive, and distorted, by classifying it as propaganda in the 'neutral' sense, they furthered the position of those who opposed the film's message. Viewing the film became difficult and any screening had to include the US government's disclaimer. Looked at this way, the decision involved a bias, though this is not an issue we need pursue here.

The important point is that propaganda in the negative sense illustrates the full extent to which the informative use of language can be abused. In this context, informative language is used to misinform rather than inform. The lesson to be learned is that as you read or listen to reports and arguments, you must try to spot any questionable biases that result in slanting or negative propaganda. The corollary of this is the principle that, as you prepare your own essays, articles, and presentations, you must make every effort to avoid slanting and ensure that you do not indulge in propaganda in the pejorative sense.

EXERCISE 1C

1. For each of the examples, discuss how the following remarks (from Exercise 1B) may have been slanted by omission or distortion.
   (a) [Former President Ronald Reagan] I want to be fair. Unemployment is 9.8 per cent. When we took office it was 7.4 per cent. Okay, I'll take blame for 2.4 per cent of the unemployment.
   (b) [From an advertisement] BALDING! AS SEEN ON OPRAH AND GERALDO. An investment that Never Stops Growing. The truth about transplants: There is no alternative to your own growing hair. Call: 416 555-6063. CHAMBERS HAIR INSTITUTE.
   (c) [Letter to the *Toronto Sun*, 1 Apr. 1996, concerning police violence in a controversial strike] It was okay for the union goons to harass citizens crossing the picket lines to the point of tears or even a scuffle or skirmish, but as soon as the shoe was on the other foot they wimped out and cried police brutality.
2. Imagine that the number of American deaths due to TB was 3 million in 1958 and 2 million in 1997 but increasing quickly. How might you slant by omission and distortion to emphasize the impression that TB is an increasing problem? To minimize the problem?
3. Is the following passage, excerpted from the University of Toronto's *The Bulletin* (No. 3, 7 Sept. 1993), an example of propaganda? Why or why not?

[The Faculty of Education] is sexist, racist and elitist. Two-thirds of the students are female, predominantly feminist, of white European middle-class background. Males are a minority as are natives, orientals, blacks and those from lower classes. The faculty has a female subculture that espouses nurturing through such stereotypical female values as care, cooperation, concern, equality, comfort and group support. Traditional male values such as individualism and aggressiveness are missing from the faculty's image of a teacher. Graduating students will disseminate these female values to the disadvantage of male pupils.

7. SUMMARY

We began by noting the different uses of language and stating that our study of reasoning will focus on the (directly) informative use of language. Having recognized this as the basis of good reasoning, we discussed the ways in which one must 'read between the lines' to recognize the full import of the claims conveyed by directly informative language. We noted problems that arise due to vested interests and the biases they produce. Most obviously, they manifest themselves in slanting by omission or distortion and, in the worst cases, in the negative sense of propaganda. Having recognized these features of informative language, we are now ready to look at the way in which it is used in reasoning. To do so, we must turn to arguments, the basic components of the reasoning process.

MAJOR EXERCISE 1M

*1. Find what you believe to be a slanted report in a student or popular newspaper or magazine and explain why you are convinced it is slanted by analysing the techniques the writer employs.

2. Find an example of propaganda (an advertisement, political pamphlet, etc.) and analyse it for slanting and other dubious ploys used to promote the cause of the organization that issued it. Explain whether it is propaganda in the general or the pejorative sense.

LOOKING

FOR AN

ARGUMENT

The argument is our basic unit of reasoning. This chapter introduces arguments and discusses:

- ◆ arguments and argument components;
- ◆ logical indicators and their role in reasoning;
- ◆ the distinction between explanations and arguments;
- ◆ argumentative and non-argumentative contexts;
- ◆ techniques for diagramming argument structure; and
- ◆ linked and convergent premises.

You may have seen the Monty Python skit in which a man enters a room and asks, 'Is this the right room for an argument?' The occupant answers 'I told you once', to which the first man replies, 'No, you didn't', and is told 'Yes, I did.' They hurl the same charges back and forth again and again.

What initially strikes us as funny is the idea of a room which is 'the right room' for arguing. We are familiar with the expression 'room for argument'. If we find ourselves disagreeing with someone else, we may interject, 'Hold on! I don't agree. There's room for argument on that point.' But 'there's room for argument' does not mean that 'there is a specific room or location where arguments can or should take place.' Arguments can take place anywhere.

Because reasoning is largely a matter of arguing pro and con, the lion's share of the remainder of this text deals with arguments of one sort or another.

In particular, it discusses how we may go about constructing good arguments, the ways we can assess other people's arguments, and the kinds of arguments that best serve a particular purpose in a given situation. Because 'good reasoning matters'—as the title of this book claims—these are essential topics if we wish to become good reasoners.

But we are not in a position to talk about kinds of arguments and the differences between good reasoning and bad until we know what an argument is and how to distinguish arguments and non-arguments. We turn to this topic now, for our first chapter on reading and writing has placed us in a position where we can easily 'make room' for it.

1. IDENTIFYING ARGUMENTS

The Monty Python skit continues:

'No, you didn't!'

'Yes, I did!'

Exasperated, the first man finally exclaims, 'Look, this isn't an argument, it's just a contradiction.'

From the point of view of logic, he is quite correct. The two men are not arguing. One is simply denying what the other is affirming.

We might contrast this 'Yes, I did'/'No, you didn't' confrontation with the kind of reasoning the famous detective Sherlock Holmes typically provides for his friend Watson. It begins with a claim, usually unexpected and usually to Watson's amazement. Let us say the claim is:

The crime was committed by someone in the house.

Holmes backs his claim by providing convincing reasons that support its truth. Suppose he provides the following reasons:

1. Although the living room window is open, there are no footprints outside, despite the softness of the ground due to yesterday's rain.
2. The clasp on the box was not broken but opened with a key that had been hidden behind the clock.
3. The dog did not bark.

We now have three reasons that support Holmes's original claim. We can describe his reasoning by saying that he has drawn a conclusion from three observations that, taken together, support his claim that the crime was an 'inside job'.

In contrast to the Monty Python skit, this is a case in which we have, from the point of view of logic, the key ingredients of an argument.

2. Definitions

Argument

In the Holmes example, the famous detective provides an argument in the sense in which most logicians understand the term. He has given reasons in support of a claim. In keeping with this, we will define an argument as any unit of discourse (oral, written, or non-verbal) that gives one or more *reasons in support of a claim*. The two individuals in the Monty Python skit do not argue in this sense, because neither gives any reasons in support of his claim. Holmes was arguing because he reinforced his claim with reasons.

In the terminology of logic, the claim an argument attempts to back is called the *conclusion* of the argument. The reasons offered in support of it are called premises. Holmes's conclusion is supported by three premises. Other arguments may be supported by more or fewer *premises*. The simplest arguments have only one premise, as in the following example:

Premise: Thinking clearly and logically is an important skill.
Conclusion: All students should study the rudiments of logic.

Although we define arguments as claims supported by reasons, we should also be aware of the arguer's intentions. First and foremost, the arguer's intention is to *convince* an audience—someone or some group of people—that a given claim is true or false, or that a proposed course of action is or is not justified. Convincing an audience usually requires that reasons be given, and the claim, along with the reasons for it, constitutes an argument.

We can, of course, be our own audience. Holmes probably reasoned through to his conclusion before he presented it to Watson. He may have first considered the hypothesis that the crime was committed by someone inside the house, and then looked to see whether there was evidence to support it. Alternatively, he may have been struck by one or more pieces of evidence and reasoned from there to his conclusion, later reinforcing it with additional evidence or premises. Either way, he acted as his own audience as he developed the argument in his mind.

After Holmes was satisfied that his conclusion was justified, he set about convincing someone else of its truth—in this case, Watson. What it takes to convince an audience depends on its background beliefs. We will have more to say about audiences in Chapter 9, where we introduce a more complete account of everyday arguments. For the moment, it is enough to note the importance of the audience when we are assessing other people's arguments and when we are constructing good arguments of our own. Convincing a hostile audience is more demanding than reinforcing people's belief in a claim they already accept. But in both cases we proceed by constructing arguments that attempt to convince an audience by providing evidence in support of our conclusion.

It is difficult to change the way other people argue, both because reasoning habits are hard to break and because poor arguments—arguments that do not satisfy the criteria for good reasoning—do successfully persuade many people. This is especially true in the case of audiences without a developed sense of reasonableness. In studying reasoning, we aim to neutralize the power of bad arguments by developing logical acumen and the ability to persuade by good reasoning rather than by other means. Our goal is 'reasonable persuasion' rather than mere 'persuasion'.

Simple and Extended Arguments

Arguments can, of course, be much more complex than the ones we have considered so far. A *simple* argument has one conclusion supported by one or more premises. An *extended* argument has a main conclusion supported by premises, some of which are, in turn, conclusions of subsidiary arguments. We can turn Holmes's argument into an extended argument by adding reasons for believing one of the premises—by backing the claim that the dog did not bark with the claim that the neighbors did not hear it, for example.

The majority of arguments we encounter in everyday life are extended arguments. This being said, we begin by studying simple arguments. After we understand them and the different ways of dealing with them, we will be ready to deal with extended arguments and the additional issues that they raise.

Box 2.1 Definitions

◆ An *argument* is a sentence or group of sentences that offers reasons in support of a claim. The reasons are called *premises*. The claim they back is called the *conclusion*. The sentence 'This animal breaths with lungs and is warm-blooded, so it must be a mammal' expresses an argument. Its conclusion is the claim that this animal is a mammal; its premise is the claim that the animal breathes with lungs and is warm-blooded.

◆ An *audience* is an individual or group toward whom an argument is directed. The audience for the sample argument in the previous definition is you, our reader. In ordinary discussion and debate, arguments are used to try to convince particular audiences of a particular point of view.

◆ A *simple* argument has one conclusion supported by one or more premises. An *extended* argument has a main conclusion supported by premises, some of which are conclusions of subsidiary arguments.

EXERCISE 2A

Identify the premises and conclusions in the following three arguments taken from the magazine *Skeptic* (vol. 4, no. 1, 1996). In each case, say whether the argument is simple or extended, and describe the intended audience.

1. Modern scepticism is embodied in the scientific method. . . . But all facts in science are provisional and subject to challenge, and therefore *scepticism is a method leading to provisional conclusions*.

2. [From a column by John Randi] The SRI lab report to Interquest [on the 'Quadro tracker', which claimed to be able to locate drugs, guns, bullets, gold, US currency, lost children, stolen property, and golf balls] stated its conclusion that the tracker is not functional and the manufacturer is scientifically highly questionable at the very least. Both [it and Randi's] analyses support the suspicion that the tracker is a fake device.

3. [Advertisement for *How to Think About Weird Things: Critical Thinking for a New Age*] Now and then a courageous publisher, more concerned with enlightening the public than with profits, will issue a book that honestly assesses pseudoscience and the paranormal. Works of this sort now in print can be counted on your fingers. It is always an occasion for rejoicing when such a book appears, and there are several ways in which *How To Think About Weird Things* is superior to most books designed to teach readers how to tell good science from bad. [Take the main point to be 'You should buy this book.']

3. Distinguishing Arguments and Non-Arguments

We have defined an argument as a unit of discourse that contains a conclusion and supporting statements or premises. Since many groups of sentences do not satisfy this definition and cannot be classified as arguments, we must begin by learning to differentiate between arguments and non-arguments.

Logical Indicators

Watch for premise and conclusion indicators.

One might compare an argument to a journey that takes one to a conclusion via a set of premises. 'Logical indicators' can be compared to signposts along the way—signposts that tell us that particular statements are premises or conclusions. 'Consequently', 'thus', 'so', 'hence', 'it follows that', 'therefore', and 'we conclude that' are important *conclusion indicators*. You can probably think of other words and phrases that function in a similar way. When you come across such words and phrases, you can usually be sure—though we shall note some exceptions—that the following statement is the conclusion of an argument. Consider the following examples:

Money is not an issue for people who have chosen to eat in this restaurant. *So* you shouldn't worry about our recent increase in prices.

All enterprising people support an open global market. You are enterprising. *Therefore I conclude that* you support an open global market.

The italicized words in these two examples indicate that a conclusion follows. In the process, they tell us that these collections of sentences are arguments. The same arguments could easily be advanced using other conclusion indicators, as in the following example:

> Money is not an issue for people who have chosen to eat in this restaurant. *Consequently*, you shouldn't worry about our recent increase in prices.

As in many simple cases, we can easily identify the premises in these examples, for they are the statements that remain after we identify the argument's conclusion.

In other cases we are alerted to the presence of an argument by *premise indicators*. Premise indicators include 'since', 'because', 'for', and 'the reason is'. Once again, you can probably think of others. The argument in our last example can be expressed with a premise rather than a conclusion indicator by wording it as follows.

> *Since* money is not an issue for people who have chosen to eat in this restaurant, you shouldn't worry about our recent increase in prices.

Here are two more sample arguments that use premise indicators:

> *Because* a human being is constituted of both a mind and a body, and the body does not survive death, we cannot properly talk about personal immortality.

> Sheila must be a member of the cycle club, *for* she was at last week's meeting and only members were admitted.

Both of these passages are arguments. As such, they contain a conclusion supported by premises. The premises are identified by the premise indicators we have italicized. In the first case, the word 'because' clearly identifies the premises, which are conjoined by the word 'and'. The remaining statement— 'we cannot properly talk about personal immortality'—is the conclusion that is claimed to follow.

In our second example, the premise indicator is the word 'for'. It tells us that the statements that follow—'she was at last week's meeting' and 'only members were admitted'—are premises for the previous statement, which functions as a conclusion. The word 'and' conjoins these two statements, emphasizing that they work together. In many cases, premise indicators eliminate the need for conclusion indicators, though some arguments use both premise and conclusion indicators. In the cycle club example, the word 'must' in the first statement acts as an oblique conclusion indicator, for it suggests that the first statement necessarily follows from the others.

In deciding whether or not a group of sentences is an argument, it is important to remember that ordinary arguments are expressed in a rich variety of ways. Sometimes the conclusion comes first and is followed by premises. Sometimes the premises come first and are followed by the conclusion. At other times, some of the evidence is given first, followed by the conclusion, after which further evidence is given. In a number of ways, other features of ordinary discourse further complicate argument presentation. Whenever a discourse is an argument, however, you will be able to detect a conclusion and one or more premises.

Box 2.2 *Common Logical Indicators*

Premise Indicators: since, because, for, given that, the reasons are, as can be deduced from, as shown by, as indicated by, may be inferred from, given that, assuming that, may be derived from.

Conclusion Indicators: consequently, thus, so, hence, it follows that, therefore, we conclude that, shows that, proves that, implies that, demonstrates that, allows one to infer that, leads me to believe that, allows us to deduce that.

Indicator Words Used in Other Contexts

Recognize and diagnose explanations.

Our major clues in identifying arguments and differentiating premises and conclusions are logical indicators. But there are times when we need to consider the logic of a chain of reasoning that contains no such indicators. An advertisement may not, for example, contain a conclusion or a premise indicator but it probably invites us to reason in a way that leads to the conclusion that we should buy this or that product.

In other cases, indicator words are used, but not to indicate premises and a conclusion. In the sentence 'Since you arrived on the scene my life has been nothing but trouble', the word 'since' does not act as a premise indicator but signals the passage of time. Likewise, 'for' does not function as a premise indicator in the sentence 'I work for Joe's Trucks', and 'thus' does not function as a conclusion indicator in the remark 'You insert the CD in the CD-ROM thus.' When you come across indicator words that have more than one use, you must therefore be sure that the word or phrase is functioning as a logical indicator in the discourse you are analysing.

In many cases—in the instance we have just noted, for example—it is obvious when indicator words do not function as logical indicators. This is not always so, however, especially in cases where indicators like 'so', 'since', 'therefore', and 'because' are used in giving explanations. Given the complexities of such cases, they require special comment.

In many cases, explanations aim to help us understand states of affairs or events, the rules of a game, different senses of a concept, or what we mean by what we have said. In such cases, explanations do not present an argument.

When someone explains how to bake a cake or build a shed, we are unlikely to mistake the instructions as premises and the result as a claim. Something similar can be said of causal explanations. Consider the following example.

> The mini van was carrying a load in excess of the maximum recommended and was hauling a trailer that had been improperly attached to the vehicle. Consequently, when the driver veered suddenly to the left to avoid a stalled truck, he lost control of the vehicle and the crash ensued.

This passage explains the cause of the crash. That the crash occurred is not in debate, and this is not a statement that requires support. What is in question is the cause of the crash. Thus, the purpose of the discourse is quite different from that of an argument. The explanation offered for the crash might be debated. It probably would be debated if it was used as expert testimony in a trial that accused the driver of traffic violations. In such a context, the explanation generates an argument. But it is not an argument and it does not use the word 'consequently' as a conclusion indicator. The causes it suggests are not presented as claims for which supporting evidence is given. The speaker simply enumerates the factors that she believes led to the event.

On the other hand, consider the following discourse.

> Germany failed because Hitler turned his attention to Russia when he had England at his mercy.

This is a contentious claim, the kind that is likely to elicit discussion and debate if proposed in a conversation about World War II. Many would say it is an overly simplistic explanation of Germany's fall from strength. Our point is that this is an explanation and not an argument: the speaker is simply offering his opinion on the cause of Hitler's defeat. He could be pressed to support his opinion with evidence, but he has not provided any in this remark.

Explanations as Arguments

Distinguish explanations that are and are not arguments.

In other cases, we explain our own or someone else's reasons for believing something and in view of this present premises and a conclusion. In such instances, the explanation contains an argument that needs to be identified and assessed like other arguments. Your first task in dealing with explanations is to distinguish those cases in which they do and do not contain an argument.

Let's imagine that someone challenges the view of Germany's World War II defeat suggested in our last example. Suppose he answers her with the following remarks.

> Sun Tzu's famous book on *The Art of War* tells us that a successful military force must act swiftly and cannot sustain a military operation for a protracted period of time. But Hitler's decision to attack Russia inevitably committed him to a protracted war. Because of this, he was bound to fail once he decided to attack Russia.

In this remark he *explains* the reasons why he believes that the decision to attack Russia precipitated Hitler's fall. One can therefore say that the word 'because' functions as an explanation indicator. But in this case it should also be clear that it functions as a premise indicator, signifying a chain of reasoning that backs his opinion. This chain of reasoning can be summarized as follows.

> First Premise: Sun Tzu's famous book on *The Art of War* tells us that a successful military force must act swiftly and cannot sustain a military operation for a protracted period of time.
>
> Second Premise: Hitler's decision to attack Russia inevitably committed him to a protracted war.
>
> Conclusion: Once Hitler decided to attack Russia, he was bound to fail.

Once we recognize this argument, we might ask a great many questions about it. Does Sun Tzu say what has been attributed to him? Is the proposed principle of military success debatable? Are there counter-examples that cast doubt on it? Did the decision to attack Russia inevitably mean a long war, or did other factors extend it? These are examples of the kinds of questions that need to be asked when we assess an argument like this one. The point to note here is that the explanation offers reasons for believing something and so contains an argument.

We can underscore the argumentative function of some explanations by considering a more mundane example. Imagine that it is the middle of the winter. Clara, who attends high school, wakes up and looks out the window only to discover a blizzard raging. Instead of getting dressed and setting off to school she thinks for a minute, smiles, and goes back to bed. Let's suppose she reasoned as follows:

> Detroit schools close down whenever there is a blizzard, so there will be no school today.

This is an argument. Clara convinces herself she need not go to school. When her father opens her bedroom door and asks her why she isn't ready for school, she explains: 'Because there's a blizzard outside and they close Detroit schools whenever there's a blizzard.' Now she has used the same ideas to explain herself. We have here another case where an explanation explains reasoning and thus contains an argument, in this case an argument for why Clara need not get out of bed.

Once we recognize Clara's argument, we can analyse it and assess it as any other argument. Given that her explanation is an attempt to convince her father by means of the reasoning it presents, he might respond by evaluating her inference. He could challenge the first premise by reminding Clara of occasions when Detroit schools remained open during a blizzard. Or he might accept her argument and her conclusion. Whether or not he agrees, he only treats her remark as an argument if he recognizes it as an attempt to provide premises in support of a conclusion.

These examples show that arguments and explanations are not in every case distinct. In logic, we have an argument whenever we have reasons suggested as premises for a conclusion. Explanations can contain reasoning in this sense and, therefore, can be classified as arguments. So we need to be alert to those that contain arguments and those that do not. The purpose of explanations, remember, is to provide understanding, while that of arguments is to convince others of the truth of a claim.

Box 2.3 Indirect Arguments

The sample arguments we have been discussing are 'explicit' arguments. In analysing such arguments we examine a piece of discourse: a set of written or spoken sentences attributed to an arguer. Most of the arguments in this book are explicit in this sense. But there are occasions, both here and in the give and take of ordinary reasoning, where we need to analyse 'implicit' arguments that someone attributes to someone else.

An example from literature may illustrate this point. In his novel *Redwork* (Toronto: Lester & Orpen Dennys, 1990), Michael Bedard describes a liaison between one of his main characters, Alison, and a philosophy PhD student she nicknamed 'Hegel'. When Alison became pregnant, 'His solution to the problem was as clear, clean and clinical as a logical equation—get rid of it. Instead, she had got rid of him. She hadn't had much use for philosophy since' (p. 24). This implies that Alison's negative experience with her boyfriend convinced her that philosophy is not of use to her. We have no direct discourse to work with, but this implies reasoning along the lines: 'My experience with Hegel was a bad one, Hegel is a philosopher who thinks like a philosopher, therefore philosophy is of no use to me.'

Implicit arguments like this, once they are recognized, can be analysed like other arguments as long as you keep in mind that you do not, in such cases, have a piece of discourse and are analysing the argument someone else has attributed to the reasoner in question. Such arguments are worth analysing for the same reason—because we want to determine whether they are instances of good or bad reasoning (in the case at hand Alison is, as we shall subsequently see, guilty of a faulty generalization).

Indicator Words: Oblique or Missing Altogether

Consider context and internal clues.

Identifying arguments is easiest when indicator words announce the premises and conclusion of an argument. Unfortunately, arguers frequently fail to use logical indicators or use oblique or ambiguous indicator words. In view of this, we must say something about how we can identify arguments and non-arguments in such cases.

When a piece of discourse contains no obvious indicator words we turn to contextual considerations and internal clues to decide whether an argument is present. We ask whether the context is one in which the writer or the speaker is attempting to justify some claim by offering reasons in support of it. The role that context plays in this regard can be seen in the case of advertisements. Though they rarely use premise or conclusion indicators, they seek to persuade us that we should buy this or that product, usually by providing reasons why we should. It is not difficult to sort out their structure, for the conclusion of an advertisement—Buy this or that!—is obvious and we need only establish what reasons are proposed for this conclusion.

Advertisements are not the only argumentative discourses free of premise or conclusion indicators. Consider the following example.

The ruins of ancient Aztec pyramids are very similar to those found in Egypt. Also, animals and vegetation found on the eastern coasts of South America bear a striking resemblance to those of West Africa. From all appearances, there was once a large land mass connecting these continents.

This passage does not contain any standard indicator words that make a conclusion 'jump out' at you. None the less, the first two sentences report observational data that appear to justify the speculative third statement—a statement of a kind that needs to be supported. Noting that the author prefaces this apparent conclusion with the expression 'from all appearances', we take this to be a context in which she offers the first two sentences as premises for the last sentence. The expression 'from all appearances' is another of the numerous expressions that can obliquely function as a conclusion indicator, equivalent to 'hence' and 'therefore'. The richness of our language provides for the possibility of many such oblique indicators.

Discerning arguments on the basis of context and internal clues is a skill everyone has to some degree, but a skill that most of us need to hone. As with most logical skills, practice breeds proficiency. The more time you spend practising, the better you will become at distinguishing arguments from non-arguments. Keep in mind that the line between these two kinds of discourse is sometimes very thin and that we must proceed with caution when there are no indicators to guide us.

An example can illustrate the issues that arise in difficult cases of argument identification. For demonstration purposes, we have adapted the following example from a letter to the editor of the *Hamilton Spectator* (10 June 1981), written on the occasion of a strike by steelworkers, steel being an important industry in Hamilton.

> Haven't we had enough letters to the editorial page of the *Spectator* every day and from cry-baby steelworkers or their wives talking about how the Stelco strike is killing them? I am sure there are hundreds of pro-union letters going into the *Spectator* office, but only the anti-union ones are printed.
>
> I would not be a bit surprised if Stelco and the *Spectator* were working together to lower the morale of the steelworkers who chose to strike for higher wages.

Even when we read this letter more than once, it is still difficult to say whether or not an argument is intended. Certainly an opinion is expressed. But does the author offer reasons to back it?

If we distil an argument from the letter, it might look something like this:

> Premise: We have had enough letters to the editorial page from cry-baby steelworkers or their wives talking about how the Stelco strike is killing them.
> Premise: I am sure there are hundreds of pro-union letters going into the *Spectator* office, but only the anti-union ones are printed.
> Conclusion: There is reason to believe that Stelco and the *Spectator* are working together to lower the morale of the steelworkers.

In proposing this interpretation of the letter we have made some linguistic adjustments. The final sentence in the published letter reads like a privately held suspicion. Assuming that the writer wants to convince readers on the basis of the considerations raised in the earlier sentences of the letter, we must reword it so that it carries the impact of a conclusion. For this reason we changed 'I would not be a bit surprised if . . .' to 'There is reason to believe that . . .'.

To create our version of the first premise, we put into statement form what appeared in the letter as a question, changing 'Haven't we had enough letters . . . ?' to 'We have had enough letters . . . .' This change highlights a stylistic feature of many arguments in ordinary language. We have already seen that an argument is a unit of discourse consisting of a group of statements. Genuine questions, however, are not statements but requests for information. As such, a genuine question cannot serve as either a premise or a conclusion. But not all questions are requests for information. In contrast, some questions are disguised statements or assertions expressed as questions for the sake of rhetorical effectiveness. We call these *rhetorical questions*. In the case at hand, the writer is not genuinely asking whether there have or have not been enough letters. Rather, her reference to 'enough letters' 'every day' in the context of a complaint about an anti-union bias is a way of stating that there *have* been enough letters. Our revised wording for the first premise clarifies the arguer's point.

We could have constructed a more complex representation of the apparent chain of reasoning in the letter before us. We could, for example, have introduced as a subconclusion the statement that 'the *Spectator* presents a biased view of the Stelco strike', which is implied in the second premise. This subconclusion might in turn be construed as a premise for the main conclusion, that Stelco and the *Spectator* are working together to lower the morale of the steelworkers. In many cases, alternative representations of the same argument are possible.

Questions remain, however. Does the writer argue, asserting a claim and providing evidence for it? Do our proposed premises and conclusion capture reasoning in the author's mind? Is this a context in which reasons are given for some claim? Perhaps so, perhaps not. It is always difficult to discern someone else's intentions if they do not use explicit or even oblique indicator words. Certainly this is a context in which an argument would be appropriate—the letter is, after all, published in the context of an exchange of opinions about the steelworkers' strike. That being said, you may think there is not enough internal evidence to show that the author of the letter should be attributed the argument we have suggested.

In cases like this, the indeterminate nature of the statements makes it a judgement whether or not an argument is intended. We chose this example precisely because it is difficult to decide. In such a case, you might take context and internal clues into account and still reasonably decide that the author is doing nothing more than expressing an opinion, or that she has moved beyond opinion into the realm of argument, or that you simply can't decide. To help you decide what to do in such a case, we offer one more principle of interpretation, 'the principle of charity'.

Box 2.4 *The Principle of Charity*

The *Spectator* example we have already discussed is a case where there are good reasons to be worried about misinterpretation. In such a case, we don't want to misinterpret, but we have no clear way to establish whether the discourse is an argument. Many logicians deal with such contexts by invoking the 'principle of charity'. We want to be fair in judging other people's arguments, so in cases where we are unsure whether a discourse is an argument we give a writer or speaker the benefit of the doubt: we try to interpret what they are saying in the best possible light. We will use this principle both when we interpret premises and conclusions and when we decide whether or not a discourse is an argument.

In the case of the *Spectator* letter, the principle of charity suggests that we should not interpret the letter as an argument. We have not yet discussed the difference between good and bad arguments, but it should still be clear that the letter is very problematic if we interpret it as an argument. So construed, its most significant shortcoming is its unsubstantiated claim that there are hundreds of union letters being ignored by the *Spectator*. A good argument has to provide evidence for such a claim.

Since it is not clear whether our letter was intended as an argument and interpreting it in this way yields weak reasoning, the principle of charity compels us to judge the letter as a strongly worded opinion rather than an argument. A concern for fairness and a determination to avoid misinterpretation leads us to this decision. This being said, we would still emphasize that this is a borderline case and that our decision could have gone the other way if the author had used indicator words, or if the context and internal evidence suggested that the author was providing support for her suggestion that the *Spectator* and Stelco are acting in collusion, or even if she substantiated her claim that several hundred pro-union letters had been sent to the editor without being published. In the absence of such evidence, the principle of charity tells us that we should not treat the letter as an argument.

Discussing Borderline Cases

Be tentative when dealing with borderline cases.

When we attempt to identify and assess arguments it is important to bear in mind the risk of *misinterpreting* someone's claims. We have already said a great deal about vagueness, ambiguity, and other causes of misinterpretation. When we construct our own arguments we want to construct them in a way that prevents misinterpretation. When we attempt to identify and assess other people's arguments we want to be equally careful to ensure that we properly interpret their remarks. We must, therefore, proceed with caution when we are trying to decide whether a particular discourse is an argument or non-argument, especially in borderline cases where the decision might go either way.

In dealing with borderline cases, it is a good idea to acknowledge the tentative nature of any analysis we propose. In cases where we wish to analyse a possible argument, this can be accomplished by introducing it with a statement like:

> It is not clear whether these remarks contain an argument, but they might be read as arguing . . .

We can then go on to outline the tentative argument we wish to discuss and to analyse it as we would analyse other arguments.

The 'rider' that we add to such analyses allows us to deal with possible arguments that may be worth discussing even if they are not intended. If we work at the *Hamilton Spectator*, for example, we might wish to take issue with the argument that may be contained in the letter we discussed, perhaps because others could interpret the letter in this way. In such a case, we can analyse the possible argument as long as we do so in a way that acknowledges that it may not be intended. We might, for example, respond to the *Spectator* letter by remarking that:

> It is not clear to us whether the author of this letter intends to argue that our newspaper is acting in collusion with Stelco, but we would like to take the opportunity to address this possibility. If she is arguing for some such conclusion, then she has failed to adequately back her claims. . . .

Here we have been careful to preface our critique of the letter's possible argument with a remark that recognizes that it may not have been intended.

Provided that we recognize the tentative nature of speculative interpretations in this or some other way—by acknowledging that we are not sure how to interpret the claims in question, that they can be variously interpreted, and so on—we can identify and assess possible arguments if we think that this is a useful way to further discussion and debate.

A Flow Chart

As you practise identifying arguments, you will come to have little difficulty distinguishing arguments and non-arguments. In time, you will be able to identify immediately many discourses as arguments or non-arguments. When you are still mastering such skills, or dealing with difficult cases, however, you may want to approach the task in a more deliberate, step-by-step fashion. You can follow the steps we have outlined in the flow chart below. Following the steps and answering the questions that they prompt will help you decide whether to treat a particular discourse as an argument.

Box 2.5 *Identifying an Argument*

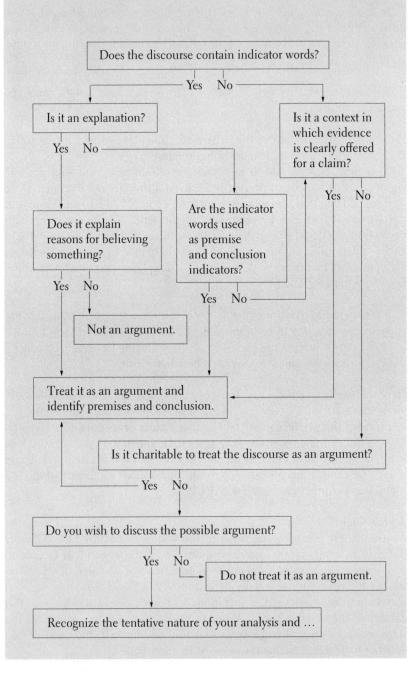

Exercise 2B

Decide whether the following passage contains any arguments or explanations. Identify any explanations that you find.

> [Albert Schweitzer, dismissing the thesis that the historical Jesus was mentally ill in *The Psychiatric Study of Jesus* (Boston: Beacon Press, 1948)] The criticism of the psychopathological writings which we are considering yields, then, the following results: (1) The material which is in agreement with these books is for the most part unhistorical. (2) Out of the material which is certainly historical, a number of acts and utterances of Jesus impress the authors as pathological because the latter are too little acquainted with the contemporary thought of the time to be able to do justice to it. A series of wrong deductions springs from the fact that they have not the least understanding of the peculiar problems inherent in the course of the public ministry. (3) From the false preconceptions and with the help of entirely hypothetical symptoms, they construct pictures of sickness which are themselves artifacts and which, moreover, cannot be made to conform exactly with the clinical forms of sickness diagnosed by the authors. (4) The only symptoms to be accepted as historical and possible to be discussed from the psychiatric point of view—the high estimate which Jesus has of himself and perhaps also the hallucination of baptism—fall far short of proving the existence of mental illness.

4. Diagramming Arguments

A simple argument consists of a conclusion supported by one or more premises. An extended argument consists of sub-arguments whose conclusions serve as premises for the main claim or conclusion. In ordinary reasoning, the conclusion may be stated first or last, or it may be sandwiched between the premises. In many cases, the premises and conclusions of an argument are repeated, in slightly different variants.

Often, remarks and comments not integral to an argument are interspersed through its premises and conclusion. They can be a confusing feature of argumentative discourse. We call these aspects of a discourse 'noise'. In dealing with arguments you need to be able to eliminate noise, which appears in a variety of forms. Sometimes it appears as introductory information that sets the stage or background for an argument that follows. In other cases, noise may consist of statements intended only as asides. They may have no direct bearing on the argument but give an article a flourish or a dash of humour. In setting out the premises and conclusion of an argument we discard noise, but in doing so we must be sure that we do not also discard something integral to the argument.

To make reasoning more readily available for inspection and analysis, we will use a procedure called 'diagramming'. We will introduce other procedures in other chapters, but diagramming will be our principal way of representing the structure of an argument. What follows is our full method of diagramming. We begin by extracting an argument's components. In difficult cases, it is easiest to begin with the conclusion, which is the overriding point that the argument aims to make. After we determine the conclusion, we can ask what evidence is given to establish it, thereby identifying the argument's premises.

For the purposes of diagramming, we create a 'legend' that lists and numbers the argument's premises as P1, P2, etc. and lists the conclusion as C. In extended arguments having more than one conclusion, we will designate the subsidiary conclusions as C1, C2, etc., and list the main conclusion as MC, but we will leave such arguments for later. After we construct a legend we put the legend symbols on a page and connect them with arrows illustrating the directions of support from the premises to the conclusion.

If we wish to diagram the argument:

Automobile accidents are the prime cause of deaths among teenagers, so high schools should teach students good driving skills.

we can create a legend as follows:

P1 = Automobile accidents are the prime cause of deaths among teenagers.
C = High schools should teach students good driving skills.

Once we have this legend, we can diagram the argument as:

The diagram portrays the essential structure of our argument. In doing so, it presents the argument in a way that allows for relatively straightforward argument assessment.

When diagramming an argument, we must frequently make linguistic adjustments. We delete the indicator words, since the legend symbols perform their task, indicating premises and conclusion and the ways in which they are connected. We also exclude any remarks we interpret as noise. In the process of listing the premise(s) and conclusion it may be necessary to make slight changes in their wording so that the diagram reads smoothly. These changes can include altering the tenses of verbs or reformulating as statements argument components that were originally expressed as exclamations or rhetorical questions.

Box 2.6 A Shortcut Method
We shall usually define our legend in the way already indicated. But there are occasions when we value a quicker method. A shortcut method is to circle each statement in the discourse and then number them consecutively. The diagram will then show the relationships between the numbered statements (and those numbers that express 'noise' can be omitted). When the diagram is set out on the page, you can clearly see which statements represent P1, or C1, etc. You might, for example, identify the P1 and C of the last example in the following way:
1. [Automobile accidents are the prime cause of deaths among teenagers.], so
2. [High schools should teach students good driving skills.].

This is a quicker method for completing practice exercises and more efficient than writing out the premises and conclusion in full. Use it when it is convenient (as we will on occasion), but be aware that for some cases this method is not suitable: as when we need to make minor revisions to the actual statements that the arguer uses (in order to eliminate 'noise', clearly express premises and conclusion more clearly, or to recognize implicit components).

Linked and Convergent Premises

Premises may support a conclusion in one of two ways. They may separately 'converge' upon a conclusion, or they may be 'linked' in support of the conclusion. Linked premises work together. Taken independently, they do not support the argument's conclusion. Convergent premises do not require each other, for they support the conclusion independently of the argument's other premises.

Consider the Sherlock Holmes argument we discussed earlier. It can be diagrammed as follows.

P1 = Although the living room window is open, there are no footprints outside, despite the softness of the ground due to yesterday's rain.
P2 = The clasp on the box was not broken but opened with a key that had been hidden behind the clock.
P3 = The dog did not bark.
C = The crime was committed by someone in the house.

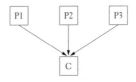

In our diagram, each of the premises is joined to the conclusion by a separate arrow indicating that it provides an independent reason for concluding that the crime was committed by someone in the house. You can see that the premises are convergent if you pretend for a moment that the only premise in the argument is P1, P2, or P3. In each case, we would have a weaker argument, but the premise would still provide some evidence for the conclusion. None of the premises requires one of the other premises for this to be the case.

Compare the two premises in the argument:

The crime was committed by someone who is strong. But George is weak. So he cannot be the culprit.

In this case, the premises depend on each other. We say they are 'linked' because the claim that the crime was committed by someone strong provides *no support* for the conclusion that George cannot be the culprit until we combine it with the second premise, which tells us that George is weak. In a diagram, we recognize the linked nature of these two premises by placing a plus sign (+) between them, drawing a line beneath them, and using a single arrow to join them to the conclusion. Our finished diagram is:

P1 = The crime was committed by someone very strong.
P2 = George is very weak.
C = George cannot be the culprit.

If you have difficulty deciding whether you should join one premise P to another, ask whether the support it provides for the conclusion depends on some other premise(s). If the answer is *no*, draw an arrow directly from P to the conclusion. If the answer is *yes*, ask yourself which of the other premises must be assumed for P to provide support for the conclusion. Join P to these premises with a + sign, and use one arrow to join this whole set of premises to the conclusion.

The following diagrams of some other simple arguments we have discussed further illustrate diagramming and the difference between premises that are linked and convergent.

(i) P1 = Sheila was at last week's meeting.
   P2 = Only members were admitted.
   C = Sheila must be a member of the cycle club.

(ii) P1 = The ruins of ancient Aztec pyramids are very similar to those found in Egypt.
   P2 = Animals and vegetation found on the eastern coasts of South America bear a striking resemblance to those of West Africa.
   C = There was once a large land mass connecting these continents.

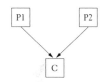

We finish with an example from Homer's *Odyssey*. In a famous incident in this ancient story, Odysseus and his men land on an island inhabited by one-eyed giants called Cyclops. When Odysseus speaks to a Cyclops inside a cave he reminds him that Zeus requires him to treat guests well. The Cyclops responds:

'Stranger, you must be a fool, or must have come from very far afield. For you warn me to take care of my responsibilities to Zeus and we Cyclops care nothing about Zeus and the rest of the gods.'

In making this reply, the Cyclops offers the following argument.

P1 = You warn me to take care of my responsibilities to Zeus.
P2 = We Cyclops care nothing about Zeus and the rest of the gods.
C = You must be a fool or have come from very far afield.

Diagramming is very useful as a tool in the analysis of extended arguments. Extended arguments, you will recall, consist of subsidiary arguments whose conclusions constitute premises for the main claim. There may be several strata of subsidiary arguments. A subsidiary conclusion, derived from two linked premises, which serves as one of two convergent premises for the main conclusion, would be diagrammed as follows:

P1 = Premise for subsidiary argument.
P2 = Premise for subsidiary argument.
C1 = Subsidiary conclusion used as a premise for a main conclusion.
P3 = Other (convergent) premise for the main conclusion.
MC = Main conclusion.

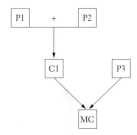

We shall demonstrate and discuss diagramming for extended arguments in a later chapter. For the moment, we shall concentrate on simple arguments, keeping in mind that the same techniques can be employed to cover the more complex instances of reasoning in extended arguments. The process of diagramming simple arguments is in Box 2.7. It completes our introduction to arguments and provides a basis for the more complex account of arguments we shall develop in later chapters.

Box 2.7 Analysing a Simple Argument
- Determine the conclusion, that is, the major point the argument is trying to establish.
- Mark the text into blocks that have a unified logical purpose, the stating of a premise or the drawing of a conclusion. Bracket digressions and noise and underline key terms.
- Express the content of each block in statement form. In doing so, try to capture the author's intended meaning.
- Create a legend listing the premises as P1, P2, etc. and listing the conclusion as C.
- Join each independent premise to the conclusion with an arrow.
- Conjoin linked premises with a + and connect them to the conclusion with an arrow.

EXERCISE 2C

In a few sentences, define each of the following concepts and illustrate it with an example of your own.
1. argument
2. logical indicators
3. diagram legend
4. premise indicator
5. linked premises
6. rhetorical questions
7. audience
8. convergent premises
9. conclusion
10. conclusion indicator
11. the principle of charity
*12. indirect arguments
13. explanation

EXERCISE 2D

Each of the following passages contains a simple argument. In each case, identify any logical indicators, create a legend, and diagram the argument.
*1. We have defined an argument as a unit of discourse that contains a conclusion and supporting statements or premises. Since many groups of sentences do not satisfy this definition and cannot be classified as arguments, we must begin learning about arguments in this sense by learning to differentiate between arguments and non-arguments.
2. All enterprising people support an open global market. You are enterprising. Therefore I conclude that you support an open global market.
3. In other cases, indicator words are used, but not to indicate premises and a conclusion. When you come across indicator words that have more than one use, you must therefore be sure that the word or phrase is functioning as a logical indicator in the discourse you are analysing.
*4. Don't worry about our recent increase in prices. Money is not an issue for people who have chosen to eat in this restaurant.
*5. In logic, we have an argument whenever we have reasons suggested as premises for a conclusion. Explanations can contain reasoning in this sense and can, therefore, be classified as arguments.
6. [Clara explaining why she hasn't got ready to go to school] 'Because there's a blizzard outside and they close Detroit schools whenever there's a blizzard.'
*7. Sun Tzu's famous book on *The Art of War* tells us that a successful military force must act swiftly and cannot sustain a military operation for a protracted period of time. But Hitler's decision to attack Russia inevitably committed him to a long war. Because of this, he was bound to fail once he decided to attack Russia.

8. In this remark he explains the reasons why he believes that the decision to attack Russia precipitated Hitler's fall. One can therefore say that the word 'because' in this passage is an explanation indicator.

9. It is important that you be alert to variations from the usual indicator words, for the richness of our language makes many variations possible.

10. We have already seen that an argument is a unit of discourse consisting of a group of statements. But genuine questions are not statements, but requests for information. As such, a genuine question cannot serve as either a premise or conclusion.

11. Misinterpreting someone else's thinking is a serious mistake and we should therefore proceed with caution when we are trying to decide whether a particular discourse is or is not an argument.

12. When we construct our own arguments we want to construct them in a way that prevents misinterpretation. When we attempt to identify and assess other people's arguments we want to be equally careful in ensuring that we properly interpret their remarks. We must, in view of this, proceed with caution when we are trying to decide whether a particular discourse is an argument or non-argument, especially in borderline cases where one might argue one way or the other.

13. It is not clear whether the letter was intended as an argument, and interpreting it in this way yields a weak one. In view of this, the principle of charity compels us to judge the letter as a strongly worded opinion and not an argument.

14. We delete the indicator words, as the legend symbols perform their task, indicating premises and conclusion and the ways in which they are connected.

*15. We deduce that these premises are 'linked'. Why? Well, the claim that the crime was committed by someone strong does not support the conclusion that George cannot be the culprit until we combine it with the second premise, which tells us that George is weak.

MAJOR EXERCISE 2M

For each of the following passages, decide whether an argument is present and explain the reasons for your decision. Diagram any arguments you find. In two cases, rewrite the arguments you find, changing the order of the premises and conclusion and using different indicator words that will clearly convey in English the structure that your diagram depicts.

*1. Religion is nothing but superstition. Historians of religion agree that it had its beginnings in magic and witchcraft. Today's religious belief is just an extension of this.

*2. The first time I went out onto the ice and saw the seal hunt it sickened me. I could not believe that a Canadian industry could involve such cruelty to animals and callous brutalization of men for profit.

3. [Josef Joffe, discussing America's role in the world, *Time*, 3 July 1995] But why not be a 'cheap hawk', letting the others take care of the world's business? The answer is easy. The Japanese won't take care of free trade. . . . The Russians, if left alone, will happily sell nuclear-weapons technology to Iran, and the French would be similarly obliging about lifting the embargo on Iraq. And who will contain China, the next superpower?

4. The following letter appeared in the Toronto *Globe and Mail*, 25 June 1987] Re: your front-page story about Sandra Bernier, the 11-year-old Roman Catholic altar girl who has been serving Mass at Sacre-Coeur Church for four years, and Emmett Cardinal Carter's order barring Sandra from the service to mark the parish's hundredth anniversary ('Girl Not Allowed To Help At Altar When Cardinal Presides Over Mass'—June 19): As practising Roman Catholics we are saddened by the Cardinal's order, and by the Vatican attitude that inspired it.

5. [The following letter concerns the incident discussed in number 4 (*The Globe and Mail*, 25 June 1987)] Re: 'Pulled From The Altar' (June 20): A Cardinal of the Roman Catholic Church is caught in the midst of a blatant case of discrimination against women when Sandra Bernier is told that her gender prevents her from serving at a Eucharist. How can we, as responsible citizens of Ontario, allow our righteous legislators to continue to use public money to support [a separate Roman Catholic] school system whose leadership denies the most basic of Canadian human rights?

6. [*Time*, 13 July 1995] To expect entertainment moguls to stop peddling lucrative scum is just about as realistic as to expect hyenas to become vegetarians.

7. [Letter to *Sports Illustrated*, 14 Feb. 1984] True. Wayne Gretzky's scoring streak is amazing. But to compare Gretzky's streak with Joe DiMaggio's 56-game gem is ludicrous—it's no contest. Gretzky kept his streak alive by scoring into an empty net in the closing seconds of a game against Chicago. Tell me, how many times did Joe D. come to bat in the bottom of the ninth with no one playing in the outfield? Case closed!

8. [From Jonelle P. Weaver, 'Salad Days', *New Woman*, July 1995] Today, there is a tendency to reduce oil [in vinaigrette salad dressing] and make up the volume in acidic liquid. That is a gross error, because the tongue-puckering results annihilate the gentle flavors of other ingredients.

9. [From a letter in defence of the Serb decision to take UN peacekeepers hostage, *Time*, 3 July 1995] They have responded, in accordance with appropriate military procedure, by . . . taking POWs—not hostages, because they are soldiers in combat . . . having the right to fire and bomb. . . .

*10. [From another letter defending the Serbs in the same issue of *Time*] What right have we to deny the Bosnian Serbs their wish to form a separate state of their own in Bosnia. . . . Would that be a crime? It certainly wasn't the case when the Slovenes and Croats—as well as the Bosnian Muslims—sought independence from the then very viable state of Yugoslavia.

11. [Letter to *New Woman*, July 1995] I am disgusted that *New Woman* printed the letter from B.A. Showalter. . . . Showalter said, 'You don't see straight people pushing their lifestyle on everyone else.' But straight people and straight society do just that. From day one, children are assumed to be heterosexual. They are exposed to tales of heterosexual romance, pushed to enjoy the company of the opposite sex, and given little opportunity to explore the alternative.

*12. The island of Antigua, located in the Caribbean, boasts secluded caves and dazzling beaches. The harbour at St John's is filled with the memories of the great British navy that once called there.

*13. [Letter to *New Woman*, July 1995, in support of a commitment to cover New Age issues] When I was going through a recent bout with depression, I discovered the 'goddess spirituality' movement. I chose Artemis as the goddess I would seek comfort in. . . . I built an altar to her in my room, burned incense, and meditated, and I found comfort in these ritualistic practices. I think this type of paganism can be an important tool for women to discover their inner strengths . . . .

14. [Advertisement for Ceasefire, the Children's Defense Fund and Friends, 1995] Each year, hundreds of children accidentally shoot themselves or someone else. So if you get a gun to protect your child, what's going to protect your child from the gun?

15. [From a passage in John Grisham's *The Chamber* (London: Century, 1994, p. 430), where his protagonist, Adam, and the Governor discuss whether his client will name an accomplice and be granted clemency] It won't happen, Governor. I've tried. I've asked so often, and he's denied so much, that it's not even discussed any more.

CHOOSING

YOUR

WORDS

In Chapter 1 we discussed the language used in reasoning. In Chapter 2 we discussed arguments—the building blocks of reasoning. In this chapter, we return to questions of language, discussing it in the context of specific issues that arise when we construct and analyse arguments. To this end, we will look at:

♦ vagueness and ambiguity;
♦ equivocation and verbal disputes;
♦ extensional and intensional definitions;
♦ definitions by genus and differentia; and
♦ ways you can ensure that you express what you mean.

It has happened to everyone. In the course of a conversation we say something that we believe is perfectly clear and intelligible. Then someone interrupts us with the comment, 'I'm not sure what you mean.' After two or more interpretations are explained we realize that our statement was unclear.

In live conversation—in seminar settings, meetings, over coffee—you are there to clarify your remarks. It is more difficult when someone is reading what you have written. Thus it is particularly important to choose your words carefully when you commit yourself on paper, both when you are critiquing someone else's argument and when you are developing your own position on an issue. Others must do the same if they expect you to understand their claims.

This chapter will alert you to some of the considerations that can ensure precision in your language when you are composing arguments. You must learn to keep them in mind when you are constructing arguments (and especially written arguments) and be able to discuss them when you are analysing and critiquing other people's reasoning.

1. Using Words Precisely

Choose words that communicate your meaning with precision.

Words mean what the users of the language use them to mean. Because language is fluid and dynamic the meanings of words shift over time, new words are coined, and old words acquire additional meanings. In its original sense the word 'apology' meant a defence of one's beliefs and behaviour. Now it usually refers to an 'I'm sorry' statement. The word 'megaton' entered our vocabulary as a measurement of the destructive force of nuclear weapons. The prefix 'mega' has since come to be used in many other contexts where the speaker or writer wants to emphasize superlative size or strength.

And the fluidity of language is not only a function of time. Spatial and social contexts also produce changes in expression and meaning. Britons, Australians, Canadians, and Americans all speak English, but each has a fund of words and phrases that do not find currency with the others.

For our purposes, the significance of the fluidity of language is that the meanings of words are not always definite and clear, and that there is considerable room for interpretation when it comes to specific words.

Euphemisms are one class of expressions in which the fluidity of language raises issues relevant to reasoning. Euphemisms substitute mild and indirect ways of speaking for those that are blunt and harsh. Euphemistic terminology reflects the influence of social factors on our language. Many euphemistic words are part of our normal and approved vocabulary. In the interests of social grace or politeness they are inoffensive substitutes for coarse, harsh, or inelegant expressions. 'Passed away' is not as harsh as 'died'. The veterinarian does not 'kill' the family pet but 'puts it to sleep', and advertisements recommend laxatives to 'relieve irregularity' rather than 'move the bowels'. Euphemisms of this sort are not only acceptable, they are desirable as long as they do not muddle someone's intended meaning.

In contrast, there are times when meanings are distorted by the use of euphemisms. Political activists accuse politicians and militarists of using intentionally misleading euphemisms to play down the horrific dangers inherent in developing nuclear weapons and nuclear power. They cite as examples the use of phrases like 'normal aberration' to refer to the Three Mile Island nuclear station breakdown, the expression 'clean bomb' to denote the neutron bomb (which kills people but leaves buildings standing), and the words 'nuclear exchange' to refer to a nuclear war. We leave it for you to decide whether George Orwell was too cynical when he contended—in 'Politics and the English Language'—that 'political language has to consist largely of euphemisms, question begging, and sheer cloudy vagueness. . . . Such phraseology is needed if one wants to name things without calling up [disquieting] mental pictures of them.'

Extension, Intension, and Tone

When we remember that the meanings of many words are in flux and that new words are constantly infiltrating our vocabulary, we can appreciate the need for constantly updating our dictionaries. The purpose of dictionaries is to collect and collate the words of a given language, to identify their meanings, and to keep abreast of changes in word usage. What a particular word means can be defined in terms of its 'extension' (sometimes called its 'denotation'); its 'intension' (sometimes called its 'connotation'); and its 'tone'.

The extension of a word is the class of things named by that word. Thus the extension of the word 'game' includes all activities to which 'game' refers. As a subset of this class, the term 'card game' includes all games within the larger class of games in which the players use one or more decks of cards.

In contrast, the intension of a word is the group of identifying characteristics that characterize the members of the class named by that word (i.e., each member of the word's extension). The intension of the word 'game' is given in the following definition: 'a game is an activity pursued as a diversion or form of entertainment, in accordance with established rules, the outcome of which may depend on skill, strength, or luck.'

The tone of a word is the group of emotional associations it elicits and the mental pictures it conjures up. Some words are essentially neutral in tone. This is usually the case with scientific and academic terms. Other words carry a negative tone, that is, we generally react with repugnance to them. Words like 'pimp', 'bastard', and 'derelict' fall into this category. Other terms carry a positive tone: 'motherhood', 'patriotism', and the like. Most terms are neither negative nor positive but neutral—words such as 'wine', 'house', 'telephone', and 'stapler'. We need also note that negative terms may be used neutrally ('Henry played the part of a pimp in last night's play') and that neutral words, depending on the context, may be given a positive or negative tone, as in: 'You waste money on two bottles of wine a day?' she asked her brother.

2. Vagueness and Ambiguity

A word or phrase is *vague* if it has no clearly specifiable meaning; it is *ambiguous* if it has more than one specifiable meaning. We are, for example, hard put to assign any clear meaning to 'the American dream' or 'existential situation' or 'conservative' or 'liberal'. These are examples of linguistic vagueness, and when we use such words and phrases without a further qualification, our audience has no alternative but to read into them whatever meanings they associate with them—just as people supply the details to a horoscope by interpreting it in light of their personal situation. Today's horoscope for Sagittarians says, among other things, 'Hang in there.' Precisely what that means will vary for Sagittarians, so much so that virtually any Sagittarian (or Gemini or Aquarian, for that matter) will be able to interpret it according to his or her individual objectives and ongoing projects.

Words or phrases are ambiguous when they have more than one specifiable meaning in the context in which they appear. Sometimes ambiguity (called 'amphibole' or 'syntactic ambiguity') results from unclear grammatical constructions. A sign over the dispensary in a drugstore that reads 'We dispense with accuracy' is ambiguous because the structure of the sentence makes it unclear what the verb 'dispense' applies to: the sentence could, therefore, be interpreted to mean 'We fill prescriptions accurately' or 'We pay no attention to accuracy in filling prescriptions'. Other cases of ambiguity (called 'semantic ambiguity') turn on the multiple meanings of words. The joke that 'The trouble with being a writer in a dictatorship is that the government keeps revoking your poetic licence' elicits a smile because 'revoking your licence' in this context can be interpreted to mean an official permit, or a writer's freedom to violate rules of syntax, rhyme, and the like.

Equivocation and Verbal Disputes

Although ambiguity is indispensable to entertainment and creative writing, it is usually a problem in directly informative discourse. And it is a frequent fault. The form of bad argument, or 'fallacy', called equivocation consists of using a term, phrase, or sentence that is semantically or syntactically ambiguous more than once in an essay or article, but with two or more meanings that are confused. If it is a key term or phrase or sentence, an unwarranted conclusion may be drawn. Consider the argument:

> If, as scientists tell us, energy neither comes into being nor goes out of being, I can't understand why there should be an energy crisis.

The problem with this reasoning concerns the meaning of the word 'energy'. In its first occurrence it refers to the total amount of energy in the universe. In its second occurrence, it refers to our diminishing gas and oil reserves.

Consider a second example:

> Science has discovered many laws of nature. This surely constitutes proof that there is a God, for wherever there are laws, there must be a lawgiver. Consequently, God must exist as the Great Lawgiver of the universe.

We can diagram this argument as follows.

P1 = Science has discovered many laws of nature.
P2 = Wherever there are laws there must be a lawgiver.
C = [Science shows us that] God, the Great Lawgiver of the universe, must exist.

This argument might initially seem convincing, but not if you think carefully about the meaning of the word 'laws', which is used in this argument in two different senses. Prescriptive laws are laid down by a legislative body or lawgiver, but descriptive laws simply identify regularities or uniform patterns in the behaviours of things within the universe as observed by scientists. P1 is clearly true only if 'laws' is interpreted to mean 'descriptive' laws, but P2 is true only if 'laws' is interpreted to mean 'prescriptive laws'. The conclusion seems to follow only because the argument equivocates these two different senses of the word 'law'.

When discourse, spoken or written, is not the product of a single thinker but a discussion or debate between two or more persons or groups, equivocation may take the form of a 'verbal dispute', which must be distinguished from a 'real dispute'. For there to be a real dispute, each party to the dispute must affirm what the other denies, and vice versa. In a verbal dispute, each of the disputants uses a key term or phrase with a different meaning. It follows that they are not talking about the same thing and cannot be denying what each other is affirming. What appears to be a real difference between them is not a real difference at all. Their dispute is only apparent, merely verbal.

Imagine two people arguing the morality of euthanasia (popularly known as mercy-killing) and whether or not it should be legalized. One maintains that euthanasia is morally justifiable because it confers on terminally ill patients the opportunity to die with dignity rather than being kept alive by life-support systems. The other argues that you cannot disguise the reality with euphemisms and that euthanasia is morally wrong because it is, in the final analysis, nothing less than murder. 'Euthanasia is morally justifiable' and 'Euthanasia is not morally justifiable' appear to signify a real dispute until it is recognized that the first person is talking about 'passive' euthanasia, which is a matter of withholding extraordinary life-support systems, thereby allowing the individual to die, and the second is talking about 'active' euthanasia, which is a matter of effecting the death of the individual by, for instance, the injection of a lethal drug. This is not to say that the morality of either type of euthanasia cannot be debated, only that our two debaters in this case cannot proceed as long as each is focusing on a different aspect of the issue.

Agreements also may be merely verbal. A real agreement requires that key terms in the agreement be understood in the same sense. A verbal agreement, like a verbal dispute, is only apparent because each party to the agreement is operating with a different understanding of crucial terms and phrases.

David Hume, an eighteenth-century Scottish philosopher, claimed to have reconciled the advocates of two extreme positions with respect to human freedom—the 'determinists', who argued that our sense of freedom is illusory because 'Every event has a cause', and the 'libertarians', who insisted that 'Man is a free being.' But the reconciliation of the two was purchased at the cost of defining 'free' differently from the way it was used by the libertarian. Whereas the libertarian held that an individual's actions are not determined by forces beyond his or her control, Hume defined 'freedom' as a lack of coercion. Hume's definition does not get to the bottom of the issue because it does not, in the opinion of the libertarian, provide a sufficient basis for moral responsibility.

Particularly in writing and in formal oral presentations, you must strive for clarity and precision if you are to write or say what you mean. Clarity is largely, though not entirely, a result of care in your choice of words. Invest time and thought in selecting the words best suited to communicating your claims. Striving for such precision involves ensuring that, given the context, the words you choose have a single and specifiable meaning. To avoid equivocation it must be clear that key terms are used consistently with the same meaning throughout your text. Keep your dictionary handy and identify the meaning of a key term that suits your needs, and stay with it. If the term that comes to mind is used for other purposes, announce that it has a nuance alien to your intended meaning, and check a thesaurus for a synonym that carries just the shade of meaning you want. Remembering that readers of a written text have only what you write to help them grasp what you intend to say should motivate you to invest the time and effort necessary to state clearly what you want to say.

Sometimes, despite your search, you cannot come up with the word with just the shade of meaning you want. In that case, you have to take a word that comes close to the meaning you intend and amend its definition to suit your purposes. Many significant words, as we shall subsequently see, simply do not have a clear and universally accepted meaning. Others have several clear, universally accepted and associated meanings. Given such conditions, communication requires that you specify the meanings of the terms you use whenever necessary, and especially of your key terms. It may be a matter of identifying one of several meanings reported in the dictionary as the one you have in mind, or of stipulating precisely how you propose to use a given term whose dictionary definition is too vague or slightly inappropriate. Defining any key terms that admit of misunderstanding is a precaution that cannot be overemphasized. Nor is it an easy undertaking. Accordingly, we need to discuss various kinds of definitions and how to formulate them.

EXERCISE 3A

1. Are the following claims vague or ambiguous or both? If vague, explain why. If ambiguous, state at least two alternative meanings.
    a) Alex is an outdoors lover.
    *b) Jennifer is a wealthy woman.
    c) 'I'll lose no time reading your essay.' (Professor to student submitting an overdue essay.)
    d) 'The best investigator is one who will stop at nothing,' Holmes asserted confidently.
    *e) Vitamin E is good for aging people.
    *f) Democracy is government by the people.
    g) You say nothing eloquently.
    h) The chicken is ready to eat.
    i) At the dinner table Harry told Garry that he had committed a grave error.
    *j) 'Play the Blushing Bride Game and win a $100 prize for you and your husband.'
    k) HUGE MONTREAL RALLY APPEALS TO THE HEARTS OF QUEBECKERS (headline, *Kitchener-Waterloo Record*, 28 Oct. 1995).
2. Each of the following claims has two plausible senses that might easily give rise to equivocation or a verbal dispute. To practise avoiding such problems, distinguish these senses and express each interpretation as an alternative version of the original.
    *a) Convicted criminals must be made to pay for their crimes.
    b) The good life is a life of pleasure.
    *c) Life continues after death.
    d) The universe is a giant thought.
    *e) Enabling legislation should be introduced to make euthanasia permissible.
    f) Genetic experimentation must be restricted.
    g) Rape trials are unfair to victims.
    h) When I made that decision, I could have decided differently.
    i) Machines can think.
    j) God is omnipotent.

3. FORMULATING DEFINITIONS

The purpose of a definition is to enable your reader or hearer to understand quickly and precisely how a term is being used. When you are writing and when you are attempting to make explicit the meaning of a term used by another author, you should recognize that there are several kinds of definition. Three of them relate to the distinctions we made earlier with respect to the extension, intension, and tone of words; a fourth kind relates to context.

The kind of definition related to tone, since it has no legitimate place in informative writing, can be dismissed quickly. A colourful definition of a term designed to give it the tone the writer wants to convey is called a 'persuasive definition'. Slanters and propagandists are adept at formulating persuasive definitions that are readily identifiable. In a public address in Manchester, England, for example, a London chief constable and one-time Methodist lay preacher spoke of AIDS as 'the most recent and dramatic example of the results that come from forsaking God's rules in human relations' (*The Globe and Mail*, 20 Jan. 1987, p. A13). If this is intended as a definition rather than a description, then it reflects personal biases and is acceptable only to those who share them. Even as a description it is problematic. This leaves us with three kinds of definition acceptable in informative discourse.

Extensional Definitions

'That', as one points to people engaged in a particular activity, 'is a game'.
'Humanistic studies' means 'studies in language, literature, philosophy, fine arts, religion, and music.'

In definitions such as these you seek to clarify the meaning of a term by identifying members of the class of things named by that term, that is, by reference to its extension. You may do so either by pointing to or by naming instances of the thing to which the term is applicable, as in the first of the above definitions, or, as in the second case, by breaking down the larger class of things into a series of representative subclasses.

Intensional Definitions

'Rubella' means 'measles'.
'Scapula' means 'shoulder blade'.
'Nom de plume' means 'pseudonym'.

Intensional definitions clarify the meaning of a term by identifying the essential qualities that make something a member of the class named by that term, that is, by reference to its intension. The definitions above are instances of the simplest form of intensional definition. By substituting a familiar term for an unfamiliar one you can draw your readers' or hearers' attention to the essential characteristics of the thing in question.

But you won't get off that easily very often. More often than not you will have to provide an intensional definition by *genus* and *differentia*.

A 'chair' is 'a piece of furniture (genus) designed for the purpose of seating one person and providing a support for the back (differentia).'

'Happiness' is 'a state of mind (genus) characterized by the satisfaction that one has achieved what one deems to be worthwhile, and by the absence of mental anguish (differentia).'

In each of these examples, the genus is the larger class of things to which something belongs. The differentia specify what it is that marks off the thing named by the term being defined from other members of the larger class. A 'chair' belongs to the larger class (genus) of 'pieces of furniture', but what 'differentiates' a chair from other items of furniture is that it is 'designed for the purpose of seating one person and providing a support for the back'.

Intensional definitions by genus and differentia are particularly useful in informative discourse, but constructing them can be difficult. We shall have more to say about them momentarily.

Contextual Definitions

'Unless' in the statement 'Unless I win the grand prize in the lottery, I will not take a trip to Europe', functions in such a way that I could have expressed myself in a logically equivalent manner by saying, 'If I do not win the grand prize in the lottery, I will not take a trip to Europe.'

The Nazis won many a battle because they had 'psyched out' young green enemy recruits with propaganda films depicting military strength.

Contextual definitions are used primarily when a term lacks extension and intension. Linguistic connectives such as 'if . . . then', 'and', 'either . . . or', 'but', and the like cannot, for example, be defined by referring to their extension or intension, so we must define them by showing how they function in the context of the language of which they are a part. Other terms (like 'psyched out') may also be defined contextually.

Conventional and Stipulative Definitions

So far, we have dealt with definitions from a conventional perspective. Conventional definitions report how a term is customarily used within the community of people using the language. But there are times when you must use stipulative definitions that specify how you will use a given term.

The meaning of a term that is inherently vague must be pinned down. In addition, you will sometimes want to use a term in a way that deviates from its conventional usage. In that case, too, you must specify precisely the meaning you attach to it. 'Democracy' normally means 'government by the people either directly or through elected representatives'. But for your purpose you may want to use the term in a more restricted sense. As long as you inform your audience that the definition you are providing is a stipulative one, you are free to use the best definition for your purposes. You could use an extensional definition: 'By the term "democracy" I mean the kind of rule by the people found in Canada and the US, not in Korea and Singapore.' Or you could use an intensional definition: 'By the term 'democracy' I mean rule by the people through the representatives chosen by periodic popular votes in free multi-party elections.'

Kinds of Definitions: Relative Merits

The special merit of contextual definitions is that they are the only means we have for defining terms that have no extension or intension. But contextual definitions of terms other than linguistic connectives leave the audience in the position of having to intuit the meaning of the term from the context in which the definition sets it. Would a person who had never encountered the phrase 'psyched out' readily grasp from the above definition the fearful and demoralized psychological state of the enemy recruits?

Extensional definitions link our words to the world of experience. Without our awareness of the extension of terms, the definitions in our dictionaries would be circular, for they would be defining terms by means of other terms, none of which has a foothold in reality. But while extensional definitions point to or name things in the world, they obviously cannot point to every instance of the term in question. At most they focus on a fair and representative sample of the things denoted by the term. The problem is that a fair and representative list of instances belonging to the class named by the term is likely to be unwieldy. And even after providing such a list, we have still not identified the common features that justify their membership in the extension.

In view of this, an intensional definition that defines a term in a single, relatively simple, well-constructed sentence specifying the essential qualities belonging to all members of its extension will have the merits of clarity, convenience, and universality.

The kind of definition you should use in particular circumstances depends largely on your purpose, your audience, and the term to be defined. If you are giving a minimally informative and entertaining talk to a primary school assembly, extensional definitions will probably do the trick better than intensional ones. But if you are writing an article for a professional journal or giving a seminar paper to your peers, precision is best achieved by intensional definitions. In scholarly circles definitions by genus and differentia generally are expected. In the interests of ensuring clarity, it is often helpful to illustrate the intensional definition with instances of the extension.

To the extent that communication with clarity requires it, you must be prepared to define key terms, especially unfamiliar and technical terms as well as terms that are vague or ambiguous, or used in a way that deviates from conventional usage. This task may sound more formidable than it is. Normally the number of terms requiring definition is small. The vast majority of the words you will use are common ones with whose meanings your readers will be familiar; and if some words happen to carry several meanings, the context will usually make the intended meaning apparent. This being said, remain alert to the need for providing definitions.

Rules for Definitions by Genus and Differentia

To help you construct good definitions by genus and differentia, we provide you with four rules.

The rule of equivalence: The defining phrase should include neither more nor less than the term being defined.

If A stands for the term being defined and B for the defining phrase, you must be satisfied that all As are Bs and that all Bs are As. The definition of 'violin' as 'a stringed musical instrument' is too broad because there are many stringed musical instruments that are not violins. The definition of 'portrait' as 'a large oil painting of a person's head and shoulders' is too narrow because portraits are not necessarily large and are not always done in oils.

The rule of essential characteristics: The defining phrase must specify the essential features of the thing defined, i.e., the traits that are indispensable to its being what it is.

The definition of 'shoplifting' as 'a way of getting things for nothing' violates this rule since it bears no reference to theft, which is intrinsically part of shoplifting. Likewise, the definition of an 'anarchist' as 'a person whose head is filled with lost causes' does not get at the essence of anarchism.

In specifying essential characteristics it may be appropriate to list peripheral characteristics relative to a specific context, though such a definition would not be applicable beyond that context. Thus, in introducing a book on the history of comic strips, one might begin by saying, 'Man is the only animal that reads comic strips', though such a definition of man would not be a useful one in a lecture on moral responsibility.

It is a corollary of the rule of essential characteristics that negative definitions are to be avoided. Saying what something is not does not say what it is. To define a 'trinket' as 'something that serves no useful purpose' does not tell us what a trinket is. It follows that antonyms must also be avoided because their use would make the definition negative. Although a 'good person' may be 'a person who is not evil' and 'night' is 'not day', such definitions fail to specify what a 'good person' is or does, or what 'night' is as distinct from 'day'.

The rule of clarity: The defining phrase must clarify the meaning of the term being defined by using words that make it readily understood.

Since this, after all, is the purpose of providing definitions, definitions that obscure are useless. Plato's definition of 'time' as 'the moving image of eternity' presupposes familiarity with his theory of reality. Apart from that theory and, some would argue, even against the background of that theory, his definition of 'time' is vague. Given a specific audience and an intention that is not straightforwardly informative and argumentative, vague definitions may serve your purpose. Defining 'architecture' in terms of 'frozen music' may suit an informal talk to a group of non-professionals, but this would not be appropriate in a formal lecture to architects.

A corollary of the rule of clarity is that a definition should not be circular. A circular definition is one that defines a word in terms of the word itself, which accomplishes nothing toward clarifying meaning. 'By "human rights" I mean the rights of human beings' is circular. More subtly circular are defining phrases that use synonyms and correlative phrases. Defining a 'homosexual' as a 'gay person' is an example of the use of synonyms, and defining a 'cause' as 'that which produces an effect' illustrates the use of correlative terms. Both definitions are circular. Although synonyms are acceptable for definitions by word substitution, they are unacceptable when a term requires the precision of a definition by genus and differentia. Note, however, that when defining a term consisting of two components in which one modifies the other, such as 'isosceles triangle' or 'watchdog', the modified term ('triangle', 'dog') may be repeated as the genus.

The rule of neutrality: The defining phrase must avoid terms heavily charged with emotive tone.

This rule warns against offering persuasive definitions that betray ulterior motives. We gave one example earlier. Another example would be the definition of 'socialism' as 'that form of government that takes wealth from energetic people and divides it among the lazy poor.'

It is easier to learn the rules for framing intensional definitions by genus and differentia than it is to apply them. Formulating definitions that satisfy the rules can be extremely taxing, and both theoretical and practical considerations may necessitate some latitude in specifying the differentia.

Usually it is simple enough to name the genus or larger class to which the phenomenon named by a term belongs. But problems arise with respect to identifying the unique, essential, and defining properties that mark off the things named by the term from other members of the larger class. Sometimes the defining properties are not at all obvious. What, for instance, are the uniquely defining characteristics of a 'human being'? Rationality? A capacity to create symbols and communicate by means of them? A sense of moral responsibility? The enjoyment of comic strips? If you see the latter three characteristics as expressions of human rationality, where do you propose to draw the line between 'higher animals' such as chimpanzees and human beings with a very low IQ?

If, sometimes, several qualities seem to be unique, there are also cases where no one quality can be considered absolutely essential. What, for instance, is the identifying mark of religion? Belief in a supernatural being? Belief in life after death? Rarefied feelings of creatureliness? Cultic ritual? Morality tinged with emotion? A way of life?

Problems encountered in connection with the attempt to define 'human being' and 'religion' are but expressions of yet another difficulty, namely, that of deciding the extension of the term being defined. Does the fertilized female human ovum belong within or outside the class of 'human beings'? If the latter, at what point does it become a human being? If the former, is it entitled to 'rights and freedoms', including the right to life, liberty, and security of the person? The bearing of these considerations on the abortion issue is apparent.

Aside from these more theoretical problems related to formulating good intensional definitions, there is the practical problem of ensuring that your definitions are geared to your purposes and your audience. The definition of 'water' as 'a liquid compound of 11.188 per cent hydrogen and 88.812 per cent oxygen by weight, which freezes at zero and boils at 100 degrees Celsius' may be useful in an introductory science lecture, but it would be quite unserviceable in a talk or magazine article about sailing or about what measures to take when our bodies retain too much fluid. But it is not only your purposes that guide you in framing definitions. You must also adjust your definitions to what you judge to be the abilities of your audience and the language with which they are familiar.

Given problems such as these, you may have to settle for something less than the ideal in the formulation of definitions. You may, for instance, have to substitute for the differentiating characteristics of whatever you are defining, phrases that describe its functions or associated behavioural characteristics. Perhaps you will have to settle for an assortment of characteristics, none of which is uniquely essential though all are relevant. Finally, if all else fails, you may be forced to resort to extensional definitions.

EXERCISE 3B

1. What kind of definition is each of the following?
   a) By 'western provinces' I mean Saskatchewan, Alberta, and British Columbia.
   *b) A kitten is an immature cat.
   c) A textbook is the sort of thing you are now reading.
   d) A human being is a featherless biped who uses language and is capable of higher emotions such as indignation and resentment.

  e) 'Macabre' means 'gruesome'.
  f) A mammal is a four-legged creature that suckles its young.
*g) By 'social sciences' is meant economics, political science, anthropology, sociology, and psychology.
*h) 'And' is a connective joining two or more statements, as in 'It is Tuesday "and" we are in Miami.'
  i) A house is a dwelling unit that has distinct living areas such as a kitchen, bedrooms, dining room, etc.
  j) The Macdonald-Cartier Freeway is a superhighway running from Montreal, P.Q., to Windsor, Ontario.
2. What rule(s) of definition by genus and differentia, if any, does each of the following definitions violate? In each case explain your answer in one brief sentence.
  a) Child abuse is the physical and/or psychological violence inflicted on a child as an expression of parental anger and frustration.
  b) Noon means 12 o'clock.
  c) Nonsense is what one is speaking or writing when what one speaks or writes is devoid of all sense.
*d) Prayer is a form of religious mumbo-jumbo.
*e) A burp is a proximal eructation.
*f) Canada is a country that lies north of the 49th parallel.
  g) Taxation is a form of theft in which the government acts as a criminal victimizing citizens by taking a big bite of their income without their willing co-operation.
  h) A circle is a geometric plane figure.
  i) A laser printer is the pen of the contemporary scribe.
*j) Distance is the space between two points measured by the yard.
*k) French is a Romance language.
3. You must define a key term for the audience you are addressing. Formulate an extensional definition and a definition by genus and differentia that would be appropriate for each of the following circumstances.
  a) You are telling prospective freshmen what constitutes a 'major' at your university.
  b) You are explaining to your parents who are not college or university graduates the nature of the discipline (anthropology, sociology, etc.) in which you are majoring.
*c) You are a candidate in a forthcoming election addressing a public meeting on the merits of 'liberalism'.
  d) You are a financial adviser speaking to a group of middle- and upper-class homemakers about 'preferred shares'.
  e) You are explaining AIDS to a high school class.
  f) You are the keynote speaker at a convention of newspaper journalists talking about 'objectivity' in reporting.

g) You are a participant at a political rally speaking to whomever will listen about 'peace activism'.

h) You are writing a letter to the editor of the *Washington Post* protesting the US government's designation of three Canadian films (two on acid rain, one on nuclear war) as 'propaganda'.

i) You are addressing an assembly of college and university students on sexual 'ethics'.

j) You are urging the local Board of Education to adopt a sabbatical policy as a measure to prevent teachers' 'burnout'.

Box 3.1 *Definitions*

Extensional definitions define a term by referring to its extension, the group of things to which it refers.

Intensional definitions define a term by referring to its intension, the set of characteristics that determines to what it refers.

Definitions by *genus* and *differentia* are intensional definitions that define a term by referring to a general kind (genus) that subsumes it, and by explaining how it differs from other things of this kind (differentia).

Contextual definitions define a term by referring to the context of its normal use.

---

4. Expressing Your Intended Meaning

Up to this point we have discussed the role of definitions in ensuring clarity and precision in our choice of words. But concern with the meanings of particular words and phrases is merely preliminary to the further task of formulating statements in a way that communicates the claims we want to make. It is quite possible for each of the component words in a statement to be clear while the statement as a whole remains unclear.

For a variety of reasons you often will find yourself at a loss to grasp clearly the claim an author is making. The problem may be psychosocial. As individuals we have differing backgrounds, environmental influences, peer groups, political commitments, problems, loves, and loyalties, all of which contribute to or constitute a network of beliefs that we bring to bear on the material we read and that colour our interpretation of it. We discuss such belief systems in Chapter 10. Alternatively, as we have seen, the problem may be vagueness or ambiguity in the author's claims.

Whatever the reason for your bafflement, you are faced with the task of sorting out what you believe you may legitimately take to be the author's intended meaning. Your awareness of the difficulties you encounter in the process of searching out the meanings of the claims of others will alert you to the painstaking care you must invest in the formulation of your own.

Getting at an author's intended meaning involves identifying plausible senses or interpretations of what is said and, with clues provided by various contextual considerations, determining which of the plausible senses is the intended one. In distinguishing between plausible and intended senses or interpretations of a claim, we deliberately use 'plausible' rather than 'possible'. The multiple and disparate meanings of various words may generate many possible meanings but some of them may be immediately discarded as nonsensical or inappropriate, leaving us with those that are at least plausible. The identification of plausible senses may hinge on alternative meanings of particular words and phrases or on alternative meanings of whole sentences.

Obviously a claim as a whole lacks meaning as long as the reader has no idea at all what a given term in that statement means, and it will be susceptible to alternative meanings if a given word or phrase is ambiguous. In view of our earlier discussions, our comments on word selection here will be brief. If an author stipulates definitions of key terms, ensure that those terms are used consistently throughout the text. To use a key term now in one sense and later in another is to equivocate and to render a claim subject to more than one interpretation. If an author uses a crucial but familiar term without stipulating the specialized sense in which it is being used, you must identify plausible alternatives. If an author uses an unfamiliar term without providing a definition for it, you will have to identify the meaning or meanings justified by the author's use of it, perhaps with the help of a dictionary. In the writing you do, you will want to spare your readers such frustrations through careful consideration in your choice of words and, where necessary, in your stipulation of meanings of terms, which you will then use consistently.

The use of a familiar but key term without stipulating the sense in which it is being used—probably because the author takes its meaning as self-evident—is the most frequently encountered of the scenarios mentioned above. Consider the claim 'The law of the church forbids the marriage of priests' and suppose that the context does not make it clear whether the marriage of priests is forbidden by the church's understanding of the will of God or whether it is forbidden by the church's administration for strictly practical purposes. The former circumstance would make the non-marriage of priests a 'divine law', the latter an 'ecclesiastical law'. The claim, then, is subject to two interpretations: (i) divine law forbids the marriage of priests, and (ii) ecclesiastical law forbids the marriage of priests. In this example the alternative meanings pivot around the single term 'law'.

Even after taking care of problems of meaning created by specific words and phrases, the claim as a whole may be susceptible to alternative senses or interpretations. Having sorted out plausible meanings of an author's claims, the final step is to determine which interpretation the author intended. This you do by a process of elimination guided by a sense of fidelity to the text, common sense, and the principle of charity. Use whatever hints there may be in other parts of the article to help you identify the author's intended meaning. If one of the plausible senses stands in blatant contradiction to what is clearly the main claim of the text, common sense dictates that you reject it. If other interpretations appear irrelevant or trivial or uninteresting or obviously false, the principle of charity would require you to eliminate them unless you have good reason for not doing so. Eventually you will be left with what you are confident is, and what you believe you can defend as, the author's intended meaning or, perhaps, two alternative restatements of the author's claim, each of which could qualify as the intended meaning. Although this process can be arduous, it is necessary insofar as the meaning of the author's claim is not perfectly evident; and it is only after this procedure that you can proceed with the task of assessing its truth or falsity.

This entire procedure should not be necessary, and would not be necessary if the author had communicated clearly and precisely. The lesson for you, as you go about constructing extended units of informative and argumentative discourse, is clear. Be prepared to undergo labour pains in giving birth to your claims! After formulating a claim, mull it over, asking yourself whether it says precisely what you mean or if it can be interpreted in different ways. And if the latter is the case, be prepared to amend it—several times, if necessary. Don't be satisfied with a first draft. Don't be satisfied until what you have written says exactly what you mean.

5. LOOKING AHEAD

We are now at the end of the chapters of this book that introduce the basic aspects of reasoning and arguing. We devoted Chapter 1 to the issues that arise when language is used informatively. It cautioned against emotional commitments that distort our perception of facts, the course of our reasoning, and our vocabulary. In Chapter 2 we identified what marks arguments off from other units of discourse, to isolate the various components of an argument with the help of indicator words, and developed diagrams for arguments. This chapter has emphasized the importance of stating with precision the claims that make up our arguments. We must define key terms, as necessary, and hone what we write until we are satisfied that our intended meaning is the only plausible meaning. But precisely stated premises and conclusions do not alone guarantee a good argument. In order to have a good argument we must have true or acceptable premises that sufficiently establish the proposed conclusion. We begin to discuss these aspects of good reasoning in the next chapter.

MAJOR EXERCISE 3M

1. Diagram the reasoning in each of the following arguments and then, in a few paragraphs, assess the strengths and weaknesses of the language employed.

Look in particular for problematic instances of vagueness, ambiguity, and emotional language, and determine whether any key terms are left undefined and whether stated definitions are acceptable.

*a) You can consult all the experts you like, write reports, make studies, etc., but the fact that pornography corrupts lies within the common sense of everybody. If people are affected by their environments, by the circumstances of their lives, then they certainly are affected by pornography. The mere nature of pornography makes it impossible that it should ever effect good. Therefore, it must necessarily effect evil. Even a fool has the sense to see that someone who wallows in filth is going to get dirty. This is intuitive knowledge. People who spend millions of dollars to try and prove otherwise are malicious or misguided, or both.

b) As a true American, I wish to speak for what is near and dear to the hearts of Americans. I wish to speak against what is as foreign to these shores as communism, socialism, totalitarianism, and other foreign 'isms', except, of course, Americanism. I speak of the administration's Medicare bill, better known as 'socialized medicine'.

If Medicare is sound, then a government-sponsored, -financed, and -controlled program is sound for every aspect of our life. But this principle must be rejected. As Americans, freedom must be our watchword. And since freedom means no control, no regulation, no restraint, government programs like Medicare are quite contrary to the American concept of freedom.

Unlike pseudo-Americans who want to socialize this country, I believe that socialized medicine would be an insult to true Americans. For true Americans don't want handouts. They want to stand on their own feet. They're willing to meet their obligations. They're willing to work and pay for their medical bills. As convincing proof of this, the AMA has advertised that it will give free medical care to anyone who wants it, and practically no one responds to these ads (adapted from a letter to the *New York Times*, March 1982).

4

BUILDING

ARGUMENTS

Chapter 2 introduced arguments as the basic unit of reasoning. This chapter carries our account of arguments further, introducing some complexities that characterize arguments in ordinary discourse. Topics of discussion include:

- ◆ abbreviated arguments;
- ◆ hidden premises and hidden conclusions;
- ◆ a visual argument; and
- ◆ general guidelines for constructing good arguments.

You should by now be able to differentiate between arguments and non-arguments and to diagram many simple arguments. Some further common features of ordinary arguments now need to be discussed. This chapter introduces two topics that will take our basic account of argument one step further. The first is abbreviated arguments, which characterize much of the discussion and debate we must contend with in our day-to-day reasoning. Such arguments introduce the further features we must master if we wish to be able to understand and assess ordinary discourse.

Our second topic is argument construction. A detailed account of good arguments must wait for later chapters, but we can prepare the way for this account by establishing some basic guidelines for argument construction. By paying attention to these guidelines you can make the structure of your arguments clear and unambiguous, and ensure that they do not commit errors that impede understanding. Following the guidelines for argument construction in this way will allow you to create arguments with fewer rather than more complications.

1. Abbreviated Arguments

Extract and state hidden components.

In setting out their arguments, writers and speakers do not always explicitly state their premises and conclusions. This is something we have already seen in the case of rhetorical questions, which are used to make implicit statements. In other cases, an arguer will provide premises that obviously lead to a conclusion but not explicitly state this conclusion. This can be an effective rhetorical device that forces the audience to draw the 'obvious' conclusion for themselves. On other occasions it is not a conclusion but a premise that an arguer leaves unstated, rendering obvious gaps in the evidence offered for a conclusion. In both cases argument components have been hidden and need to be revealed. We call arguments of this sort 'abbreviated' arguments.

An abbreviated argument might be compared to a journey with missing signposts. We follow a familiar sequence of events but feel lost and suspect a missing signpost. However, we see that we will have no trouble proceeding to our destination if we hypothesize a line of reasoning hinted at along the way. When something like this happens in an argument, we have an abbreviated argument and must make the hidden reasoning explicit by filling in the conclusion or premise that has been hinted at or left unstated.

Bear in mind two competing concerns. On the one hand, you want to uncover *all* aspects of an argument that are relevant to its assessment: you want to recognize the full argument. This requires that you turn implicit premises or conclusions into explicit argument components, for an account of them must play a central role in argument assessment.

On the other hand, there are limits to what we can do when we are reconstructing hidden argument components. When we build our own arguments we can add premises to improve them. But we cannot do this to a great extent with other people's arguments. If we add extra premises to someone else's argument to strengthen it, it becomes our argument. We are more archaeologists than architects when we deal with other people's abbreviated arguments, for we are bent on reconstructing them in the way the author originally intended them. Instead of adding to the argument, we want to discover what is already there, albeit implicitly, in the abbreviated form. We call an argument's implicit components 'hidden' components and must learn to recognize them when we identify and diagram an argument.

In supplying hidden components, whether premises or conclusions, you need to rely on your sense of what makes an argument a coherent whole. Cultivating this sense requires practice.

Hidden Conclusions

An argument has a hidden conclusion when its premises invite a conclusion that is left unstated. In many such cases the arguer makes it clear, in one way or another, that his statements are offered as reasons for accepting the conclusion that is not given. Consider the following comment on seat-belts.

> I think there is enough evidence to justify a reasonable conclusion. In the vast majority of cases that have been examined, the wearing of seat-belts has prevented injuries that would have resulted from automobile accidents. And these cases appear to vastly outnumber the relatively few cases in which people have avoided injury because they were not wearing seat-belts and were thrown clear of a vehicle.

The first line of this passage suggests that a conclusion follows from the evidence. It is left unstated, but the rest of the passage makes it clear that the hidden claim is the conclusion that the wearing of seat-belts is a good way to avoid injuries in automobile accidents. The abbreviated argument can be diagrammed as follows.

P1 = In the vast majority of cases that have been examined, the wearing of seat-belts has prevented injuries that would have resulted from automobile accidents.

P2 = These cases appear to vastly outnumber the relatively few cases in which people have avoided injury because they have been thrown clear of a vehicle.

HC= It is reasonable to conclude that the wearing of seat-belts is a good way to avoid injuries in automobile accidents.

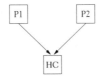

Within legends and diagrams, we indicate hidden components by prefixing 'H' to the symbols that represent the relevant components, in this case the conclusion. In this way, our diagram makes it clear that we are dealing with a hidden, rather than an explicit, conclusion.

In supplying the hidden conclusion in this argument we have tried to do so in a way that captures, as precisely as possible, the tone and content of the author's remarks. In this case, it is significant that he emphasizes that some of the accidents investigated do not confirm his point, qualifies one of his statements with the word 'appear', and says that his conclusion is 'reasonable'. These qualifications imply a meaning of 'reasonable' that does not include 'infallible'. In view of this, we would overstate his intentions if we expressed the conclusion as 'Wearing seat-belts always prevents injury.' A conclusion such as 'The wearing of seat-belts should be required by law' is also out of place, for it introduces an issue—legislation—that the writer has not touched upon.

A second example concerns a remark made by Mahatma Gandhi, the famous Indian philosopher, in a discussion of children's education. It is from *All Men Are Brothers: Life and Thoughts of Mahatma Gandhi* (Ahmedabad, India: Navajivan, 1960, p. 201), a collection of his remarks edited by Krishna Kripalani.

> Reading comes before writing and drawing before tracing the letters of the alphabet. If this natural method is followed, the understanding of the children will have much better opportunity of development than when it is under check by beginning the children's training with the alphabet.

Strictly speaking, this remark might be described as two statements. The first is the claim that the natural order of learning places reading before writing and drawing before printing letters of the alphabet. The second is the claim that children will learn better if parents and teachers substitute this natural progression for the teaching of the alphabet. Though no conclusion is actually stated, one is obviously invited, for these two statements suggest that we should educate children by following the natural progression that Gandhi recognizes. When we diagram the argument, we include the hidden conclusion as follows.

P1 = In the natural progression of learning reading occurs before writing and drawing before tracing the letters of the alphabet.

P2 = If this natural progression is imitated in teaching methods, children's understanding will have a much better opportunity of development than when it is held under check by beginning the children's training with the alphabet.

HC = Children should be introduced to reading before writing and to drawing before the letters of the alphabet.

The diagram portrays P1 and P2 as linked premises because P1 is an explanation of the 'natural method' referred to in P2. In view of this, P2 is not understandable without P1 and depends on it.

Two further examples of hidden conclusions appear in the following advertisements for psychics in a recent magazine.

Voted #1 Psychic Michelle Palmer will bring lover back to stay forever. Removes evil influences. 817-555-3345

ESP Psychic/Harvard PhD Melinda Meyers
God-gifted spiritualist, 20 yrs. Discovers problems, solutions in 1st minutes of conversation. 817-555-0039 Returns lovers within hours. Successful!

This is a case where context tells us that we are dealing with arguments, for these discourses are advertisements inviting us to conclude that we should call these psychics for advice. The evidence put forward is not likely to be misunderstood, though it is presented in a very succinct way. This is typical in printed advertisements of this sort, for one pays for such advertisements by the word or line. In diagramming the arguments involved, we express each piece of information provided as a premise.

The argument of the first advertisement is diagrammed as follows.

P1 = Michelle Palmer was voted the number 1 psychic.
P2 = Michelle Palmer will bring lovers back to stay forever.
P3 = Michelle Palmer removes evil influences.
HC = You should call Michelle Palmer for advice.

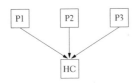

Perhaps we do not need to say that there are many ways in which this is a poor argument. P1 is vague—we are not told who voted Palmer the number 1 psychic—and there is no solid evidence supporting the claims about her abilities. This being said, it only matters for our present purposes that the discourse is an argument, i.e., a clear attempt to give us reasons for believing a hidden conclusion.

The second advertisement can be diagrammed as follows.

P1 = Melinda Meyers is a Harvard PhD.
P2 = She has been a God-gifted spiritualist for 20 years.
P3 = She discovers problems and solutions in the first minutes of conversation.
P4 = She returns lovers within hours.
HC = You should call Melinda Meyers for advice.

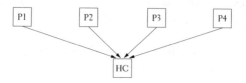

As with the first advertisement, there are many ways in which this argument could be criticized. In the present context, it is enough to note the hidden conclusion, designated as 'HC'. We turn now from hidden conclusions to the other hidden components that complicate many ordinary arguments.

> **Box 4.1 Finding Hidden Conclusions**
> Ask yourself whether the discourse in question defends or invites some unstated conclusion. If the answer is yes, represent this claim as a hidden conclusion, HC.

Hidden Premises

It is often more difficult to supply hidden premises than hidden conclusions, for we must choose between different possibilities and must be able to justify what we claim is hidden. The most complete justification is one that shows an arguer is necessarily committed to any unstated premise we uncover.

When you think that an argument may contain hidden premises, you need to ask yourself whether there is a gap in the reasoning from premises to conclusion that must be bridged before the conclusion is supported. Consider the following argument, adapted from *Time*, Nov. 1984.

We should stop aborting innocents, as that would eliminate the need of bizarre and unnatural methods of making babies.

This is an interesting example because the argument is so condensed. It is clear from the passage that the author is opposed to both abortion—which is described as 'aborting innocents'—and to the 'bizarre and unnatural methods of making babies' (surrogate motherhood, in vitro fertilization, etc.). We see further that opposition to the latter is being given as a reason for opposing abortion. Abortion, on this account, is objectionable because it creates a shortage of babies, which is being satisfied by making babies in 'bizarre and unnatural' ways. Understanding this, we diagram the argument as follows.

P1 = By stopping the abortion of innocent fetuses we could eliminate the need for unnatural methods of making babies.

HC = We should stop aborting fetuses.

There is something right and something wrong with this diagram. It does seem to reflect the general structure of the reasoning, but there is something missing from our diagram — there is a gap in the reasoning from premise to conclusion that must be bridged. As the argument stands, it is entirely possible that one might accept P1 and not draw the proposed conclusion, so the author must be committed to some other premise that allows this conclusion to be drawn. If you think about it, you will see that this extra premise is the claim that unnatural methods of making babies are wrong and should be avoided. It is this claim *together with* P1 that takes us to the conclusion. We recognize the claim in question as a hidden premise and include it in the diagram.

P1 = By stopping the abortion of innocent fetuses we could eliminate the need for unnatural methods of making babies.
HP2 = Unnatural methods of making babies are wrong.
HC = We should stop aborting fetuses.

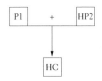

It is important to recognize the hidden premise in this argument as it is a controversial claim that might be debated. Many people would respond to it by arguing that unnatural methods of doing things are not wrong. We can well imagine them backing this claim by arguing that we constantly depend on unnatural methods of doing things that are based on science and technology. We could debate whether this would justify unnatural methods of making babies, but this is not an issue we will pursue in the present context. For our purposes, it is enough to note that we need to recognize the hidden premise in the initial argument we are analysing.

When we supply hidden premises to an argument we make its links explicit so that they can be scrutinized. We must therefore recognize as hidden premises any assumptions that might be debated. This does not mean that we treat *all* assumptions as hidden premises, for every argument presupposes an endless number of assumptions. In view of this we distinguish between assumptions that may be debatable and assumptions that are not debatable, and recognize the former but not the latter as hidden premises.

In the above argument we have not, therefore, treated as hidden premises the obvious assumptions that 'Abortion is a way of killing a fetus', that 'Science has made unnatural ways of making babies possible', that 'Making babies naturally is not wrong', and that 'The words used in this argument are meaningful English words'. *Every* argument makes many obvious assumptions we should not recognize as hidden premises because it is, from the point of view of reasoning, uninteresting to enumerate uncontroversial assumptions. The assumptions that we ignore usually reflect widespread agreement about the world, language, and what is right and wrong.

In contrast with uncontroversial assumptions, those that are speculative or debatable are represented as hidden premises in the diagramming of an argument. Failure to include them results in an incomplete diagram. A further argument about abortion, from a philosophy class discussion, illustrates this.

Abortion is not murder. The soul does not enter the body until the first breath is taken. Up to this point, the fetus is a biological entity only.

Although it contains no indicator words, the context and the sense of the passage suggest that the first statement is a conclusion supported by the remaining statements. If we diagram it without its hidden premise, our diagram would appear as follows:

P1 = The soul does not enter the body (which is only a biological entity) until the first breath is taken.
C = Abortion is not murder.

In constructing this diagram, we have treated the two sentences that support the conclusion as one premise because they make essentially the same point. The diagram captures the explicit reasoning in the passage we began with, but it is missing an important hidden premise that needs to be recognized if we are to assess the argument properly.

We can begin to extract the missing hidden premise by noting that the word 'murder' is a key term in the argument's conclusion, yet the stated premise says nothing about murder. This alerts us to a gap in the reasoning that needs to be bridged by some assumption. When we set about to identify this assumption, it turns out to be a controversial one. We can express the assumption as follows.

HP2 = An entity without a soul (i.e., one that is only biological) cannot be murdered.

The arguer is obviously committed to this assumption to get from the stated premise (P1) to the conclusion (C). We include HP2 in the diagram:

In recognizing HP2 we unearth a key component of the argument that must be discussed when the argument is assessed. Settling the issues that it raises would require that we become much clearer about what it means 'to have a soul', and would need to consider other cases where it might be said that something without a soul (say, a person who is brain dead) might be murdered.

The next example is taken from an article on Chinese-American relations published in *Time* in July 1995. It describes poor relations with China that began with 'the bloody suppression of the Tiananmen Square democracy movement' and were worsened by a series of subsequent disputes. When China's leadership looks at these developments, 'the only logical conclusion', according to the article, 'is that Washington is making a concerted and coordinated attack' on the Chinese government. The article thus attributes to the Chinese the following argument.

P1 = A series of disputes have arisen with the United States.

C = Washington is making a concerted and coordinated attack on us.

There is something missing from this diagram, for the stated conclusion follows only if one accepts another premise, i.e., that American disputes with China reflect a co-ordinated plan. In the *Time* article, this hidden premise is attributed to the Chinese by Charles Freeman, an Assistant Secretary of Defense, who comments that 'The Chinese are congenitally incapable of believing that a great country can conduct foreign policy by spastic twitching.' Including this statement in the diagram, we eliminate the tone of this remark, for we must be cautious about the premises we attribute to other people's reasoning. We, therefore, express the argument's hidden premise as:

HP2 = A great country like the US must be acting according to a co-ordinated plan.

The amended diagram becomes:

Once again, the hidden premise plays a key role in the argument. If one is arguing with the Chinese, it is probably this premise that one will wish to dispute.

As a last example, consider the controversial assumption in the following passage from a column by Bob Talbert in the *Detroit Free Press*.

> Airlines are funny. They make sure you aren't carrying a weapon of destruction and then sell you all the booze you can drink.

In calling airlines 'funny', Talbert presumably means that they are hypocritical or inconsistent. Understood this way, this passage is recognizable as an argument giving reasons for the charge of hypocrisy. Having clarified the meaning of 'funny', we can recognize the following argument components.

P1 = Airlines make sure you aren't carrying a weapon of destruction.
P2 = They sell you all the booze you can drink.
C = Airlines are hypocritical ('funny').

Someone looking at these premises might question how they support the charge of hypocrisy. The answer is that they do so by relying on the following hidden premise.

HP3 = Booze is a weapon of destruction.

After this premise has been recognized, the reasoning can be straightforwardly diagrammed as follows:

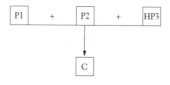

Again, the hidden premise is controversial and the argument would have to be evaluated according to the criteria for good analogical reasoning, which we will introduce in Chapter 11.

Box 4.2 Finding Hidden Premises
Ask yourself whether the stated premises lead directly to the conclusion or depend on some unstated assumption. If the latter, and if this assumption needs to be assessed, present the unstated assumption as a hidden premise.

Exercise 4A

Each of the following passages can be read as an argument but has hidden components that should be made explicit. Diagram each argument, supplying hidden conclusions or premises as necessary.

1. No politicians are statesmen because statesmen are honest.
2. All forms of murder are wrong, so euthanasia is wrong.
3. Bill's gone bowling, so he won't be back till 4:30.
4. Free coupons will be given to the first 500 shoppers, so if you want them, be there early!
*5. Either Bill's bus didn't get in on time or there was no cab available. If his bus was in on schedule and he could get a cab straightaway, he'd be here by now.
6. How can you be so inconsistent? You argue against capital punishment and say you are opposed to the taking of human life. Yet you argue for a pro-choice stand on abortion.
7. True democracy requires communication and debate. In the case of large-scale democracy, this means that it requires large-scale communication systems that are available to everyone. It follows that the Internet makes global democracy feasible for the first time.
*8. [From a discussion in *Time*, 3 July 1995, of Bill Moyers's PBS television series on poetry] 'Moyers makes virtually no attempt to place the poet in a larger social context—to view poetry as a profession (or, perhaps more to the point, to analyze what it means that ours is a culture where it's all but impossible to be a professional poet). Ezra Pound once pointed out that history without economics is bunk. To which one might add that poetry without economics—without some sense of the ebb and flow of the megamercantile society surrounding the poet—is bunk too.'
9. [Al Strachan in his sports column in *The Globe and Mail*, 5 Jan. 1987, commenting on the expulsion of the Canadian junior hockey team from the world championship tournament after they responded to rough play by the Soviets with a bench-clearing brawl] The Canadian juniors did little more than any sane, healthy person would do in similar circumstances, be it in a hockey arena or on a public street.
10. [Pierre Théberge, the organizer of an exhibit of automobiles at the Montreal Museum of Fine Arts, 1995] In design circles the automobile is still something of an 'orphan', because it has been looked upon as essentially an outgrowth of technological development.

*11. [Aristotle, *Rhetoric*, Book II, ch. 21.6] Being a mortal, do not cherish immortal anger.

12. Diagram the implicit argument in the following quote [from Laczniak and Murphy, *Ethical Marketing Decisions* (Lexington, Mass.: Lexington Books, 1993), p. 263]: A final argument that can be made for televised political advertising is that it motivates voters. TV advertising is thought to reach and vitalize individuals who otherwise might not participate in the election.

13. [Tom McIver, 'A Walk Through Earth History', *Skeptic* 4, 1 (1996), p. 35] This then, is the real argument against evolution: its supposed moral consequences. Creationism is the necessary foundation of fundamentalist biblical belief and thus the only basis for morality.

14. [Adapted from *Skeptic* 4, 1 (1996)] With notable exceptions, the discipline of sociology is like alchemy trying to transmute lead into gold. It has failed to graduate to the status of a fully scientific enterprise because it has yet to take seriously the limitations imposed on social engineering by the facts of human biology.

Box 4.3 A Visual Argument

In many situations, it may not be immediately obvious how you can apply the basic logical skills to analyse more unusual attempts to convince us of this or that point of view. In such cases, remember that you can apply your basic skills in logic to reduce an attempt to convince an audience to a clear argument.

We can illustrate this point with the following example.

Posters like this have frequently been employed by the US Department of Health, Education and Welfare in its anti-smoking campaigns. In this instance—and in many other cases like it—we can deal with visual attempts to persuade us of a claim by 'translating' visual images into corresponding verbal statements that can be analysed in the ways already noted.

In this case, the poster suggests that we should be wary of smoking in the same way a fish should be wary of biting on a fish hook, for in both cases the result is being 'hooked'. We can diagram this argument as follows.

P1 = Like a fish's biting on a fish hook, your smoking can injure or kill you.

HP2 = You don't want to get hooked.

C = You should be wary of the addictive nature of smoking.

We have designated the second premise in this argument 'HP2' because it is a necessary premise but it is not explicitly acknowledged—verbally *or* visually—in the poster. (One might also discuss a sub-argument that seems to support HP2— the fish looks miserable, unhappy, remorseful, suggesting that you don't want to get hooked because it will make you miserable, unhappy, and remorseful.)

Once we diagram such arguments, we can assess them in the same ways that we assess other arguments. In this case, the key question is whether we have a case of equivocation, for someone might claim that the argument conflates two different meanings of the word 'hook'. After all, being hooked on a fish hook is a physical phenomenon, but being hooked on smoking is psychological as well as physiological. This difference being noted, one might argue that it does not matter, for in both cases one is tied to something bad for one's health but difficult to let go of.

Our point is that we can deal with the argument in the poster by employing the techniques we have discussed. More generally, we can use such techniques whenever we 'translate' a non-standard argument, like one detailed throughout an entire book, into a corresponding argument of the sort already treated. In this case it meant translating visual cues into verbal statements. In other cases, it may mean recognizing an extended argument as a series of simple arguments that can be dealt with individually.

If you keep such possibilities in mind and proceed carefully and clearly in a step-by-step fashion, you will be able to apply your skills to a great variety of elaborate arguments that might at first seem beyond logical analysis.

2. CONSTRUCTING GOOD ARGUMENTS

So far, we have stressed how to identify and diagram simple arguments. Now it is time to say something about the construction of good arguments. A detailed account of good arguments is left for the remainder of this text, which explains what makes good arguments good and, by contrast, what makes bad arguments bad. In the remainder of this chapter, we prepare the way for this discussion by making some general remarks on the construction of good arguments.

Presenting Arguments

Many of the problems that characterize ordinary arguments are not due to faulty reasoning so much as to faulty presentation. Even if we have a good argument, it will not be convincing if it is presented in a way that is not accurate and forceful. The discussions of clarity and precision in Chapters 1 and 3 are instructive in this respect.

The construction of good arguments begins with the requirement that you not present your audience with difficulties in deciding what you mean. You will recall that one of the primary causes of this is a failure to use indicator words when presenting arguments. We can avoid any possible misinterpretation of this kind by always using indicator words when we present an argument. By so identifying our premises and conclusions, we will spare our readers and listeners the trouble of speculating about our intended claim and our reasons for claiming it. A commitment to the use of indicator words need not cramp your style, for there are many indicators available that can fit your style of writing or speaking. By carefully using logical indicators, you avoid reliance on context or the principle of charity to communicate the meaning of your claims.

A further thing to avoid is a reliance on hidden argument components. At times they may be an effective rhetorical device, but we should not have to resort to such devices in the attempt to convince our audience. While rhetorical considerations do play a role in argumentation, they often mask poor reasoning, and it would be wise to keep them to a minimum until you are more experienced at using models of good reasoning. Sometimes we discover that our arguments contain unintentional hidden components—we all have a tendency to assume claims that others may see as controversial—but this should not prevent us from striving to keep them to a minimum.

A commitment to the use of logical indicators and the attempt to avoid hidden components is one way to ensure the clarity of our arguments. This is one of the commitments stressed in Chapters 1 and 3. Further commitments of this nature are those involving the avoidance of ambiguous and vague expressions, discussed in Chapter 3, and slanting, propaganda, and euphemisms, discussed in Chapter 1. This means retaining the standards of clarity set in those chapters, defining key terms clearly, clarifying possible ambiguities and vagueness, and formulating our statements with precision. Even where we attempt this through the use of logical indicators, since many of them have non-argumentative meanings, we must be sure to use indicators in ways that do not yield unintended interpretations of our arguments. In brief, four principles for presenting good arguments are:

- ◆ use indicator words;
- ◆ avoid hidden components;
- ◆ clarify ambiguities;
- ◆ be precise.

Diagramming Arguments

Diagramming other people's arguments is useful because it clarifies their structure. In the same way, diagramming our own arguments encourages us to organize our reasoning in a way that makes clear the relationships between premises and conclusion. The use of diagrams will also help our readers and listeners picture the flow of our reasoning when they assess it.

Though initially time-consuming, diagramming our own arguments can be a rewarding and revealing exercise. How rewarding depends on our objectives. We can dispense with diagramming when we prepare a presentation of little consequence—say, a light-hearted address at a social function—but it is usually wise to diagram when we organize our reasoning in a major paper, speech, or thesis.

Extended arguments exhibit a more complicated structure. We deal with them by breaking them into their subsidiary arguments, depicting those as simple argument diagrams, and then putting the simple arguments together to show their relationships in the extended argument. It is often useful to diagram one argument for our conclusion and then another that answers likely objections to it. In this way, we prepare ourselves both to support our claim and to respond to later objections.

A carefully constructed diagram, whether of a simple argument or an extended one, shows how the various parts of our reasoning fit together. It acts like a road-map that summarizes the journey from our premises to our conclusion. Among other things, it makes the linked nature of linked premises explicit, distinguishing them from convergent premises.

Studying a diagram often reveals gaps in our reasoning that we need to rectify before our remarks are presented or published. The confidence that comes from securing all the links in your reasoning will allow you to discuss and debate your claims without hesitation. You will appreciate the significance of this confidence if you recall, as we all can, occasions when people became confused and inarticulate when challenged to explain or defend their reasoning.

Having extolled the virtues of diagramming, we offer you a few words of caution and some practical suggestions. In diagramming—and in constructing arguments—aim for simplicity. Plot the structure of your argument so that it is relatively simple and stands out as clearly as possible. Do not defeat your purpose by creating a small-scale version of a Greek labyrinth. Do not push the possibilities for diagramming to extremes. All you need is a diagram that shows clearly the role that each premise plays in the total scheme of your argumentation. Additional elaboration tends to be confusing.

Some of us are less comfortable with diagrams than others. A person's facility for constructing diagrams seems to depend on his or her ability to visualize abstract structures and on having had experience with such instruments as graphs and flow charts. If you are a person who finds diagramming difficult, what you need is practice. We suggest you work with very simple structures first and then proceed to more complex diagrams where the benefits of diagramming will be more readily apparent. Rest assured that your mastery of diagramming will be directly related to the amount of time you are prepared to invest in cultivating it.

In summary, the following principles should be adhered to in preparing and diagramming arguments:

- ◆ diagram an argument for your conclusion;
- ◆ diagram an argument against likely objections;
- ◆ keep your diagrams as simple as possible;
- ◆ base your finished argument on your diagrams.

Knowing Your Audience

We interpret what we read and hear according to the way we understand the world, the general truths we believe other people hold, and the issues we expect to be the focus of discussion and debate. Because we must argue differently depending on the audience we are trying to convince, we cannot decide what evidence to present and how best to present it if we do not have relevant information about our intended audience.

The priest or minister who argues within the context of a sermon makes assumptions and states premises that would be unacceptable to people who do not hold the basic beliefs of the congregation. He or she can none the less be confident that most parishioners will not take exception to these assumptions and beliefs. Likewise, Sherlock Holmes can argue effectively with Watson because he has in advance a good knowledge of Watson's fund of knowledge, of what he is likely to believe, and, consequently, of what reasoning should convince him. For a different audience, such as the police or the press, Holmes alters his presentation of the evidence to be convincing.

When we argue we assume that our audience consists of reasonable people capable of being convinced by logical arguments. If we did not make such an assumption, there would be little purpose in arguing. The question we must ask ourselves is whether other assumptions can and should be made about our audience. A politician may not have to convince the party faithful of the wisdom of a new piece of legislation, but must expect to have to do so when facing members of an opposing party.

We leave a detailed discussion of audiences for Chapter 10. At this stage it is enough to say that you must keep audiences in mind when you are constructing arguments in ordinary life. Typically, this means that you must ask yourself what your immediate audience believes and what kinds of reasoning will be most effective in convincing them of your conclusion. In dealing with individuals you know well, you probably do this intuitively, for you already know their basic beliefs and ways of thinking.

This book will not be so specific in dealing with individual arguments and audiences. Instead, our aim will be the construction of arguments that are plausible to reasonable people who understand the basic topics and issues the argument considers. We call the audience consisting of such people the 'universal' audience, and anyone who follows the principles of good reasoning will be deemed to belong to this audience. Because we are still restricting ourselves to simple arguments, there are limits to what we can expect to accomplish with our practice arguments. But in constructing them, keep this knowledgeable, reasonable audience in mind.

Reflecting

When we are the audience for an argument, we must read or listen perceptively. This requires that we pay close attention to context and the audiences being addressed and that we reflect on the assumptions implicit in what is said, on the evidence for what is said, and on the implications of an author's claims. In the process of questioning these assumptions, premises, and implications, you will find that they logically commit the author to related beliefs or courses of action that he or she has not anticipated or has ignored.

Reflective reading and listening of this sort will permit you to discern and discuss problems in other people's arguments. To ensure that such problems do not afflict our own arguments, we must pair our ability to reflect carefully on the reasoning of others with an ability to reflect critically on our own reasoning. In constructing good arguments we must, therefore, reflect on our claims and assumptions, and on the consequences they imply. We must think through each claim we propose to ensure that it is lucid and to see how it relates to other claims. We must know what our assumptions are and be satisfied that they are acceptable to ourselves and our audience. We must consider carefully the logical implications of our claims to protect ourselves against the criticism that we have failed to notice how our position commits us to dubious beliefs or to questionable grounds for behaviour.

In a word, we must, before we set about the task of writing or speaking, think through (i) what we want to say, (ii) what we must say to support our claim and defend it against possible objections, and (iii) how we can organize our thoughts to state our case most effectively.

Good Reasoning

In emphasizing again and again that 'good reasoning matters', we want to encourage you to set your sights high. At the same time, we don't want you to panic in the process of striving for an elusive ideal. However convinced you may be of the correctness of a given claim, that judgement should always be open to revision as new evidence comes to your attention. We never have all the evidence and are always limited by the evidence available to us at a certain time and place. This means that our knowledge is always incomplete, and that our views and our reasons for them will constantly be changing and open to revision. Far from a cause for disillusionment, our inability to construct 'perfect' arguments can foster an atmosphere of intellectual challenge that can invigorate creative and constructive thinking.

Although this text will not attempt to teach you how to construct a perfect argument, it does present criteria for constructing good arguments and assessing whatever arguments you meet. To understand them, we need to understand argument evaluation, a complicated topic to be addressed in the next chapter.

Exercise 4B

Go back to Exercise 3M. Pick four arguments in the exercise. In each case, dispute the argument's conclusion by constructing a (simple) argument for the opposite conclusion. Present the argument in a paragraph.

Exercise 4C

Construct and diagram simple arguments supporting or disputing five of the following ten claims. Present the argument in a sentence or two and then diagram it.
*1. A college education is not a right.
*2. Television beer advertisements should be banned.
*3. Capital punishment is wrong.
 4. The next President will be a Republican.
 5. The next Prime Minister will be a Liberal.
 6. The drinking age should be a uniform 21 across the nation.
 7. Newspapers should not exploit their position by supporting causes.
 8. Violent pornography should be censored.
 9. Restrictions on assault weapons are a good idea.
10. The Australian system of free university education is a good one.

EXERCISE 4D

Go to your local newspaper or your favourite magazines and find five examples of simple arguments (if you find extended arguments, lift the simple structures out of them).

MAJOR EXERCISE 4M

For each of the following passages, decide whether the passage contains an argument. If it does, diagram it and construct another argument for the same conclusion or the opposite conclusion, or for or against one of the premises in the argument. After you have presented your argument in a paragraph, diagram it. In the process of constructing your argument, keep in mind the basic guidelines we have discussed in this chapter.

1. What machine is more intimate with you than your phone? It listens—patiently—to everything you say. It hears things your best friend never hears. It brings you both good news and bad news, and it isn't offended when you neglect it.

*2. [Pat Curran, Canadian Automobile Association, quoted in *TransMission* 4, 3 (1995)] We at the CAA believe that reducing the speed to 30 kilometres per hour on city streets would be unreasonable and unenforceable. Motorists will only obey the speed limits that they perceive as reasonable. Further, we feel that such a low speed limit . . . could have the detrimental effect of increasing fuel consumption and exhaust pollution.

3. According to many experts, laughter is a potent healer. Physiologically, laughter reduces hormones that cause stress: the muscles relax, endorphins produce a feeling of well-being, and one's heart rate slows. If you want to be healthy, laugh!

*4. [Joe Kita, 'Lounge Act', *Men's Health* 10, 10 (1995)] Ever notice how relaxed you feel after a yawn or a sigh? That's because it's the body's natural way of venting tension, says yoga expert Lilias Folan in *The Big Book of Relaxation*.

*5. [Greg Gutfeld, 'Be a Jerk', *Men's Health* 10, 10 (1995)] A long time ago, I had this health problem. . . . Almost immediately, my doctor laid my worries to rest. He told me to relax. He sat with me and we talked for a long while. . . . We bonded. We became pals. . . . But there was a small problem. I was still sick.

Finally, I gave up and went to see another doctor. He was not a pleasant guy, more like a scowl in a white jacket. He took one look at me and spat out a diagnosis. . . .

A week later I was cured.

I learned something valuable here: When it comes to your health and other important matters, you can usually count on a jerk.

6. Lipton College was a better school because it was tough. When what you said made no sense, someone jumped on you. It wasn't pretty but it taught you to be careful and be ready to defend yourself.

*7. [Aristotle, *Nichomachean Ethics*, tr. W.D. Ross (New York: Charles Scribner's Sons, 1927)] And politics appears to be [the master art]; for it is this that ordains which of the sciences should be studied in a state, and which each class of citizens should learn and up to what point they should learn them; and we see even the most highly esteemed of capacities to fall under this, e.g. strategy, economics, rhetoric. . . .

8. [From a report of the research and statistics group of the Department of the Solicitor-General of Canada, *The Globe and Mail*, 9 Jan. 1987] It seems jurors are more willing to convict for murder since the abolition of the death penalty. The over-all conviction rate for capital punishment was about 10 per cent for 1960–1974. From 1976, when capital punishment was abolished, until 1982, the conviction rate for first degree murder was about 20 per cent.

9. [A comment on a debate about Bill 179, Ontario legislation that would ban strikes by public employees] Not only does Bill 179 take away the right to strike, but the right to collective bargaining, through which both the employer and employee mutually agree to the terms and conditions under which they [employees] will work. As anyone who follows the news will know, the Pope has repeatedly stated that man has the right to demand what he feels is just compensation of his labours, including the right to strike.

10. [From *One World*, the monthly magazine of the World Council of Churches, June 1987] In answer to the question how he would explain to the Christian pacifist his endorsement of violence in the name of Black justice, Zimbabwean President Canaan Banana replied: '. . . look at John 15:13—"Greater love has no man than this, that he lay down his life for his friends." When a young man disenchanted by the suffering of his people says "I must give my life to bring freedom", I see this young man dying for the love of his country.'

11. [From Carl Sagan, *The Dragons of Eden* (New York: Random House, 1977), p. 92] At the same time that the hominid cranial volume was undergoing its spectacular increase, there was another striking change in human anatomy . . . there was a wholesale reshaping of the human pelvis. This was very likely an adaptation to permit the live birth of the latest model large-brained babies.

12. [From Raymond Chandler, *Goldfish* (London: Penguin, 1995), p.41] There didn't seem to be any hurry . . . they didn't know anything about Westport. Sunset hadn't mentioned the name in their presence. They didn't know it when they reached Olympia, or they would have gone there at once.

13. [Adapted from a public advertisement from Canada Post] The people who send you ads-in-the-mail do a lot of nice things for you, and for us. Advertising Mail allows you to shop from the comfort of your home. Advertising Mail adds $50,000,000 revenue to the Post Office and that keeps postal rates down. Advertising Mail creates employment for tens of thousands of men and women all over Canada. Probably someone you know.

14. [From an advertisement for the book *Judaism Beyond God*, by Rabbi Sherwin Wine, *Humanist*, Aug. 1987] Judaism is more than a religion. It's a four-thousand-year-old culture. It has a secular history, secular roots. Einstein and Freud are as much a part of it as Abraham and Moses. Throughout Jewish history there has been a non-establishment pragmatic Jewish humanist tradition. . . . Most Jews, without knowing it, embrace it. You too may be part of the secular Jewish tradition.

15. [From an advertisement for a vitamin pill called 'Within', in *Ms.*, Aug. 1987] Most multivitamins don't know you from Adam.

WITHIN

With the extra calcium and extra iron women need. . . . The most complete multivitamin created for women.

16. [From Bercuson, Bothwell, and Granatstein, *The Great Brain Robbery* (Toronto: McClelland & Stewart, 1984)] It is an axiom that anything worthwhile is difficult to get. . . . It was once difficult to achieve the academic qualifications to enter a Canadian university, but it is difficult no more.

*17. [From Machiavelli, *The Prince*, tr. Quentin Skinner and Russell Prince (New York: Cambridge University Press, 1988), p. 35] . . . the nobles cannot be satisfied if a ruler acts honourably, without injuring others. But the people can be thus satisfied, because their aims are more honourable than those of the nobles: for the latter want only to oppress and the former, only to avoid being oppressed.

18. [From a letter to *Harper's*, Dec. 1986] Cigarettes are the greatest public health problem we have, and the most flagrant example of drug pushing, since most tobacco is pushed on teenagers, who are led by advertising into thinking it's cool to smoke.

19. [From Robert F. Hartley, *Business Ethics: Violations of the Public Trust* (Toronto: John Wiley & Sons, 1993)] Lest we conclude that all takeovers involving heavy borrowing are ill-advised, reckless, and imprudent, let us look at a positive example. A&W root beer is part of America's motorized culture. . . . In 1986, Lowenkron engineered a leveraged buyout for $74 million, with $35 million in junk bonds. . . . By 1989, the company's sales surpassed $110 million, more than triple what they were before the buyout; profits reached $10 million, compared to a small loss in 1986.

*20. [From a letter to the editor of the *Toronto Sun*, 3 Sept. 1987] I think it is sad that some members of our society still enjoy watching a spectacle like the

Media Pig Race (page 2, Aug. 27 *Sun*). Those pigs were not racing. They were terrified animals running in a panic from the noise of the crowd. It is a display of cruelty that the *Sun* should not condone by endorsing one of the unfortunate participants. We kill pigs for food. We do not need to torment them first.

EVALUATING

ARGUMENTS

Chapters 2 and 4 introduced arguments. The present chapter introduces argument evaluation. As a first step in elucidating the difference between good and bad reasoning, it discusses:

◆ the essential ingredients of good reasoning;
◆ valid and invalid arguments;
◆ forms of argument; and
◆ the laws of thought.

As earlier chapters have demonstrated, the first prerequisite of a good argument is clarity. Whoever reads or hears the argument should have no trouble identifying it as an argument with specific premises leading to a clear conclusion. But a good argument requires more than clarity. It must also convince reasonable people who accept its premises that they should accept its conclusion. In short, it should be an instance of good reasoning.

In this chapter, we begin to elaborate those features of good arguments that make them instances of good rather than bad or questionable reasoning. After a very general overview of the requirements for good reasoning, we will focus on one type of reasoning that encompasses the kinds of arguments we discuss in Chapters 6, 7, 8, and 9.

1. GOOD ARGUMENTS

Before we explore the nature of good arguments in detail, we can say something very general about the criteria for good reasoning. There are two essential aspects of good arguments: (i) acceptable premises and (ii) a conclusion that follows from these premises. An argument without acceptable premises cannot convince a reasonable audience because they will not accept the claims upon which it is based. An argument without a conclusion that follows from its premises will fail to convince a reasonable audience because they can accept its premises and still reject its conclusion.

Consider an argument that Arthur Conan Doyle attributes to his fictional detective, Sherlock Holmes, in *A Scandal In Bohemia*. It occurs at the end of the story, when Holmes explains to the King why he hopes that the woman who is his suspect is in love with her husband.

> Because it would spare your majesty all fear of future annoyance. If the lady loves her husband, she does not love your majesty. If she does not love your majesty, there is no reason why she should interfere with your majesty's plan.

This explanation gives reasons for believing Holmes's opinion, so we can treat it as an argument. In doing so, we need to recognize that the 'would' in Holmes's initial response tells us it is a statement about what would be true if the woman does love her husband. In view of this, we can express the premises and conclusion in Holmes's reasoning as follows.

P1 = If the lady loves her husband, she does not love your majesty.
P2 = If she does not love your majesty, there is no reason why she should interfere with your majesty's plan.
C = If the lady loves her husband, it would spare your majesty all fear of future annoyance.

To be sure that we have fully captured Holmes's reasoning, we can make the connection between P2 and C clear by adopting as HP3 the implicit claim that 'If there is no reason why she should interfere with your majesty's plan, then this should spare your majesty of all fear of future annoyance.' Once this is done, we can diagram the argument as follows.

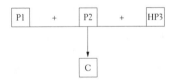

As the King himself admits, this is a good argument that is difficult to criticize. What we need to note is that this is so because premises 1-3 are reasonable premises, and because Holmes's conclusion clearly follows from them. Like the other arguments that make Holmes a famous reasoner, this argument is characterized by the two basic ingredients of good reasoning.

As a second example, consider the following argument on American water policy, taken from an article called 'The Trouble With Dams' (*Atlantic Monthly*, Aug. 1995). According to the author, we should change water policy to enforce conservation measures because 'we squander so much [water] that following through on just the easiest conservation measures would save vast amounts of water.' We can diagram this argument as follows:

P1 = Following through on just the easiest water conservation measures would save vast amounts of water.

C = We should follow through on conservation measures.

If we want to be sure that the diagram captures all of the author's reasoning, we may include as a hidden premise the implied assumption that it is wrong to waste water that could easily be saved. With HP2 included, the diagram appears as follows:

A detailed discussion of the premises of this argument would take us away from the topic that concerns us, so we will simply say that we find both P1 and HP2 to be acceptable premises (in support of P1 we could cite studies of conservation measures). Because the premises are acceptable, and the conclusion follows from them, this is another instance of good reasoning.

The recognition that someone might wish to debate P1 underlines an important point. Whenever we deal with complex and controversial issues, it is usually difficult to treat them in a definitive way without propounding long and involved extended arguments. This is especially true in the case of moral and political debates, which typically involve a variety of issues that can be discussed from a variety of points of view. Given such complexities, we must often accept premises, arguments, and conclusions that are reasonable and plausible rather than certain and irrefutable. This being said, such reliance does not contradict what we have said about the basic criteria for good reasoning, for as long as we recognize their limits, plausible premises are acceptable in such circumstances, and conclusions that they make plausible can be said to follow from them.

In summary, there are two essential criteria for good arguments. A good argument has (i) acceptable premises, and (ii) a conclusion that follows from them.

Box 5.1 *Diagnosing Bad Reasoning*

The criteria for good reasoning can be used to explain bad arguments as well as good arguments, a bad argument being one that fails to satisfy one or both criteria. For a good criticism of an argument along these lines, let's turn to an article by Steve Marantz (*The Sporting News*, 24 July 1995), which takes issue with the common claim that pitching in major league baseball has declined. In passing he criticizes a comment by the Mets general manager, who backs the claim that pitching has declined with the remark: 'Go watch a high school pitcher. Nine of 10 have major mechanical flaws.'

We can represent the GM's argument as follows:

P1 = Nine of 10 high school pitchers have major mechanical flaws.
HP2 = Such flaws were not so prevalent in earlier years.
C   = Pitching in the majors is declining.

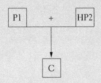

We include the hidden premise HP2 in the diagram because the issue here is whether pitching is poorer now than in the past, hence the GM's remark makes sense only if he is claiming that the situation has declined in high school.

Having diagrammed the GM's argument, let's turn to Marantz's criticism of it. He writes:

One [problematic] inference is that those flaws carry into the major leagues. Another is that in a long-ago golden age of sandlot baseball, mechanical flaws were nonexistent.

Consider the second criticism first. It is overstated but it effectively raises the question whether the GM's argument satisfies the first criterion of a good argument. As Marantz implies, it is questionable whether we should accept HP2, for we have no reason to believe that mechanical flaws in high school pitchers were not as prevalent (not 'nonexistent') in a previous era.

Marantz's other criticism raises doubts about the second criterion of good reasoning, for even if we grant the premises, the conclusion does not clearly follow. It does not follow because we do not know that mechanical flaws in high school pitchers will carry over to the big leagues. If they can be routinely corrected then their existence does not suggest the conclusion that pitching has declined in the major leagues.

In raising his two criticisms of the GM's argument, Marantz implicitly adopts the role of a good reasoner, showing that the argument he criticizes fails to satisfy our two criteria for good reasoning.

Good Arguments in More Detail

To take our account of good arguments further, we need to elaborate some aspects of good reasoning that warrant much more detailed comment.

In discussing the criteria for good reasoning, some would say that the premises of an argument must be true rather than 'acceptable'. It is natural to reply by asking what it means to say that an argument's premises are 'true'. This question raises age-old issues that are addressed by philosophical theories of truth. The intricacies of such theories are intriguing, but they lie beyond the scope of the present book. We will not, therefore, speak of the truth of premises directly. Instead, we say that the premises of good arguments must be *acceptable*, i.e., accepted as true by an arguer and the audience.

Because acceptable premises are accepted as true, truth still plays an implicit role in arguments and argument evaluation. The second criterion for good reasoning tells us that a good argument takes an audience from premises accepted as true to a conclusion that must, in view of them, be accepted as true as well. Here we need to distinguish conclusions that follow from premises in different ways. Some reasoning is structured so that a conclusion *necessarily follows* from a set of premises: it is impossible for the premises to be true and the conclusion false. In such cases, someone who accepts the premises obviously should accept the conclusion. Such arguments are said to be 'valid'. It follows that an argument is invalid if it is possible for its conclusion to be false when its premises are true. In checking validity or invalidity we assume the truth of the premises. Whether the premises are in fact true is another question, which we will address at a later point.

A second category of argument consists of arguments in which a conclusion follows from an argument's premises with, at best, a high degree of probability. We continually use such arguments when we analyse what we believe to be 'the facts' about ourselves and our world. They are not valid in the logical sense—it is possible for the conclusion to be false even if the premises are true—but it would be a mistake to conclude that they must be rejected as a group. In comparison with valid reasoning, such arguments are characterized by a more tentative link between their premises and their conclusions, but they are still an essential part of ordinary reasoning and it is possible to distinguish reasonable from unreasonable cases.

When we deal with good reasoning of the second variety, it is useful to distinguish two further criteria that may be used when judging whether a conclusion follows from a set of premises. First, we can ask whether the premises in an argument are 'relevant' to the conclusion. We count a premise or group of premises as relevant when it provides some—i.e., any—evidence that makes the conclusion more likely. A good argument always advances premises that are relevant to the conclusion it proposes.

Relevant premises do not guarantee a good argument. In good reasoning, premises must also be *sufficient* to establish that a conclusion is more likely than not. This implies something more than relevant premises, for the latter may provide some support for a conclusion without providing enough to convince a reasonable audience. In this way, we can elaborate on the second criterion for good reasoning by saying that a conclusion follows from a set of premises if the premises are (i) relevant to the conclusion and (ii) sufficient to establish it as probable.

The difference between relevant and sufficient premises will be clear in many cases. Consider the following *Vanity Fair* letter, which responds to an article that profiled Kathleen Brown, the 1992 Democratic candidate for California governor. In answer to the article's speculation that she would be able to 'deliver' California's electoral votes to Clinton during the 1996 presidential election campaign, Lawrence H. Wallach wrote:

> No governors will be able to 'deliver' their states' electoral votes to President Clinton or anyone else. Clinton will win or lose California based on the voters' perception of . . . his record. Note that in 1992 Clinton easily carried California even though the state had a Republican governor who fully supported George Bush.

Wallach here claims that governors cannot 'deliver' electoral votes. Because he provides evidence to back his claim, we can extract the following argument from his letter.

P1 = In 1992, the California governor could not deliver his state's electoral votes to President George Bush.

C = No governors are able to deliver their states' electoral votes to a particular presidential candidate.

We judge that P1 is relevant to the argument's conclusion. It successfully shows that governors sometimes fail to 'deliver' electoral votes to their preferred presidential candidates. The problem is that Wallach makes the much stronger claim that no governor can succeed in doing so. Instances like the one he cites are relevant to this claim, but one example is not enough to show that his conclusion is even likely. For all we know, a more comprehensive look at examples might show that this instance is unusual.

Deciding when we have sufficient evidence for a conclusion can be difficult at times. In 1992, for example, the Canadian National Breast Screening Study published the results of a major study of mammography, which concluded that it is not reliable for women in their forties. Given the careful way in which the study was conducted and the remarkably large number of women surveyed, one would expect that it provided sufficient evidence for this conclusion. Later research suggested that the study was flawed, however. The major problem was the seven-year follow-up period it examined—a period that was too short to register the positive effects of detecting small tumours that may not become life threatening for eight or more years. This example illustrates that it can be difficult to decide when the evidence offered by an argument is sufficient for a conclusion.

Much more could be said about relevance and sufficiency, but we will leave a detailed discussion for Chapter 10. In the meantime, we will focus on models of inference and argumentation that do not require this type of evaluation. To understand such arguments we need to better understand validity in the logician's sense.

2. VALID AND INVALID ARGUMENTS

An argument is valid whenever it is impossible for its premises to be true and its conclusion false. Validity thus encompasses the strongest possible link between premises and a conclusion. When we learn to distinguish valid and invalid arguments we are learning to judge when they are characterized by this link.

In many cases, we can judge validity by relying on our own understanding of what follows and does not follow from a set of premises. In doing so, we can learn from Sherlock Holmes. Following his investigations and reflections on his findings, he usually announces the unexpected verdict that 'So-and-so committed the crime in question.' In response to his partner's quizzical response, he claims that his reasoning is 'Elementary, my dear Watson.' By this, he means both that it is simple once it is understood and that his conclusion is inescapable once the evidence is understood. Holmes then goes on to demonstrate that this is in fact the case.

Because we have all listened to and proposed many arguments in our lifetime, most of us can quickly test the validity of arguments that are relatively straightforward and uncomplicated. We rely on this skill when we follow Holmes's reasoning step by step. By resorting to this skill we can, like Holmes, usually demonstrate that our inferences are valid.

Consider an example that might arise in the course of reading this book. In working through its exercises, you wonder whether the answer to a particular question is included in the answers collected at the back of the book. In the process, you employ the following reasoning.

P1: All the exercise questions answered at the back of this book are starred.
P2: Exercise question number 5 is not starred.
C: Exercise question number 5 is not answered at the back of the book.

This argument is valid, and your reading of it should tell you this. If you are unsure, try and imagine that the premises are true and the conclusion is false. This would mean that exercise question number 5 is, contrary to what the conclusion states, answered at the back of the book. But it would also mean that P1 is true, i.e., that all answered questions are starred. It would necessarily follow that question 5 is starred, but this contradicts P2.

This 'mental experiment' shows that it is impossible for C to be false when P1 and P2 are true, i.e., that the argument is valid. Having seen that this is the case, we might note that it does not necessarily follow that our example is a good argument. If we invoked it while we were looking at question number 1b in the major exercise at the end of this chapter, then it would have a false conclusion. This is not because there is a problem with the way the conclusion follows from the premises, but because one of the premises (P2) is in this case false. This underscores the point that valid arguments are full-fledged instances of good reasoning only if they have acceptable premises. This is a natural consequence of our basic criteria for good reasoning, for validity guarantees only that an argument's conclusion follows from its premises, and this is only one of two ingredients of a good argument. Because the other essential ingredient is acceptable premises, a valid argument can fail to be good reasoning because its premises are not acceptable.

In studying validity we will, for the most part, ignore the question of whether the premises of an argument are acceptable. Doing so allows us to isolate the issue of validity and concentrate our attention on this one particular aspect of good reasoning. We will turn to other criteria later.

In providing our previous examples of valid reasoning, we have assumed that you are already familiar with the structure of simple arguments. We have made this assumption because we believe that you have read the section of this book that discusses them. If asked why we believe this, we might answer with the following reasoning.

> If you have read Chapter 2, you have read the section of the book that introduces simple arguments. But you have read Chapter 2. We conclude that you have read the section of the book that discusses simple arguments.

Here again, the validity of this argument should be immediately clear to you. The premises would be true and the conclusion false only if you have not read our discussion of simple arguments, even though it is contained in Chapter 2 and you have read Chapter 2. As in the earlier example, this is a situation where validity is 'elementary' once we understand the argument in question.

Of course, not all arguments are valid. We must, therefore, be able to detect invalidity as well as validity. In many cases, we can do so in the same way that we have been determining validity—by relying on our prior understanding about what follows and does not follow from a set of premises. Here we can model ourselves on Sherlock Holmes once again, though in this case we must compare ourselves to the great detective when he criticizes someone else's—say Watson's—faulty chain of reasoning.

Your grasp of invalidity probably asserts itself in many cases where you find yourself rebelling against an argument. 'Hey,' you may say, 'that doesn't follow.' If you are pushed, you may go further and back your claim by constructing a similar argument with premises that are obviously true and a conclusion that is clearly false. 'You're arguing like this', you may say, and then provide a counter-example.

Consider the following argument about AIDS.

P1 = All people who suffer from AIDS are infected with HIV.
P2 = Paul does not have AIDs.
C = Paul is not infected with HIV.

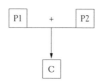

Such reasoning was common when it was first discovered that AIDS victims were HIV carriers. At first glance, it might seem to be a valid argument. But this impression will not last if you think about it carefully. The problem is that P1 — the claim that all people who suffer from AIDS are infected with HIV — is compatible with the claim that other people also carry the virus. Paul can, therefore, be infected with HIV even though he does not have AIDS. It follows that the conclusion of the argument can be false when the premises are true, and that the argument is invalid.

To back our claim that this example is invalid, we may want to construct a parallel argument that makes its invalidity clearer. We construct an argument with parallel premises that are clearly true and a parallel conclusion that is clearly false. In the present instance, we can do so by saying 'You can't argue about AIDS that way. That's like saying: All Canadians speak English, the President of the United States is not Canadian, so the President of the United States does not speak English. Don't you see? Your argument involves the same kind of reasoning!'

If the point of this counter-example is not clear, we can show that it is parallel to our initial argument by comparing their components one by one as follows:

Premise 1:
   [Original:]   All people who suffer from AIDS are infected with HIV.
   [New:]   All Canadians speak English.

Premise 2:
   [Original:]   Paul does not have AIDS.
   [New:]   The President of the United States is not Canadian.

Conclusion:
   [Original:]   Paul is not infected with HIV.
   [New:]   The President of the United States does not speak English.

The structure of these two arguments is the same, so we can judge the validity of one by considering the validity of the other. In fact, a whole class of arguments has this structure and can be treated in the same way.

Parallel cases can be used to demonstrate validity as well as invalidity. In both circumstances, the aim of a parallel argument is the same: to portray the logical structure of the argument one is judging. Constructing parallel arguments is one good way to develop logical skills, but we will not dwell on this technique here. Instead, we will learn to deal with cases of validity and invalidity by discussing general patterns of argument. In learning to recognize these forms, we will learn to recognize parallel arguments, but at a higher level of generality than we have discussed so far.

3. FORMS OF ARGUMENT

Though a comparison might initially seem far-fetched, the distinction between an argument's form and content might usefully be compared to the distinction between a steel tube and liquid that it carries. The tube is a rigid structure that functions in a particular way in different circumstances: it delivers the liquid it contains from one place to another. This being said, there is a way in which the tasks the tube performs may be drastically different in varied circumstances. After all, a steel tube may carry oil, coffee, spring water, medicine, or sewage. In a similar way, a particular form of argument is a logical structure that works in a specific way but can be filled with different contents and in this way deliver different conclusions.

An example may make this clearer. Consider the following argument.

P1: Everyone who gets a degree from the University of Southern California has taken a course in critical thinking.
P2: Ted got his degree from USC.
C: Ted must have taken a course in critical thinking.

This is an argument about Ted and courses in critical thinking at USC. Looked at from this point of view, it is very much an individual argument. But this particular content resides within a logical structure that this argument shares with many other arguments.

To isolate the logical form of this particular argument, we let X stand for 'people who get a degree from USC', let Y stand for 'people who take a course in critical thinking', and let Z stand for 'Ted'. Once we define these letters in this way, we can represent the form of our example as follows.

Form 1: P1: All X are Y.
         P2: Z is X.
         C: Z is Y.

This is a useful way to represent our argument because it shares this structure with many other arguments that can be represented in the same way. An example with completely different content is the following.

> All professors at the University of Amsterdam have PhD degrees. Jan Yulti is a professor at the University of Amsterdam, so Jan Yulti must have a PhD.

If we let X = professors at the University of Amsterdam, Y = people with PhD degrees, and Z = Jan Yulti, then we can represent this new example as 'form 1'. Our ability to do so shows that we have two arguments that share the same form even though their contents are entirely different.

Because form 1 presents the logical structure of our two examples, we can use it to explain why both these arguments are valid. Indeed, form 1 can be used to show that any argument of this form is valid. In any case like this it will be impossible for the conclusion to be false (for Z not to be Y) if its premises are true, regardless of its content, for premise 1 would imply that 'Z is not X' and this would contradict premise 2.

The argument form that we have labelled 'form 1' demonstrates the validity of the initial argument we noted, as well as any argument that shares this form. Argument forms can also demonstrate ways in which many arguments become invalid. Consider the following argument.

> All people who read novels are library users. Paul does not read novels. Paul is not a library user.

Like our first example, this is an argument about groups (or 'sets' or 'classes') of things. In this case, we can let X = people who read novels, let Y = people who use libraries, and let Z = Paul, and can represent the argument as follows.

Form 2:   Premise 1: All X are Y.
             Premise 2: Z is not X.
             Conclusion: Z is not Y.

Once again, many arguments share this form. Among them, we can include the similar parallel reasoning we used to demonstrate that this form is invalid. It can be represented as form 2 by letting X = Canadians, Y = people who can speak English, and Z = the President of the United States.

More generally, we can see why arguments of this form are invalid, for the conclusion would necessarily follow from premise 2 ('Z is not X') only if it were true that 'All Y are X', and this is not what is claimed in premise 1, which states a very different relation, namely that all X are Y.

It would be possible to continue this discussion by identifying various forms of argument, but we will not do so here, for this is the goal of subsequent chapters. Chapters 6 and 7 are devoted to the forms of argument studied in 'syllogistic' reasoning, which is the logic of arguments about groups or classes. It deals with argument forms like the one we have taken as our first example (form 1). Chapters 8 and 9 are devoted to 'propositional' reasoning, which deals with argument forms like the one we have taken as our second example of a valid argument. In syllogistic reasoning, the content in an argument form is made up of statements about categories and classes. In propositional reasoning, the content is made up of propositions joined by 'ifs, ands, and buts'. In both cases, our dealings with particular forms of argument can be seen as an extension and an elaboration of our present discussion.

4. The Laws of Thought

We will end this introduction to the role that validity plays in argument evaluation with the so-called 'laws of thought'. They are regarded as the most basic principles of sound reasoning. Though Aristotle is usually credited with having formulated these laws, he did not create them. At most, he identified them as axiomatic structures that govern reasonable thinking. This is another way of saying that the principles they embody are elementary, self-evident principles by which all reasoning must abide. They are worth noting in the present context because we implicitly rely on them when judging validity and invalidity, and because they tell us how we should reason.

The Law of Identity

The laws of thought are three in number. The first is the *law of identity*, which states that 'x is x' where 'x' refers in both cases to the same thing at the same time and in the same respect. The truth of this principle should be apparent: it states that it makes no sense to claim or think that 'A fork is not a fork' or that 'The Prime Minister of Australia is not the Prime Minister of Australia.'

Statements that appear to contradict the law of identity invariably involve an equivocation on the meaning of the first and second 'x' in the statement 'x is x'. When a fork is twisted beyond recognition, we might laugh and say that 'A fork is not a fork' but this means only that 'This utensil is a fork in one sense but not another.' More specifically, our 'fork' is a fork in the sense that it was manufactured to be a fully functioning fork, but not in the sense that it can function in this way now. The word 'fork' in 'A fork is not a fork' does not, therefore, refer in both cases to a fork at the same time and in the same respect.

Explicit statements of the law of identity are rare because they are so obviously true that we usually assume them. This being said, many logically important statements are statements of identity that depend on the law of identity. Usually, such statements have the form 'x is y', where x and y are two different descriptions of one thing. In such a case we will say that the expressions x and y are 'equivalent' because they refer to the same thing.

In discussing politics we invoke the law of identity when we say that 'The President of the United States is the chief executive officer of the US' or that 'The official residence of the Prime Minister of Canada is 24 Sussex Drive, Ottawa.' We implicitly rely on the law of identity whenever we make statements of this sort using different designations of the same thing interchangeably, substituting one designation for another.

The principles of identity also apply when we deal with statements rather than things. Statements are identical when they are exactly the same. They are equivalent when they communicate one thought in different words. The sentence 'I think of work only from nine till five' is equivalent to the sentence 'I don't think of work before nine or after five.'

In the chapters that follow we will constantly rely on our ability to recognize equivalent statements. Consider the following version of an earlier example.

P1 = Refusing to follow through on easy conservation measures would squander vast amounts of water.

HP2 = It is wrong to waste large amounts of water.

C = We should follow through on such conservation measures.

In some logical contexts it is useful to recognize that this chain of reasoning is equivalent to the following argument: 'If we do not follow through on easy conservation measures we will waste large amounts of water. We shouldn't squander water. We should follow through on such conservation measures.'

The equivalence of these arguments is a consequence of the equivalence of the various argument components that make them up. If we want to set out their equivalence in more detail we can do so by setting out the equivalences of those components.

Premise 1: 'Refusing to follow through on easy conservation measures would squander vast amounts of water' *is equivalent to* 'If we do not follow through on easy conservation measures we will waste large amounts of water.'

Premise 2: 'It is wrong to waste large amounts of water' *is equivalent to* 'We shouldn't squander water.'

Conclusion: 'We should follow through on such conservation measures' is *justifiably identical to* 'We should follow through on such conservation measures.' [by the law of identity]

Whenever we exchange equivalent components the result is an equivalent argument that advocates the same point of view.

It is important to keep equivalences and identities in mind when we are dealing with arguments and argument components, for good reasoning often requires that we be able to recognize when the same argument is expressed in different but equivalent ways.

The Law of Non-Contradiction

The second law of thought is the *law of non-contradiction*. It says that statement x and its negation cannot both be true. Alternatively, we can express the law as the principle that a statement cannot be both true and false. It cannot, for example, be both true and false that you hold the world record for discus throwing. The same can be said of any statement.

As we saw in the case of the law of identity, apparent violations of the law of non-contradiction usually depend on shifts of meaning that are easily detected. You don't deny the second law of thought when you say, 'Well, it is raining and it isn't raining. It's drizzling.' Instead, you shift the meaning of 'raining' in your sentence. As soon as a precise meaning is specified, you will have to admit that it cannot be said that 'It is raining here at this moment' and that 'It isn't raining here at this moment.'

In logic, we implicitly rely on the law of non-contradiction whenever we decide that an argument is valid, for this is so only if the assumption that the premises are true and the conclusion is false leads to contradiction. In other circumstances, we invoke the law of non-contradiction when we accuse some-one or some argument of logical inconsistency. We have good reason to protest when someone maintains that God must exist as the causal source of the universe on the grounds that everything must have some causal explanation, and at the same time holds that we may not legitimately ask 'What caused God?'

Inconsistent conduct by individuals, groups, and governments implies moral contradictions that violate the law of non-contradiction. In controversial cases, we must assess the apparent contradiction carefully. An example is the accusation that a state or province is inconsistent because it claims to disapprove of gambling but operates a lottery, sports pools, and casinos. The government might reply that its actions and claims are not inconsistent because it approves of controlled gambling and disapproves of uncontrolled gambling. To see whether this successfully undermines the charge of inconsistency, we would have to consider whether the distinction between 'controlled' and 'uncontrolled' gambling withstands careful scrutiny. If it does, there is no contradiction. If we cannot make sense of this distinction, then there is no way around the contradiction and the government can legitimately be criticized.

The Law of the Excluded Middle

The final law of thought is the *law of the excluded middle*. It states that any meaningful claim x is true or false. There are, in other words, no middle alternatives between these two truth values. This is the 'middle' that the third law of thought excludes. In a great many ordinary arguments, it is on the basis of explicit or implicit 'or' statements that the arguer declares that some state of affairs 'does or does not' pertain.

As with the two other laws of thought, counter-examples to the law of the excluded middle are almost always founded on problems of meaning. It must be granted that it is true or false that you can throw a discus 20 metres, though this might not seem to be the case if we cannot decide what we mean by 'throw', or if you can sometimes throw it 20 metres and sometimes not. So long as we make the meaning of the word 'throw' precise, it will be clear that the law of the excluded middle does hold (in certain contexts, some philosophers called 'intuitionists' deny the law of the excluded middle, but these contexts do not matter here).

Arguments implicitly rely on the law of the excluded middle when they take issue with a claim in order to establish its negation. In such a case, we proceed by criticizing one of the two alternatives the law allows, leaving one alternative that must be accepted. A lawyer may, for example, defend Tyler's innocence by showing that it makes no sense to claim that he is guilty. In another circumstance, a scientist may criticize a particular theory by assuming that it is true and showing that this leads to contradiction (in such an argument one appeals, of course, to the law of non-contradiction and the law of the excluded middle). In the next four chapters we shall see a number of important forms of argument characterized by reasoning of this kind.

Box 5.3 The Laws of Thought

The *law of identity* states that 'x is x', where x is a statement or a thing.

The *law of non-contradiction* states that a proposition x and its negation cannot both be true.

The *law of the excluded middle* states that a meaningful proposition, x, must be either true or false.

We rely on all three laws of thought when we identify and assess forms of argument. The law of identity justifies transitions between statements that make the same claim. The law of non-contradiction is employed whenever we judge that some set of claims is contradictory and inconsistent. The law of the excluded middle allows us to argue for some claim by arguing against its contradiction.

MAJOR EXERCISE 5M

1. For each of the following four arguments from *The Sporting News* (24 July 1995), diagram the argument and discuss whether it is a good argument in terms of the two basic criteria for good arguments. Explain any doubts you may have.

*a) [Dave Kindred, arguing against Major League Baseball's decision to institute new rules designed to speed up the game] There is pleasure knowing that events and not an expiring clock will decide when the evening's entertainment is done.

*b) [Mike Schmidt, talking about the content of his speech on his induction into the Baseball Hall of Fame] Children and their dreams must have positive reinforcement from parents, coaches and friends. I truly believe that this reinforcement is not only important, but imperative. . . . Without parental encouragement to reach their goals, it is more difficult for children to develop self-esteem and become successful.

c) [Letter to 'Voice of the Fan'] So Rockets' General Manager John Thomas . . . doesn't think changing the logo after back-to-back titles won't hurt their luck? Well, I subscribe to Crash Davis' theory, as stated in the movie, 'Bull Durham'—'Never (mess) with a winning streak.' . . . Ask the Penguins if they're sorry they changed logos. They did after their second consecutive Stanley Cup title but haven't made it past the second round since.

d) [Steve Marantz, defending the view that pitching is better than in the past] Strikeouts are a trademark of power pitching. Games are averaging 12.7 strikeouts this season. . . . Never has the game seen more strikeouts than today.

2. Diagram each of the following arguments and say whether they are valid or invalid. Explain your decision.

a) [Letter to 'Voice of the Fan'] So Rockets' General Manager John Thomas . . . doesn't think changing the logo after back-to-back titles won't hurt their luck? Well, I subscribe to Crash Davis' theory, as stated in the movie, 'Bull Durham'—'Never (mess) with a winning streak.' . . . Ask the Penguins if they're sorry they changed logos. They did after their second consecutive Stanley Cup title but haven't made it past the second round since.

*b) [Steve Marantz, defending the view that pitching is better than in the past] Strikeouts are a trademark of power pitching. Games are averaging 12.7 strikeouts this season. . . . Never has the game seen more strikeouts than today.

c) The conclusion of the argument can be false when the premises are true, so the argument is invalid.

d) Most people find that their logical abilities improve with practice. So you should do fine if you work regularly on the exercises in this book.

*e) In order to avoid the intricacies of theories of truth, we will rely on our earlier remark that the objective of an argument is to convince an audience. If this is so, then it is sufficient for our purposes that the premises of a good argument be accepted as true by both us and our audience. So this is what we will aim for.

3. For each of the following forms of argument, say whether the form is valid or invalid and construct three examples of arguments that fit this form. [Replace capital letters with names of groups, replace lower-case letters with sentences.]

a) All X are Y. All Y are Z. Therefore all X are Z.

b) If x, then y. If y, then z. So if x, then z.

*c) Some X are Y. Some X are Z. So some X are Y and Z.

4. Each of the following sentences appeals to one of the laws of thought. In each case, say which one.

*a) 'The man in the big hat' in Jerry Jeff Walker's song is the cowboy, so it is a song about the passing of the cowboy's way of life.

b) Your honour, we plan to show that the defendant could not possibly have committed the crime. In view of this we will call on the jury to acquit her.

c) Venus is the morning star and Venus is the evening star. So the morning is the evening star and it is not a star!

*d) [From a letter from William A. Homes, Jr, to 'Voice of the Fan', *The Sporting News* (24 July 1995)] Lupica quotes Sparky [Anderson] as saying, 'There is a river everybody has to cross at some point in their life, and that river is the one with fear running through it. I crossed it when I refused to manage those replacement players. . . .' Well now, it would seem that since that initial crossing, ol' Sparky has come back across that river, because at least twice this month, he's called on—gasp!—a replacement player (reliever Mike Christopher) to win two games for him.

e) He couldn't have been in Seattle because I was with him in Vancouver.

f) You can't have your cake and eat it too.

g) You were there or you weren't. You were wearing a red shirt or you weren't. You ran into the bank or you didn't. Stop beating around the bush and tell us which it is.

CLASSIFYING

ARGUMENTS

Chapter 5 introduced arguments whose conclusions follow necessarily from the premises, if those premises are true. This chapter looks at one type of such argument: the categorical syllogism. It discusses::

◆ categorical statements;
◆ immediate inferences;
◆ categorical arguments (syllogisms); and
◆ tests for validity using Venn diagrams.

The last chapter introduced us to reasoning that allows us to conclude what has to follow given that certain other statements (the premises) are the case. Within this domain of reasoning we find the categorical syllogism. This chapter will treat *categorical reasoning*, or reasoning about classes.

Consider the following argument, where the conclusion is separated from the premises by a solid line:

All astronomers are highly educated.
All highly educated people are assets to society.

All astronomers are assets to society.

If someone knew the first two pieces of information independently, then once those ideas were brought together in a piece of reasoning, the person would be able to draw the conclusion that must follow. Many advertisers depend on this process when preparing campaigns. It adds to the effectiveness of an advertisement if potential customers can be expected to draw the correct conclusion for themselves. The following advertisement illustrates this:

> Domino's pizza gets there sooner, and anything that gets there sooner has to be better.

This can be recast as:

> All Domino's pizzas are things that get there sooner.
> All things that get there sooner have to be better.

From these two statements the advertiser expects us to draw the conclusion, 'All Domino's pizzas are things that have to be better.' Given the amounts of money involved in such advertising, we can appreciate how much trust is being placed in that expectation, that is, in the deductive process. The fact that members of an audience are able to draw the conclusion for themselves, through their own reasoning, adds to its potential effectiveness.

You will notice that each of the examples above, when complete, involves three statements, and each statement expresses a relationship between two categories or classes of things. 'Domino's pizzas' comprise a class of things, as do 'things that get there sooner'. All categorical syllogisms express relationships between three classes of things. Such statements relating classes of things are called *categorical statements*. In the next section we examine the various types of categorical statements that can make up syllogisms. Later, we will explore the syllogism itself and ways it can be tested for strength. If the conclusion of a categorical syllogism follows necessarily from its premises, that argument is deemed to be *valid*. If there is no necessary entailment between premises and conclusion, the argument is deemed *invalid*. In this chapter we will introduce a simple method for testing validity by means of Venn diagrams. In the next chapter we provide a more technical, but more reliable method, using schematization and rules.

1. CATEGORICAL STATEMENTS

Categorical statements are subject-predicate statements expressing relationships between classes of things. In the statement 'All crows are black', 'crows' is the subject and blackness is being predicated of that subject. Thus we speak of a subject class (crows) and a predicate class (black things). The subjects and predicates are always expressed as classes of things. This is particularly important to remember about the predicate class. In 'Domino's pizza gets there sooner', 'Domino's pizzas' is the subject class, but the predicate class is expressed as 'things that get there sooner' since there is no class of 'gets there sooner'.

Pure Forms

There are four distinct types of these categorical subject-predicate statements. We will look at each of these as a pure form and then consider some of their common variations in ordinary language. Using the letters 'S' to represent the subject class of any categorical statement and 'P' to represent the predicate class, we can present and formulate the four types of categorical statement.

(i)   All S are P. The *entire* membership of the subject class is *included within* the predicate class. We call this a *universal affirmative* statement or UA, since it affirms something about all members of S. 'All police officers are public servants' is a UA statement.

(ii) No S are P. The *entire* membership of the subject class is *excluded from* the predicate class. We call this a *universal negative* statement or UN, since it denies something about all members of S. 'No children are senators' is a UN statement.

(iii) Some S are P. At least one member of the subject class is *included within* the predicate class. We call this a *particular affirmative* statement or PA, since it affirms something about only a portion of the membership of S. 'Some animals are carnivores' is a PA statement.

(iv) Some S are not P. At least one member of the subject class is *excluded from* the predicate class. We call this a *particular negative* statement or PN, since it denies something about only a portion of the membership of S. 'Some people are not actors' is a PN statement.

These are the 'pure forms' of categorical statements, and all statements expressing class relationships are logically equivalent to one or other of these forms. Hereafter we shall refer to these four forms by the letters UA, UN, PA, and PN. When interpreting these forms there are a few points to note.

1. We must be careful to distinguish between the statement that *excludes* some S from the class of P and a statement that *includes* some S within the class of non-P. Thus 'Some S are not P' is read as a PN statement, while 'Some S are non-P' is a PA statement.

2. Persons, things, and places designated by proper names such as the President, Apollo 11, and Belgium, as well as defined groups such as 'these cows' or 'the players on the field at the moment' or 'that bus' (said while pointing to a bus) should all be interpreted as referring to an entire class

and statements in which they are the subjects will be expressed as universal statements. This is because proper names are names of classes with only one member and in ordinary usage statements with limited phrases denoting the subject term are intended to be universal. Thus 'Belgium is a member of the European Economic Community' is a UA statement, and 'No players on the field at the moment are Native Americans' is a UN statement.

3. Finally, note that the UN is *not* expressed as 'All S are not P' because such a statement is ambiguous. On the one hand, it could mean that *all* Ss are *excluded* from the class of P, in which case no S are P. On the other hand, it could mean that it is *not* the case that *all* S are *included* in the class of P, in which case some S are not P. Consider, for example, the statement, 'All TV evangelists are not frauds.' Does the speaker mean that all TV evangelists are excluded from the class of frauds? Or is the speaker only excluding some TV evangelists from the class of frauds? The first alternative would be expressed as a UN statement: 'No TV evangelists are frauds.' The second interpretation is a PN statement: 'Some TV evangelists are not frauds.'

Since the principle of charity dictates that we not attribute to a writer a stronger claim than he or she may have intended, you should interpret statements of the 'All S are not P' variety as PN statements unless you happen to know that the classes of things denoted by S and P are logically exclusive. Thus, 'All triangles are not four-sided figures' would have to be interpreted as a UN statement because, by definition, no triangle can be a four-sided figure.

Common Variations

We have already seen some of the variations that express categorical relationships. Here are some (but only some) further variations:

UA

All astronauts are intelligent people.

Astronauts are intelligent.
Every astronaut is an intelligent person.
Anyone who is an astronaut must be intelligent.
None but intelligent people are astronauts.
Only intelligent people are astronauts.
No astronauts are unintelligent people.

UN

No astronauts are cowards.

No one who is an astronaut can be a coward.
No cowards are astronauts.

No one who is a coward can be an astronaut.
All astronauts are non-cowards.
All cowards are non-astronauts.
If X is an astronaut, X is not a coward.

PA

Some women are priests.

At least one woman is a priest.
Most women are priests.
A few women are priests.
There are some women who are priests.
Several women are priests.
Some women are not non-priests.

PN

Some women are not priests.

Many women are not priests.
Most women are not priests.
Few women are priests.
All women are not priests.
Not all women are priests.
Some women are non-priests.

These variations do not exhaust all the possibilities and you may well think of others. It is also important when dealing with particular propositions to recognize that while 'many', 'few', and 'most' are all read as meaning 'some', the reverse is not the case. That is, if you have a proposition referring to 'some x', you cannot assume that it means 'many' or 'most' unless the context indicates as much.

As you read through the next sections of this chapter, you will see how some of the stranger variations are indeed equivalent to the pure forms. Where you must decide which pure form you have, think through the class relationship that is intended. Is the intent of the statement to include or exclude? Is it referring to the entire subject class or only a portion of it? Rather than trying to decide what form a statement is, it is often helpful to eliminate the forms it is not in order to come to the one it has to be.

One error so common it should be noted here involves statements that begin with 'Only'. There is a temptation to render 'Only intelligent people are astronauts' as 'All intelligent people are astronauts.' This is wrong. 'Only' indicates the predicate class. While the statement involved is a UA statement, the effect of the 'only' is to reverse the classes, giving us 'All astronauts are

> **Box 6.1 Recognizing Pure Forms**
> Until you become practised at recognizing pure forms, you might want to employ the following three-step process for arriving at them. Take the statement 'Busy people are never at home when you want them.'
>
> *Step #1*: Determine the classes involved.
> [Busy people] are never [at home when you want them = people who are at home when you want them].
>
> *Step #2*: Determine whether the statement is affirming (including) or negating (excluding).
> Busy people are *never* = excluded from people who are at home when you want them.
>
> *Step #3*: Determine whether the statement is universal or particular.
> No busy people are people who are at home when you want them. UN

intelligent people.' To see that this must be so, consider that while *only* students at your institution take the particular course in which you are covering this material (there are similar courses elsewhere, but not the *same* course), it would be quite wrong to say that all students at your institution are taking the course (would that they were!). What is the case is that *all* students taking this particular course are students at your institution.

EXERCISE 6A

Classify the following statements as UA, UN, PA, or PN, and express each in its 'pure form'. Be sure to express both the subject and predicate terms as classes with members.
Example: A few students own Volvos.
Step 1:   A few [students] [own Volvos = Volvo owners].
Step 2:   A few students *are* Volvo owners.
Step 3:   Some students are Volvo owners. PA

*a) Most dentists have six-digit incomes.
*b) Dinosaurs are extinct.
*c) Most people are not prepared to pay higher taxes.
 d) No one who has paid attention should be confused.
 e) None of my sons is greedy.
 f) Laws are made to be broken.
*g) Only the lonely know the way I feel tonight.
 h) A few students in this class wish they weren't.
 i) There are some extremely wealthy people who pay no income tax.

j) Many wealthy people do not pay income tax.
k) People who live in glass houses shouldn't throw stones.
l) Stephen is far from being fastidious.
*m) New York is in New York.
*n) None but the courageous will survive.
o) Beauty is in the eye of the beholder.
p) Many children of planned pregnancies turn out to be battered children.
q) The vast majority of murders are crimes of passion.
r) All that glitters is not gold.
s) Most labour leaders are not supporters of the North American Free Trade Agreement (NAFTA).
t) Those who support NAFTA see it as a recipe for economic prosperity.
*u) Under no circumstances should the courts deal leniently with people who drive vehicles while inebriated.
v) Several renowned physicists are religious mystics.
*w) Those cars parked on the street whose permits have expired will be towed away.
x) Lotteries breed avarice.
y) Whatever will be will be.

2. IMMEDIATE INFERENCES

It is useful for understanding the pure forms, and necessary when preparing some syllogisms for testing, to appreciate the basic relationships between the four forms. These are usually called immediate inferences. This does not mean that they are immediately obvious to everyone, but that no mediate term is involved. We will begin with the traditional square of opposition.

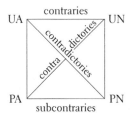

This allows us to ascertain quickly what must be the case when various statements are known to be true or false.

The UA and UN statements are contraries. This means that they cannot both be true, but could both be false, and would both be false whenever PA and PN are both true. The PA and PN statements, on the other hand, being subcontraries, *cannot* both be false, but could be true whenever the UA and UN are both false.

Also, the UA statement implies the PA, such that when the UA is true so is the PA (the opposite inference cannot be made). The same relationship holds between the UN and PN. One immediate inference that you can expect to use when working with categorical syllogisms is that of contradiction.

Contradiction

Contradiction has to do with what statement must be true if a given statement is false, and what statement must be false if a given statement is true. Two statements are contradictories if they cannot both be true and they cannot both be false, but one of them must be true and the other one must be false.

You might be inclined to think that the contradictory of a UA statement is a UN statement, but, as we have seen, these two are contraries because it is possible for them both to be false. Examining the square of opposition reveals that the relationship of contradiction exists between the UA and PN, and between the UN and PA.

When it is true that 'All astronauts are intelligent', then it must be false that 'Some astronauts are not intelligent.' Likewise, if we are told that 'Some astronauts are not intelligent' is true, then we can infer that 'All astronauts are intelligent' has to be false. The same relationship holds between the UN and PA statements. When it is true that 'No astronauts are cowards', then it must be false that 'Some astronauts are cowards.' Also, if we are told that 'Some astronauts are cowards' is true, then we can infer that 'No astronauts are cowards' must be false.

Obversion

A second immediate inference of interest to us is called obversion. Since a syllogism has three statements expressing relationships between only three classes of things or terms (each appearing twice), then the existence of more than three terms means that we do not have an acceptable syllogism that can be tested. But due to the variety of ordinary language, what looks like more than three terms may often be reducible to three because the additional terms are complementaries of one or more of the other terms. For example, the class of 'dogs' has as its complementary class 'non-dogs'. If 'dogs' is the subject class 'S', then the complementary class will be written as 'non-S'. Everything in the world can be divided into its class and complementary class. 'Presidents' and 'non-Presidents', 'things that are amusing' and 'things that are not amusing'. In fact, in translating ordinary language we may often be prepared to take liberties and translate, for example, 'dull people' and 'interesting people' as complementary classes, whereas the traditional logician would insist that the complementary class of 'dull people' is 'non-dull people'.

Obversion is a tool we can use to get rid of complementary classes and reduce the number of terms in a syllogism to three, thereby making it testable. We have already seen that 'No astronauts are non-intelligent' is a common variation of 'All astronauts are intelligent.' This is because each is the obverse of the other. They mean the same thing; when we obvert a statement we do not change its meaning. To obvert:

i) Change the statement from negative to affirmative or affirmative to negative. That is, if it is a UA, make it a UN, and vice versa; and if it is a PA make it a PN, and vice versa.

ii) Negate the predicate term.

Obversion works for each of the pure forms as follows:

	Given		*Obverse*
UA	All S are P	UN	No S are non-P
UN	No S are P	UA	All S are non-P
PA	Some S are P	PN	Some S are not non-P
PN	Some S are not P	PA	Some S are non-P

Conversion

Conversion applies directly to only two of the pure forms and in a limited sense to a third one. The PN statement does not convert. Conversion allows you to switch the position of the S and P terms. In fact, that is how you convert: exchange the position of the S and P.

But this can be done only to UN and PA statements. The converses of UA and PN statements are not logically equivalent. The UN statement converts easily because both classes are being excluded from *each other*. Hence, if 'No astronauts are cowards', it must also be the case that 'No cowards are astronauts.' Likewise, if 'Some women are priests', the converse, 'Some priests are women', must also hold. To appreciate further why UN and PA statements convert so easily, you should read the section on distribution in the next chapter.

The UA statement does not convert in this way. While 'All astronauts are intelligent' may be true, we would not want to say 'All intelligent people are astronauts'. However, the reversal of the terms would be possible in a limited sense. That is, if 'All astronauts are intelligent', it must be the case that 'Some intelligent people are astronauts'. So the converse of a UA statement is a PA statement.

No such qualification is possible with PN statements. While 'Some animals are not dogs' is true, we cannot accept the converse, 'Some dogs are not animals.' The converse of the PN statement is not its logical equivalent, and so we say that it does not convert. Conversion, then, works as follows:

	Given			Converse
UA	All S are P		PA	Some P are S (by limitation)
UN	No S are P		UN	No P are S
PA	Some S are P		PA	Some P are S
PN	Some S are not P		X	

Contraposition

A final immediate inference we can perform is contraposition. Whereas with conversion it was in the cases of UN and PA statements that the original and the modified statements were logically equivalent, with contraposition it is the UA and PN for which this is true. This is so because contraposition consists of obverting, then converting, and then obverting again.

Given	Obverse	Converse of Obverse	Obverse of Converted Obverse (Contrapositive)
UA All S are P	UN No S are non-P	UN No non-P are S	UA All non-P are non-S
UN No S are P	UA All S are non-P	PA Some non-P are S	PN Some non-P are not non-S
PA Some S are P	PN Some S are not non-P	—	—
		—	—
PN Some S are not P	PA Some S are non-P	PA Some non-P are S	PN Some non-P are not non-S

The PA cannot be contraposed because its obverse, a PN statement, cannot be converted. The UN statement is subject to contraposition with limitation since its obverse is a UA statement that, upon conversion, becomes a PA. While contrapositives strike many people as cumbersome, reflection will show you that 'All non-intelligent people are non-astronauts' is simply an alternative, if unusual, way of saying that 'All astronauts are intelligent.'

EXERCISE 6B

Provide at least two immediate inferences for each of the following:
Example: Some farmers are subsidized.
Some subsidized people are farmers.

It is false that no farmers are subsidized people.
*a) Only ticket holders will be admitted.
*b) Many New Yorkers vacation in Florida.
 c) No non-famous people are listed in *Who's Who*.
 d) Some areas of North America are not populated.
 e) It is not true that all hard workers are successful people.
 f) Not all mushrooms are edible.
*g) Many donors to the club are non-users.
 h) No non-citizens are refused legal assistance.
 i) The Meadowlake circus is unpopular with animal lovers.
 j) It is false to say that some illegal acts are moral.

3. CATEGORICAL SYLLOGISMS

A categorical syllogism consists of three and only three categorical statements that relate three and only three classes of things. More precisely, a categorical syllogism is an argument consisting of three categorical statements related in such a way that two of them, having one class-term in common, yield a third categorical statement relating the other two class-terms.

Consider one of our earlier syllogisms:

All astronomers are highly educated.
Highly educated people are assets to society.

All astronomers are assets to society.

Each statement is a UA statement. The first two are the premises of the argument, the last one is the conclusion. These three statements relate three classes of things, namely: 'astronomers', 'highly educated people', and 'assets to society'. Each of these classes appears twice in the syllogism. Each of the classes in the conclusion ('astronomers', 'assets to society') appears in a different premise. The remaining class ('highly educated people') appears once in each premise. Depending on the particular positions the classes occupy in a syllogism, the syllogism will be valid or invalid.

Up to this point we have used S and P to represent the subject and predicate terms for categorical statements. Now we will restrict the use of S and P to the conclusion of a syllogism and introduce a third symbol, M, to represent the third class.

S = subject of the conclusion
P = predicate of the conclusion
M = class common to both premises, or middle term

Consistent with this convention, we would identify S, P, and M in the above syllogism as follows:

S = astronomers
P = assets to society
M = highly educated people

This identification of the meanings of S, P, and M we call the *legend*. Note again that each symbol represents a *class* of things and is always expressed in those terms.

The syllogism with which we are working can now be shown to have the following 'symbolic form'.

All S are M		S UA M
All M are P	or	M UA P
All S are P		S UA P

Preparing Syllogisms for Testing

The question of a syllogism's *validity* is a question about its *structure*. We are interested in whether the conclusion follows necessarily from the premises, and at this stage we will not worry whether the premises are true or acceptable. This is why you might see quite bizarre examples offered as instances of valid syllogisms. The following is a case in point:

All dogs are highly educated.
All highly educated creatures are baseball fans.

All dogs are baseball fans.

The statements are ridiculous, but as they are represented here, they constitute a valid syllogism. This argument has exactly the same form as the previous argument about 'astronomers', 'assets to society', and 'highly educated people'. That is, it is also of the form:

All S are M
All M are P

All S are P

By a 'valid argument' we mean that, should the premises be true, the conclusion would have to be true. The conclusion follows necessarily from the premises, and to deny it while accepting the premises would commit us to a contradictory position. So we must not confuse validity with truth. They are quite separate concepts. While we are dealing with syllogisms, we must try not to be distracted by what the statements say. Translating the syllogisms into their 'symbolic form' will help us to concentrate solely on validity.

From what has been said about validity, it should be clear that an *invalid* argument is one in which the conclusion does not follow necessarily from the premises. Even assuming the truth of the premises, the conclusion of an invalid argument could still be false.

The first things we need to do when preparing syllogisms for our tests of validity are to identify the types of categorical statements involved, assign S, P, and M, and then set out the argument in its standard form.

We will begin with the conclusion because S and P are identified by assigning them to the terms of the conclusion. The M class can *never* appear in the conclusion.

The use of physical discipline towards children is known to encourage aggressive tendencies. Aggressive behaviour results in difficulty for the child later in life. Therefore, physical discipline is not good for children. (Laura E. Beck, *Child Development*, 2nd edn [Boston: Allyn and Bacon, 1991].)

One of the advantages of working with syllogisms over a period of time is being able to recognize arguments like this as ones that relate classes of things. Since we are dealing with ordinary language, we need to make decisions about different phrases and terms that can be interpreted as equivalent. In this argument, the conclusion is easily identified by the indicator 'therefore'. This is then followed by: 'Physical discipline is not good for children.'

This statement relates the classes of things that are 'acts of physical discipline' and 'things that are good for children'. And it does so by excluding the classes from each other. So it is either a UN or PN statement. Since there is no qualifier to suggest that only some acts of physical discipline are intended, we interpret it as a UN. In its categorical form the conclusion reads:

No acts of physical discipline are things that are good for children.

Now we assign S and P to the subject and predicate of this conclusion:

S = Acts of physical discipline
P = Things that are good for children

The middle term, M, will be the one with both premises in common. But we have yet to determine the premises and cast them in their categorical form. The first of the two remaining statements, though, clearly includes the S term. It tells us that acts of physical discipline (towards children) are things that encourage aggressive tendencies. 'Things that encourage aggressive tendencies' would then be a candidate for our M class. To decide on this, we would have to interpret the remaining sentence ('Aggressive behaviour results in difficulty for the child later in life') as one that relates the potential M class with P. Assuming that experiencing difficulty in later life is not good for children, we can interpret the ordinary language statement given as having the meaning: 'No things that encourage aggressive tendencies are things that are good for children.'

This confirms M as 'things that encourage aggressive behaviour' and we can rewrite the argument in categorical form as:

All acts of physical discipline are things that encourage aggressive behaviour.
No things that encourage aggressive behaviour are things that are good for children.

No acts of physical discipline are things that are good for children.

All S are M
No M are P

No S are P

In fact, if we had been unsure about how to phrase the second premise, we could have derived it as the hidden premise required to get from the first premise to the conclusion. Having cast the argument in its categorical form, use the legend to check that it now has the same meaning as the original formulation.

Any syllogism can be translated into categorical form following this procedure. The critical step to remember is the first one of identifying the conclusion and assigning S and P to the terms of the conclusion.

EXERCISE 6C

Prepare the following syllogisms for testing, identifying S, P, and M. Example:

All members of the United Nations are expected to meet their obligations with respect to peacekeeping. Since the United States is a member of the United Nations, it must therefore meet its peacekeeping obligation.

All members of the United Nations are nations expected to meet their peacekeeping obligations.
The United States is a member of the United Nations.

The United States is a nation expected to meet its peacekeeping obligations.

S = The United States
P = Nations expected to meet their peacekeeping obligations
M = Members of the United Nations

All M are P
All S are M
_____
All S are P

a) Nobody with a history of heart disease should take up jogging. Because jogging is a strenuous form of exercise, and no one with a history of heart disease should engage in strenuous forms of exercise.
b) Some professional clowns have personality disorders and some people with personality disorders are deeply depressed. So some professional clowns are deeply depressed.
*c) For a vegetable to be considered fresh, it must have been harvested within the last 48 hours. These beans were picked just last night. So they should certainly be considered fresh.
d) Only healthy people can join the army, and so people suffering from debilitating illnesses cannot join the army, since they are not healthy.
e) Some polls have been skewed by unrepresentative samples. But any poll like that cannot be trusted. So some polls are untrustworthy.

4. TESTING VALIDITY BY DIAGRAMS

We now turn to our tests for determining validity or invalidity. Remember, if the syllogism is a valid one, the truth of the premises will guarantee the truth of the conclusion. Consider the following syllogism:

P1 All astronomers are highly educated people.
P2 All highly educated people are assets to society.
_____
C All astronomers are assets to society.

We can see that, if every member of the class of astronomers belongs to the class of highly educated people (P1) and every member of the class of highly educated people belongs to the class of assets to society (P2), then it must be the case that every member of the class of astronomers belongs to the class of assets to society, which is what the conclusion tells us. Hence, we can see that this is a valid syllogism. To accept the premises but deny the conclusion would put us in a contradictory position.

To recognize validity is easy with simple arguments. But there are some arguments that seem valid when they are invalid. Consider the next example:

All people who oppose the trade bill are people with conservative values.

Smith has conservative values.
_____

Smith opposes the trade bill.

This argument has a superficial appeal to it; it sounds right. (Even more so if we substitute for Smith the name of a well-known conservative.) But, as we will see when we test the argument, the conclusion is not guaranteed by the premises and could be false when the premises were true. Also, when it comes to invalidity, we want not just to be able to recognize it, but to have ways of accounting for that invalidity in an explanation.

A more exacting method of testing is by what are called Venn diagrams, named after the British logician John Venn. Most syllogisms you are likely to encounter can be tested using this method. Venn diagrams should not be confused with your regular method of diagramming the direction of flow of reasoning in an argument. On that scheme all three-statement syllogisms would be depicted:

Venn diagrams, by contrast, use circles to depict the relationships between the classes of things represented by S, P, and M. There are certain procedural matters to remember about this method. We shade those portions of circles that our statements tell us are empty. When we are told that some members of a class either are or are not members of another class, we use X to represent this on the diagram. These points can be illustrated by using two circles to depict each of the four pure forms of categorical statement.

UA

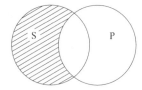

All S are P, so we shade all the circle representing S that is not included in P. This indicates that any portion of S outside of P is empty, which is what the UA statement tells us.

UN

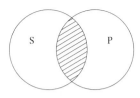

No S are P, so we shade the intersection between the circles representing S and P to show that this area is empty because nothing is both S and P.

PA

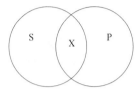

Some S are P, so we put an X in the intersection between the circles representing S and P to show that at least one member of the class of S is also P.

PN

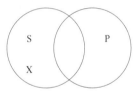

Some S are not P, so we put an X in the area of the circle representing S that does not intersect the circle representing P to show that at least one member of S is not P.

A Venn diagram has three circles representing the three classes involved in the syllogism.

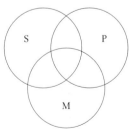

The statements of the syllogism tell us how the classes stand in relation to each other, and as we represent these statements on the three-circle diagram we look to see whether the premises guarantee the conclusion.

In terms of the Venn diagram this means that for a valid syllogism, once the premises have been represented on the diagram, the conclusion should be already there. This is because the conclusion of a valid argument contains no more information than was in the premises. The test for validity using Venn diagrams is expressed as follows: if, after representing the premises, the conclusion is already represented on the diagram, then the argument is valid; if the conclusion is not already represented, the argument is invalid.

We will begin illustrating this by confirming our judgement of an earlier argument:

P1 All astronomers are highly educated people.
P2 All highly educated people are assets to society.

C All astronomers are assets to society.

It has the *legend*:   and the *form*:

S = astronomers   All S are M
P = assets to society   All M are P
M = highly educated people   All S are P

Each is a UA statement, so this is a relatively straightforward example.

P1 is represented

All S are M

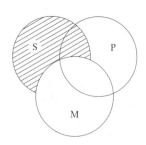

P2 is represented

All M are P

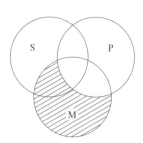

C is represented

All S are P

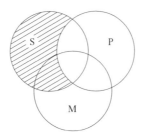

We put P1 and P2 together on a Venn diagram:

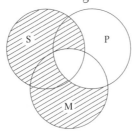

Now, as our test, we look to see whether the conclusion, All S are P, is represented on this diagram. And it is. The area of S outside of P is completely shaded, indicating that it is empty and that indeed All S are P. So this syllogism is a valid argument. It has a valid form or structure, and any syllogism with the same form will also be valid.

Another relatively simple syllogism is the following:

P1 All people who oppose the trade bill are people with conservative values.
P2 Smith has conservative values.

C Smith opposes the trade bill.

This is another argument with all UA statements, but its form is different from the previous syllogism.

Legend: *Form:*
S = Smith   All P are M
P = people who oppose trade bill   All S are M
M = people with conservative values   All S are P

P1

All P are M

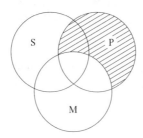

P2

All S are M

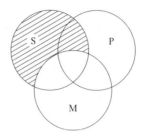

C

All S are P

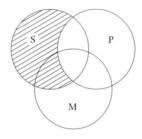

We put P1 and P2 together on a Venn diagram:

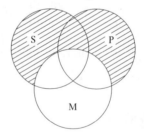

This time we find the conclusion, All S are P, is not already represented on the diagram. The area intersecting S and M, and which is outside of P, should be shaded, but it is not. This means that the conclusion contains more information than was given in the premises and, therefore, the conclusion does not follow necessarily from the premises. The syllogism is *invalid*, and *any* syllogism with the same form will also be invalid.

Having shown simple examples of a valid and an invalid syllogism, we can turn to more complex examples. The following is an advertisement from *Vogue* (Oct. 1992).

No ordinary beauty fluid can deliver the continuous moisture every skin needs to counteract the drying effects of the environment. New Hydra-Renewal Continuous Moisturizing Cream can.

The advertisement makes two claims. The first claim excludes the class of ordinary beauty fluids from the class of beauty fluids that can deliver the continuous moisture every skin needs to counteract the drying effects of the environment. It is a UN statement. The second claim includes New Hydra-Renewal Continuous Moisturizing Cream within that second class. It is a UA statement. As noted earlier, advertisers expect audiences to be able to draw conclusions from statements that are given. In this case, the obvious hidden conclusion is a UN statement that excludes New Hydra-Renewal Continuous Moisturizing Cream from the class of ordinary beauty fluids.

Our procedure requires us to begin with the conclusion, and in this case the conclusion was hidden. But there can be no doubt that the conclusion uncovered here was intended (it is a belief held by the writers). Testing this syllogism will tell us whether the writers have produced their copy wisely.

Legend:	*Form:*
S = New Hydra-Renewal Continuous Moisturizing Cream	No P are M
P = ordinary beauty fluids	All S are M
M = beauty fluids that can deliver the continuous moisture every skin needs to counteract the drying effects of the environment	No S are P

P1

No P are M

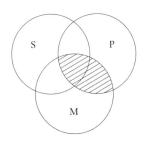

P2

All S are M

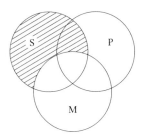

C

No S are P

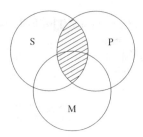

We put P1 and P2 together in a Venn diagram.

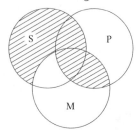

If the syllogism is valid, the conclusion ('No S are P') will already be on the diagram. And it is; the advertisers have exploited their audience's ability to make deductive inferences. The entire area in which S and P intersect is shaded, showing it to be an empty class. The argument is valid. (But whether or not this is a good product depends on the acceptability of the premises.)

The next example is taken from a report in *The Globe and Mail* (17 Mar. 1987, p. A1). The report involved the rejection of public service AIDS announcements by a committee that screens commercials for private broadcasters in Canada. The committee's reasoning included the following:

Most (3 out of 4) public service AIDS announcements urging the use of condoms condone casual sex. Therefore, most (3 out of 4) public service AIDS announcements urging the use of condoms are not acceptable for broadcast.

Since these statements refer to 'most' and not to 'all', we can identify them as particular statements. The first statement (a premise) includes some public service AIDS announcements within the class of announcements that condone casual sex. It is a PA statement. The conclusion, identified by the indicator 'therefore', excludes those announcements from the class of announcements suitable for broadcasting. It is a PN statement. With this example we will proceed first to assign S, P, and M (we have enough information to do so), and then decide on how to express the hidden premise.

P Some public service AIDS announcements urging the use of condoms are announcements condoning casual sex.

C Some public service announcements urging the use of condoms are not announcements acceptable for broadcast.

Legend:

S = public service AIDS announcements urging the use of condoms

P = announcements acceptable for broadcast

M = announcements condoning casual sex

Form:

Some S are M

Some S are not P

The hidden premise must involve a relationship between M and P. What does someone using the expressed reasoning in this argument believe about M and P? It seems likely that they believe the two classes to be mutually exclusive of each other. No announcements acceptable for broadcast are announcements condoning casual sex, and vice versa. Either way, it is a UN statement.

No M are P   or   No P are M

(Does it make a difference which way we write this?)

P1

No M are P

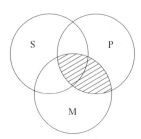

P2

Some S are M

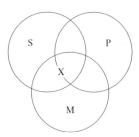

C

Some S are not P

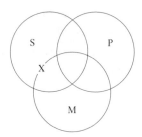

We put P1 and P2 together in a Venn diagram. Notice that when we have a universal and a particular statement, the universal is always depicted first.

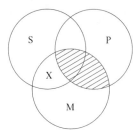

Is there an X anywhere in S outside of P, as the conclusion requires? Yes, there is. The argument is valid.

One further example should suffice in illustrating the complexities of the Venn diagram method of testing.

> Some medical professionals are not supporters of euthanasia and some supporters of euthanasia are liberals. From this it follows that it is false to say that all medical professionals are liberals.

'It follows that . . .' introduces the conclusion from which we may identify S and P, and M is the class common to the two premises. We are told in the conclusion that a UA statement ('All medical professionals are liberals') is false. If this is the case, its contradictory statement must be true, and the contradictory of a UA statement is a PN statement. Now our syllogism is revealed as comprising three particular statements and we can proceed to the legend and to setting out its form.

P1 Some medical professionals are not supporters of euthanasia.
P2 Some supporters of euthanasia are liberals.

C Some medical professionals are not liberals.

Legend:
S = medical professionals
P = liberals

M = supporters of euthanasia

Form:
Some S are not M
Some M are P
_____
Some S are not P

P1

Some S are not M

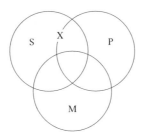

P2

Some M are P

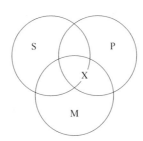

C

Some S are not P

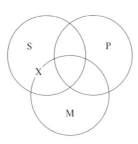

We put P1 and P2 together in a Venn diagram:

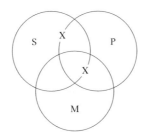

Since there are no universal premises, there are no empty (shaded) areas. So we do not know whether the X of P1 should go in the areas of S outside or inside of P. Consequently, we put it on the line. Likewise with P2, we do not know whether the M that is P is also S, so we put it on the line. Now, for the argument to be valid there should be an X in the area of S which is outside of P. But we cannot be sure of this; the X is on the line. Thus, this syllogism is invalid because the premises do not guarantee the conclusion.

This example shows one of the drawbacks of the Venn diagram method. It has worked well with our other examples but the possibility of error arises when we are unsure where to place the X for particular statements. What we have provided in this chapter is sufficient to introduce the syllogism and equip you for most everyday arguments that involve relationships between classes of thing.

MAJOR EXERCISE 6M

1. For each of the following syllogisms: identify S, P, and M in a legend; provide its form; and determine its validity using the Venn diagram method. Example:

You will agree that all husbands are married and that no wives are husbands. Surely it follows that no wives are married.

Legend:
  S = wives
  P = married people
  M = husbands

Form:
All husbands are married people
No wives are husbands
No wives are married people

P1

All husbands are married people

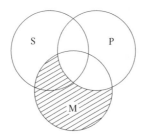

P2

No wives are husbands

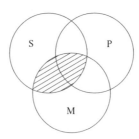

C

No wives are married
people

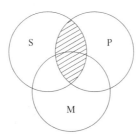

We put P1 and P2 together in a Venn diagram:

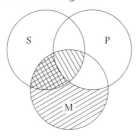

The intersection between S and P is not completely shaded. Therefore, the conclusion is not contained in the premises and this argument is *invalid*.

*a) Some cats aren't pests but all cats are pets, so no pets are pests.

*b) All buildings over 50 feet tall are in violation of the new city by-law and the bank building is over 50 feet tall. Therefore, it is in violation of the by-law.

c) No one who fails this course can major in Psychology and all Psychology majors are assured a good career, so no one who fails this course is assured a good career.

d) Only courses that involve disciplined thought provide good training for law. And since most philosophy courses involve disciplined thought, they must provide a good training for law.

e) Some habits are not harmful and some vices are not habits, so some vices are not harmful.

f) From measuring the footprints we are convinced that the murderer is a man who wears size 9 shoes. That description fits Jim, so he must be the murderer.

g) It is simply not true, as many people suppose, that all professors of political science are socialists. I am convinced of this because, first, it is false to say that no political science professors are money-grubbers and, second, it is certainly true that no socialists are money-grubbers.

h) No courteous people are rumour mongers and all discourteous people lack friends. Clearly it must be the case that no rumour mongers have friends.

*i) To make love is to engage in battle! This must be true because it takes two to stage a fight and it also takes two to make love.

j) Only if they are quick and capable readers can students easily master the books required for the English courses here. But many students are poor readers. Therefore, they will have problems. (T. Govier, *A Practical Study of Argument* [Belmont, Calif.: Wadsworth, 1992])

k) Your ideas are immaterial. But whatever is immaterial does not matter. Therefore, your ideas do not matter.

2. Wherever possible, supply the hidden component that would make the following syllogisms valid and exhibit validity (or invalidity) by the Venn diagram method. Example: Capital punishment is wrong because it is itself a crime.

All acts of capital punishment are crimes.
_____
All acts of capital punishment are wrongful acts.

Legend: *Form:*
S = acts of capital punishment   [   ]
P = wrongful acts   All S are M
                                                    _____
M = crimes   All S are P

P

All S are M

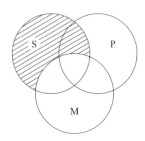

C

All S are P

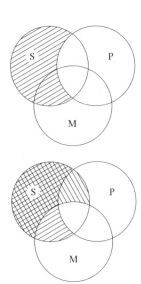

For the conclusion to be contained in the diagram (indicating validity), all of S outside of P must be shaded. The hidden premise must express a relationship between M and P, and the only possible statement that would fit these two requirements is: All M are P.

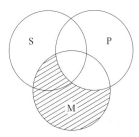

*a) No person who values integrity will go into politics because the realities of political life force people to compromise their principles.

b) Only men are serial killers, and Carmelia Louise is certainly no man.

c) Most students can afford to pay more for tuition because most students make between $4,000 and $6,000 each summer. (*The Globe and Mail*, 12 May 1988.)

d) It's not the case that all media stories are reliable because many media reports from foreign news agencies are unreliable.

e) Some of the things parapsychologists tell us about are outlandish because they utterly contradict the laws of nature.

3. In each case, construct a valid syllogism by supplying premises for the following conclusions. Example: All Picasso paintings are costly.

S = Picasso paintings	All M are P
P = costly things	All S are M
M = items prized by the world's leading art collectors	All S are P

*a) This syllogism is valid.

b) Most trade books are not worth the paper they are printed on.

*c) No one does wrong voluntarily.

d) Only cool-headed people will prosper.

e) Some heavy smokers die of causes other than lung cancer.

f) Human colonization of the outer planets is currently beyond our capabilities.

g) All non-union members are non-employees.

h) You will not get a better deal on a new car than at Dave's Motors.

TESTING

SYLLOGISTIC

ARGUMENTS

Chapter 6 introduced the categorical syllogism and explained how to construct such arguments and test their validity by means of Venn diagrams. This chapter takes that discussion one step further by introducing a method for testing syllogisms using rules. It discusses:

- ◆ schematization;
- ◆ distribution;
- ◆ rules of validity and their application; and
- ◆ some additional procedural points.

1. SCHEMATIZATION

When we became acquainted with the four basic forms of categorical statements, we learned them as UA, UN, PA, and PN. Now we will adopt their traditional labels as, respectively, A, E, I, and O statements (from the Latin for the verbs to 'affirm' and to 'negate': AffImo and nEgO). This change will help us learn the features of the remaining parts of this chapter.

A represents the universal affirmative statement 'All S are P.'
E represents the universal negative statement 'No S are P.'
I represents the particular affirmative statement 'Some S are P.'
O represents the particular negative statement 'Some S are not P.'

From this point on we will schematize these statements as:

S A P	All S are P.
S E P	No S are P.
S I P	Some S are P.
S O P	Some S are not P.

2. DISTRIBUTION

We must add a further component to this schematization. We need some way of indicating whether the subject and predicate *terms* in each case (rather than the statements) give us information about the entire class of things to which they refer or whether they give us information about only a portion of the classes they name. This information is indispensable to applying the rules of validity. If information is given about an entire membership of a class named by a term, the term is said to be *distributed*. If information is given about only a portion of the membership of the class named by the term, the term is said to be *undistributed*.

Given these definitions, it is apparent that the subject term of the A and E statements is 'distributed', since we are told something about *all* S and *no* S. Likewise, the subject term of the I and O statements is 'undistributed', since we are told something about only *some* of the membership in each case. The predicate term of E and O statements must be distributed since these statements exclude some or all the membership of the subject class from the *entire* membership of the predicate class. In the A and I statements, the predicate term is undistributed because such statements do not give us any information about the entire predicate class but only about a portion of the predicate class with which the subject terms of those statements are coincident. All this is conveyed on the following chart:

Statement	Subject term	Predicate term
A	distributed	undistributed
E	distributed	distributed
I	undistributed	undistributed
O	undistributed	distributed

This chart also gives further information as to why we were only able to apply straightforward conversion to the E (UN) and I (PA) statements in Chapter 6. Only with these two statements is the distribution or non-distribution of the subject and predicate classes balanced, thus allowing us to switch them.

In our schematization, we will use a lower-case 'd' following the class symbol to indicate distribution and 'u' to indicate non-distribution. This enables us to complete the schematization of the four types of categorical statement as follows:

A	Sd A Pu	All S are P
E	Sd E Pd	No S are P
I	Su I Pu	Some S are P
O	Su O Pd	Some S are not P

Note that whatever S and P (or M) represent, the A, E, I, and O statements will *always* be schematized with the distribution/non-distribution indicators as shown here. You will not have to figure out the distribution of terms in each syllogism with which you work, but need simply remember the pattern of distribution/non-distribution associated with each type of statement.

3. RULES OF VALIDITY

Particularly when dealing with complex syllogisms, using rules to determine validity is likely to be more reliable for the student than analysing language or even the Venn diagram method. There are three rules of interest to us.

Rule 1. The middle term, M, must be distributed at least once.
M is the class that is related to each of S and P in the premises, and it is on the basis of these relationships that a relationship between S and P is said to be deduced in the conclusion. If the class represented by M in the premises is undistributed in both instances, then each premise could be giving information about a different portion of the M class. In that case, there would be no basis for expressing a relationship between S and P. It is not a violation of Rule 1 if M is distributed in both premises, but it is a minimum requirement that it be distributed at least once.

If the M term is undistributed in both of its occurrences, the syllogism is invalid. The fallacy associated with this type of invalidity is called 'the fallacy of the undistributed middle'.

Rule 2. Any term distributed in the conclusion must be distributed in the premise in which it occurs.
The point of this rule is to ensure that the conclusion does not contain any more information than is given in the premises. A term undistributed in a premise gives information about only a portion of the membership of the class named by that term. If that term is distributed in the conclusion, the conclusion would be saying something about the entire membership of that class. Clearly the conclusion may not refer to *all* members of a class if the premises refer only to *some* of them. Since only S and P appear in the conclusion, it is to these two terms that this rule applies.

If a term is distributed in the conclusion but is undistributed in the premise in which it appears, the syllogism is invalid. In this case, the argument would be guilty of what is called 'the fallacy of illicit process'.

Rule 3. There can be only as many negative premises as there are negative conclusions, and if there is a negative conclusion, there must be one negative premise.

This rule governs the presence of negative statements (E or O) and needs to be invoked only in the case of syllogisms containing them. There cannot be two negative premises, nor can there be a negative conclusion drawn from two affirmative premises. There can only be one negative premise, in which case there must be a negative conclusion, and vice versa.

Since negative statements *exclude* classes from others, if the S and P classes are both excluded from M, then there would be no basis on which to conclude anything about the relationship *between* S and P. Likewise, if both premises are affirmative and include S and P in a portion of the M class, then that is no basis for excluding S and P from each other in the conclusion. If, however, one premise expresses a relationship of inclusion and the other a relationship of exclusion, then, given that the other rules are satisfied, the conclusion can legitimately express a relationship of exclusion.

The fallacy involved depends on the specific manner in which the syllogism violates Rule 3: two negative premises; a negative premise with an affirmative conclusion; affirmative premises with a negative conclusion.

A valid syllogism must satisfy all three rules. If any one rule is violated, the syllogism is invalid.

4. APPLYING THE RULES

Let us test two syllogisms we know to be invalid by means of the rule method.

(i)

All people who oppose the trade bill are people with conservative values.
Smith is a person with conservative values.

Smith opposes the trade bill.

Legend:	Form:
S = Smith	Pd A Mu
P = people who oppose the trade bill	Sd A Mu
M = people with conservative values	Sd A Pu

Note that because they are all A statements, the distribution is 'd u' in each case.

Test:
Rule 1: *Violated:* The middle term is undistributed in both premises.
Rule 2: *Okay:* Only S is distributed in the conclusion and it is also distrib-
uted in the premise. [It is not a problem for P to be distributed in the
premise but undistributed in the conclusion.]
Rule 3: *Not applicable:* There are no negative statements.
This syllogism is *invalid* because it violates rule 1, thereby committing the fal-
lacy of the undistributed middle.

(ii)
Some medical professionals are not supporters of euthanasia.
Some supporters of euthanasia are liberals.

Some medical professionals are not liberals.

Legend:	*Form:*
S = medical professionals	Su O Md
P = liberals	Mu I Pu
M = supporters of euthanasia	Su O Pd

Test:
Rule 1: *Okay:* The middle term is distributed once in the premises.
Rule 2: *Violated:* P is distributed in the conclusion, but it is undistributed in
the premise.
Rule 3: *Okay:* There is only one negative premise and there is a negative
conclusion.
This syllogism is *invalid* because it violates rule 2, thereby committing the fal-
lacy of illicit process.

A Further Consideration
For many logicians, a syllogism cannot be valid if it has two universal premises
(A or E) and a particular conclusion (I or O). Such a concern follows from
what is called a *hypothetical* interpretation of universal statements. It may
have occurred to you that a statement like 'All shoplifters will be prosecuted'
does not assume that either class, 'shoplifters' or 'those who will be prosecuted', has any members. In fact, the statement's intent is to keep both classes
empty of members. So we make sense of the statement with a hypothetical
reading, i.e., '*If* there is a shoplifter, that person will be prosecuted' (we
allowed for such statements in our list of 'Common Variations' in Chapter 6).
The hypothetical reading of universal statements does not assume that either
class has members. But particular statements, since they refer to *some*, are
assumed to have members. Thus a syllogism like the following is invalid
under the hypothetical reading of universal statements, because the premises

could refer to classes without members but the particular conclusion asserts that there are members of the classes:

> Not all major diseases are curable because AIDS is a major disease and it is incurable.

After providing the contradictory of the conclusion ('Not all major diseases are curable') and obverting the premise with the complement of the 'P' term ('AIDS is incurable') we derive:

> All cases of AIDS (M) are cases of major diseases (S)
> No cases of AIDS (M) are curable diseases (P)
> _____
> Some major diseases (S) are not curable diseases (P)

Throughout our discussion of categorical syllogisms, we have been assuming not a hypothetical reading of universal statements but an *existential* interpretation. That is, we have been assuming that the statements have been expressing assertions about classes with members, about things that are real and exist. This is because most instances of syllogisms drawn from ordinary circumstances (like the AIDS example above) favour the existential interpretation. Unless you know that the universal premises of a syllogism refer, or are intended to refer, to classes that have no members, we suggest you adopt the existential interpretation of those statements. But where the hypothetical interpretation is clearly warranted, you should invoke a fourth rule:

Rule 4: A syllogism with two universal premises that do not assume the classes have members cannot have a particular conclusion.

5. PROCEDURAL POINTS

We will close this chapter with some procedural points that will assist you as you test syllogisms using the rule method.

(i) Watch for classes and their complements in arguments, for example, 'suitable things' and 'unsuitable things'. Where these appear together in an argument, try using immediate inferences to reduce the number of terms to three and explain the process you are employing.

(ii) When assigning symbols in the legend, always identify S, P, and M as positive classes and then, if the complements are present, assign them as non-S, non-P, and non-M. This will avoid the confusion of having, for example, S represent immortal beings and non-S represent mortal beings.

(iii) If a syllogism involves a hidden component, then, wherever possible, use the rules to supply whatever unstated component yields a valid argument.

This is a way to use the principle of charity to give the benefit of doubt to the arguer. But you will find that some syllogisms cannot be made valid, no matter what hidden component is suggested. Also, remember that, if proving validity in this way seems overly generous, doing so does not guarantee the argument will be a good one. We still must be convinced that the premises are acceptable.

One last example will illustrate these three procedural points.

No problems are welcome because all undesirable things are unwelcome.

The premise indicator 'because' tells us we have a premise and a conclusion:

P All undesirable things are unwelcome.
_____
C No problems are welcome.

We have a hidden premise to supply. We also have at least four classes of things: 'problems', 'welcome things', 'undesirable things', and 'unwelcome things'. But 'welcome things' and 'unwelcome things' we can take as complementary classes and look to reduce one to the other by means of immediate inferences.

We have the conclusion, so S and P are identified for us. The remaining class is 'undesirable things', but since this is a negative class, we will assign M to 'desirable things'.

Legend: *Form:*
   S = problems
   P = welcome things   All non-M are non-P
                                       _____
non-P = unwelcome things   No S are P
   M = desirable things
non-M = undesirable things

Our task is now to eliminate non-M and non-P. We can do this by using contraposition (or obversion, conversion, and obversion).

non-Md A non-Pu — contrapositive — Pd A Mu

If all undesirable things are unwelcome, then all welcome things are desirable. This gives us:

Pd A Mu
[   ]
_____
Sd E Pd

Now we must ask what hidden premise would be required for this argument to be valid. To decide this, we proceed through each rule, ensuring that it is not violated. The hidden premise must involve S and M. In order for rule 1 to be satisfied, M must be distributed in the hidden premise, since it is not distributed in the expressed premise. (This means the hidden premise cannot be an I statement.) For rule 2 to be satisfied, S must be distributed because S is distributed in the conclusion. The only statement that would allow both M and S to be distributed is an E statement. And we further see that in order for rule 3 to be satisfied, the hidden premise would have to be either an E or an O statement. Hence, the hidden premise must be an E statement: either 'No problems are desirable things' or 'No desirable things are problems.' And with this supplied the argument is valid.

Major Exercise 7M

Extract at least one syllogism from each of the following passages and test it for validity. Wherever necessary, supply a hidden component. Example:

Since then to fight against neighbours is an evil, and to fight against the Thebans is to fight against neighbours, it is clear that to fight against the Thebans is an evil. (Aristotle, *Prior Analytics*)
All acts of fighting against neighbours are evil acts.
All acts of fighting against the Thebans are acts of fighting against neighbours.

All acts of fighting against the Thebans are evil acts.

Legend:	*Form:*
S = acts of fighting against the Thebans	Md A Pu
P = evil acts	Sd A Mu
M = acts of fighting against neighbours	Sd A Pu

Test:
Rule 1:   *Okay:* The middle term is distributed in the first premise.
Rule 2:   *Okay:* Only S is distributed in the conclusion and it is also distributed in the premise.
Rule 3:   *Not applicable:* There are no negative statements.
This syllogism satisfies all the rules and so is valid.
  *a) It's not the case that all valid syllogisms have acceptable premises, nor is it the case that any valid syllogism has a false conclusion. So, no syllogisms with acceptable premises have false conclusions.
   b) Only foreign-owned magazines that have a substantially different Canadian edition are acceptable in Canada under current federal guidelines. Thus, *Sports Illustrated* is unacceptable.

c) Regan sets out Frey's argument schematically as follows: 1. Only those individuals who can have beliefs can have desires. 2. Animals cannot have beliefs. 3. Therefore, animals cannot have desires. (Michael P.T. Leahy, *Against Liberation: Putting Animals in Perspective* [New York: Routledge, rev. 1994])

d) That man must be extremely ignorant: he answers every question that is put to him. (Voltaire, *Dictionnaire Philosophique*)

e) Only the finest rums come from Puerto Rico. Aging has given our rums a smoothness, whether straight or mixed, that has made them preferred over all others. And only in Puerto Rico, with its heritage of fine rums, is aging guaranteed by law. (Ad for Puerto Rico rums, *Atlantic Monthly*, Nov. 1993)

*f) No beast so foul but knows some pity;
But I know none, and
Therefore am no beast. (Shakespeare, *Richard III*)

g) Black's paints have been around since 1880, and with that kind of experience you know you're getting the best that money can buy. (Radio ad)

h) [Background: On 23 September 1991, then US President George Bush addressed the United Nations on the question of the UN resolution equating Zionism with racism. In concluding that Zionism was not racism, he argued for the historical difference between them.]

Zionism . . . is the idea that led to the creation of a home for the Jewish people. . . . And to equate Zionism with the intolerable sin of racism is to twist history and forget the terrible plight of Jews in World War II and indeed throughout history.

i) A major constitutional challenge, running right up to the Supreme Court, can consume hundreds of thousands of dollars. Only those who can pay exorbitant lawyers' fees will pursue such a challenge; the logical inference is that the Charter will, in the long term, favour the rich. (R. Fulford, in *Saturday Night*, Dec. 1986)

*j) It is quite incorrect to say 'Violence cannot ever be condoned.' Violence in defence of self or family is usually acceptable. If a sniper is shooting a gun in a crowd of people then it is the duty of the police to shoot back with deadly accuracy to stop the shooting. Going to war to protect your country has an honourable tradition. In retrospect, it is obvious that the killing of Adolf Hitler and his cronies would have prevented World War II and the Holocaust, and would therefore have been quite acceptable. (Letter to the *Peterborough Examiner*, 24 Nov. 1994)

k) Murder is the unlawful killing of a human being. The murderer has preferred no lawful charge against his victim; given him no right to counsel, no right to cross-examine or make full answer and defence; denied him the right to be tried before an independent, impartial public tribunal; denied him any appeal. The murderer is prosecutor, judge and jury, all without lawful authority. Only such killing can be called murder.

In absolute contrast, society provides an accused murderer with all the rights and safeguards he has denied his victim. If then, after proof of guilt beyond a reasonable doubt, society sentences him to death, that is not murder; it is as far from unlawful killing as it is possible to get. To call this murder is to speak nonsense. (Judge Bewdley, in *The Globe and Mail*, 19 Mar. 1987)

*l) Capital punishment is uncivilized, barbaric, and merely revenge.

This is the capital-punishment-is-murder argument all over again.

What the abolitionists assert here is: 'Uncivilized barbarians kill; all killing is uncivilized and barbaric; therefore, judicially ordered executions are uncivilized and barbaric.' (Ibid.)

m) An entity with no consciousness is not a person. Because consciousness seems to imply a brain, one might say 'no brain, no person'. One can say that a person is really dead when the brain stem no longer functions. Or that something without a brain cannot be a person. But having a brain isn't the vital point. The important question is whether something has rational agency. Taking a person to be a rational sentient agent, nothing that is not a rational sentient agent can be a person. Little embryos are not rational sentient agents so they cannot be classified as persons. (Adapted from Keith Ward, 'An Irresolvable Dispute' in A. Dyson and J. Harris, eds, *Experiments on Embryos* [London: Routledge, 1990].

SOME IFS,

ANDS, AND

BUTS

Valid arguments can have a variety of forms. 'Propositional' arguments depend on relationships between propositions that are expressed by words like 'if, then', 'and', 'or', and 'not'. In this chapter we:

♦ introduce propositional arguments;
♦ discuss different kinds of propositions;
♦ learn how to represent the logical structure of a proposition;
♦ elaborate ways of judging whether propositional arguments are valid; and
♦ provide a variety of examples of simple propositional arguments.

We use categorical reasoning to assess the validity of arguments that deal with relationships between different classes. We need different techniques for assessing other kinds of valid arguments. In the present chapter we introduce techniques that allow us to construct and analyse arguments that depend on logical relations between propositions. To do so, we must first be clear about the nature of simple and complex propositions.

1. SIMPLE AND COMPLEX PROPOSITIONS

We have already introduced diagramming techniques that allow us to diagram ordinary arguments and the more narrowly defined arguments of the categorical syllogism. With propositional arguments we turn to another way of representing arguments and their components.

The basic building blocks of propositional arguments are 'simple' propositions, which affirm that some state of affairs is the case. Each of the following is a simple proposition:

Nuclear war is the most disastrous thing that could happen to the Earth.
The weather forecast predicts rain for the next 24 hours.
The mail has been delivered.
I'm going to report you to the superintendent.
Zeus and Hera head the Olympian family of gods.
Kellogg's is committed to providing foods of outstanding quality.
You are reading my e-mail.

Simple propositions express a single thought that may be true or false. 'Complex' propositions are formed by combining or adapting them. This is done by employing 'connector words' that turn simple propositions into more complex statements. Using two of the simple propositions we have already listed, we can construct the complex proposition, '*If* you are reading my e-mail, *then* I'm going to report you to the superintendent', by conjoining them with the connector words 'If . . . then'.

We can clarify the logical structure of complex propositions by letting lower-case letters stand for simple propositions that are their basic constituents. As a memory aid, it is a good idea to pick a letter you can associate with a key word or particular proposition, as in the following examples:

m = The *m*ail has been delivered.
c = You will enjoy your *c*ourse in critical thinking.
n = *N*uclear war is a terrifying possibility.
e = You are reading my *e*-mail.
r = I'm going to *r*eport you to the superintendent.

From this legend, we use the letters m, c, n, e, and r to make clearer the basic structure of complex propositions that contain these simple propositions. We can, for example, represent the complex proposition, 'If you are reading my e-mail, then I'm going to report you to the superintendent', as the statement, 'If e, then r.'

When we represent complex propositions in terms of their simple components, we need to be able to recognize the following four kinds of complex propositions and the connector words we use to form them.

Negations
A negation denies another statement. Any statement, simple or complex, can be negated by saying that 'It is not the case that . . .'. In propositional reasoning, we use the symbol '-' to negate propositions, much as we used it to represent negative classes in syllogistic reasoning. For any proposition x, -(x) is the

negation 'x is not the case' or, more simply, 'not x'. If we can drop the brackets without confusion, then we will represent the negation -(x) as -x.

If we let:

c = I am a crook.

then -c represents President Richard Nixon's famous statement, 'I am not a crook.' Negations are expressed in a variety of ways in ordinary discourse. The Richard Nixon negation could, for example, be expressed as:

It's not true that I'm a crook.
Those who say I'm a crook are mistaken.
It's false that I'm a crook.
I'm a crook: Not!

In dealing with propositional arguments we treat all these propositions as versions of the proposition -c.

A special case of negation arises when we negate another negation. Because affirming something is equivalent to denying that it is not the case, the negation of a negation is an affirmation. Looked at from this point of view, the negation of Nixon's claim that he is not a crook is the claim that he *is* a crook. We will therefore represent the latter negation (the proposition --c) as the proposition c. More generally, we will represent the negation of any negation as an affirmation. When we recognize this equivalence, and when we recognize different ways of expressing a negation, we invoke the principles of identity discussed in Chapter 5.

Conjunctions

Conjunctions have the form 'x and y'. We will use the symbol '&' as a symbol for the word 'and', and so represent a conjunction as a statement of the form 'x & y'. Each component in a conjunction is called a 'conjunct'. The conjunction states that all of its conjuncts are true. In propositional logic, we always use the connector '&' to state conjunctions. In dealing with ordinary language propositions, we can more generally treat as a conjunction any proposition claiming that two or more propositions are true. The following five sentences can all be counted as ways of expressing the same conjunction:

Lewis Carroll wrote *Alice in Wonderland* and he wrote *Symbolic Logic*.
Lewis Carroll is the author of *Alice in Wonderland* as well as *Symbolic Logic*.
Alice in Wonderland and *Symbolic Logic* were written by the same author: Lewis Carroll.

Like *Alice in Wonderland*, *Symbolic Logic* was written by Lewis Carroll.
I assure you that Lewis Carroll wrote both *Alice in Wonderland* and *Symbolic Logic*.

All five of these conjunctions claim that the two propositions 'Lewis Carroll wrote *Alice in Wonderland*' and 'Lewis Carroll wrote *Symbolic Logic*' are true. We can, therefore, represent all of them as the proposition a & s, where:

> a = Lewis Carroll wrote *Alice in Wonderland*.
> s = Lewis Carroll wrote *Symbolic Logic*.

Like many, perhaps most, examples of conjunction, this example is composed of two simple propositions. In other cases, the conjuncts included in a conjunction may be complex propositions. We can easily construct examples by imagining that we are discussing the contents of Lewis Carroll's *Alice in Wonderland*, and by letting:

> f = Alice fell down the rabbit hole.
> c = Alice met the Cheshire cat.
> h = Alice met the Queen of Hearts.
> g = Alice had a good time.

If we use this translation scheme, then c & -g represents the conjunction 'Alice met the Cheshire cat, but she didn't have a good time', -(f & c) & g represents the conjunction 'It's not true that Alice fell down the rabbit hole and met the Cheshire cat, but Alice had a good time', and f & (c or h) represents the conjunction 'Alice fell down the rabbit hole and met the Cheshire cat or the Queen of Hearts.' In these and similar cases a conjunction contains a conjunct that is a complex proposition.

Disjunctions

A disjunction is a complex proposition that claims that one of two or more component claims is true. In propositional reasoning, disjunctions have the form: 'x or y'. We call the component propositions x and y 'disjuncts'. In most cases, a disjunction has two disjuncts, but it is easy to think of exceptions. The disjunction, 'He was going to get the liquor, the food, or the entertainment', can, for example, be represented as 'l or f or e' where:

> l = He was going to get the liquor.
> f = He was going to get the food.
> e = He was going to get the entertainment.

Ordinarily, a disjunction is true if one of its disjuncts is true. If we let:

a = Glenda's going to Alberta.
m = Glenda's going to Montana.

then the disjunction 'a or m' is, for example, true if Glenda is going to Alberta, Montana, or both Alberta and Montana (the latter may be the case if she is visiting the international park that joins them).

In ordinary language, we sometimes emphasize the possibility that 'x or y' may be true because x and y are true by employing the connector words 'and/or' or 'either . . . or . . . or both'. In propositional logic, we will assume that 'w or y' asserts 'w or y or both'. This is a useful assumption because propositional logic arguments are normally characterized by such disjunctions. In the information box below, we explain how you can represent another kind of disjunction (what logicians call an 'exclusive' disjunction) with propositional logic symbols.

Box 8.1 Exclusive Disjunctions

We call ordinary statements of the form x or y 'inclusive disjunctions' because they include within themselves the possibility that all of their disjuncts are true. Logicians call disjunctions that exclude this particular possibility 'exclusive' disjunctions. We sometimes indicate the latter with the connector words 'either . . . or . . . *but not both*'. The qualifier in this phrase tells us that the disjunction in question has the form (x or y) & -(x & y). This is the standard form of an exclusive disjunction, though it is, strictly speaking, a conjunction that conjoins the disjunction x or y and the negation -(x & y).

Sometimes the exclusive nature of a disjunction must be made explicit if we are to understand instances of ordinary reasoning. Consider how we might reason in a restaurant where the menu says that 'tea or coffee' comes with the dinner special. Clearly, this means that we can have one or the other but not both: the disjunction is exclusive. If we fail to recognize that this is so, we will not be able to demonstrate the validity of the reasoning: 'The menu says you can have coffee or tea and you've had coffee so you can't have tea.' When we deal with reasoning of this sort we will do so by recognizing the disjunction in question as (t or c) & -(t & c).

Conditionals

A conditional is a complex proposition that has the form 'If x, then y.' We call x the 'antecedent' of the conditional and y its 'consequent'. We will represent a conditional as a statement of the form x → y (you can read this statement as ' If x, then y' or as 'x arrow y'). As this visually suggests, a conditional states what follows if a certain condition (the antecedent) is or was or might be the case.

A good example of a conditional is the following remark by the baseball player Jeff Blauser: 'If somebody wants to hit me (with a pitch), he's doing me a favour.' In propositional logic, this statement can be represented as h → f where:

h = Somebody wants to hit me with a pitch.
f = He's doing me a favour.

We can illustrate the different ways in which conditionals can be expressed in ordinary language by noting the following ways of expressing Blauser's thought:

A pitcher is doing me a favour if he wants to hit me with a pitch.
The pitcher is doing me a favour when he tries to hit me with a pitch.
Somebody who tries to hit me with a pitch is doing me a favour.
Trying to hit me with a pitch is doing me a favour.

Adopting the translation scheme already outlined, all of these statements can be represented as the proposition h → f. Recognizing such statements as conditionals, we capture the structure of an argument that might otherwise elude us.

Like conjunctions and disjunctions, conditionals may have components that are complex statements, and may be included in other complex propositions. The statement, 'Socrates was a great philosopher and it would be interesting to see his reaction to modern society and to modern philosophy if we could bring him back to life', illustrates both of these phenomena. If we let:

s = Socrates was a great philosopher.
m = It would be interesting to see his reaction to modern society.
p = It would be interesting to see his reaction to modern philosophy.
l = We could bring him back to life.

then we can represent this proposition as:

s & (l → (m & p))

Note that the brackets we use in this case are needed to ensure that the meaning of this propositional logic formula is clear. We shall have more to say about this aspect of propositional logic statements shortly, but first we provide some initial exercises to further acquaint you with the basic forms of propositional logic statements.

Box 8.2 *Simple and Complex Propositions*
The following are the basic forms of propositional logic statements:
1. *Simple statements* express a single true or false thought. In propositional logic we represent them as lower-case letters of the alphabet.
2. *Negations* are statements that deny some other statement. They are represented as statements of the form -x, where x is the statement negated.
3. *Conjunctions* are statements that claim that two or more other statements are true. We will represent them as statements of the form x & y (x and y are called 'conjuncts').
4. *Disjunctions* are statements that claim that one or more of a number of disjuncts are true. They are represented as statements of the form x or y.
5. *Conditionals* are statements that claim that some statement is true if some other statement is true. We represent them as statements of the form x → y (x is called the antecedent of the conditional and y is called the consequent).

EXERCISE 8A

1. Using the legend provided, translate the following propositional logic sentences into English.
   p = Pluto is the planet we should explore.
   h = There are humanoids on Venus.
   e = The humanoids eat human beings.
   s = Space is the final frontier.
   v = Venus is the planet we should explore.
   *a) p
   b) -h
   c) s & v
   *d) p or v
   e) h → v
   f) (s & h) → v
   *g) (s & h & e) → -v
   h) s & -p
   i) (s → v) & (v → s)
   j) (v or p) → s
   k) p → -v
   *l) s; s → v; therefore v
2. Using the letters indicated to represent simple propositions, represent the following as propositional logic statements. In dealing with disjunctions, be sure to consider whether they are exclusive or inclusive.
   a) You will become a famous writer, or at least a published author. (f, p)
   *b) If we let c = I am a crook, then -c represents Richard Nixon's famous statement 'I am not a crook.' (l, r)

*c) You're wrong when you say that Lee Mun Wah didn't produce the film *The Color of Fear*. (c)

d) [From a box of Kellogg's Frosted Flakes] If it doesn't say KELLOGG'S on the box, it's not KELLOGG'S in the box. (o, i)

e) [From the same box] If this product in any way falls below the high standards you've come to expect from Kellogg's, please send your comments and both top flaps to: Consumer Affairs, KELLOGG INC. (f, s)

*f) We define a 'valid argument' as an argument in which the conclusion follows necessarily from the premises. (v, n)

g) An argument is *in*valid if it is possible for the premises to be true and the conclusion false. (i, p)

*h) [From a box of Shredded Wheat] You should try Shredded Wheat with cold milk or with hot milk. (c, h)

i) [From *The Economist*, Aug. 1995] If they do not set these [sugar and peanut] programmes on a path to oblivion, any idea that these Republicans deserve the adjective 'free market' can be dispensed with, once and for all. (s, p, f)

j) [From an ad in *Mother Jones*, July-Aug. 1995] If you want to burn up to 79% more calories, WalkFit is your answer. (b, w)

*k) [Tucker Carlson of the Heritage Foundation, in a letter to *Mother Jones*, July-Aug. 1995] Safe neighbourhoods are organized. (s, o)

l) [Judith Wallerstein in *Mother Jones*, July-Aug. 1995] It isn't true that divorce is different for a poor child than it is for a rich child in its emotional content. . . . (d)

2. TRANSLATION IN MORE DETAIL

The process of representing ordinary statements as propositional logic forms is often called 'translation' because it translates ordinary sentences into the language of propositional logic. Though the translations that result are often approximations, they usually capture the sense of the original statements well enough to allow us to understand and assess their role in arguments. We have already introduced the basic principles of translation, but some aspects of the process bear repeating and others remain to be introduced. To underscore the key aspects of translation, we offer the following '10 commandments' for good translation. If you keep them in mind, you should have no difficulty translating ordinary arguments into their propositional logic symbols.

1. Use lower-case letters to represent simple propositions. This rule of translation may seem obvious, but beginning students often represent complex propositions, most commonly negations, as simple propositions. You must remember that it is a mistake to let m = Marcus Aurelius was not a good emperor, for this is a negation and must be represented as one. The proper way to deal with this proposition is by letting m = Marcus Aurelius was a good emperor, and by representing it as -m.

2. *Translate propositions literally if you can.* When ordinary sentences use propositional logic connector words, translate them literally. 'Either Cec or Margaret is the guilty party' is properly translated as c or m (where c = Cec is guilty and m = Margaret is guilty). This statement implies that 'If Cec isn't guilty then Margaret is' but it would be incorrect to represent it as -c → m. Instead, we must use propositional logic modes of inference to show that c or m implies -c → m.

3. *Do not confuse indicator words and connector words.* Remember that words like 'because', 'therefore', etc. are not propositional connectors. They are logical terms, but they function in different ways, establishing the relationship between propositions in an argument. They cannot, therefore, be translated as propositional logic symbols.

4. *Use the same letter to represent equivalent simple propositions.* It is a corollary of the principle of identity that sentences that 'propose' the same thing represent the same proposition. Thus the sentence, 'She got the highest mark in the math exam', is the same proposition as the claim that 'No one did as well as she did.' In dealing with ordinary arguments, you must treat different expressions of the same statement as the same proposition if you want to present the logic of propositional arguments properly.

5. *Ignore minor variations.* Sometimes ordinary language propositions differ in minor ways that can be ignored when you translate them into propositional logic symbols. You must judge what is and is not a minor variation by asking what matters in the context of the issue addressed by a particular argument. This being said, in most circumstances it will be possible to treat as equivalent the following variations on the proposition 'The American Anti-Vivisection Society opposes animal experimentation.'

> The American Anti-Vivisection Society opposes animal experimentation: you can count on it!
> I can tell you that the American Anti-Vivisection Society opposes animal experimentation.
> Animal experiments are vehemently opposed by the American Anti-Vivisection Society.
> Obviously, the American Anti-Vivisection Society is against experiments with animals.
> Like Peter Singer, the members of this society reject animal experiments.
> The American Anti-Vivisection Society wants to end animal experimentation.

In some sophisticated logical systems we would distinguish between these different statements but this is rarely necessary in the context of propositional logic.

6. *Use brackets to avoid ambiguity.* In Chapter 3 we emphasized the importance of avoiding ambiguity in our own arguments and diagnosing it

when we analyse other people's reasoning. In propositional logic, we use brackets to avoid possible ambiguities when we symbolize particular propositions. The statement: a → b or c, is ambiguous because it can be interpreted as the statement (a → b) or c, or as the statement a → (b or c). Logically, this is an important difference and you must make it clear which proposition you intend when you are translating a particular argument.

7. *Recognize 'unless' statements as conditionals.* In ordinary language, the connector word 'unless' precedes an implicitly negated antecedent. In propositional logic, propositions of the form 'y unless x' are therefore rendered as 'If not x, then y.' The statement 'Your kite can't fly unless there's a breeze' is, for example, properly rendered as the conditional 'If there is no breeze, then your kite won't fly.'

8. *Don't confuse 'if' and 'only if'.* In most conditionals, the statement that follows the connector word 'if' is the antecedent. An exception is conditionals that contain the connector words 'only if'. In dealing with such cases, you should translate 'x only if y' as the statement x → y. To see why this is the case, consider the conditional 'You can join the Air Force only if you are 18.' It would be a mistake to interpret this proposition as the claim that you can join the Air Force if you are eighteen, for this is only one of the requirements (other requirements include good physical health, the passing of entrance exams, and so on). More generally, 'x only if y' says that y is a necessary, but not sufficient, condition for x. Because it follows that x could not occur if y was not the case, x implies y (i.e., x → y) but y need not imply x.

9. *Recognize biconditionals.* In a simple conditional, the implication goes one way. It says that an antecedent implies a consequent, but not vice versa. In other cases, a proposition states both that an antecedent implies a consequent and that this consequent implies the antecedent. We call such statements of mutual implication 'biconditionals'. In propositional logic, we represent biconditionals as statements of the form (x → y) & (y → x).

Biconditionals are important because they give us a way to represent ordinary statements that express equivalences. One standard case occurs when propositions express definitions, which state the conditions under which a term may be used and what this use implies. The informal definition 'An alchemist is the medieval version of the modern chemist' may be rendered as the biconditional (a → m) & (m → a) where:

a = A person is an alchemist.
m = A person is the medieval version of the modern chemist.

When we want to present explicitly a statement as a biconditional we use the connector words 'if and only if'. This will eliminate any chance of misinterpretation, for such a statement explicitly conjoins two conditionals, one an 'if' conditional that flows one way and one an 'only if' conditional that flows in the opposite direction.

10. *Check your translation by translating back to ordinary English.* If you have translated a proposition or an argument properly, translating back into ordinary English should produce a proposition or an argument equivalent to the one with which you began.

Translating Arguments

The 10 commandments of good translation tell us how to translate ordinary propositions into propositional logic forms. They also tell us how to translate whole arguments, for this requires only that we use these commandments to translate the argument's premises and conclusion.

We can illustrate the process of translating an entire argument with the following simple example of a valid argument, which we discussed in Chapter 5.

If you have read Chapter 2, then you have read the section of this book that introduces simple arguments. You have read Chapter 2. Therefore, you have read the section of this book that introduces simple arguments.

We must begin by adopting a translation scheme, which we will define as follows:

r = You have read chapter 2.
s = You have read the section of this book that introduces simple arguments.

Given this translation scheme, we can represent the premises and the conclusion of our argument as:

r → s; r; therefore s.

In translating other propositional arguments, we proceed in a similar fashion by translating each of the argument's components into propositional logic forms. Because it is important to be comfortable with such translations before we go on to learn how to judge propositional validity, you should work through the following exercises before you proceed.

Box 8.3 Ten Commandments for Good Translation
1. Use lower-case letters to represent simple propositions.
2. Translate propositions literally if you can.
3. Do not confuse indicator words and connector words.
4. Use the same letter to represent equivalent simple propositions.
5. Ignore minor variations.
6. Use brackets to avoid ambiguity.
7. Recognize 'unless' statements as conditionals.
8. Don't confuse 'if' and 'only if'.
9. Recognize biconditionals.
10. Check your translation by translating back to ordinary English.

EXERCISE 8B

1. Translate the following sentences into propositional logic forms using the letters indicated.
   a) If that's Louis, we're in for trouble and if it's not we're home free. (l, t)
   b) If Angela and Karl frequent the place, then it's no place for us to go. (a, k, g)
   *c) [Paul Friedman, the public-address announcer at Wrigley Field in *The Sporting News*] One thing I've learned is that if you make a mistake, if you say it with a deep enough voice, you can get away with it. (m, d, g)
   d) Either you straighten up and get your act together or you're out of here. (s, a, o)
   e) If you want to have a good time, you should go to British Columbia or to California. (g, b, c)
   *f) If you have multimedia skills or have worked on video you can apply for the job. (m, v, j)
   g) It's a good wine, but not a great wine. (a, g)
   h) If the greenhouse effect takes place as predicted, the crocuses will not always bloom in April. (g, c)
   i) If there are any more boycotts of the Olympics, the games will lose their credibility. (b, c)
   *j) Either I'm paranoid, or you are out to get me. (p, o)
   *k) They're lying when they say they weren't there. (t)
   l) North Korea will disarm if and only if South Korea disarms. (n, s)
   *m) Only those who can stand a lot of pain can get a PhD. (s, p)
   n) The murder can't have been committed by both the chauffeur and the butler. (c, b)
   o) Whenever it rains there are dark clouds in the sky. (r, d)
   p) If you go to town, then you'll see the remains of the car on your right side if you turn right on Dundas Street. (g, r, d)
   q) If he'll buy the chair if I up the price to $400, then we'll know that he's guilty and we'll arrest him. (b, u, g, a)
   *r) I'm not interested in that car unless it is in mint condition. (i, m)
   s) When it rains there are clouds in the sky, and when it doesn't the sky is clear unless the pollution gets too bad. (r, c, p)
   t) I'll go only if Joan goes, too. (g, j)
   u) If you have a headache, it's because you drank too much last night and I can't feel sorry for you when you drink too much. (h, d, s)
   * v) [Boyle's law] The pressure of a gas varies with its volume at a constant temperature. (p, v, t)
2. Decide whether the following statements express simple conditionals or biconditionals, and put each into symbols using the letters given.
   *a) An individual is still alive as long as an EEG records brain signals. (a, s)
   b) You may become a Catholic priest only if you are male. (p, m)

c) A figure is a triangle whenever it has only three sides. (t, s)

*d) Metal does not expand unless it is heated. (e, h)

*e) Abortion is murder if and only if the fertilized ovum is a person. (m, p)

f) Whenever it rains, he's in a bad mood. (r, b)

g) If there are any more boycotts of the Olympics, the games will have to be cancelled. (b, c)

3. Translate the following propositional logic arguments into propositional logic forms using the letters indicated.

a) She's guilty only if she committed the crime and committed it intentionally. She did commit the crime, but unintentionally, so she's not guilty. (g, c, i)

b) Humans are mammals, and whales, dolphins, and elephants are mammals, so humans and whales are mammals. (h, w, d, e,)

*c) In order to avoid the intricacies of such theories we will rely on our earlier remark that the objective of an argument is to convince an audience. If this is so, then it is sufficient for our purposes that the premises of a good argument be accepted as true by both us and our audience. (o, s)

d) It should be clear that this new argument is invalid, for it is obviously possible for its two premises to be true when its conclusion is false, and if this is true then the argument is invalid. (v, t)

*e) The Conservatives will win the election if Liberal support declines in urban ridings. But there's no chance that Liberal support will decline in the urban ridings. (w, d)

f) You have a problem with your hardware or your software. If it's your software, Scott can fix it. If there's a problem with your hardware, Deb can help. But Jack said you don't have a problem with your software. So Scott can help. (h, y, s, d)

g) It appears that you have offended him or he simply dislikes you. It must be the latter, for I can't imagine you offending him. (o, l)

h) Americans or Germans or the Russians will win the most medals at next year's Olympics, but the Russians will not do well enough to win and the Americans will not do well enough to win, so Germans will win the most medals. (a, g, r)

3. VALID PROPOSITIONAL ARGUMENTS

Now that we know how to represent the structure of propositional arguments as well as simple and complex propositions, we can use the argument schemes that result to judge whether particular arguments are valid. We do so by identifying particular forms of propositional reasoning that are valid and invalid, and then deciding which forms are employed in particular arguments. It will be convenient to proceed by discussing the forms of argument that can be used with the different kinds of complex propositions.

Conjunctions

Propositional logic recognizes two valid forms of conjunctive argument. They are probably the most obviously valid propositional arguments, so it is useful to begin the discussion of validity with them. We call one of these forms of argument 'conjunction elimination' ('&E' for short) and the other 'conjunction introduction' ('&I' for short).

Conjunction elimination allows us to 'eliminate' conjunctions in the sense that we isolate a conjunct they contain. Conjunction introduction allows us to introduce a conjunction. We can summarize the rules for the construction of such arguments as follows:

&E: If some conjunction is true, we may conclude that each of its individual conjuncts is true.

&I: If the individual propositions x, y, . . . are true, we may conclude that the conjunction x & y . . . is true.

Both these forms of argument are common in ordinary reasoning—so common that we usually take them for granted. Once they are made explicit, it should be clear that they are valid forms of inference. In the first case, the truth of a conjunction implies that each of its conjuncts must individually be true, for this is precisely what the conjunction states. In the second case, the truth of a conjunction's conjuncts obviously implies the truth of a conjunction, for it must be true if they are true.

Particular instances of both forms of argument may seem contrived, for normally we assume such obvious inferences in ordinary language. However, it is useful to make them explicit in propositional logic, both because this illustrates the nature of valid forms of propositional reasoning and because it provides practice in making implicit inferences explicit. In view of this, we turn to some examples.

The novel on the desk is *Arcadia*. The cover says the author is Jim Crace. In the blurb on its back cover we read that 'He is the author of *Continent* . . . and *The Gift of Stones*.' These claims can be used as the basis of the following conjunctive reasoning when someone asks about Jim Crace.

a = Jim Crace is the author of the novel *Arcadia*.
c = Jim Crace is the author of *Continent*.
g = He is the author of *The Gift of Stones*.

Inference 1:	*Inference 2:*
c & g	c
Therefore, c	a
	Therefore, c & a

Inference 1 is a case of &E. It would probably be employed if someone asked, 'Is Jim Crace the author of *Continent*?' The answer involves remembering that the back cover of Arcadia says 'c & g', and by deducing c. Inference 2 is a case of &I. We rely on it when we conclude that Jim Crace is the author of *Arcadia* and *Continent* by deriving this from the front cover of *Arcadia* together with proposition c, from inference 1.

Both &I and &E can be used to make inferences involving any number of other conjuncts. The following, for example, is a case of &I:

j

m

p

a

Therefore, j & m & p & a

Though such inferences probably seem obvious, we shall see that isolating simple inferences of this sort will allow us to put together chains of inferences that enable us to establish quite complex inferences and conclusions.

We can already use the inference rules &E and &I to construct a variety of arguments. We can prove the validity of these and other propositional logic arguments by constructing propositional logic 'proofs'. A proof is a numbered sequence of premises and other propositions that we infer according to propositional logic rules like &E and &I. First we list premises. Then we derive intermediate conclusions justified by propositional rules that allow us to construct valid arguments. We use these intermediate conclusions as a basis for further inferences until we arrive at the conclusion we want. We justify each individual inference by applying a rule of inference to premises and/or previous lines of our proof.

Consider a simple example. Suppose we know that Jean-Paul Sartre wrote *Being and Nothingness* and *Existentialism and Humanism*, and that Victor Hugo wrote *The Hunchback of Notre Dame* and many other novels. On the basis of these propositions we can prove the validity of the conclusion that Sartre wrote *Being and Nothingness* and Hugo wrote *The Hunchback of Notre Dame* by letting:

b = Sartre wrote *Being and Nothingness*.
e = Sartre wrote *Existentialism and Humanism*.
h = Hugo wrote *The Hunchback of Notre Dame*.
o = Hugo wrote many other novels.

and by reasoning as follows:

1. b & e   P (for 'premise')
2. h & o   P
3. b   1, &E
4. h   2, &E
5. b & h   3, 4 &I

Lines 1 and 2 of this proof list our premises. The other lines are derived by constructing sub-arguments that take us at line 5 to our conclusion. At line 3 we infer that b must be true from b & e, which is true according to line 1. Our justification, '1, &E', indicates that we derived b by applying &E to line 1. In a similar way, our proof tells us that line 4 follows from line 2 by &E, and that b & h follows from lines 3 and 4 by the rule &I.

When using the forms of argument &E and &I as propositional rules of inference, remember that they can be applied to conjunctions with more than two conjuncts. Because the conjunction b & c & d & e claims that each of its conjuncts is true—i.e., that b is true, c is true, d is true, and e is true—we can use it and &E to establish each of these individual conjuncts. The rule &E can also establish b & c, for our initial conjunction can be thought of as the proposition (b & c) & d & e.

Disjunctions

The basic form of inference we use in constructing valid disjunctive arguments is called 'disjunction elimination'. We symbolize it as 'orE' and define it as follows:

> orE: If a disjunction and the negation of one of its disjuncts are true, one of the remaining disjuncts must be true.

In a particular case of orE, an initial disjunction tells that (at least) one of its disjuncts must be true. Accepting this to be the case, the further claim that a specific disjunct is false leads inevitably to the conclusion that one of the others must be true. In the most common case, a disjunction has two disjuncts and the falsity of one establishes the truth of the remaining one.

We can illustrate the way orE works by constructing a propositional proof for the inference a very confident teacher may make when she scans her class and sees several students yawning. Imagine that she reasons as follows:

> Either my students are bored with my lecture or they are tired because they partied last night. But this is one of the most scintillating lectures I've ever given. That must have been some party! They're exhausted!

If we let:

> b = The class is bored with my lecture.
> t = The students are tired after last night's bash.

then we can prove the validity of the proposed conclusion as follows:

1. b or t   P
2. -b   P
3. t   1, 2, orE

As in the previous example, we construct this propositional logic proof by listing our premises and applying rules of inference that allow us to derive our
proposed conclusion.

Though our proof successfully shows that our hypothetical teacher's reasoning is valid, it may still be a poor argument. This is because a valid argument is good reasoning only if its premises are true, and the premises in this
argument might be questioned. Students will probably say it is easy to imagine that a teacher mistakenly believes her lecture to be exciting when her students find it boring.

Though we are concerned primarily with the validity of arguments, it is
worth noting that orE inferences are frequently mistaken because they are
founded on a disjunction that overlooks alternative possibilities. In the case of
our example, the teacher may, for example, have overlooked the possibility
that her students are tired for reasons other than those she contemplates. They
may, for example, be tired because they were up late studying for a history
exam tomorrow.

Logicians call a disjunction that overlooks alternative possibilities a *false
dilemma* (or, less frequently, a 'false dichotomy'). It is important to beware of
the possibility of false dilemmas for they are a prevalent part of ordinary reasoning, which frequently reduces complex issues to two alternatives that overlook other possibilities.

We can illustrate this by considering a letter written to *Mother Jones* magazine in response to an article by Michael Castleman. The latter discussed
ways of making American neighbourhoods safe. According to Marc Mauer,
the assistant director of the Washington Sentencing Project:

> Castleman provides some good examples about ways in which neighborhoods
> can come together in crime prevention efforts. But his suggestion that 'reduc-
> ing criminal opportunity is our best bet for controlling crime' because of the
> difficulty of addressing poverty . . . raises a false dichotomy.

The Castleman argument that Mauer refers to in this letter is a classic case of
orE. Castleman proceeds from the disjunction, 'We can control crime by
reducing criminal opportunity or by addressing poverty', argues against the
second disjunct (i.e., that we can't control crime by addressing poverty), and
concludes that we must try to control crime by reducing criminal opportunity.
In propositional logic, we can represent the argument as follows:

c = We can control crime by reducing criminal opportunity.
p = We can control crime by addressing poverty.

1. c or p   P
2. -p   P
3. c   1, 2, orE

As this proof shows, Castleman's argument is a valid argument. It follows that we can question it only by questioning one of the premises on which he relies. This is what Maurer does when he charges Castleman with a false dilemma.

Using the propositional logic symbols we have already introduced, we can describe Mauer's criticism of Castleman by saying that he argues that the disjunction c or p overlooks other possibilities—in particular, the possibility that we can control crime by adopting a mix of measures that fight poverty and control criminal opportunity. As in other cases of false dilemma, Mauer maintains that Castleman's argument tries to force us to choose between two cut-and-dried alternatives, in the process overlooking other possibilities.

We finish our account of disjunctive arguments by noting that the rule orE can be applied to exclusive as well as inclusive disjunctions. Consider, for example, the following variation on our initial example of an argument that depends on an exclusive disjunction:

> The menu says you can have coffee or tea; you decided not to have coffee so you can have tea if you like.

If we let:

c = You have coffee.
t = You have tea.

then we can prove the validity of this argument as follows.

1. (c or t) & -(c & t)   P
2. -c   P
3. c or t   1, &E
4. t   3, 2, orE

In the case of this and other instances of exclusive disjunctions, the use of orE requires that we first use &E to isolate the disjunction that we want. Once this is done, orE can easily be applied in the way outlined in our definition of this form of inference.

In addition to illustrating the rule orE, this propositional proof illustrates how different kinds of rules of inference can work together in a particular proof.

Conditionals

The most basic rules of inference we use when we construct arguments that employ conditionals are called 'affirming the antecedent'—'AA' for short and traditionally known as *modus ponens*—and 'denying the consequent', 'DC' for short and traditionally known as *modus tollens*. They can be defined as follows:

AA: If a conditional, x → y, and its antecedent x are true, we may conclude that its consequent, y, is true.

DC: If a conditional, x → y, is true and its consequent y is false, then we may conclude that its antecedent, x, is false.

Both these forms of inference play a central role in ordinary reasoning. AA takes a conditional and its antecedent as a basis for the conclusion that its consequent is true. Such inferences are obviously valid, for a conditional states that its consequent is true in these specific circumstances. Inferences of the form DC are also valid, for a true conditional and a false consequent are incompatible with a true antecedent, which would imply that the consequent was true.

We can illustrate the rule AA by imagining a circumstance in which company stock we own (i) will rise in value if it is placed on a public exchange and (ii) will be placed on a public exchange if questions about the company's president are resolved. Suppose further that we are confident the president will be fired and that the problems will be resolved if this is so. In such circumstances we can let:

s = Our stock will go up in value.
p = Our stock is placed on a public exchange.
r = The company resolves questions about its president.
f = The president will be fired.

and can use the following chain of reasoning to prove that our stock will be placed on a public exchange and will increase in value:

1. p → s   P
2. r → p   P
3. f → r   P
4. f   P
5. r   3, 4, AA
6. p   2, 5, AA
7. s   1, 6, AA
8. p & s   6, 7, &I

Notice that every time we use the rule AA, we state the line numbers where the relevant conditional and its antecedent appear.

The conditional inferences in this first example are all of the AA variety. In many other cases, conditional inferences are of the DC form. Consider the following letter to Toronto's *Globe and Mail* (29 Jan. 1987):

The prize for the most erroneous statement of the week should be shared by economist John Crispo and journalist Jennifer Lewington. Both of them claim that the present value of the Canadian dollar [$0.68 US] gives our exporters an advantage of thirty per cent or more in the US market.

Nothing could be further from the truth. That would be true only if prices and costs had risen by the same amount in both countries. In fact, between 1970 and 1986, the price index of GNP rose twenty-eight per cent more in Canada than it did in the United States.

If we let:

e = Economist John Crispo is correct.
j = Journalist Jennifer Lewington is correct.
a = The value of the Canadian dollar gives Canadian exporters an advantage of 30% or more in the US.
s = Prices and costs rise by the same amount in both countries.

then the letter's argument can be translated as: e → a; j → a; a → s; -s; therefore -e & -j. Having determined that the argument has this structure, we can prove its validity as follows:

1. e → a   P
2. j → a   P
3. a → s   P
4. -s   P
5. -a   3, 4, DC
6. -j   2, 5, DC
7. -e   1, 5, DC
8. -e & -j   7, 6, &I

When you use the rules AA and DC, there will be times when the antecedent or consequent of a conditional is itself a complex proposition. In view of this, affirming the antecedent may mean affirming a conjunction, a negation, a disjunction, or a conditional. If we want to use the conditional 'It is uncomfortable in the attic whenever the temperature and the humidity are high' (which can be rendered as $(t \& h) \rightarrow -c$) as a basis for the conclusion that 'It is uncomfortable in the attic', then we must do so by affirming the antecedent 'The temperature is high and the humidity is high.'

Denying the consequent is prominent in scientific reasoning, in the rejection of inadequate scientific hypotheses. In such cases, a theory is rejected by showing that it implies certain experimental results that cannot be corroborated. Put symbolically, we can say that a theory T is rejected because T →R and -R where R are the experimental results in question.

A good historical example of this use of DC is the refutation of phlogiston theory by Lavoisier in 1775, an important event in the evolution of chemistry. According to phlogiston theory, combustion is a process in which a substance called 'phlogiston' departs from a burning substance. This implies that a substance will lose weight when it combusts (since it has lost phlogiston) but Lavoisier demonstrated that this consequence does not hold when mercury combusts. If we let:

p = Phlogiston theory is correct.
w = Mercury will weigh less after combustion.

then we can represent that Lavoisier's reasoning is a clear case of DC, for it has the form p → w; -w; therefore -p.

Box 8.4 A Conditional Variation

In our earlier account of propositional logic forms, one of our 'commandments' for good translation emphasized that we should ignore minor variations. One variation of the rule DC that merits comment has the form:

x → y
We do not want y.
Therefore we do not want x.

This is an obvious variant of the rule x → y, -y therefore -x, which we will, in propositional logic, treat as a valid instance of DC.

An example of such reasoning is found in the following drawing of a David Low cartoon. Low was a famous cartoonist during World War I and World War II who was ultimately knighted for his insightful political commentary.

'PERHAPS IT WOULD GEE-UP BETTER IF WE LET IT TOUCH EARTH.'

This particular cartoon illustrates the situation at the end of World War I, after Germany had been defeated and France and Britain were determining the size of the war reparations Germany would have to pay. Low criticizes unlimited indemnity, arguing that it will make it impossible for Germany to pay its reparations. We can represent the argument as a variation of denying the consequent as follows.

g = Germany is forced to pay unlimited indemnity.
a = Germany will be able to pull the load that we require.

1. g → -a   P
2. a   P (what we want to be the case)
3. -g   1, 2, DC (what we want to be the case)

To be very clear about what is going on in this case, we have added explanatory brackets beside lines 2 and 3 of this proof.

Conditional Fallacies

In contrast to the valid inferences AA and DC, the inferences called 'affirming the consequent' and 'denying the antecedent' ('AC' and 'DA') are fallacious. The first occurs when one affirms a conditional's consequent and concludes that its antecedent is true, the second when one denies its antecedent and concludes that its consequent is false.

That these are invalid forms of argument can be shown by the following examples. While it is probably true that you'll amass a great deal of money if you're a financial genius (that $f \rightarrow m$, where f = you're a financial genius, and m = you'll amass a great deal of money), it would obviously be a mistake to make the following inferences, which exemplify the fallacies AC and DA:

1. If you're a financial genius, you'll amass a great deal of money.
   You've amassed a great deal of money.
   Therefore, you're a financial genius.
2. If you're a financial genius, you'll amass a great deal of money.
   You're not a financial genius.
   Therefore, you won't amass a great deal of money.

Both inferences are invalid because they overlook the fact that one may end up with a great deal of money for any number of reasons, and it follows that one can do so without being a financial genius. One can, for example, amass large sums of money by winning a lottery, being lucky in the stock market, inheriting a fortune, and so on. The conditional that is the basis of inferences 1 and 2 ($f \rightarrow m$) states that being a financial genius is one way to amass a great deal of money, but it does not say that this is the *only* way to amass a lot of money.

Biconditionals

The fallacies affirming the consequent and denying the antecedent are often confused with AA and DC because conditionals are incorrectly interpreted as biconditionals. We have seen that they are conjunctions composed of two conditionals and can work with them by isolating these conditionals (by using the rule &E) and applying the rules AA and DC to one or both of them.

We can appreciate biconditional inferences by looking at circumstances in which they play a prominent role. Consider, for example, a scientific attempt to explain a state of affairs y. In constructing such an explanation, a scientist tries to identify some proposition x that accounts for y. In the process, he or she must show that x implies y (that $x \rightarrow y$), but this itself is not enough. Indeed, a reliance on this conditional alone would imply an instance of the fallacy AC.

To be convincing, the scientist must, therefore, try to show that the given account of y is the one we should accept. The extent to which this is possible is a matter of philosophical dispute, but the whole process can be seen as an attempt to establish the biconditional $(x \rightarrow y) \& (y \rightarrow x)$, for this entails that x implies y *and* that y implies x.

Let us take a particular example. A controversial geological hypothesis claims that the extinction of dinosaurs and other species in Earth's early history is the result of a meteorite or comet collision with the Earth. To establish this explanation as the proper one is to establish the likelihood of the biconditional $(i \rightarrow e) \& (e \rightarrow i)$, where

e = Extinctions occurred at specific places.
i = A comet or meteorite collided with the earth at these places.

The initial evidence for this hypothesis was found by Canadian geologist Digby McLaren, who discovered fossil records indicating that certain species of coral and shellfish abruptly died out at some point between the Frasnian and Framennian stages of geologic time (the latter about 370 million years ago, the former about 7 million years later). Speculating on the reasons, he hypothesized that a meteorite at the end of the Frasnian period sent huge tidal waves to ocean shores and disrupted the shallow-water environment and caused the extinctions.

Digby's explanation is initially plausible, for $i \rightarrow e$, but holders of this theory would be guilty of affirming the consequent if they interpreted e as definitive evidence of a meteorite collision with Earth. To defend this hypothesis satisfactorily one must go further and demonstrate that alternative explanations of the extinctions are not feasible. In doing so, one must attempt to establish i as the only plausible cause of the extinctions. In other words, the possibility as $e \rightarrow i$ must be established. In this vein, subsequent discussions have focused on whether there are alternative conditions that could account for the extinctions.

The strength of biconditional propositions is seen in our ability to use them in conjunction with the truth or falsity of their antecedents *or* consequents as a basis for a conclusion about their remaining components. As the following proofs show, the rule &E prepares the way for the use of AA or DC in such circumstances:

1. $(x \rightarrow y)$ & $(y \rightarrow x)$ P
2. -x   P
3. $y \rightarrow x$ 1, &E
4. -y   3, 2, DC

1. $(x \rightarrow y)$ & $(y \rightarrow x)$ P
2. x   P
3. $x \rightarrow y$ 1, &E
4. y   3, 2, AA

Conditional Series

The last propositional form of inference we will consider in this chapter is also useful when we reason with biconditionals or simple conditionals. It is called 'conditional series' ('CS' for short) and can be defined as follows:

> CS: If x, y, and z are any propositions and $x \rightarrow y$ and $y \rightarrow z$ are true, then we may conclude that $x \rightarrow z$ is true.

Essentially, CS tells us that an antecedent entails not only its consequent but any further consequent entailed by that first consequent. If it is true that (1) if Hitler had attacked Britain two months earlier, he would have won the Battle of Britain; and that (2) if he had won the Battle of Britain he would have won World War II; then CS allows us to conclude that if Hitler had attacked Britain two months earlier he would have won World War II. More formally, we can demonstrate the validity of this inference by letting:

t = Hitler attacked Britain two months earlier.
s = Hitler would have won the Battle of Britain.
w = Hitler would have won World War II.

and by constructing the following propositional logic proof:

1. $t \rightarrow s$ P
2. $s \rightarrow w$ P
3. $t \rightarrow w$ 1, 2, CS

As you will observe in the exercises ahead, it is often useful to employ CS in conjunction with conditional rules of inference like AA and DC.

This account of the rule CS completes our discussion of the most basic forms of argument we use as rules of inference in propositional logic. We summarize these rules at the end of this chapter. As you begin to construct propositional proofs for yourself, refer to this summary. But you should try and learn the rules well enough to make this unnecessary. The following general principles will also help you construct propositional logic proofs.

4. CONSTRUCTING SIMPLE PROOFS

Equipped with rules for constructing valid propositional arguments, and with your ability to translate ordinary sentences into standard propositional logic forms, you are ready to construct simple proofs that demonstrate the validity of specific arguments. For those who initially find proofs difficult, we offer the following guidelines for proof construction.

(i) *Good proofs depend on good translations.* If you do not translate an argument into propositional logic properly, your proof cannot (however ingenious it is) prove that the argument is valid. So be sure that you translate an argument carefully. Among other things, this means that the premises and conclusion must be represented using the connectors we have already discussed (-, &, or, →) and lower-case letters that represent simple sentences. In translating each argument component, follow the guidelines we introduced in the earlier sections of this chapter. If you know that an argument is valid but cannot provide a proof to show its validity, you may not have translated it properly.

(ii) *Good propositional reasoning, like other kinds of good reasoning, proceeds by breaking an extended argument into a series of smaller steps that lead to the main conclusion.* The validity of an extended piece of reasoning may be difficult to see and can be more readily appreciated when one breaks the reasoning into a series of more manageable steps.

(iii) *If the validity of an argument is not obvious, do not try to grasp it immediately.* In keeping with (ii), you should instead proceed by taking one part of the proof and confining your attention to it. You may find it useful to begin by asking what follows from the stated premises, what follows from the propositions they imply, and so on. As you work through such steps, remember that your overall proof must be a sequence of shorter inferences that conform to one of the rules we have discussed.

(iv) *One useful strategy begins with an argument's conclusion and works backward.* Adopting this strategy, you may want to proceed by asking a series of questions. What must be true to make the conclusion true? What must be true to make these other propositions true? What rule will probably be used to establish the final conclusion? What propositions will have to be established for this rule to produce the desired proposition?

If your conclusion is a conjunction, you may speculate that it should be established by the rule &I. The next question to ask is how each individual conjunct can be introduced. Perhaps this will require the rule orE in one case, and the rule AA in the other. Perhaps that will require that you first isolate the negation of a disjunct. And so on.

(v) Derive as much information as you can from an argument's premises. Especially when you are unsure how to proceed, you may wish to do so by deriving what you can from an argument's premises and seeing where this takes you. If a premise is a conjunction, you can isolate each conjunct. If a premise is a conditional and another its antecedent, then AA can be used to derive the consequent. Ask yourself what forms of argument are invited by the premises.

(vi) Keep track of premises. In most arguments, the conclusion depends in some way on all of the premises. In view of this, it is probably the premises you have not yet employed that will be the key to progressing further with your argument.

(vii) Familiarize yourself with the rules of inference. You cannot be comfortable constructing propositional logic proofs if you are unsure of basic rules of inference. Begin with the summary of rules in Box 8.5 but try to learn the rules well enough so that you can dispense with it.

Box 8.5 Propositional Rules of Inference

&E: If some conjunction is true, we may conclude that each of its individual conjuncts is true.

&I: If the individual propositions x, y, . . . are true, we may conclude that the conjunction 'x & y . . .' is true.

orE: If a disjunction and the negation of one of its disjuncts are true, at least one of the remaining disjuncts must be true.

AA: If a conditional, $x \rightarrow y$, and its antecedent x are true, we may conclude that its consequent, y, is true.

DC: If a conditional, $x \rightarrow y$, is true and its consequent y is false, then we may conclude that its antecedent, x, is false.

CS: If x, y, and z are any propositions and $x \rightarrow y$ and $y \rightarrow z$ are true, then we may conclude that $x \rightarrow z$ is true.

EXERCISE 8C

As a review of what we have covered so far, and as preparation for what lies ahead, fill in the following crossword puzzle.

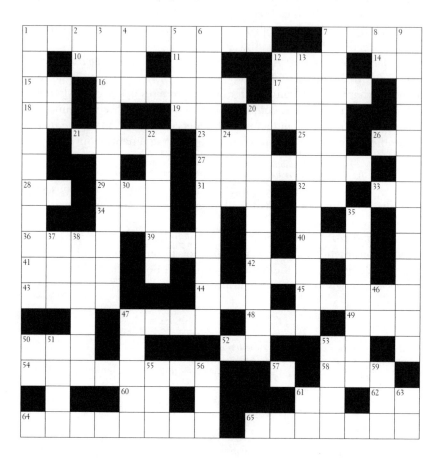

CLUES ACROSS:
1. What follows from premises.
7. Booby _____.
10. If g = It's a girl, then -g = It's a _____.
11. If p = Paul goes out, c = Chris goes out, m = Mary goes out, then m → (p & c) and -c imply that Mary is _____.
12. 'Lion' is equivalent to '_____'.

CLUES DOWN:
1. If . . . then statement.
2. Latin for 'note well'.
3. a & b.
4. Sounds, but is not, equivalent to a dishonest practice.
5. If t = Go to Thailand, and e = You like exotic places, and it is true that e and e → t, then you should go here.

CLUES ACROSS *(cont.)*

14. If you have a PhD you are a _____.
15. If x = yes, then -x = _____.
16. -(a & b) _____ s a & b.
17. _____ Fitzgerald, singer.
18. If x then y, -y, so -x.
19. Man's title.
20. _____ of rope.
21. Sounds like our disjunctive connector.
25. Same as 61 down.
26. First word of a proverb equivalent to h → e, where h = You're human.
27. _____ the antecedent.
28. The principles of identity tell us to treat 'that is' as interchangeable with this abbreviation.
29. If m = Catch me, then c → m is a common saying if c = you _____.
31. If d = The stock market has its downs, then -d is the statement that the stock market has its _____.
32. Short for Nova Scotia.
33. (a → b) & (b → a) is a _____ conditional.
34. In a race between two individuals, it is a false dilemma to say that one or the other will win, for it may be a _____.
36. Degree _____.
39. Word used to form negations.
40. We've discussed conditionals and biconditionals, but not _____ conditionals.
41. Food for Lassie.
42. The laws of thought apply _____ versally.

CLUES DOWN *(cont.)*

6. Some propositional rules of inference—e.g., &I—are rules of _____.
7. Denying the consequent is traditionally called *modus* _____.
8. The next chapter discusses *reductio* _____ *absurdum*.
9. The topic of this chapter is _____ logic.
12. Let g = Leo, c = Chris, and l = Linda, and apply orE twice to the following: g or c or l, -c, -l.
13. a & b, therefore b is a case of and _____.
20. b in a → b.
22. A word traditionally associated with AA.
24. Short for a Democrat's opposite.
30. Logic plays an important role in _____ research.
35. A rule yet to be introduced: x or y, x → z, y → z, therefore z.
37. French equivalent to 'island'.
38. Famous baby doctor, Star Trek personality.
46. Grand __ Opry.
47. The law of the excluded middle says statements can be true or false but not _____ or more false.
50. One of the forms of argument discussed in later chapters of this text is called _____ *hominem*.
51. Trigonometric function.
53. One might awkwardly say that &E _____ s a conjunction.
55. A verb that implies repeated use of equivalent propositions.
56. The number of rules of inference introduced in this chapter, plus four.

CLUES ACROSS *(cont.)*

43. _____ Uris, famous author.
44. The proposition a & b can be false in three ways. How many ways are there for it to be true?
45. t → m, t = you go to a theatre, m = you may go to an _____.
47. 'b when a' is equivalent to 'If a, _____ b.'
48. -(x & -x) is an instance of the principle of _____-contradiction.
49. s → m, s = She's a member of the Legislative Assembly, m = She's an _____.
50. First word of a biblical saying equivalent to a → b, where b = shall be given.
52. Abbreviation for 'light'.
53. m or a, where m = a form of meditation, and a = advertising abbreviation.
54. Half of x or y.
57. See 57 down.
58. A rule in propositional logic: Assume x, derive y & -y, conclude -x.
60. If we treated AA as a rule of elimination, its abbreviation would be this.
61. _____5, British agency.
62. a or i, where a = abbreviation for 'pound', i = first initials of an American president.
64. Apply the rule &E to f & d, where f and d are the names of two great logicians, Frege and De Morgan.
65. Argument building block.

CLUES DOWN *(cont.)*

57. First letter of the abbreviation of the rule used to derive a consequent.
59. h & p & j, where h = Hirt, p = Pacino, and j = Jolson.
61. If m = The culprit is me, y = The culprit is you, and s = The culprit is someone else, and y → r, r → m, s → (s & m), then we can be sure that one culprit is _____.
63. Hamlet asks whether he should x or -x, where x = _____.

MAJOR EXERCISE 8M

1. Fill in the missing steps in the following proofs. Each '?' indicates a missing step. All the premises are identified.

   *a) 1. a → b   P
       2. a   P
       3. ?   ?

   b) 1. c → d   P
       2. c → e   P
       3. c   P
       4. ?   ? AA
       5. e   2, 3, AA
       6. ?   4, 5, &I

   *c) 1. (e or d) & f   P
       2. -d   P
       3. ?   ??
       4. e   ??
       5. ?   ??
       6. e & f   4, 5, &I

   d) 1. m → n   P
       2. n → o   P
       3. m & r   P
       4. m   3, ?
       5. n   1, 4, ?
       6. o   ???

   e) 1. a & -c   P
       2. c or e   P
       3. -c   ???
       4. ?   2, 3, ?

   *f) 1. a → d   P
       2. d → e   P
       3. a & b   P
       4. a   ???
       5. ?   1, 4, AA
       6. ?   ???
       7. a & e   4, 6, ?

2. Using the letters given, translate the following arguments into propositional logic and either prove them valid or identify them as invalid. Identify any fallacies committed.

*a) [Galileo's reasoning for the conclusion that the solar system revolves around the sun] If the planetary system is heliocentric, Venus will show phases. But Venus does show phases, so the planetary system is heliocentric. (h, v)

b) Katie can't be guilty, for she didn't act suspiciously and that's how someone acts when she is guilty. (g, s)

c) [A.M. Turing in 'Computing, Machinery and Intelligence', *Mind* 59, 236 (1950)] If each man had a definite set of rules of conduct by which he regulated his life he would be no better than a machine. But there are no such rules, so men cannot be machines. (d, b)

d) That violin isn't worth anything unless it was made by a famous violin maker like Stradivarius. Wow! It's a Stradivarius. It must be worth a fortune! (s, f)

e) [From an ad in *The Economist*, Aug. 1995] If you are looking for a bank committed to a straightforward approach to helping you protect your wealth, consider Bank Julius Baer. (l, b)

*f) If the government minister is not honest, she is not to be trusted, and if she's not to be trusted she should not hold a government post but go back to her law firm. But I know that the minister is not honest, so she should return to her law firm. (h, t, g, r)

*g) As a patriot I can tell you what attitude you should have to this great nation of ours: love it or leave it! You obviously don't love it, so why don't you go ahead and leave? (l, g)

h) If they asked for 'Jazz' they wanted him. If they wanted him he's in trouble. And if he's in trouble he's gone home. So if they asked for Jazz, then he's probably gone home. (a, t, h)

i) [From a letter to the *Kitchener-Waterloo Record*, 25 June 1995] The only negative aspect of being a No supporter in the Quebec referendum is finding oneself alongside Brian Mulroney. If keeping Canada together means accepting the company of Mulroney, then maybe we had better rethink our positions.

3. Prove that if the biconditional (a → b) & (b → a) is true and b is false, then a is false.

4. Translate the following arguments into propositional logic form using the letters indicated and construct a proof of their validity.

*a) [Zen Master Dogen in Yuho Yokoi, *Dogen* (New York: Weatherhill, 1976)] You should listen to the Zen master's teaching without trying to make it conform to your own self-centred viewpoint; otherwise you will be unable to understand what he is saying. (l, a)

b) She's guilty only if she committed the crime and she's guilty only if she committed it intentionally. She did commit the crime, but unintentionally, so she's not guilty. (g, c, i)

c) Humans are mammals, and whales, dolphins, and elephants are mammals, so humans and whales are mammals. (h, w, d, e)

*d) In order to avoid the intricacies of such theories we will rely on our earlier remark that the objective of an argument is to convince an audience. If this is so, then it is sufficient for our purposes that the premises of a good argument be accepted as true by our audience. (o, s)

e) It should be clear that this new argument is invalid, for it is obviously possible for its two premises to be true while its conclusion is false, and if this is true then the argument is invalid. (t, v)

*f) The Liberals will win the election if and only if Conservative support declines in the rural ridings. But there's no chance that Conservative support will decline in the rural ridings. (l, c)

g) If there's a problem, it's a problem with your hardware or your software. If it's your software, Deborah can fix it. If there's a problem with your hardware, Scott Reaume can help. But I don't think it's a problem with your software, so Scott can help. (p, h, s, r, d)

h) It appears that you have offended him or he simply dislikes you. It must be the latter, for I can't imagine you offending him. (o, l)

*i) Americans or Germans or Russians will win the most medals at next year's Olympics, but the Russians will not do well enough to win and the Germans will not do well enough to win, so Americans will win the most medals. (a, g, r)

5. Translate into propositional logic symbols and prove valid the following arguments. Use the letters in parentheses to represent your simple sentences.

*a) We do not want anarchy. When criminals are not punished, the result is rising crime—in a word, anarchy. When corporations don't break the law, the result is falling stocks—in a word, anarchy. So we should punish criminals and support corporate crime! (c, b, a; adapted from a cartoon by Jules Feiffer, 16 Apr. 1972)

b) If capital punishment does not deter capital crimes, it is not justified, and if it's not justified it should not be a part of criminal law and should be abolished everywhere. Capital punishment does not, however, deter capital crimes, so it should be abolished everywhere. (c, j, l, e)

*c) [Start by changing the rhetorical question into statement form.] If you're so smart, why aren't you rich? (s, r)

d) Rumour had it that Sam Stone or a look-alike was having dinner at The Steak House. When Tom asked whether he had made a reservation and had showed up on time, the hostess replied affirmatively. 'In that case', said Tom, 'the person having dinner can't possibly be Sam Stone.' (s, l, r, t)

e) [Look for the hidden conclusion in the following example.] If the Rev. Jerry Falwell evaluates his ministry by the money it makes, then he is serving mammon, not God. Now the newspapers reported a complaint by him that his ministry has probably lost $1 million, maybe closer to $2 million, in revenues over the past month as a result of infighting at PTL. If he complains in that way, he is evaluating his ministry by the money it makes. (e, m, g, c)

f) [REAL Women is a Canadian organization promoting some of the traditional women's roles.] If you belong to REAL Women, you believe in its ideals. But if you believe in its ideals, you believe that men should be our leaders. If you believe that men should be our leaders, you must believe that REAL Women should not lead us. But if you believe that REAL Women shouldn't lead us, you don't really believe in REAL Women. So if you believe in REAL Women, you don't! (r, i, m, l)

*g) [Look for the hidden component in the following argument.] Zsa Zsa Gabor, who recently got married for the eighth time, gave her age as 54. If that's true, she was only five when she entered and won the Miss Hungary beauty title in 1933.

h) [Adapted from an argument in T. Govier, A *Practical Study of Argument*, 3rd edn (Belmont, Calif.: Wadsworth, 1992), p. 253] Elephants have been known to bury their dead. But they would do so only if they have a concept of their own species and understand what death means. If they understand what death means, they have a capacity for abstraction, and if they have a capacity for abstraction, they can think. Yet you admit that elephants have no moral rights only if they can't think, so elephants have moral rights. (b, c, u, a, t, m)

6. Construct two proofs of the following propositional logic argument, one that uses the rule CS and one that does not.

   Campbell was Prime Minister for the shortest time in Canadian history, but it wasn't her fault if the party didn't fully support her. The party didn't fully support her if Mulroney didn't support her and Mulroney did not support her, so it wasn't her fault. (c, f, s, m)

7. Prove the validity of the following arguments:
   a) $b \rightarrow c, c \rightarrow d, d \rightarrow e, b$, therefore e.
   *b) $b \rightarrow c, a \rightarrow b, d \rightarrow a, -c$, therefore -d.
   c) a & b, b & c, therefore a & c.
   d) $b \rightarrow c, c \rightarrow d, -d, a$, therefore a & -b.
   *e) $a \rightarrow (b \& c), c \rightarrow d, a$, therefore a & d.
   f) b & -c, c or d, $d \rightarrow a$, therefore a.
   g) $a \rightarrow (b \& -c)$, c or d, a, therefore d.

DILEMMAS

AND

REDUCTIOS

Chapter 8 introduced the most basic forms of propositional reasoning. In this chapter we continue our account of propositional logic by discussing more complex forms of argument. It introduces:

- ◆ a rule for proving conditionals;
- ◆ *reductio ad absurdum* arguments;
- ◆ two kinds of reasoning by dilemma;
- ◆ instructions on how to take a dilemma by its horns or escape between them; and
- ◆ rules for equating conjunctions and disjunctions.

We have already introduced all the connectives we need to represent propositional logic arguments and statements. We have also introduced the basic rules of inference for constructing propositional logic proofs. You have had an opportunity to practise proof construction in the exercises at the end of the last chapter. Your familiarity with these aspects of the logic of 'ifs, ands, and buts' provides a basis for more elaborate forms of propositional inference. The forms we introduce in this chapter are integral to ordinary reasoning and capture further features of day-to-day debates. We will proceed by discussing four new forms of argument.

1. CONDITIONAL REASONING

The rules AA and DC are rules of conditional 'elimination'. They allow us to use a conditional to establish the truth of its consequent or the falsity of its antecedent. In the process, we 'eliminate' the conditional in the sense that we replace it with the component we isolate. We now contrast this process with one encompassed by the first of the additional rules of inference. This rule allows us to prove and thereby introduce a new conditional, in this way showing that certain things are or would be the case if the conditions specified in the antecedent hold. Because we frequently argue for conditionals, the rule captures an important aspect of ordinary propositional reasoning.

We will call our new rule 'conditional reasoning' ('CR' for short). To see how it works, consider the way in which we might establish a conditional in the context of an ordinary disagreement. Imagine that a group of us are arguing about what should happen to an old city market. Someone offers the opinion that 'If I owned the old city market, I'd take it down and sell the property.' We can easily imagine someone else retorting:

> If you did, you'd be a fool. For suppose you did close down the market and put the property up for sale. Then the municipal government would refuse to change the zoning by-laws and a buyer would not be able to build anything more profitable. You'd have to settle for an absurdly low price and only a fool would sell in those circumstances.

This argument consists primarily of claims about what would be the case if the antecedent of the proposed conditional were true—i.e., if the person in question decided to close down the market and sell the property. The structure of the argument is a case of conditional introduction. We illustrate this by letting:

    c = You close down the old city market.
    s = You sell the property.
    m = The municipal government would refuse to change the zoning by-laws.
    b = A buyer would be able to build something more profitable.
    l = You would have to settle for an absurdly low price.
    f = You would be a fool.

Using this translation scheme, we can summarize our sample argument as follows:

Conclusion: $(c \& s) \to f$
For suppose $c \& s$
Then m
But $m \to -b$ and $-b \to l$, so l
And $l \to f$, so f

Within propositional logic we can formally prove the validity of arguments like this by invoking the premise for conditional reasoning, called the rule CR, which we will define as follows:

CR: Introduce a premise x (listed as P/CR), infer y by propositional logic rules of inference, and conclude that x → y.

The hypothetical premise that we introduce for the purpose of the rule CR is justified in our proof as 'P/CR'. Once we show that it entails some other proposition y, we can conclude that y is true if x is true, i.e., that x → y.

We can illustrate the rule CR by proving the validity of our first example of a conditional argument. In this case, we need to introduce c & s as our conditional premise and conclude f, for c & s is the antecedent of the conditional we wish to prove and f is its consequent. A complete proof follows:

1. (c & s) → m	P	
2. m → -b	P	
3. -b → l	P	
4. l → f	P	
5. c & s	P/CR	
6. m	1, 5, AA	
7. -b	2, 6, AA	
8. l	3, 7, AA	
9. f	4, 8, AA	
10. (c & t) → f	5-9, CR	

We use this kind of reasoning in ordinary circumstances whenever we assume a proposition 'for the sake of argument', show that another proposition follows, and conclude that the second proposition is true if the first is true.

To ensure that the rule CR is not used to justify any illegitimate inference, we stipulate that the lines used for conditional introduction (the lines that extend from our conditional premise to the line where we deduce our consequent) must not be used elsewhere in the proof. This restriction is needed to ensure that the conditional premise is employed (explicitly or implicitly) only when we are speculating on what would be the case if it were true.

In our first example, this restriction on CR means that lines 5-9 may not be used elsewhere in the proof. They must be treated in this way because they contain statements about what would be the case if the person in question closed the old city market and sold the property (if c & s were true), not statements about what actually is the case. A proof that did not respect this restriction might go on to mistakenly conclude, among other things, that the city market was in fact closed and sold.

Consider another example to illustrate how CR works. Suppose that you believe we can solve the problems of the Third World and still enjoy a reasonable standard of living if we develop alternative forms of energy, and that there will be a greater chance of lasting peace if we solve the problems of the Third World. Given these premises, we can use CR to prove the validity of the conclusion that there will be a greater chance of lasting peace if we develop alternative forms of energy. If we let:

a = We develop alternative forms of energy.
s = We can solve the problems of the Third World.
e = We will enjoy a reasonable standard of living.
g = There will be a greater chance of lasting peace.

we can construct the following proof:

1. $a \rightarrow (s \& e)$		P
2. $s \rightarrow g$		P
3. a		P/CR
4. $s \& e$		1, 3, AA
5. s		4, &E
6. g		2, 5, AA
7. $a \rightarrow g$		3-6, CR

Here as elsewhere, the key to a good CR proof is the proper use of other propositional rules of inference after we have adopted our initial conditional premise P/CR. Something similar can be said when we construct arguments and proofs that depend on the next form of propositional reasoning.

2. REDUCTIO AD ABSURDUM ARGUMENTS

The forms of argument we have discussed so far offer 'direct' evidence for their conclusions—i.e., evidence that implies it. In ordinary reasoning we may also argue for a conclusion by offering what we call 'indirect' evidence. We do so whenever we establish our own views by demonstrating that opposing views are mistaken. In propositional logic, we call this form of indirect reasoning a 'reductio ad absurdum' argument.

Literally, reductio ad absurdum means 'reducing to absurdity'. In keeping with this, 'RAA' arguments attempt to establish the absurdity of the positions they reject. They disprove a claim x by assuming it ('for the sake of argument') and deriving a consequence y that is clearly false. This demonstration shows that x can be true only if y is true, and allows us to use y's falsehood to show that x implies that y & -y. Because y & - y is absurd, we conclude that x itself is false (-x). We formally define the rule RAA as follows:

RAA: Take any proposition as a *reductio* premise (P/RAA), deduce an absurd consequence that leads to a contradiction, and conclude that the negation of the initial proposition must be true.

Some logicians distinguish between strong and weak versions of *reductio ad absurdum*. The rule works in the same way in both cases, but is characterized by different kinds of contradictions. The strong form of RAA attacks an opponent's views by demonstrating that he or she is committed to contradictory views. Because such views cannot, as the principle of non-contradiction emphasizes, be true, it follows that his or her position must be false. The weaker form of the *reductio* derives a contradiction from an opponent's position together with a claim that others (ourselves, a universal audience, those participating in discussion, etc.) accept as true. We employ *reductios* of this form when we reject the consequences of an opponent's claims because they conflict with beliefs that are generally accepted.

Both kinds of RAA arguments insist on logical consistency. A strong RAA argument puts in question an opponent's claims by showing that they entail consequences that demonstrate an inconsistency in his or her own thinking. In contrast, a weak RAA argument alleges that a claim is inconsistent with the beliefs of reasonable people.

The important point is that a position must be rejected in both cases, though the charge of inconsistency is less serious in the first case, implying as it does that persons must, if they are reasonable, revise their beliefs to eliminate the inconsistency. In contrast, it is always possible that they will respond to the weaker form of RAA by maintaining their own beliefs and rejecting what other reasonable people allegedly believe.

Some of the best examples of RAA arguments are found in geometric and mathematical reasoning, but they lie beyond the scope of the present book. We will, therefore, take our examples of RAA from ordinary discourse. The following remarks are adapted from election material that criticized the position taken by a candidate for the Progressive Conservative Party of Canada.

> The Conservative candidate says that he would introduce a bill adding five years in prison to the sentence of anyone convicted of a crime committed with a gun. He also claims he is for fiscal restraint. So much for his credibility. A person who wants to undertake huge expenditures is not for fiscal restraint and his penal reforms would require the expenditure of hundreds of millions of dollars for the construction and maintenance of new prisons.

In this case, our writer is clearly charging that the Conservative candidate's views are contradictory and should be rejected. In doing so she proposes a variant of the strong version of *reductio*. In keeping with our account of such arguments, the crux of this passage is the claim that it is inconsistent to advocate fiscal restraint and a costly new policy for penal reform.

We can show the validity of the proposed argument with the following propositional proof, which invokes the rule RAA.

a = The Conservative candidate proposes to add five years to the sentence of anyone committing a crime with a gun.

f = He is for fiscal restraint.

h = His programs would require the expenditure of hundreds of millions of dollars.

1. a   P
2. (h → -f) & (a → h)   P
3. h → -f   2, &E
4. a → h   2, &E
5. f   P/RAA (RAA Premise)
6. h   4, 1, AA
7. -f   3, 6, AA
8. f & -f   5, 7, &I
9. -f   4-7, RAA

Here the contradiction that we derive at line 8 shows that our *reductio* premise at line 4 must be mistaken, for it leads to this absurdity.

You have probably noticed that the rule RAA might, like the rule CR, be described as a process of constructing a proof within a proof. In one case, the subproof deduces a consequent from an antecedent. In the other, it deduces a contradiction from a hypothetical *reductio* premise. In both cases, the lines within the subproof we construct cannot be used elsewhere in our proof. In the case of RAA, this means that the lines beginning with our P/RAA and ending with our contradiction (lines 4-7 in our example) cannot be employed elsewhere in our proof. This stipulation ensures that the conclusions we deduce on the basis of our RAA premise are restricted to conclusions about what would be the case if it were true.

The weak version of RAA works in the same way as the strong version, but the contradiction it highlights is between someone's views and views that we ourselves assert. Consider a discussion in which someone argues that we must always return what has been borrowed from a friend when asked to do so. We may answer that 'always' allows for no exceptions and construct the following scenario: imagine that you have borrowed a gun for target shooting and your friend wants it back, but he has suffered a nervous breakdown and is determined to kill himself. Presumably we should not return the gun and it follows that the proposed ethical principle—that we should always return what has been borrowed when the original owner requests it—is mistaken.

We can prove the validity of this example of weak RAA as follows:

r = One should always return what was borrowed when the owner requests it.
g = One should return a gun to an owner who is bent on suicide.

1. r → g   P
2. -g   P
3. r   P/RAA
4. -r   1, 2, DC
5. r & -r   3, 4, &I
6. -r   3-5, RAA

In constructing this proof, we construct a weak RAA since the contradiction occurs because our opponent's position contradicts what we believe an audience of reasonable people will accept. In view of this, he or she may in principle reject -g (regardless of how odd that may seem to us) and we cannot be sure that he would find our reasoning convincing. Hence, our opponent may not be guilty of inconsistency in the strong sense. We can do little more than lament his poor judgement if he continues to maintain r and fails to show what is wrong with our argument against it.

Note that our last example could be proven valid by applying the rule DC to the premises. This is not surprising insofar as any propositional argument may be proven valid in a variety of ways. In this case it is notable that a proof using the rule DC is much simpler than a proof using the rule RAA and is, therefore, preferable in ordinary circumstances, though both succeed in proving the validity of our argument. We used the example that we did because it is a simple case of RAA that clearly illustrates the general form of *reductio* arguments.

3. DILEMMA

In ordinary language, a dilemma is a situation that asks us to choose between two alternatives, both of which are unpleasant. The following offhand comments offer a dilemma:

I feel sorry for politicians. Either they vote according to their own lights or vote as their constituents want. If they vote as their constituents want, they compromise their conscience; but if they vote according to their own lights, they alienate their constituents. So either they compromise their conscience or they alienate their constituents.

The word 'so' in this passage is a conclusion indicator, which makes it clear it is an argument. Reasoning like this has a specific logical structure governed by a rule of inference we will call 'dilemma'. Before we define it, we need note that it may also apply to situations in which the alternatives in question are both pleasant. An instance of the latter is found in the following argument, which has the same logical structure as the previous example.

> I won $200. If I celebrate by yielding to my gastronomic desires I'll indulge myself at the Restaurant *Elite*. If I celebrate by yielding to the aesthete in me I'll take in a play off Broadway. I'll yield to one or the other, so I'll dine at the *Elite* or see a play tonight.

The only unpleasant aspect of this 'dilemma' is the choice between the alternatives, which exclude each other. The form of this argument is none the less identical to the form of the first example and we will describe both as 'dilemmas'.

In propositional logic, we distinguish two kinds of dilemma argument. The examples we have already noted are governed by a rule we call 'dilemma to disjunction' (symbolized 'Dor') and defined as follows:

> Dor: For any statements w, x, y, and z, if w or x and w $\rightarrow$ y and x $\rightarrow$ z are true, then y or z is true.

The validity of Dor arguments can be understood in terms of our earlier discussions of disjunctions and conditionals. The initial disjunction in a Dor argument states that one of the disjuncts is true, but each affirms the antecedent of one of the conditionals, thereby justifying the conclusion that one of the consequents must be true.

We can prove the validity of our first example of dilemma by letting:

> l = He votes according to his own lights.
> c = He votes as his constituents want him to.
> h = He compromises his conscience.
> a = He alienates his constituents.

and by constructing the following propositional logic proof:

> 1. l or c   P
> 2. c $\rightarrow$ h   P
> 3. l $\rightarrow$ a   P
> 4. h or a   1, 2, 3, Dor

A second form of dilemma argument occurs when the two consequents of the premise conditionals are identical, as happens in the following example.

If I tell my boss how I bungled the contract, he'll fire me; and if he finds out from someone else, he'll fire me. Either I tell him myself or he'll find out from someone else. Woe is me! I'm about to be fired.

In dealing with this kind of dilemma we invoke the rule 'Dilemma', abbreviated 'D'. It works on the same principles as Dor but does not result in a disjunction.

D: If a disjunction is true and each disjunct implies z, then z is true.

Given the disjunction x or y and the conditionals x → z and y →z, the rule D allows us to validly infer the conclusion z. It can be used to prove the validity of our example as follows.

    b = I tell my boss how I bungled the contract.
    f = He'll fire me.
    s = He finds out from someone else.

    1. (b → f) & (s → f)   P
    2. b or s   P
    3. b → f   1, &E
    4. s → f   1, &E
    5. f   2, 3, 4, D

4. Answering a Dilemma

In discussing simple disjunctive arguments in the previous chapter, we noted that they are sometimes guilty of the fallacy 'false dilemma'. In a similar fashion, we acknowledge that dilemma arguments may be problematic. Two specific problems may arise.

First, a dilemma argument may be problematic because the initial disjunction may be a false dilemma: it may not exhaust the alternatives. This is not a concern if the disjuncts are contradictories, for then the law of the excluded middle tells us that there is no middle ground. If, on the other hand, the disjuncts are not contradictories, there may be some other alternative that allows us to 'escape' the dilemma by asserting this alternative.

A second problem arises when the implications asserted in a dilemma's conditionals are debatable. Here again, the problem is not the validity of the argument, which is guaranteed by the rule D or Dor. Rather the problem is premise acceptability, for the premises are mistaken or at least dubious.

In ordinary language, we have distinct expressions that we use when we talk about these two problems with dilemmas. When someone is faced with a dilemma, we say that they are caught on the 'horns' of a dilemma. 'Escaping between the horns of a dilemma' consists of showing that the disjunctive premise is false because it overlooks a legitimate alternative. 'Taking the dilemma by the horns' consists of showing a dilemma to be false because one (or both) of the conditionals it assumes is false.

The politician's dilemma with which we began might be answered by trying to escape through its horns. If we want to criticize it in this way, we must argue that it is guilty of false dilemma and thus simplifies the alternatives a politician faces. Politicians can, we may argue, reject the black and white alternatives offered and choose to vote according to their own lights on matters of conscience, and vote as the majority of their constituents want on other issues. By 'escaping between the horns' in this way, they need not compromise their consciences and will on many, or even most, issues please their constituents rather than alienate them.

We can illustrate the technique of taking a dilemma by the horns through another example. Imagine a woman who is contemplating an abortion. Suppose she reasons as follows:

If I have an abortion, I'll be haunted by guilt. But if I don't, I'll ruin my career. So I'll be haunted by guilt or I'll ruin my career.

If we let:

    a = I have an abortion.
    c = My career will be ruined.
    h = I'll be haunted by guilt.

then we can represent the argument as having the form:

    a or -a
    a → h
    -a → c
    Therefore, h or c

The disjunction this argument relies on ('Either I'll have an abortion or I won't') is clearly true. It follows that the only way to refute the argument is by taking the dilemma by the horns and arguing that one of the dilemma's conditionals is false, i.e., that either -(a → h) or -(-a → c). This we may attempt to do in any of our standard ways of arguing—by constructing an RAA argument, for example. Because such arguments raise very complex issues, we won't pursue this strategy here, except to say that the proponents of the different sides of the abortion debate are likely to take hold of different horns of the dilemma.

In principle, we support both attempts to escape through the horns of a dilemma and attempts to take it by the horns by developing propositional logic proofs, showing that the conclusion, the disjunction, or one of the conditionals is false. Any such proof would be very complex, however, so we shall treat the ways of refuting dilemmas more informally: by translating a dilemma into propositional logic symbols, and then by explaining where it goes wrong.

> **Box 9.1 Criticizing a Dilemma**
> Escaping between the horns of a dilemma consists of showing that the disjunctive premise is false because it overlooks a legitimate alternative.
> Taking the dilemma by the horns consists of showing a dilemma to be false because one (or both) of the conditionals it assumes is false.

5. DE MORGAN'S LAWS

The final form of propositional argument we will discuss also figures prominently in ordinary reasoning. It consists of one of two forms of argument called De Morgan's laws ('DeM' for short). They are named after the nineteenth-century British logician Augustus De Morgan and can be defined as follows:

DeM: 1. If a disjunction is false, then all its disjuncts are false, and vice versa.
 2. If a conjunction is false, then at least one of its conjuncts is false, and vice versa.

Essentially, De Morgan's laws establish equivalences that hold between certain kinds of conjunctions and disjunctions. Given two statements x and y, DeM(1) asserts that -(x or y) is equivalent to the conjunction -x & -y. DeM(2) asserts that -(x & y) is equivalent to the disjunction -x or -y.

Though the validity of DeM should be evident, we can easily illustrate it with an example. DeM(1) says the claim that I'll go to neither Salzburg nor London is equivalent to the claim that I won't go to Salzburg and I won't go to London. DeM(2) says that the falsity of the claim that I will go to Salzburg and to London is equivalent to the claim that I won't go to Salzburg or I won't go to London (perhaps neither).

The rule DeM is an effective way to move from conjunctions to disjunctions and vice versa in propositional logic proofs. We can illustrate its use by supposing that you won't pass your logic course unless the final exam counts for more than 50 per cent and you pass the mid-term exam. If you subsequently discover that either one of these conditions is not met, you can then deduce that you will not pass the course by letting:

p = You pass the mid-term exam.
f = The final counts for more than 50 per cent.
c = You pass the course.

and by reasoning as follows:

1. -(f & p) → -c   P
2. -f or -p   P
3. -(f & p)   2, DeM
4. -c   1, 3, AA

Note that there is no need to indicate which part of DeM the proof depends on, as that will be obvious to anyone who knows propositional logic.

We hasten to add that the reasoning in this last example is not necessarily good reasoning, once again because the premises are debatable. In *your* case, we are confident that such premises are false, so we will carry on with our discussion of forms of inference.

6. Summary: Rules of Inference

Having completed our examination of forms of propositional argument, we conclude this chapter by listing our new rules of inference in Box 9.2. You may use this for handy reference until you no longer need it.

As you go about constructing propositional logic proofs, keep in mind the guidelines for proof construction we discussed in our last chapter, for they are directly applicable here as well. It is important that you construct a proof in a step-by-step manner, proceeding from your premises to your conclusion. Keep in mind that one way to do this is by working back from your conclusion to your premises. Using these further rules of inference you may be able to move beyond an impasse in a complex proof by invoking the rule CR or RAA, for both allow you to introduce a provisional premise with which you can then work.

In conclusion, note that we have emphasized valid forms of argument in our account of propositional reasoning. This emphasis notwithstanding, we have also noted some invalid forms of argument and problems that commonly arise when we ask whether particular premises are acceptable. Even when we have a valid argument, it is an instance of good reasoning only if its premises are acceptable. If you keep this in mind, then your ability to detect validity should provide a good basis for the construction of good arguments.

> **Box 9.2 Complex Rules of Inference**
> CR: Introduce a premise x (listed as P/CR), infer y by propositional logic
>   rules of inference, and conclude that x → y. (Note that the lines of the
>   proof that lead from x to y cannot be used elsewhere in the proof.)
> RAA: Take any proposition as a *reductio* premise (P/RAA), deduce an absurd
>   consequence that leads to a contradiction, and conclude that the nega-
>   tion of the initial proposition must be true. (Note that the lines from
>   P/RAA to the contradiction may not be used elsewhere in the proof.)
> Dor: For any statements w, x, y, and z, if w or x and w → y and x → z are true,
>   then y or z is true.
> D: If a disjunction is true and each disjunct implies z, then z is true.
> DeM: 1. If a disjunction is false, then all its disjuncts are false, and vice versa.
>   2. If a conjunction is false, then at least one of its conjuncts is false, and
>   vice versa.

MAJOR EXERCISE 9M

1. Translate into propositional symbols and prove the validity of the following
   arguments. Use the indicated letters to represent simple sentences and use
   the rule CR to prove conditionals.
   a) [From an article on determinism—the view that we do not really choose
      to do what we do because our actions are caused by things beyond our
      control, such as heredity and environment.] If a man could not do other-
      wise than he in fact did, then he is not responsible for his action. But if
      determinism is true, then the agent could not have done otherwise in any
      action. Therefore, if determinism is true, no one is responsible for what
      he does. (d, o, r)
   b) If Nick does not become a poet, he will become a social worker or a doc-
      tor. If he is a social worker or a doctor, he will be financially better off
      but unhappy. So Nick will be unhappy if he doesn't become a poet. (p,
      s, d, f, h)
   *c) You can join the Air Force only if you're eighteen, so you can't join the
      Air Force unless you're eighteen. (j, e)
2. Provide a *reductio ad absurdum* argument for each of the following claims.
   Construct it in an ordinary English paragraph and then translate your argument into propositional logic and construct a proof of its validity.
   a) Every occurrence has a cause.
   *b) Religion fulfils some deep human need.
   c) 'Never tell a lie' is a rule that should not be followed in all circumstances.
   d) People in medieval times were wrong in thinking Earth saucer-shaped.
3. Set up propositional logic proofs of the following dilemmas. In each case, discuss briefly how you would attempt to refute the dilemma.

*a) The most unfair question one can ask a spouse is: 'If I die, would you marry again?' It's unfair because if one says 'yes', that will be taken to mean that one is waiting for his/her spouse to die; and if one says 'no', that will be taken to mean that one's marriage is not a happy one!

b) If we censor pornographic films, we will be denying people the right to make their own choices and thereby causing such people harm. But if we do not censor pornographic films, we run the risk of exposing society to crimes of a sexual nature committed by those who have been influenced by such films and thereby causing people harm. Either way, some people must be harmed.

d) Take, for example, the Chrysler worker with a home and family. If he tries to sell his home and seek employment elsewhere, he faces a substantial financial loss. On the other hand, if he stays on with frozen wages and guaranteed layoffs while the cost of living continues to spiral upwards, he still faces financial disaster. Some choice!

e) Death is one of two things. Either it is annihilation, and the dead have no consciousness of anything, or, as we are told, it is really a change—a migration of the soul from this place to another. Now if there is no consciousness but only (something like) a dreamless sleep, there is nothing to be afraid of. . . . If, on the other hand, death is a removal from here to some other place, then what we are told is true, and all the dead are there. But then we should look forward to meeting them. So death is nothing to be afraid of, gentlemen. (Adapted from Plato's *Apology*, 40c-41a)

4. Translate into symbols and prove the validity of the following chains of reasoning by using the rule DeM.

   a) The robbers took the Ming vase or the Buddhist statue, and she'll be angry if they're not both here. I don't want to be around when she gets angry, so I think that I should leave. (m, b, a)

   b) I saw Maryanne in Pittsburgh on the 13th at 2 p.m., so she couldn't have been in Toronto at that time. (p, t)

   c) A professor cannot be both a reputable scholar and a popular teacher. She is popular in the classroom, so she must have abandoned a life of reputable scholarship. (s, t)

   *d) Jacinth pulled through without complications, but Francis has a black eye the size of a football, Kirstin has a fever of 39 degrees, and I see that Fred or Paul is in the hospital. So it is false that Fred and Paul are well. (j, f, k, f, p)

5. Prove the validity of the following arguments:

   a) (b → c) and (c → b), -b, therefore -c.
   b) (a or b) → c, -(c or d), therefore -a.
   *c) -(a & b), a, therefore -b.
   *d) a & b & c & d, therefore c or e.
   e) -(a or b), a or c, therefore c.

f) -(a & b), a, therefore -b.

g) (b & c) → a, c, -a, therefore -b.

h) -(a & b), -a → c, -b → c, therefore c.

6. Prove the validity of the following arguments.

a) You'll get a passing or a failing grade on the exam. If you get a failing grade, then my confidence in you has been misplaced. But I'm sure my confidence has not been misplaced, so I'm sure you'll get a passing grade.

*b) If you do your homework assignments, you'll learn informal logic, and if you learn informal logic, you'll be a good reasoner. But if you're a good reasoner, you'll probably succeed in your chosen field. So you'll probably succeed in your chosen field if you do your homework assignments.

c) I hope the Prime Minister can use the forthcoming Commonwealth meetings to good advantage by persuading New Zealand to alter its sporting relationships with France after the latter's nuclear tests in Tahiti. If New Zealand continues to associate with France, Pacific Island nations will boycott the Commonwealth Games, and if they do that the Games will be cancelled. But if the Games are cancelled, millions of dollars spent in preparation and millions of athlete-hours spent in training will go down the drain. So if New Zealand continues to associate with France, millions of dollars and millions of athlete-hours will go down the drain.

*d) [Look for the hidden conclusion.] If you're a great singer, then you're Shakespeare and the moon is made out of green cheese. So there.

e) The murder of Sir Robert was motivated by the hatred he inspired or by a calculated desire to gain his fortune. If it was a calculated crime, it must have been perpetrated by both Lord Byron and his mistress, Kate; but if it was done out of hatred, then either the butler, Robert, or Lord Byron's brother, Jonathan, did it. Now Kate was too frightened a woman to have done it and Jonathan has the unassailable alibi of being in Brighton on the evening of the murder. Therefore, it's obvious the butler did it.

f) If you enjoyed both Hemingway and Faulkner, you'd like Steinbeck, but you despise Steinbeck, so you must dislike either Hemingway or Faulkner.

g) It will rain if and only if the wind changes, but the wind will change if and only if a high pressure area moves in and a high pressure area will move in if and only if the arctic front moves southward. It follows that it will rain if the arctic front moves southward.

*h) According to a famous story in Greek philosophy, the great sophist Protagoras agreed to give Euthalus instruction in law on the following terms: Euthalus was to pay half of the fee in advance and the remainder if and when he won his first case. After the instruction, Euthalus did not take any cases and Protagoras grew impatient waiting for the remainder of his payment. He finally took Euthalus to court himself, arguing as follows: Either the court will decide for me or against me. If it decides for me, then Euthalus must pay. If it decides against me, then Euthalus has won his first case in court. But if he wins his first case in court, then he must pay me (for that is our agreement). So Euthalus must pay me.

i) [Euthalus learned his logic well, and replied as follows.] Protagoras is wrong, for either the court will decide for or against me. If it decides for me, then I do not have to pay. But if it decides against me, then I have lost my first case in court. But if I lose my first case in court, then I do not have to pay (for that is our agreement). So I do not have to pay.

j) If the patient has a bacterial infection, she will have a fever. If she does not have a bacterial infection, then a virus is the cause of her illness. So, if she has no fever, she must be ill from a virus.

k) Either I'll go to France or I won't. If I go, I'll have an interesting time and send you a card from Metz. If I don't go to France, I'll go to Spain and send you a card from Barcelona. But if I go to Barcelona, I'll have an interesting time, so I'll have an interesting time no matter what.

l) It is wrong to think that we can both value life and be opposed to abortion and birth control. If everyone in the world were against abortion and birth control, can you imagine the terrible poverty, the starvation, the suffering? We would literally have wall-to-wall people, the whole world would be one big slum like we see in South American countries. Life wouldn't be worth living. (*Toronto Sun*, 10 Feb. 1983)

*m) [Adapted from Jack Miller, Science Column, *Toronto Star*, 9 June 1987, p. A14] Kepler offered the theory [that the night sky should be an unbroken canopy of starlight] . . . to disprove the then popular idea that the universe stretched forever and was filled with an infinite number of stars. If that was true, he said, then there would be so many stars that no matter which way you looked at night, you would see one. In every direction there would be a star at some distance or other. There would be no dark spaces between the spots of light, so the sky would be all light. And since the sky obviously is dark at night, the universe does not stretch out forever, or does not have an infinite number of stars in it.

n) [From an article on Senator John Glenn in the *Manchester Guardian Weekly*, 23/10/83] 'We are not flying into that and there's no way around it,' he told the small band of aides and correspondents. . . There was no argument. . . . When one of the world's greatest pilots says it isn't safe, you don't fly.

7. Using the information provided, deduce by means of propositional logic proofs answers to the questions asked.

a) [*Will someone from the humanities be appointed president of the university you plan to attend?*] The president has just turned 46. She is a responsible person but her birthday has been spoiled by a financial scandal. Now she is in trouble with the board of governors or senate. If the board of governors are unhappy, they'll fire her and she'll go somewhere else. If she goes somewhere else, one of the vice-presidents will be appointed president. But the vice-presidents are from the humanities. (The president is from physics.) If the senate is unhappy with the president, they'll make it impossible for her to carry out her programs, and no responsible person will stay in those conditions.

*b) [*Are you likely to survive?*] You are at sea in a terrible storm. You can run for a lifeboat or stay where you are. If you run for it, then you will be lost at sea. If you don't run you will be safe unless the storm continues. If the storm continues you can survive only if you run to one of the lifeboats. If the sky is dark, the storm is likely to continue. You look up and sea a dark and stormy sky.

8. Prove that the following forms of argument are valid and provide a sample argument to illustrate the form in question.

   *a) (p or q) & -(p & q), p, therefore, -q.

   b) p or q, therefore q or p.

   *c) p → q, therefore -q → -p.

   d) -r → p, -p & q, s → -r, therefore -s.

   e) (a → b) & (b → a), therefore (a & b) or (-a & -b).

   f) The law of the excluded middle (i.e., p or -p) from no premises.

   *g) The law of non-contradiction (i.e. -(p & -p)) from no premises.

   h) p & (q or r), therefore (p & q) or (p & r).

*9. THE CASE OF THE MISSING BROTHER: A case from the files of Super Sleuth.

   I still remember it clearly. That day I burst into your office with the news. I was flustered, but you sat there cool and unmoved.

   'Calm down', you said, 'and tell me what's the matter.'

   'He's gone', I spluttered. 'He's disappeared!'

   'It happens all the time', you mused philosophically.

   'But he was here just yesterday, and now he's gone—poof—like a little puff of smoke.'

   'Calm down', you said again. 'Calm down and tell me all the details.'

   So it began, the case of the missing brother. You've probably had more exciting cases, but it required a tidy bit of deduction, as far as I recall . . .

   So much for intro. It's up to you to solve the case. The goal is to determine what happened to Louis, the missing brother. Was he kidnapped? murdered? something else? Who perpetrated the crime? What, if any, were the weapons used? And where is Louis now? To deduce the right conclusion, work your way through each day of the case file below. From the information gathered on each day, you should be able to construct a propositional proof that provides some relevant information (e.g., that 'If Mary did it, revenge must have been her motive'). By the time you solve the case, you should be more comfortable constructing proofs in propositional logic.

Example:

Day 1. You discover that one of the suspects, Joe, would have done something to Louis if and only if (1) he needs a lot of money or (2) he and Louis were still rivals. Yet you discover that Joe doesn't need any money (he's rolling in it!) and that Louis and Joe are no longer rivals.

Let: j = Joe is the culprit.
　　　 m = Joe needs a lot of money.
　　　 r = Joe and Louis are rivals.

Then we can deduce the conclusion that Joe is not the culprit:

1. (j → (m or r)) & ((m or r) → j)　　P
2. -m & -r　　　　　　　　　　　　　　P
3. -(m or r)　　　　　　　　　　　　　 2, DeM
4. j → (m or r)　　　　　　　　　　　　1, &E
5. -j　　　　　　　　　　　　　　　　　4, 3, DC

Now you're on your own.

Day 2. Louis runs a house for homeless men in Montreal. If he was working on Thursday (the day of his disappearance), he would have been serving the men dinner at 5:00 p.m. If he was serving dinner, then Michael and Leo (two of the homeless men) would have seen him. Michael didn't see him. [If you can't sort out what conclusion you should try to prove, then turn to the answers at the end.]

Day 3. If Louis wasn't working, he must have been headed to the grocery store or have gone for a run when he left on Thursday morning. If he goes for groceries, he walks past 121 rue Frontenac where there is a big dog chained to the post. Whenever he walks past the big dog at 121 rue Frontenac, it barks furiously. The dog did not bark on Thursday morning. [Begin your deduction with what you proved on Day 2, i.e., use it as your first premise.]

Day 4. A psychic (who's always right) says Louis is kidnapped or lost. If he's lost, he can't be in Montreal (he knows it too well). If he's kidnapped and in Montreal, the police would have found him. They haven't. [Try an RAA.]

Day 5. I receive a note demanding a ransom of a thousand dollars. The note is either from Louis and the real kidnappers or from someone trying to make some easy money. If they wanted to make some easy money, I wouldn't have received a note asking for a thousand dollars (which will be hard to get from a poor man like myself). If it is from the real kidnappers, then they and Louis are in Quebec City. [Deduce a conjunction answering the following two questions: Is the note from the real kidnappers? and where is Louis?]

Day 6. Checking on the suspects, you find that Mary is awfully squeamish. This tells you that she had a hand in Louis's disappearance if and only if she hired someone else to do her dirty work. If she hired someone, it would be Joe and Betty Anne, or her brother Ted. But we already know that Joe is not the culprit.

Day 7. An anonymous phone caller tells you that Louis is held captive by some strange cult called Cabala (there's more to this case than meets the eye). If she's right, Chloe will know about it, though she won't say anything. Yet if Chloe or Sam knows about it, Bud will tell you if you slip him a twenty. You slip him a twenty and he has nothing to tell.

Day 8. Arriving in Quebec City, looking for some leads, you see Mugsy. There are three reasons why Mugsy might be here. Either he is going to mail another note, or he's helping hold Louis in Quebec City, or he's vacationing. If he's mailing another note, he's a culprit, and if he's helping hold Louis he's a culprit. As you go to find out, Mugsy sees you and runs down an alley before you can apprehend him. He wouldn't be running away if he were vacationing.

Day 9. An anonymous phone caller tells you that the whole case is 'A SP___', but he chokes and the phone goes dead after he gets out the first three letters. No one would have killed the caller unless he was right.

Day 10. Mugsy has been reported going into an old warehouse. You sneak in the back door and along a narrow corridor. There are two doors at the end of the hall. The police have said that Louis must be held in one of these two rooms. A thick layer of dust covers the door on the left.

Day 10 ½. Your heart pounds. You slip your pistol out of your pocket and bust through the door. Much to your chagrin, there's no one there. [This requires a revision of the conclusion reached on Day 10. Using your new information, go back to it and prove that the police were wrong when they said that Louis must be in one of these two rooms. Use a *reductio* argument.]

Day 11. You turn to the other door at the back of the warehouse. It leads to the only other room in the warehouse. You know that this is the warehouse Mugsy entered and he would have entered it only if Louis was captive here.

Day 12. The minutes seem like hours as you sneak to the door and quietly open it. You see Louis, Mary, and Mugsy sharing a bottle of good French wine, laughing at how upset I must be. If this were a serious kidnapping, they would not be laughing.

Day 13. Having discovered the whole thing is a spoof, you deduce the motive and the reason why Mary and Ted were involved when you note that either Louis or Mary wanted to fool me; that whoever wanted to fool me must have had a lot of money; that Mary and Mugsy are broke; and that if Louis wanted to fool me, Mary and Mugsy must have participated because he paid them.

Day 14. You wonder whether you should charge me the full rate, given that it was all a spoof. You believe you should get paid the full rate if you did the regular amount of work, however, so . . .

Day 15. Not having my brother's sense of humour, and thinking that one should pay for the consequences of one's actions, I decide that I should . . .

ASSESSING

THE

BASICS

The last four chapters dealt with arguments the structures of which meant that the conclusions followed necessarily from the premises, if those premises were acceptable. In this chapter we take up the question of premise acceptability as well as the type of good arguments that don't have premises that guarantee the conclusions. It introduces:

- ◆ ordinary reasoning and probability;
- ◆ acceptability;
- ◆ relevance;
- ◆ sufficiency; and
- ◆ applies these basics to an extended argument.

Our concern in chapters 6, 7, 8, and 9 focused around valid forms of arguments that purport to give conclusions that necessarily follow from a set of premises. Checking the validity of such arguments is a necessary and important task. But it is also a very narrow aspect of what goes into good reasoning.

For the purposes of testing an argument for validity, we assumed the truth of the premises. We saw that it is quite possible to have a valid argument in which the component statements are false. Validity simply means it is impossible for the premises of an argument to be true and the conclusion false. In other words, it means that if the premises are true, then the conclusion would have to be true. That's a big 'if'. Now we must focus on whether the premises are acceptable claims.

In ascertaining facts, the other major category of arguments plays a particularly significant role. Arguments of this kind offer varying degrees of probability for their conclusions, but do not pretend to guarantee them. It is to such reasoning that we often turn to decide whether the premises of a valid argument are factually reliable and, generally, whether any given factual claim warrants our belief.

1. ORDINARY REASONING AND PROBABILITY

When we ask concerning any claim whether it is true, we are asking whether it is acceptable. By this we understand that it should describe some state of affairs, that it should accord with reality, and that it should be acknowledged by a universal audience with access to appropriate specialized knowledge.

The truth or falsity of a claim that purports to be factual can be decided in a variety of ways. One way is to construct a valid argument leading to the claim in question. In the argument: 'If Susan wants to date the taller man, then she should date John, because John is taller than Jim', the truth of the premise 'John is taller than Jim' may be established by the further argument: 'If John is taller than Bill, he is taller than Jim. Since John is taller than Bill, he must be taller than Jim.' Proving the truth of a claim in this way simply pushed the question of truth back a step, since the truth of the premises of the supporting argument would then need to be established.

The alternative is to seek to establish facts by appealing to the kinds of reasoning that extrapolate from what we already know. In this kind of reasoning, unlike the forms of argument we studied in Chapters 6–9, the truth of a set of premises does not guarantee the truth of a conclusion, but establishes them with some degree of probability.

The role of this kind of reasoning in determining factual claims can be illustrated with reference to the claim 'All astronomers are highly educated people.' You will recall that this is a premise in the following syllogism:

All astronomers are highly educated people.
All highly educated people are assets to society.
_____
All astronomers are assets to society.

This, as we have seen, is a valid argument. Its strength depends on the truth of its premises. The first premise, 'All astronomers are highly educated people', seems a reasonable enough assertion, given our experience.

But this last phrase should give us pause. Clearly we do not have experience of all professional astronomers (we'll set aside the amateurs for this point), and certainly not with regard to their education. We believe that, given the complexity of their discipline, all previous professional astronomers have been highly educated people, and we are prepared to project this belief onto present and future professional astronomers. But it is at least logically conceivable that the occasional charlatan may slip into the ranks of professional astronomers or that society and its institutions may change so as to require less rigorous standards of education of its astronomers.

Whatever can be conceived without contradiction is at least theoretically possible even though, on the basis of past experiences, we may consider it quite improbable. Our point is that 'All astronomers are highly educated people' cannot be known with certainty because we do not and never will have all the evidence we would require to draw a necessary conclusion. 'All astronomers are highly educated people' is, then, only probable and has been arrived at through reasoning that supports a high degree of probability.

Since good reasoning of any kind depends on the acceptability of premises, we must recognize from the outset that premises purporting to be factual claims can only be established with some degree of plausibility or probability. This is because claims about the world depend on our experience within it, which is always open-ended. We will never have all the experience we require to establish such claims with certainty.

Generally we believe that future experiences will conform to our past experiences. We expect the egg shell to break when we hit it against the lip of the bowl. We expect the road to be slippery when it is covered with ice. To lesser degrees, we expect to be happy with our new car if we have been happy with five previous models built by the same manufacturer, and we expect we will enjoy the latest Stephen King novel because we have enjoyed all his previous novels.

The danger is that the regularity of our experience will lead us to assume certainty where only probability is warranted. The egg does not *have* to break. They always have in the past, but nothing in logic demands that this should hold in the future. And the same applies to our other examples. The point is that we cannot draw any *necessary* conclusion about the breaking of eggs because not all of the data are in. Given that the source of our belief is experience of the world, it is in principle impossible to justify factual claims as necessarily true.

The Scottish philosopher David Hume was making just this point when he argued that all of our expectations about the world are based on no more than habit. We see things have been a particular way in the past, and we conclude that they must continue to be that way in the future, that there is necessity in the world. But no sound argument can support this reasoning. This does not change the way we live. As Hume pointed out, the regularities in experience give us enough probabilities to enable us to get by quite comfortably.

Although our experience does not yield certainty, it does tell us something about our world and, as a consequence, the kinds of reasonable conclusions we can draw. Conclusions drawn from arguments about conditions in the world and the states of affairs between human beings will be probable or improbable to greater or lesser degrees, but they will never be certain. This lack of certainty underscores the importance of good reasoning in our efforts to determine what we consider to be 'the facts' about the world and ourselves.

Criteria for Assessing Probable Reasoning

In Chapter 5 we introduced basic criteria for good reasoning: acceptable premises and a conclusion that follows from those premises. When we turn to the construction of good arguments that do not purport to guarantee their conclusions the specific criteria that concern us are: acceptability, relevance, and sufficiency. These same criteria must be employed in analysing the arguments of others, of course. In introducing various specific argument forms, such as causal arguments and analogies, we will formulate in each case more specific criteria by way of applying the general criteria. But, should we fail to identify a given argument form, we can still do a good job of assessing the overall strengths and weaknesses of a piece of reasoning by applying these general criteria. Consequently, it is important that we investigate each of these criteria in detail before demonstrating how they can be jointly employed in the assessment of extended arguments.

2. ACCEPTABILITY

It is important that we distinguish between the acceptability of an argument and the acceptability of its premises. To make an overall judgement about the strength or weakness of a particular argument requires that we consider all the criteria appropriate to good reasoning. We will illustrate the assessment of an argument's acceptability at the end of this chapter and in the final chapter of the text.

Here we are concerned with the acceptability of the premises. In judging acceptability, whether we are assessing another's claims or supporting our own, we ask whether the specific audience being addressed, along with a universal audience of reasonable people, would accept the statement without further support.

For each premise provided in support of a conclusion, ask yourself whether evidence conflicts with the statement that directly undermines its claim to be acceptable, or whether you lack the evidence needed to decide either way. In the first case, the premise is unacceptable and there are grounds for rejecting it. It may conflict with a known state of affairs existing in the world, or it may be rejected by definition, or it may be inconsistent with another premise in the same argument. We will consider each of these ways of being unacceptable in due course. In the second case, the premise is questionable. It cannot be accepted as given but we do not have grounds to judge that the statement itself is unacceptable. However, given that the onus is on the arguer to provide acceptable premises, the presence of questionable ones is a weakness in the argument.

For your part, you must support your judgement that a premise is questionable by indicating what evidence would make it acceptable. That is, what are you looking for that has not been provided? You may find that, when you scrutinize a premise this way, what you had thought to be questionable is in fact unacceptable since the evidence that would be required to make it acceptable could not, in principle, exist.

For example, an arguer claims that women who object to men watching Playboy television are selfish because (and here is the first premise) 'The hormonal chemistry of the sexes is such that women do not derive pleasure from watching semi-nude buxom blondes.' At first blush this premise appears to be questionable: no support is provided for it; on the other hand, we have no initial reason to reject it. But when we ask what sort of evidence we *would* need to accept this statement we begin to recognize it as a quasi-scientific claim. It purports to depict a *fact* about women generally and the relationship between their chemical make-up and what they are able to enjoy. Minimally, what we require here is some social-scientific study to corroborate this. Of course, the existence of women who do derive pleasure in this way creates a state of affairs that contradicts the generality of the premise and is a reason to reject it.

But a further premise the arguer provides is even more problematic: 'Women derive analogous sexual titillation from soap operas and romance novels.' No matter how charitable we wish to be, this premise seems unsupportable in principle. It is difficult to conceive of a legitimate scientific study that would corroborate this statement (particularly the 'analogous' part). Hence, a premise that seemed questionable is, on reflection, judged unacceptable.

Remember that it is never enough to simply dismiss a premise as unacceptable or questionable. Those judgements must be supported by the grounds for the unacceptability or a statement of what is missing that is needed for acceptability/unacceptability to be decided.

Box 10.1 Determining Acceptability

There are three decisions we can make with respect to a claim's acceptability:

(i) It is *acceptable* without further support.
    The statement itself is of such a nature, or it is supported by other statements, such that the audience will accept it.

(ii) It is *unacceptable*. That is, the statement conflicts with what is known to be the case such that the audience (and evaluator) has reason to reject it.

(iii) It is *questionable*. The statement is neither acceptable nor clearly unacceptable because insufficient information is presented to decide either way.

Belief Systems and Acceptability

In judging acceptability, we need to consider it in relation to our audiences. In Chapter 4, we distinguished between a specific audience that shared particular commitments and a universal audience consisting of reasonable people. As a prerequisite to the acceptance of our conclusions, the premises and assumptions on which our argument is based must be acceptable to our immediate audience. Our audience must be able to understand their meaning and assent to them without further support. If our audience consists of rational people, their acceptance of our premises will, of course, remain open to revision in the event that new data come to light.

A central consideration in fairly evaluating acceptability is the role of perspective in reasoning. In addressing ourselves briefly to the problems of communication in Chapter 1, we saw that communication is rendered difficult by virtue of the fact that communicators are 'persons', individuals distinct from one another in terms of their heredity, background experiences, conditioning influences, loves, loyalties, values, commitments, politics, religion, and other involvements. These factors constitute for each of us a system of beliefs and commitments.

Such systems have an enormous impact on the way we argue and the claims for which we argue, as well as the way we assess acceptability. It is important for us to examine the notion of belief systems in order to become more sensitive to the nature of audiences and appreciate further the context within which arguments take place. Understanding the nature of belief systems will prove helpful to us both as we construct arguments and as we evaluate the arguments of others.

All our arguments are formed within a belief system and conform, whether or not we realize it, to the world view or perspective that we have adopted. The make-up of the belief system comprises a number of factors, of which some are with us from early in our development and others are more transitory. Our birth determines our sex, race, nationality (although this can change), and, often, our religion. Among the more transitory components are the careers we choose, the organizations and clubs we join, and the friendships we form. We can also think of other associations or commitments that do not fit neatly into either of these categories. Many people reject or change an earlier religious perspective, for example, and this has a major and often dramatic effect on their world view. Again, some of our strongest attachments, such as those to parents or siblings, arise at birth, whereas attachments to our children arise later in life.

Our commitments and beliefs are integrated to the point that it is usually difficult to determine which have been inherited and which originate with us. They define our self-identity, comprise our personal perspective, and give rise to the opinions we hold. Strong opinions, in turn, are the embryos from which arguments develop.

Even when we engage in legitimate reasoning, deeply held beliefs may still influence our arguments in ways we do not expect. Quite often this is evident not so much in what we say, but in the assumptions behind our reasoning and the consequences that follow from it. Consider the following excerpt from an extended argument by George Grant (from 'The Case Against Abortion', *Today Magazine*, 3 Oct. 1981, pp. 12–13). Opposed to abortions for convenience, he introduces into the debate an unusual consideration:

> Mankind's greatest political achievement has been to limit ruthlessness by a system of legal rights. The individual was guarded against the abuses of arbitrary power, whether by state or by other individuals. Building this system required the courage of many. *It was fundamentally based on the assumption that human beings are more than just accidental blobs of matter. They have an eternal destiny and therefore the right to rights.* But the large-scale destruction of human beings by abortion questions that view.

We have italicized the two sentences important to what concerns us. Our system of legal rights, Grant insists, is 'based on the assumption that human beings are more than just accidental blobs of matter.' What this 'more' is, he tells us, is that human beings have a 'right to rights' because they 'have an eternal destiny'. An 'eternal destiny' stands in contrast to being an 'accidental blob'. This must mean that we are planned, that our existence is intentional, that there is something eternal or immortal about us, presumably as individuals. All this makes us more than 'accidental blobs'. Ours is a planned, spiritual existence. But planned by whom? Though no mention is made of 'God', belief in a deity is implied.

In drawing out Grant's meaning, we have strayed far from what is stated, but reasonably so. There is ample reason to conclude that Grant's reasoning is grounded in a religious commitment, that he believes we are part of a divine plan. Although this is never stated, it is implied by and follows as a consequence from what is stated.

Elements of our belief systems can have a conscious or unconscious influence on our arguments. Given that our beliefs can show up in the implications and consequences of what we say, it is important that we identify them if we are intent on convincing our audience. Failure to do so explains why so many arguers miss each other's meaning and why premises we deem acceptable are judged unacceptable by others. Grant's argument needs to be reinforced because his premises are unlikely to be accepted by people who do not share his religious beliefs.

We cannot remove our belief system to prevent its influence, nor is it necessary or advisable to try to do so. Our belief system is an integral part of us; to deny it is to deny ourselves. But we must guard against its unconscious or illegitimate influence on our reasoning by being aware of it. Awareness of it requires self-evaluation. We should ask ourselves why we are members of certain audiences. What is it that we hold in common? Which beliefs and commitments do we hold most strongly, and how did they arise? As we construct a profile of our belief system, we can begin to assess the impact of our commitments and associations on our thinking and actions.

Beyond sex, race, religion, and nationality, we should reflect on our educational background—commitments to schools and to a segment of society educated at our level, as well as the beliefs that arise from our economic and social environment and how these influence our views on society, social standing, and politics. We should reflect, too, on our value system—where it comes from and the commitments it entails, personally, nationally, and globally.

Such reflections will give us a profile of our belief system and help us to understand why we reason as we do. It is one thing to discuss how we would construct arguments defending capital punishment or opposing censorship. But it is quite a different matter to ask why we would come to argue such issues in the first place and why we happen to view the issues the way we do. At some deep level both these activities are connected.

If you catch yourself responding emotionally to an issue instead of employing reasoned argument, you will have to judge the acceptability of your emotive claims. For this, familiarity with your belief system is essential. But we encourage you to test the rationality of your beliefs. Emotional responses are not necessarily irrational. But are they reasonable? Are you able to support your passionately held beliefs with good and sufficient reasons? You need not give up such a belief because you may yet discover rational support for it. But if you cannot support it at present, you should be aware that this is the case and that you will have little success convincing a reasonable audience.

Belief Systems and Audiences

What we have said about ourselves as arguers also applies to audiences—both the audiences of which we may be a part and the audiences we may have occasion to address. The belief systems of an audience predispose its members toward certain claims and arguments. Familiarity with the belief systems of audiences enables us to judge more effectively what is required to ensure the acceptability of the premises of an argument.

If you are a person with a college or university education, you are likely to favour the maintenance and support of universities and colleges and to see them as playing a valuable role in society. Accordingly, you are likely to be sympathetic to arguments proposing a reasonable level of government funding for the university system. The extent of your sympathy is also likely to affect the degree of evidence you will require to be convinced. An arguer does not need to provide you with evidence that a university education is valuable; this can be assumed. She need only provide reasonable grounds for believing the universities are underfunded, and you will agree with her conclusion for increased funding. But convincing people without your educational background may require much more evidence. They are not necessarily sympathetic to the cause and will not accept without further support the premise that a university or college education is valuable.

As we saw in the discussion of bias in Chapter 1, there is a danger that our sympathies for a cause or position may make us lax in our critical assessment of an argument supporting it. We may not give such arguments the same scrutiny we reserve for neutral arguments or those supporting causes we do not favour. It is difficult to be objective in such cases, but it is important that we attempt to be. Just because we believe there are good arguments in favour of a position does not mean that the next one we see supporting that position will be good. We can strengthen the general support for a position we hold by pointing out the flaws in arguments made for it and by showing how those flaws may be remedied or avoided. On the basis of other reasons, we may accept the conclusion of an argument without accepting the premises supporting it, just as we may agree that a conclusion follows necessarily from its premises but reject the premises.

These comments also apply to our audiences. They, too, have belief systems that a responsible reasoner will not exploit. While our arguments may quite legitimately touch the hearts of our audiences, our primary obligation as responsible thinkers is to consider their minds and speak to them with reasoned arguments. Generally, you can anticipate three types of specific audience: one *sympathetic* to what you are arguing; one not predisposed to your position but *open* to considering it (this is also a key characteristic of the universal audience); and one *hostile* to your position.

While each of these audiences requires the same standards of argumentation, it should be easier to convince an audience of the acceptability of a claim if they share your perspective than if they do not. The hostile audience will be the hardest to convince and your skill as a critical thinker is put to the test when you address such an audience. Doing so demands that you be sensitive to the belief system the members of such an audience share. Quite often, the only way they will be convinced of your point is if you can get them to see it *from their perspective*. Think carefully about the shift of focus this entails. It requires that you think in terms that are hostile to your own position. This audience, more than any other, asks for a reason to be convinced. Its members expect you to consider them and what they believe and argue to *this*.

Audience consideration is not a casual feature of arguing well. Awareness of the belief system of an audience is one of the more important prerequisites for effective argumentation. Without it, all your skills in structuring arguments may prove worthless. Your aim in arguing with a hostile audience is to bring about a change in their thinking. Make it a point to meet people where they are, to understand the thinking on their side, and to lead them from there.

One important qualification concerns the acceptance of standards held by the universal (or ideal) audience—that audience comprised of reasonable, objective people. This consideration always has greater priority over any specific audience you address, because the universal audience is governed by the principles of good reasoning. With the specific audience we aim to respect the beliefs they hold, the assumptions behind their perspective, and the particular knowledge to which they have access. If the principles of good reasoning and the entrenched beliefs of an audience conflict, it is reasonable to favour the former. This way we avoid the apparent trap of treating as 'reasonable' the arguments of fanatics, racists, and their ilk. The following captures this division in a general condition of acceptability:

Premise Acceptability:
A premise is judged acceptable if
(i)   it would be accepted *without further* support by the audience for which it is intended, given the background knowledge of its members and the beliefs and values they hold,

and

(ii)   it conforms to (does not violate), alone or in combination with other premises, the principles of good reasoning.

What do we mean here by 'the principles of good reasoning'? Generally, we have been discussing such principles throughout this text and will continue to do so. You should already have a fairly developed sense of the kinds of things a reasonable audience will accept. What follows are some key ways in which a premise can be judged acceptable for a universal (and often specific) audience.

Universal Conditions of Acceptability
(i) Acceptable by definition or self-evidently acceptable.
One way to establish a factual claim is by appealing to definitions. We know from the meanings of its component terms that the statement 'All squares are four-sided figures' must be acceptable. Closely linked to the appeal to definitions is the recognition of a claim as self-evident. 'Your phone bill will be more, less, or the same as last month's bill' is obviously the case because it exhausts all the possibilities with respect to this month's bill. Sometimes we appeal to moral principles we take to be self-evident. 'One should not cause unnecessary pain' is an example of a moral principle many people consider to be self-evident.

Claims that are acceptable by virtue of the meaning of the terms relate to how we use language and so rely to some extent on what is commonly known (as will be discussed below). But they are the strongest type of such claims, because if we attempt to deny them we commit absurdities or contradictions. Thus, there is no onus on the arguer to support such claims. Any support would be redundant.

(ii) Acceptable as a factual statement reporting immediate perception or as a statement of personal testimony.

Immediate perception is another way of establishing the acceptability of some claims. It is on this basis that we would determine whether it is or is not the case that 'There has been virtually no snowfall during the last few hours.' If someone presents us with such a statement, we really have no grounds to reject it unless it contradicts our perception of the same event.

This leads to the more difficult cases of claims that are based on a person's own testimony and are not verifiable by shared perceptions. While carrying less force as evidential statements for conclusions, such appeals to personal testimony often arise in argumentation and we need to deal with them. In general, we have no reason to dispute what someone claims to have experienced. If people want to convince audiences it is in their interests to be truthful and we can grant statements such as 'I have driven my Toyota every day for two years without any mechanical problem' as acceptable based on the personal testimony of the utterer.

There are obvious qualifications to this, and we need to be cautious. If a person has proved repeatedly to be untrustworthy, then that is a reason not to accept what he or she says. Likewise, if the statement lacks plausibility, as with a claim that someone was removed from his car in broad daylight and taken up into an alien spacecraft, then we are justified in not accepting it. We expect personal testimony claims to conform to the general structure of experience.

(iii) Acceptable by common knowledge.

Both of the first two conditions bear on common experience in some way, but common knowledge is so often invoked as a reason for the acceptability of a statement that we need to treat it cautiously. Students tend to believe that virtually any claim can form part of some community's shared experience and so judge claims accordingly. This is where we need to consider both the specific audience being addressed and the underlying universal audience. Important also is the distinction between descriptive claims and evaluative claims. 'The government has proposed a separate justice system for minority groups' is a descriptive claim—it simply describes a state of affairs. 'The government's proposed separate justice system for minority groups is an outrage' is an evaluative claim; it conveys the same information as the descriptive claim but adds an assessment of it. The first statement may be common knowledge within a community; the second is not.

Under 'common knowledge' we are judging factual claims of a descriptive nature that we can *expect* to be *commonly* known. Two terms emphasized here need to be considered in more detail. The breadth of the common knowledge depends on the nature of the topic being argued and the goals of the arguer. We could dismiss a lot of the premises aimed at specific audiences because they report or depend on information not generally known by a larger (universal) audience. But that is being uncharitable. Unless the argument is specifically aimed at a universal audience or has overstepped the boundary between descriptive and evaluative claims, we can allow statements based on the common knowledge of the community being addressed.

At the other extreme, people sometimes reject statements because they are not commonly known by all members of an audience. This again is uncharitable and points to the need to consider what we might reasonably *expect* an audience to know. For the most part, we do not know what is actually known by all individuals making up audiences and communities. We cannot see into other minds, and certainly not the minds of large groups of people. To this extent 'common knowledge' is a bit of a misnomer. But we do know what we expect people to know, that is, what they have access to in their daily lives. We live in environments where certain ideas and information are readily available, and by appealing to these environments we can make sense of the common knowledge condition. Thus when we speak of common knowledge we are not speaking about what people actually know, but what we can reasonably expect them to know given the environments in which they live and work. This allows us to accommodate those individuals who don't know what everyone else does.

So the common knowledge condition is a judgement we make about environments, and we make that judgement considering the universality of the argument and the audience being addressed. Thus we can, generally, allow statements like 'The Roman Catholic Church does not allow women to be priests' or 'The Soviet Union disbanded in 1991' because these are common bits of information that form part of the environments of most people.

More difficult is a statement like 'The United Nations' Fourth World Conference on Women was held in Beijing.' People's access to this information depends on how widely it has been reported in their communities, on how much media exposure has been given to it. Also, it will be of greater interest to some audiences than to others. We would allow for these things in judging its use in a premise. But insofar as the audience was appropriate, and the statement is descriptive rather than evaluative, it is the kind of statement that could pass as common knowledge for a specific audience.

(iv) Acceptable due to its being defended in a reasonable sub-argument.
When we judge the acceptability of premises, what we expect is that an arguer will support those premises that would not be otherwise acceptable to the audience being addressed. Where an arguer has fulfilled this obligation, and the support provided is reasonable, then we have grounds for finding the supported premise to be acceptable. Of course, once supported in this way, the premise

in question becomes a conclusion. But when we evaluate the acceptability of an argument's premises it is important not to overlook subconclusions because these also constitute premises for the main claim. Consider the following:

> It seems jurors are more willing to convict for murder since the abolition of the death penalty. The over-all conviction rate for capital punishment was about 10 per cent for 1960–1974. From 1976, when capital punishment was abolished, until 1982, the conviction rate for first degree murder was about 20 per cent. There is reason to believe, then, that the consequence of returning capital punishment to Canada will be to see more murderers sent back onto the streets by reluctant juries. (From a report of the research and statistics group of the Department of the Solicitor-General of Canada. Source: *The Globe and Mail*, 9 Jan. 1987)

We can diagram the four statements of this argument as follows:

1. [Canadian] jurors are more willing to convict for murder since the abolition of the death penalty.
2. The over-all conviction rate for capital punishment was about 10 per cent for 1960–1974.
3. From 1976, when capital punishment was abolished, until 1982, the conviction rate for first degree murder was about 20 per cent.
4. There is reason to believe that the consequence of returning capital punishment to Canada will be to see more murderers sent back onto the streets by reluctant juries.

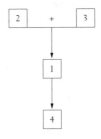

When evaluating the acceptability of the premises in this argument we begin with statement 1, which is a premise in support of the main claim, 4. Statement 1, '[Canadian] jurors are more willing to convict for murder since the abolition of the death penalty', is a controversial, interpretive statement, and even the specific audience of the Canadian public could not accept it as it stands. Recognizing this, the authors have provided the statistical data needed to support 1 in statements 2 and 3. Each provides a description of a state of affairs with respect to murder convictions, statement 2 prior to the abolition of capital punishment, statement 3 after the abolition. Thus, 2 and

3 represent the right kind of premises needed to support subconclusion 1 and render it acceptable. Of course, attention would then shift to the acceptability of the premises in 2 and 3, and the acceptability of those factual statements would rely largely on the authority of the source. Such appeals constitute our final condition for acceptability.

(v) Acceptable on the authority of an expert.
A premise can be accepted because it carries the support of, or appeals to, an expert or authority. The appeal to authority is an argument form that will be treated in detail in Chapter 12. Here, we wish only to introduce the notion of expertise and indicate its role in assessing premise-acceptability. Experts are people, institutions, or sources who, by virtue of their authority, knowledge, or experience, can be used to support the claims made in premises. Consider this example:

> Premise: The Surgeon General says smoking is bad for your health.
> Conclusion: Smoking is bad for your health.

Here, the sole support given for the claim is the word of the Surgeon General. If such an authority is appropriate here—the right kind, speaking on the right issue, with the right motive—then the premise is acceptable. Note that the premise may not be enough to carry the conclusion. But in cases (and there are many of them) where we do not have access to the information we would need to judge a premise, or where we simply lack the expertise to make such an assessment ourselves, it is quite legitimate to rely on an authority. Authorities act as proxy support for a premise. The information they have is available somewhere so their support provides a presumption in favour of the premise. They will rarely be enough to carry an argument, but many extended arguments include them somewhere.

Experts and authoritative sources come in many forms, like the Department of the Solicitor-General of Canada in the earlier argument, which, as an objective body, gives legitimate support to the premises given there. Other possibilities include the Bible and Koran, professionals who are renowned in their fields, objective consumer advocacy groups, documentaries, dictionaries, and textbooks.

Box 10.2 Universal Conditions of Acceptability
  i) Acceptable by definition or self-evidently acceptable.
 ii) Acceptable as a factual statement reporting immediate perception or as a statement of personal testimony.
iii) Acceptable by common knowledge.
 iv) Acceptable due to its being defended in a reasonable sub-argument.
  v) Acceptable on the authority of an expert.

Universal Conditions of Unacceptability

In some instances, a premise will be judged unacceptable because it fails to satisfy, i.e., it specifically violates, one or more of the conditions for acceptability. In many cases the failure to support a premise with a reasonable sub-argument, or with an appeal to common knowledge, may simply render the premise questionable but not explicitly unacceptable. The absence of such support prevents us from making a firm judgement. But when a premise contradicts a state of affairs in the world, and the contradiction is apparent from immediate perception or common knowledge, then we have cause to judge the premise unacceptable. Likewise, a premise might be found unacceptable due to the meanings of its component terms, if those meanings were contradictory, referring to married bachelors or some such things. Beyond these considerations, there are a few other more specific conditions of unacceptability.

(i) Unacceptable due to an inconsistency with another premise.
Inconsistency is a weakness in argumentation that is brought to light by carefully reading an argument's components and considering their meaning. It is possible for two (or more) premises in an argument to be perfectly acceptable when considered individually. But when they are appraised together we encounter a situation where they cannot both be acceptable as support for the same conclusion. Consider the inconsistency between the following premises:

P1: Only claims that can be verified or falsified in some way can be trusted.

P2: Enough people have reported encounters with ghosts to make their existence likely.

Two such statements could issue from the belief system of someone who had not carefully evaluated her or his own beliefs and considered how they sit together. At first glance, P2 might seem to be consistent with P1, since a person's experience is a type of verification. But the kind of verification intended by P1 is objective, third-person verification. If claims are to be trusted, there must be some way of subjecting them to testing. P2 relies on common (or not so common) reportage rather than an objective method of testing. As they stand, P1 and P2 appeal to quite different criteria and if both were to be used in a single piece of argumentation, the inconsistency between them would render them unacceptable.

(ii) Unacceptable due to begging the question.
Begging the question is a violation of the principle of good reasoning that requires us to avoid circularity, or not to assume in our premises what we are attempting to establish in our conclusions. The following argument illustrates this point:

How do we know that 1[we have here in the Bible a right criterion of truth]? 2[We know because the Bible claims it is a right criterion of truth]. 3[All through the Scriptures are found . . . expressions such as 'Thus says the Lord', 'The Lord said', and 'God spoke'.] 4[Such statements occur no less than 1,904 times in the 39 books of the Old Testament]. (adapted from *Decision Magazine*, Jan. 1974)

1. The Bible is a right criterion of truth.
2. The Bible claims it is a right criterion of truth.
3. All through the Scriptures are found expressions such as 'Thus says the Lord.'
4. Such statements occur no less than 1,904 times in the Old Testament.

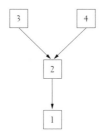

The sub-argument in support of 1 (the main claim) would probably be judged sufficient and accepted by an uncritical audience already sympathetic to it. But the argument would not be — or, at least, should not be — convincing to a universal audience.

By definition, whatever reasons you give to back up a claim must be supporting statements. A statement is not a supporting statement if it merely restates the conclusion or implicitly contains it. What makes statement 2 unacceptable as a premise to a universal audience is that it assumes precisely what it is supposed to prove. It begs the question. No reasonable person who has doubts about the truth of the Bible and who is looking for an argument to support the claim that 'the Bible is the right criterion of truth' will be convinced by the argument given. To accept statement 2 as a reason for statement 1, one must already assume that statement 1 has been established.

One way to avoid the problem of begging the question is by resisting the temptation to use premises that merely restate the claim you are trying to establish. The premise: 'People living below the poverty line ought to receive a basic income' is not a separate and distinct reason for the claim: 'The poor should be given financial subsidies up to a pre-established minimum.' It simply recasts the same idea in different language.

(iii) Unacceptable due to problems with language.
As a result of our investigations of language in Chapter 3, we can recognize several semantic problems that would be grounds for finding a premise

unacceptable. There may be cases where a specific audience would understand an arguer's meanings while a universal audience would not. But there are also clear-cut examples where no audience could be certain of a premise's meaning, where the statement is essentially vague and the context cannot resolve that vagueness, or where a definition, although not internally contradictory, is too broad or narrow or persuasive. (A definition that is missing, though, would be a problem of sufficiency. This will be discussed later.)

Even premises that report personal testimony and would otherwise be allowed can be rejected because they fail to communicate clearly. The statement: 'I have driven my 1993 Ford every day for three years without any major problem' founders on the vagueness of 'major problem'. If the person has experienced a constant series of 'minor' problems, that itself might be considered a major problem to someone else.

Box 10.3 Universal Conditions of Unacceptability
- i) Unacceptable due to an inconsistency with another premise.
- ii) Unacceptable due to begging the question.
- iii) Unacceptable due to misuse of language.

EXERCISE 10A

1. Construct audience profiles for each of the following:
   *a) university students
   b) Native North Americans
   c) sports fans
   d) citizens of industrialized countries
   e) pet owners
   f) labour union members
   g) farmers
   h) newspaper and media people
2. Consider your own belief system and construct a profile of its major features.
3. List the features you would include in the belief system of the universal audience.
4. Explain the grounds you would use in judging the acceptability or unacceptability of each of the following statements:
   *a) The presence of a cause is demonstrated by the existence of its effects.
   *b) The Soviet Union exists today just as it did in 1980.
   c) The intersection of these two major roads is the worst location for accidents in the city. (stated by the chief of police)
   d) Of all the countries I have visited in South America, I have found the people of Chile to be the most hospitable.
   e) Human beings cannot always be trusted to tell the truth.

f) Several extinct species exist in the rain forest.

*g) Prisoners in federal penitentiaries should be allowed to vote because they still retain their citizenship and elected officials oversee the regulations that govern the running of penitentiaries.

h) Emily Dickinson was an American poet.

5. From the perspective of the universal audience, assess the acceptability of the premises in each of the following arguments. Be sure to explain fully the grounds for your decisions.

a) Nobody likes a quitter. So I won't give up smoking.

*b) To every man unbounded freedom of speech must always be on the whole advantageous to the state; for it is highly conducive to the interests of the community that each individual should enjoy a liberty perfectly unlimited of expressing his sentiments.

c) What is really interesting about the recent discoveries in genetics is the potential they provide for more mischief. It is quite likely these discoveries will cause many people to conclude that there is no hope of redemption for people with 'bad genes', and they will write them off. The next step would be to reason that the bad genes should be weeded out and the best way to do that is to phase out the people who bear them.

d) The gods must not be blamed, for they do no wrong, willingly or unwillingly; nor human beings, for they do no wrong except unwillingly. Therefore, no one is to be blamed. (Marcus Aurelius, *Meditations*, Book XII)

e) [Background: On 14 February 1989, Ayatollah Khomeini of Iran imposed a *fatwa* (death sentence) on author Salman Rushdie for his allegedly blasphemous book *The Satanic Verses*.]

With all that has been written about the Rushdie affair, I have not yet heard any non-Muslim voices raised in criticism of the writer himself. . . . To my mind, he is a dangerous opportunist.

Clearly he has profound knowledge of the Muslim religion and its people and he must have been totally aware of the deep and violent feelings the book would stir up among devout Muslims. In other words, he knew exactly what he was doing and he cannot plead otherwise. (From a letter to *The Times*, 28 Feb. 1989, by British author Roald Dahl)

3. RELEVANCE

Beyond having acceptable premises, the second major condition that good arguments must meet is having a conclusion that follows from those premises. When we looked at arguments where the premises purported to guarantee the conclusion, we saw a tight relation between the premises and the conclusion such that if the premises were acceptable or true the conclusion had to be acceptable or true. It is often said that the premises entail the conclusion. In considering arguments where the premises do not guarantee the conclusion we turn our attention to the more general criterion of *relevance*. Like entailment, relevance relates premises to conclusions, but in a less rigorous way. We can recognize a conclusion's premises to be relevant to it yet still have questions about that conclusion. Consider the following argument:

Premise: Six member countries of the UN support the US proposal.
C: Most members of the UN support the US proposal.

For reasons we shall shortly discuss, the premise is relevant to the conclusion: it is the right kind of evidence needed to begin establishing the conclusion and increases the likelihood of the conclusion. But, it is clear, the premise does not entail the conclusion. We can accept the premise without having to accept the conclusion. We see, then, that relevance is something apart from entailment.

Let us add a second premise to our example:

Premise 2: The US proposal will soon be debated in the General Assembly.

Like the first premise, premise 2 could be accepted on the basis of immediate perception. But unlike the first premise, the second one makes no obvious contribution to establishing the conclusion—it is not a reason for believing the conclusion. Premise 2, then, is not relevant to the conclusion.

Internal Relevance

Demonstrated above is what we call *internal relevance*: a relation that exists between a premise or premise set and a conclusion. For premises to be relevant to a conclusion it is not enough for them to be acceptable or to 'talk about the same subject'. The premises must act on the conclusion so as to increase (or decrease) the probability of the conclusion being accepted.

> **Box 10.4 Internal Relevance**
> If a premise increases the probability of the conclusion it is intended to support, or if it decreases the probability of that claim, then the premise is relevant to the conclusion. If neither of these conditions holds, then the premise is not relevant.

Usually, when we argue our goal is to increase the degree of probability attributed to a claim. But it is possible to introduce evidence that actually undermines the claim, and we have to allow for such instances. Also, when we engage in counter-argumentation we do think of relevance in this negative way as we look to introduce premises that take away from a claim and decrease its probability.

Our earlier example illustrates the nature of internal relevance. The first premise, 'Six member countries of the UN support the US proposal', actively increases the probability that the conclusion will be accepted. If six members support the US then this goes toward supporting the conclusion that 'Most members of the UN support the US proposal.' It is the kind of evidence that we would look for to establish the claim. What we require further is information about the other member nations. As more indicate their support of the proposal, so the probability of the conclusion increases further. But if we learn that a number of members oppose the proposal, that counts as negatively relevant evidence that starts to decrease the likelihood of the conclusion.

In contrast to premise 1, premise 2, 'The US proposal will soon be debated in the General Assembly', has a neutral relation to the conclusion, neither increasing nor decreasing its probability. It simply does not work as a reason for the conclusion, in spite of its being acceptable and related to the conclusion in subject-matter. We need to learn from this that premises we have judged acceptable should not be considered relevant because of their acceptability. Relevance is a quite different consideration, and acceptable premises can still be found irrelevant to the conclusion they are intended to support. Also, that a premise and a conclusion are talking about the same subject does not guarantee that the premise will be relevant to the conclusion in the active way necessary.

Note that in extended arguments not all the premises are relevant to the main claim, because many of them are intended only as support for subsidiary claims. The claim for which a premise is given as evidence is the claim for which the relevance of the premise should be decided.

The following example, excerpted from an editorial in *The Globe and Mail* (6 Feb. 1987), serves as a fuller application of our rule:

1[The right to a lawyer is crucial to our justice system]. . . . 2[An accused is vulnerable to intimidation, conscious or not, by the authorities who arrest him]. Since 3[our society considers him innocent unless proved guilty], and 4[believes he should not be compelled to testify against himself], 5[justice requires that he be counselled by someone who knows the law and can advise him on which questions he must legally answer].

The opening statement appears to be the conclusion for which the reasons that follow are offered as evidence. Diagrammed, the argument looks like this:

1. = (MC) The right to a lawyer is crucial to our justice system.
2. = (P1) An accused person is vulnerable to intimidation, conscious or not, by the authorities who arrest him.
3. = (P2) Our society considers the accused person innocent unless proved guilty.

4. = (P3) Our society believes the accused should not be compelled to testify against himself.
5. = (P4, C1) Justice requires that the accused person be counselled by someone who knows the law and can advise him on which questions he must legally answer.

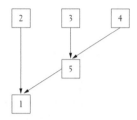

The diagram shows us a subsidiary argument within the main argument. Accordingly, in assessing relevance, we must look at the bearing each of statement 2 and statement 5 has on statement 1, the MC, and the bearing each of statement 3 and statement 4 has on statement 5. Although we may legitimately wonder whether a paralegal could take the place of a lawyer in providing the required service, we have no difficulty seeing that statement 2 and statement 5 are the right kind of evidence needed to increase one's acceptance of statement 1. Likewise, statements 3 and 4 actively increase the likelihood of statement 5 being accepted. Applying our rule of internal relevance, of course, requires judgement on our part. But there seems to be nothing in this argument with which we can legitimately disagree.

Box 10.5 *Relevance and Hidden Premises*

Those of you still having trouble identifying hidden premises may find the rule of internal relevance useful. Before you dismiss a premise as irrelevant to a conclusion consider whether there is a hidden premise that, once drawn out, combines with the explicit premise to support the conclusion. Of course, you won't find this in every case. Consider the following:

1[It is morally permissible to experiment on human embryos at a developmental stage prior to the formation of the brain] since 2[there is no possibility of causing pain or distress to the organism].

1. It is morally permissible to experiment on human embryos at a developmental stage prior to the formation of the brain.
2. There is no possibility of causing pain or distress to the organism.

    Statement 2 is given as a reason for statement 1, but at first glance we might judge it as irrelevant to that conclusion. How do we get from causing pain to having a brain? What would make the premise relevant to the conclusion, that is, provide active support for it, would be if the author explicitly related having a brain and feeling pain. Drawing out the following hidden premise is, then, a reasonable assumption to attribute to the author. Once drawn out, it combines with the explicit premise to provide relevant support for the conclusion.

HP = A brain is required for any entity to receive messages of [feel] pain.

4. CONTEXTUAL RELEVANCE

Another form of relevance concerns the relationship of a segment of the argument or the argument's conclusion to the correct context. You should note that an argument can pass the test of internal relevance, with all its premises judged relevant to the conclusion they are intended to support, yet still prove to be contextually irrelevant. The rule here is to ensure that the context of an argument has been correctly recognized and that all components relate to it. If an argument correctly addresses the context in which it arises, including the issue with which it is concerned and any prior argument to which it responds, then it is contextually relevant. If the argument misrepresents the issue or a prior argument and attacks the misrepresentation, or if it deviates from the issue and doesn't return to address it, then the argument is contextually irrelevant and is guilty of being either a 'straw-man argument' or a 'red herring'.

Straw-man Arguments

We often find ourselves summarizing an opponent's position for purposes of clarifying it or attributing certain consequences to it, and then arguing against it. When we do this, we must be sure that the opposing position has been fairly and accurately represented. If our version is wrong, whether it is deliberate or through an oversight—if we take our opponent's position to be A when she intended B, and then proceed to attack A—we are guilty of the type of contextual irrelevance known as a 'straw-man argument'. A straw-man argument is always a misrepresentation of a position, usually weakening it to make the response easier and apparently more effective.

We must address the real argument advanced by a person or held by opponents, not some weakened version of it. The rule of contextual relevance requires that our interpretation of an opposing position be fairly and correctly represented.

Consider the following argument, excerpted and adapted from a letter to the *New York Times* (Mar. 1982):

> 1[It should be obvious the new Medicare Bill will not accomplish the utopia claimed for it]. Because 2[it will not make everyone healthy overnight]. Therefore, 3[the new medicare bill should not be passed].

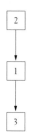

Here we have two arguments: statement 1's support of statement 3, and statement 2's support of statement 1. Both arguments satisfy the requirement of internal relevance. Statement 2 to statement 1 clearly does, since the failure to make everyone healthy overnight actively increases the likelihood that the bill will not achieve a state of utopia. Statement 1 to statement 3 does so less clearly, but it is charitable to allow that the failure to achieve a promised utopia would be a relevant (though far from sufficient) reason the bill should not be passed.

But here we pause and wonder about the first argument. Who promised that the Medicare Bill would achieve a utopia? Presumably, the proponents of the bill, this arguer's opponents. But did they claim this? And if so, did they mean by such a claim that the Medicare Bill would make everyone healthy overnight? It seems implausible that anyone would make such a claim and more like an exaggeration on the arguer's part. From this point of view, we have a strong reason to think that the arguer has created a caricature of the opposing position in order to attack that misrepresentation. In short, we have every reason to suspect that we are dealing with a straw argument that is contextually irrelevant to the real issue.

In the Medicare argument we had to use our judgement to detect an exaggeration. In the next example no such exaggeration is apparent. A sincere attempt to support a position has led to an oversight. The example is a letter to the *Peterborough Examiner* (20 May 1992).

> I am concerned by the recent letters to the editor which portray the Women's Health Care Centre as an abortion clinic.

I would like to point out that the Women's Health Care Centre provides many valuable services . . . pregnancy non-stress testing; colposcopy clinic; lactation consultant (breast feeding support); counselling and information on a wide range of health issues of concern to women and their families; workshops covering PMS, menopause, body image, living alone and many others.

I feel that the services provided by the Women's Health Care Centre . . . provide comprehensive information and support for the women of Peterborough and the surrounding areas.

The nature of the issue and the context indicate this is an argumentative attempt to defend the Women's Centre against recent attacks. For the most part, that defence is well made. The writer claims that the Centre provides many valuable services and supports that claim in an internally relevant way with a detailed list of appropriate services. But when we consider the context in which the debate arises and the point to be addressed, we are led to ask: 'Is the Women's Health Care Centre an abortion clinic?' The writer indicates that it is certainly much more than an abortion clinic and if the charge had been that it was *only* an abortion clinic then her response would have forcefully addressed that charge. But that was not the charge, and it remains that the writer has not addressed the claim that it was an abortion clinic. We do not know whether she agrees or not. For all its merits, the writer's argument has not addressed the point that the context required to be addressed, and on that ground it is contextually irrelevant.

Red Herring

The second type of contextual irrelevance is what has been traditionally termed the 'red herring'. What distinguishes this from the straw-man argument is that there is no misrepresentation of a prior position or context. Rather, the shift takes place within the argument as the boundaries of the context are altered through the introduction of a quite irrelevant consideration.

Consider the following example, this time in the form of a dialogue between two speakers, A and B:

A: Why are you not willing to support the gun-control legislation? Don't you have any feelings at all for the thousands of lives that each year are blotted out by the indiscriminate use of handguns?

B: I just don't understand why you people who get so worked up about lives being blotted out by handguns don't have the same feelings about the unborn children whose lives are being indiscriminately blotted out. Is not the sanctity of human life involved in both issues? Why have you not supported us in our efforts at abortion legislation?

B does not misrepresent A's position; he simply avoids it by shifting attention to something else altogether. His response is something like:

> P: The lives of unborn children have been indiscriminately blotted out.
> P: You haven't supported our abortion legislation.
> P: The sanctity of human life is involved in both issues.
> HC: I won't support the gun-control legislation.

This conclusion has to be hidden because we can only assume that this is B's reaction. His shifting of topics really allows him to avoid addressing the issue of gun control, so our reconstruction is at best hypothetical.

A red herring arises whenever there is a shift of topic within an argument and the argument is not brought back to the real issue. This is an important point to note. The third premise identified above—'The sanctity of human life is involved in both issues'—could be the beginning of a return to the issue and the establishment of an argument from analogy. But such a return is never completed and we bring the charge of red herring. But it will be important later to resist the temptation to judge all arguments from analogy as red herrings. In an argument from analogy the arguer does turn aside to another topic or subject, but does so to suggest a comparison. That comparison then has a bearing on the conclusion where the argument is brought back to its original issue. With red herrings we have no return.

Watch closely for instances of contextual irrelevance. Check that the context is appropriately served by all arguments. Otherwise you may be misled by an argument's internal relevance to accept it as a legitimate argument when you should not do so.

EXERCISE 10B

Assess the relevance of the reasons offered for the following claims. For the purposes of this exercise, assume each reason is acceptable. It is appropriate to employ common beliefs and assumptions when making these assessments.

*1. Claim: It is wrong to inflict suffering on animals.
   Reasons:
   a) It is wrong to inflict suffering on any creature that can experience pain.
   b) All animals can experience pain.
   c) Circuses exploit animals for human profit.
   d) Some medical advances for humans can only be achieved at the price of inflicting pain on rats and rabbits.
   e) Under Christian doctrine, we are to be the stewards of Nature.

2. Claim: There should be stricter gun-control laws.
   Reasons:
   a) Children already witness too much violence on television.

b) Few people would be killed by handguns if those guns were more rigidly controlled.

c) The right to bear arms is written into the Constitution.

d) Police associations across North America support stricter gun laws.

e) Stricter gun-control laws would assist police in keeping law and order.

3. Claim: Government-sponsored day care is needed to promote equality of the sexes.

   Reasons:

   a) Welfare costs will be reduced if single parents are free to take remunerative employment.

   b) Sexual equality requires that women be free to pursue the same employment opportunities as men.

   c) The lack of government-sponsored day care is an impediment to equality of the sexes.

   d) Day-care centres provide young children with an environment in which they can learn to interact and acquire essential social skills.

   e) Economic pressures often force women to choose between motherhood and a career.

4. Claim: Drunk drivers who are convicted of causing accidents in which others are injured should be compelled to compensate the victims or their families.

   Reasons:

   a) This would force repeat offenders to take responsibility for their actions.

   b) The costs arise as a result of the drunk driver's actions.

   c) Courts often treat drunk drivers too leniently.

   d) Costs incurred in accidents are the responsibility of the insurance companies.

   e) It's unfair to expect the victims to bear the costs of someone's negligence.

5. Claim: Vikings visited North America centuries before Columbus.

   Reasons:

   a) The Vikings were exceptional sailors and their ships were built to withstand the travails of long voyages.

   b) What is believed to be a Viking burial ground has been found on the coast of the eastern United States.

   c) Native North American legends speak of contact with white men long before Columbus.

   d) Vikings were known to be fearless warriors.

   e) No replica of a Viking ship has been able to traverse the Atlantic Ocean in modern times.

5. SUFFICIENCY

To the major criteria of acceptability and relevance we need to add one other to allow us to complete our analysis of examples like this earlier one:

Premise: Six member countries of the UN support the US proposal.
C: Most members of the UN support the US proposal.

Here, we allowed that the premise was acceptable, judged it to be relevant to
the claim, but still felt that the argument fell short of being an instance of
good reasoning. What the premise fails to give the conclusion is *enough*
evidence, and this is our final criterion: sufficiency.

What a good argument should do is create a presumption in favour of its
conclusion such that its audience is more likely to adopt it, and so that anyone
who does not do so has the onus shifted to him or her to provide a counter-
argument. But how much is enough evidence? Experience tells us that this
will vary from argument to argument. There are no precise rules for determining when enough evidence has been put forward. Nor can we think in
terms of the number of premises, since a single premise in one argument can
carry as much evidence for its claim as three or four premises in another argument. But some important considerations can assist you in making judgements of sufficiency.

(i) *Assess the sufficiency of evidence in relation to how strongly the claim has
    been expressed.*
Suppose a resident of an average-size city argues on the basis of her experience that the federal postal service is inadequate, by which she means deliv-
ery is slow and unreliable. There is no denying the details of her personal
testimony, and we may sympathize with her, given our own frustrations with
the postal service. Yet we can see that the evidence of her experience alone is
not sufficient to convince a reasonable audience. In fact, it is difficult to see
what nontrivial conclusion can be drawn from her experience.

But suppose the same person undertakes to canvass her neighbours and
other neighbourhoods throughout the city and finds numerous households
with similar complaints. If she can argue on the basis of a broader range of
experience, her argument becomes stronger. But it is still not strong enough
to support the claim that the postal service in general is inadequate. What she
may have is sufficient evidence, if it is representative of all neighbourhoods, to
show that the postal service *in her city* is inadequate.

Finally, if she could cull supporting evidence from regions and cities right
across the country, then she might have sufficient evidence to support her
claim about the postal service in general. But this, we recognize, would be
very difficult for an individual to accomplish.

The point of this example is that what constitutes sufficiency of evidence
must be decided relative to the claim the evidence is intended to support. The
more general the claim, the more evidence is needed. For this reason you are
advised to keep your claims as specific as possible. Without the support of
something like a national poll behind you, you are likely to experience
difficulty in marshalling sufficient evidence for general claims like this one.

Claims that are expressed with high degrees of certainty are also difficult to support unless you are in possession of the evidence to do so. Consider the following example:

Thor Heyerdahl crossed the Atlantic in a raft designed after carvings on an ancient Egyptian tomb. Heyerdahl landed at the island of Barbados. This proves that Barbados was the first landing place for humans in the Western world.

The two premises do not come close to proving what is required of them. But they do provide the right sort of relevant evidence that would be adequate for a weaker claim such as 'This raises the possibility that . . .'.

(ii) Do not draw a conclusion too hastily.
We sometimes find ourselves 'jumping to conclusions' that we need to modify or withdraw when the excitement abates. Traditionally, arguments of this sort have been termed 'hasty conclusions' or 'hasty generalizations' and involve drawing conclusions before enough evidence is in. This does not mean that we can't make claims that we then test to see if we can gather the evidence for them. Scientific progress often proceeds this way, with hypotheses being put forward and then subjected to rigorous testing. But we would be quite alarmed to learn that the latest drug on the market had been tested on only a few subjects before it was concluded that it 'worked'. In fact, our government agencies would not allow this to happen. A similar check needs to be made on our own hypotheses. But still some judgement is required. How many tomatoes in the basket do we have to check before we decide they are generally okay and a good value for the money? At least 50 per cent plus one for a reasonable conclusion. But beyond that, circumstances will determine what we consider to be enough to put out our money.

On the other hand, less evidence may be enough to draw negative conclusions. No matter how many times a hypothesis is verified, if there is one instance in which it fails, and the prediction had not allowed for any failures, then that one instance can be enough for our rejecting the hypothesis. In a similar, but not identical vein, one negative experience of touching a hot stove is enough to convince a child not to do so again. Of course, given the openness of our experience of the world, the next time the hot stove might not burn. But the negativity of the experience is enough to prevent further testing, and we would be reluctant to charge the child with drawing a hasty conclusion, because to do so would be to expect that he should have gathered further evidence.

(iii) Ensure that the arguer has provided a balanced case and discharged all her or his obligations.
Better arguments, that is, arguments more likely to receive serious attention from others and to impress them with our reasonableness, are those that try to give a balanced picture of an issue. If you present only the evidence support-

ing your position and ignore evidence that detracts from it, your audience is likely to be suspicious about what you have left out. It does not help the postal critic's argument if she presents a lot of supporting evidence only to have her opponents present evidence indicating that most people are satisfied with the service.

To present selectively only one side of an issue is to engage in the argumentative version of what Chapter 1 called 'special pleading'.

> The government should not be returned for another term in office. It has hurt the country by paying too much attention to foreign policy and neglecting domestic affairs.

Beyond the vagueness of the charges, the argument overlooks anything positive the government may have done. It is possible that the arguer believes that nothing positive has been done. But a more complete evaluation of the government's performance will have a wider appeal to a broader audience.

We should strive wherever possible to dress our arguments with a sense of objectivity and balance. If evidence goes against your position, honesty demands that you introduce it and respond to it. If you cannot counter it, you probably should not be advancing that argument in the first place. In assessing the arguments of others, however, do not judge them too harshly for not anticipating all the objections to their claim. Rarely are all conditions for sufficiency satisfied, but a well-constructed argument should make a reasonable attempt to respond to key objections.

Finally, ensure that an arguer has discharged all her or his obligations, particularly those arising from the arguer's own charges and promises. If the arguer claims a position is inconsistent, then the onus is on him or her to substantiate the charge. The failure to do so is a violation of the sufficiency condition. Likewise, if the arguer promises to show that a position has no reasonable objections to it, then the subsequent argument should be judged on whether that promise is fulfilled.

Another obligation is to define key terms in an argument. If a definition required to establish a claim is omitted, then the evidence for that claim is insufficient.

EXERCISE 10C

Assess the sufficiency of the premise sets offered for each of the following claims:
*1. Claim: Boxing should not be outlawed.
   Reasons:
   a) Boxing gives many young men the opportunity to escape lives of poverty.
   b) Boxing is no less dangerous than other contact sports.
   c) The art of boxing reflects an age-old human love of physical challenge and excellence.

d) While there are some serious injuries, these are relatively rare and proportionately fewer than in other popular sports.

e) No one is coerced into boxing or watching the sport.

2. Claim: Critical thinking courses are certainly the most important courses in the curriculum.

   Reasons:

   a) Critical thinking teaches the fundamentals of good reasoning.

   b) It helps people detect bad reasoning in the arguments they hear and read.

   c) Critical thinking principles underlie all the academic disciplines.

   d) Critical thinking teaches skills that are useful in the everyday world.

   e) A critical thinking course is part of a well-rounded education.

3. Claim: The service in the local department store is always excellent.

   Reasons:

   a) I was there yesterday and three assistants asked if they could help me.

   b) There's a sign over the main entrance which says 'We Aim to Please'.

   c) The store is usually busy when I'm there, unlike its competitor.

   d) I've always been treated courteously by the sales staff.

   e) My father has had the same good experience with the store.

4. Claim: Lee Harvey Oswald probably did not act alone in assassinating President Kennedy.

   Reasons:

   a) He was alleged to have shot Kennedy from the sixth floor of the Texas School Book Depository where he worked, but shots were also fired from a grassy knoll to the side of the President's car.

   b) Several witnesses report seeing armed men running away from the vicinity of the shooting.

   c) Studies of the direction of the bullets that hit the President indicate they came from more than one direction.

   d) Investigations found that Oswald, who was known to have Cuban sympathies, was involved in the assassination.

   e) The 1976 US Senate inquiry concluded that more than one gunman had been involved.

5. Claim: A critical thinking course is useful for most post-secondary students.

   Reasons:

   a) These courses discuss the basic elements used in producing strong, convincing arguments.

   b) Students who have taken a critical thinking course generally perform well in other courses.

   c) Such courses force students to defend the decisions they make and the claims they advance.

   d) Such courses aid students in recognizing themselves as thinking creatures with specific beliefs.

   e) Critical thinking fosters an environment in which students are required to consider the beliefs and perspectives of others.

6. APPLYING THE CRITERIA

In completing this chapter, we want to apply what we have learned about the basic criteria of argument assessment.

The failure of an argument to be relevant to its context is the most detrimental fault of all. Likewise, if there is a major flaw of internal irrelevance, the argument probably cannot be salvaged. But do not assume because one chain of reasoning in an extended argument is internally irrelevant to the MC that the argument has no merits. If there are sufficient other relevant premises, the MC may be adequately supported, despite the fault in the argument that needs to be noted or, if it is your argument, eliminated.

Likewise, do not take the insufficiency of support for a subclaim to be reason enough to dismiss an entire argument, nor a few unacceptable premises that play only a minor role in your diagram as rendering the entire argument worthless. Remember, although irrelevance remains a major problem, often more premises can be added to an argument to rectify insufficiency and premises can be further supported to remedy unacceptability. In the following example we apply the criteria to an extended argument.

1[Many people dismiss out of hand the suggestion that certain children's stories should be banned because of things like violence and stereotyping]. But 2[there is at least one reason to consider censoring some children's stories]. 3[In several common children's stories the stepmother is an evil person who mistreats her stepchildren and wishes them ill]. For example: 4[Her stepmother wishes Snow White dead and later tries to poison her]. 5[Cinderella's stepmother treats her as a servant and mocks her in front of her stepsisters]. And 6[the stepmother of Hansel and Gretel has them abandoned in a deep forest]. Since 7[children hear these stories at an impressionable age], 8[such stories may be instrumental in creating for young children a negative image of stepmothers].

2 (MC) = There is at least one reason to consider censoring some children's stories.

3 (C1) = In several common children's stories the stepmother is an evil person who mistreats her stepchildren and wishes them ill.

4 (P1) = Her stepmother wishes Snow White dead and later tries to poison her.

5 (P2) = Cinderella's stepmother treats her as a servant and mocks her in front of her stepsisters.

6 (P3) = The stepmother of Hansel and Gretel has them abandoned in a deep forest.

7 (P4) = Children hear these stories at an impressionable age.

8 (C2) = Such children's stories may be instrumental in creating for young children a negative image of stepmothers.

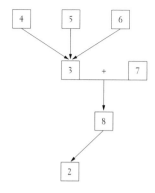

The first statement in this discourse is taken as background. It announces the context in which the argument arises, indicating its controversial nature, and stating the position with which the author disagrees. Statement 1 will be useful in assessing contextual relevance.

We have three arguments here: the support proposed for statement 3 by statements 4, 5, and 6; the support proposed for statement 8 by statements 3 and 7; and the support proposed for statement 2, the MC, by statement 8. In judging acceptability, we work backwards through the diagram starting with statement 8.

The claim that certain children's stories may be instrumental in creating a negative image of stepmothers for young children (8) is weakened in a positive sense by the qualifying phrase 'may be'. The writer does not have to establish that the stories *do* have this affect, only that they may. While the claim is still not acceptable as it stands—if it was common knowledge, there would be little need to argue for it—it is supported, and we can look to see if that support is reasonable.

The claim that children hear these stories at an impressionable age is unsupported so must be evaluated on its own merits. While it may suffer from the vagueness of what constitutes an 'impressionable age', we are prepared to allow the premise on the grounds that people commonly understand young children to be impressionable and these stories are usually told to quite young children. A reasonable audience should accept it. To assess statement 3 we need to again consider the evidence offered for it. Each of statements 4, 5, and 6 reports a central and commonly known element in a very popular children's story. Each is acceptable, given the common currency of these stories. And they are enough to establish statement 3 with its reference to 'several common' stories. Together, then, 3 and 7 are acceptable as support for 8 (and, we will soon see, relevant to it). So this argument fares very well on the acceptability condition.

The context, proposed in the first statement, does not seem exaggerated. We do encounter such charges, particularly during times when children's reading material comes under close scrutiny. The argument as developed responds to this context and without diversion from it. The argument is contextually relevant.

To consider internal relevance we look at the arrows in the diagram. They indicate five decisions to be made about internal relevance. The structure of the diagram is important here. The irrelevance of statement 8 to the MC (2) would be far more detrimental to the argument than the irrelevance of one of the premises given in support of statement 3. As it happens, statement 8 is relevant to the MC. We are told there is at least one reason to consider censoring some children's stories. We expect statement 8 to provide such a reason, and it does. The creation of a negative image for young children is a reason to consider censorship.

Statements 3 and 7 are linked in support of 8. Why should we believe the stories may be instrumental in creating a negative image for young children? The premises give us the kind of information relevant to answering this question: each story conveys the stepmother as an evil character and children hear these stories at an impressionable age. Finally, three arrows lead to statement 3. Statement 3 claims the image of the evil stepmother exists in 'several common' stories. The kind of evidence that would be relevant to establishing this claim would involve examples of such stories. That is exactly what each of statements 4, 5, and 6 provides. So each of them is internally relevant to statement 3. The argument passes the relevance condition.

Finally, we must decide whether the evidence is sufficient to establish the main claim and its subconclusions. It is important to note that both the MC and the subconclusion in statement 8 are expressed in a qualified way with no suggestion of certainty. The MC reads that 'there *is at least one* reason to *consider* censoring some children's stories'. It falls short of actually advocating censorship (for which this argument would not be sufficient), nor does it concern all children's stories. Hence, evidence concerning one reason to raise the possibility of censorship would be enough, and this the argument provides. The subconclusion in statement 8 states that the stories *may be* instrumental in creating a negative image of stepmothers in young children. Again, it does not suggest a firm causal relationship between children's stories and negative attitudes toward stepmothers. Such a claim would be harder to defend. Thus, we judge that statements 3 and 7, together, are enough support for 8. To decide otherwise would require us to say what more would be needed and there is little more that we could expect (beyond, perhaps, the testimony of children or stepmothers who have felt this influence). Whether the three instances cited in statements 4, 5, and 6 are sufficient support for statement 3 is a matter of judgement. But statement 3 refers only to 'several' stories and the supporting premises provide three.

Note that the sufficiency of the evidence in this argument has been judged according to the expectations raised by the argument's own claims. This is a point to take to heart when constructing your claims. Applying the general criteria to the 'stepmother' argument reveals it to be strong all round. We could charge that it lacks balance because no instances are provided of stories containing good stepmothers, but the many merits uncovered far outweigh this minor defect.

In this chapter we developed by discussion and then illustrated by example the general criteria you must keep in mind in constructing good arguments and in evaluating the strength of arguments put forward by others. In the next two chapters we will develop several specific argument forms governed by more precise applications of the general criteria.

MAJOR EXERCISE 10M

Assess each of the following passages in terms of the basic criteria of acceptability, relevance, and sufficiency. Be sure to defend your assessments and comment on the overall strength of the argument in each case.

*1. Elementary school teachers should be better paid than university professors. The reasons for this are as follows. The complex material dealt with at university requires that students be well grounded in basic skills of reading and writing. And according to many educators elementary school teachers teach students in their most formative years when basic skills are best taught. Therefore, the job of elementary school teachers is more important than that of university professors.

Furthermore, people should be paid according to the importance of their jobs to society. And lastly, university professors are already overpaid.

*2. [Phillip Flower, *Understanding the Universe* (St Paul: West Publishing Co., 1990)] Astronomy, however, is accessible to everyone. For only a modest investment, anyone can purchase or build a telescope and begin viewing the sky. . . . Magazines such as *Sky & Telescope* and *Astronomy* are written for amateurs and help them keep up with the latest research results. In addition, many books for the nonscientists have been written on a variety of astronomical subjects, from the origin of the solar system to the future of the universe.

3. [*New York Times*, 1 Nov. 1992, section 2, p. 14] [A]udiences don't want to see male nudity because it's too private, less attractive than female nudity, and somewhat threatening, so directors avoid it (male nudity) at almost any cost.

4. [From a subscription renewal letter from the *London Review of Books*] The *London Review of Books* is becoming a 'must-read' among scholars, journalists and opinion leaders—not only in Britain but in North America, too. And until recently, you were among this select group, participating in the international exchange of ideas. You were in an enviable position. Many people who would enjoy the *London Review of Books* do not yet know about it. You did. You took advantage of that. I can't imagine that you would want to forgo the pleasure of subscribing, especially since we have made the

renewal rates so attractive. Surely, your not renewing must be an oversight. This is your last chance to correct it.

5. [From Daniel D. Polsby, 'The False Promise of Gun Control', *Atlantic Monthly*, Mar. 1994] Everyone knows that possessing a handgun makes it easier to intimidate, wound or kill someone. But the implication of this point for social policy has not been so well understood. It is easy to count the bodies of those who have been killed or wounded by guns, but not easy to count the people who have avoided harm because they had access to weapons. Think about uniformed police officers, who carry handguns in plain view not in order to kill people but simply to daunt potential attackers. And it works. Criminals generally do not single out police officers for opportunistic attack. Though officers are expected to draw their guns from time to time, few even in big-city departments will actually fire a shot (except in target practice) in the course of a year. This observation points to an important truth: people who are armed make comparatively unattractive victims. A criminal might not know if one civilian is armed, but if it becomes known that a large number of civilians do carry weapons, criminals will become warier.

6. [In the following piece, from the *Times Literary Supplement*, 13 Jan. 1995, extract and assess the argument attributed to Salman Rushdie. Most of the background is provided, although it may help to know that Imran Khan is a high-profile cricket player.]

On July 30 last year, P.D. James . . . wrote a *Spectator* diary meditating upon physical handicaps of one kind and another. 'The depressing fact is that no government can totally compensate for biological disadvantage. And the greatest biological disadvantage is undoubtedly suffered by the ugly and the plain', she argued, observing that nowadays politicians need perfect teeth. 'We writers are fortunate: beauty is neither required nor expected of us . . . .'

However, she did not leave it there. 'I suspect that few of us are free from the tyranny of the physical self', she continued. 'I wonder whether Salman Rushdie would have written *The Satanic Verses* if he had been born as handsome as Imran Khan?'

[Rushdie] went ape, sending a letter of complaint to the paper. . . . 'For what I take her remark to mean is that I wrote a novel she considers poor—or, not to mince words, 'ugly'—because I was myself lacking in beauty. Ergo, ugly writers write ugly books, and beautiful writers write beautiful ones. Thus, Naomi Campbell is the best novelist in Britain. And we must move swiftly to re-evaluate the novels of, oh let's say P.D. James, in light of her own jacket photographs.'

7. [Advertisement: *Good Housekeeping*, Mar. 1992] Trees aren't the only plants that are good for the atmosphere. Because nuclear plants don't burn anything to make electricity, nuclear plants don't pollute the air. In fact, America's 111 operating nuclear electric plants displace other power sources and so reduce

certain airborne pollutants in the US by more than 19,000 tons every day. Just as important, nuclear plants produce no greenhouse gases.

*8. [In the early 1980s pay TV was introduced to parts of Canada. One of the channels, First Choice, provoked a great deal of controversy when it aired adult programs from the Playboy Network. The programming was deemed degrading to women and there was a concern that children would have access to it, despite the late hours at which it aired. The following is a letter to the *Toronto Sun*, 26 Jan. 1983.]

The noisy demonstrations against First Choice television are a blatant display of malicious selfishness. The hormonal chemistry of the sexes is such that women do not derive pleasure from watching semi-nude buxom blondes. Women derive analogous sexual titillation from soap operas and romance novels. Therefore, women objecting to male enjoyment of the female form are like deaf people demanding prohibition of music because they are incapable of enjoying it themselves.

9. [Adapted from I.F. Stone, *The Trial of Socrates* (Toronto: Little, Brown and Company, 1988), p. 62] It seems paradoxical for Socrates to say that he was not a teacher. One can imagine three possible reasons for such a claim. They are political, philosophical, and personal. The political reason is tied to Socrates's rejection of democracy. He held that 'one who knows' should rule, but such rule would be undermined if knowledge and virtue were things that one could teach. The philosophical reason is the impossibility of attaining the absolute certainties that Socrates wanted to attain. The personal reason may be Critias and Alcibiades, two of Socrates's students who turned out badly and did Athens a great deal of harm.

*10. [From Norman Kretzmann's 'Introduction' to *William of Sherwood's Introduction to Logic* (Minneapolis: University of Minnesota Press, 1968), pp. 3-4] Whether or not [William of Sherwood] was a student at the University of Paris, we have several reasons for believing that he was a master there. In the first place, he lived at a time when 'scholars were, indeed, to a degree which is hardly intelligible in modern times, citizens of the world' and when 'almost all the great schoolmen . . . taught at Paris at one period or other of their lives.' Secondly, in each of his two main works Sherwood uses an example with a Parisian setting: in one case the Seine, and in another the university. Finally, all the philosophers who show signs of having been influenced directly by Sherwood or his writings were in Paris at some time during a span of years when he certainly could have been lecturing there.

11. [From a letter to the *Toronto Sun*, 17 Nov. 1983] Canadian military men died in foreign fields because Canada declared war on other countries, not vice versa. The mere fact that we fought does not necessarily make our cause or causes virtuous.

Few Canadians really paused long enough to really investigate the reasons for our foreign adventures.

I had a long talk with a veteran of World War II. He was a hand-to-hand-combat instructor and a guard at Allied headquarters in Italy. I questioned him on the reason for Canada's involvement. He replied unhesitatingly that we fought because Britain told us to. That was the only reason.

It is quite clear that the only reason for world wars is that countries that have no business in the conflict get involved.

12. [Environment Canada, Ottawa, *State of the Environment Reporting Newsletter*, no. 7, Dec. 1991] Canada is truly a forest nation. The forest sector provides important social, environmental and economic benefits to every Canadian. Forests not only supply wood and fibre, they also provide a habitat for many plants and animals and a retreat from the pressures of daily life. Canada's forests are a backdrop for a multi-million dollar tourism and recreation industry. They also play an important environmental role by recycling carbon, nitrogen and oxygen, influencing temperature and rainfall, protecting soils and supplying energy.

FORMS

OF

REASONING

In this chapter we begin the discussion of different forms of reasoning. We outline the basic structure and conditions of each kind of argument, and provide a sketch of what would constitute a good 'counter-argument' in each case. The forms of reasoning include:

- ◆ generalizations;
- ◆ causal reasoning;
- ◆ slippery slope arguments;
- ◆ arguments from analogy; and
- ◆ appeals to precedent.

Chapter 10 discussed the general criteria for good arguments. As we have seen, every good argument must have premises that are relevant, acceptable, and sufficient to establish its conclusion. When we are presented with a specific argument, or with different kinds of arguments, we have to determine how these general criteria will be applied in the case at hand. In other words, what are the specific conditions that must be satisfied to construct a good argument of that type? These conditions will vary from one type of argument to another, because in each case we are tailoring the general criteria of relevance, sufficiency, and acceptability to the specific form of argument. In the next two chapters we examine different types of arguments as various 'forms of reasoning' and specify how the general criteria function when applied to these different arguments.

In each case, we will take a specific kind of argument and describe its structure and the conditions that must be satisfied to construct a good argument of that type. We will then examine what would constitute a good 'counter-argument' to that argument type. We use counter-arguments whenever we argue that someone else's reasoning—or the claim based on this reasoning—is mistaken. The criteria for judging any argument we make against a claim based on that reasoning—i.e., a counter-argument—are the same criteria for a good argument of any particular kind.

We may now proceed to a discussion of various distinct forms of ordinary reasoning. Keep in mind that this list is not exhaustive; the particular conditions we identify for each kind of argument are simply specific applications of the general criteria for a good argument, and these criteria will serve you even when you encounter a type of argument that is not dealt with here.

1. GENERALIZATIONS

'Generalization' is the process of moving from specific observations about some individuals within a group to general claims about members of the group. Generalizations take the following form:

> Some members of a group have characteristic x.
> Therefore, members of the group have characteristic x.

Occasionally we make generalizations on the basis of a single incident. One painful experience may convince a child that fire is too hot to touch or, satisfied with the work done in our home on a particular occasion, we may conclude that 'The Magic Carpet Cleaning Co. usually does a good job cleaning carpets.' More often, however, generalizations are based on a series of observations or experiences. Polls, surveys, and studies of past experience aim to give us information, for example, concerning whether the majority of the population favours capital punishment or whether mandatory seat-belt legislation reduces injuries in traffic accidents by the alleged 40 per cent. These are examples of generalizations, and in most cases such generalizations are based on an incomplete survey of the evidence.

Because the evidence is often necessarily incomplete, some people have tended to think that generalizations are not a very good way of reasoning. You hear people say, for example, 'It's not good to generalize', suggesting that generalizing is never legitimate. However, generalizations are not only a prevalent and necessary form of reasoning in various matters, but they are largely legitimate forms of reasoning. Of course, as we discussed in Chapter 10, some generalizations are not legitimate—for example, when they are based on insufficient evidence or contain bias, or when they are arrived at too quickly. In these cases we can refer to them as hasty generalizations, or simply as poor generalizations. The point is that if the proper conditions are met, generalizing is a legitimate tool in our reasoning.

Let's take an extended example to illustrate the process of making generalizations. Suppose that you operate a small business that assembles computers and you have ordered a thousand microchips for those computers from a firm in Japan that has agreed to produce them to your exact specifications. Upon their arrival, you open one of the 10 boxes at random, pull out five of the 100 chips it contains, and examine each one carefully to ensure that it meets your requirements. You find that all five do. Again at random you open another box from the 10 and test five more chips, finding once again that they operate as they should. The same is done with a third and a fourth box, always with the same results. By this time you have carefully examined 20 of the 1,000 chips and are fully satisfied. Twenty out of 1,000 is a small ratio, but you conclude none the less that 'The computer chips meet our specifications.'

As we shall see shortly, this is a good inference, even though the premises, consisting of limited observations, obviously do not guarantee the truth of the conclusion about the entire order. You could guarantee the truth of the conclusion if you examined all 1,000 of the chips and found each and every one to meet your specifications. But we are usually not in a position to undertake such a task; nor should it be necessary, given that we have the basis for a reasonable generalization. By the same token, it remains possible that a significant portion—most or even all of the remaining chips—are not what you had ordered. You may have been merely lucky (or rather, unlucky) and picked out 20 good ones. However, since the chance of this happening is still small, the reasoning here can be accepted and the generalization can stand.

The end result of such a generalization is often a *universal* claim of the form 'All Xs are Ys.' We discussed such claims in Chapter 6. In the present example, the universal conclusion would read, 'All the microchips are good.'

What we call a *general*, as distinct from a universal, claim would be expressed as 'Xs are, in general, Ys' or 'Xs are Ys' or 'Each X is probably Y.' With respect to your microchip order, you could adopt as your conclusion the proposition that 'Generally, the microchips meet our specifications.' The point to be underlined here is that general claims are not as strong as their universal counterparts: stating that 'Generally, the microchips meet our specifications' is not as strong a claim as 'All the microchips meet our specifications.' The general claim that the microchips meet your specifications means that they are, on the whole, satisfactory; but unlike the universal claim, the general claim leaves open the possibility that some chips may be defective. Even so, the possibility that *some* might be defective does not negate the conclusion that, generally, the chips are good. When we say 'Salmon is good to eat', we mean that it is usually palatable and our claim is not refuted if we are served a piece of salmon that does not measure up to our general expectations. In other words, salmon does not suddenly become 'not good to eat'—it's just this particular piece of salmon.

Because generalizations may be expressed as either general or universal claims, and because the former are not as strong as the latter, general claims are easier to defend than universal claims, where there is less latitude. It's wise, therefore, to make general claims rather than universal ones when constructing arguments, unless you can absolutely guarantee the truth of the universal claim. In the case of the microchips, the general claim is more easily defended than the claim that 'All the microchips meet the specifications', although this, too, is supported by the sampling.

Depending on your findings, your sample could be used to support what we call *proportional* generalizations. Let us suppose that on examining the first five microchips, you find that one of the five is defective. In that case, you would probably pull out a few more, say, four more chips, from the same box and inspect them. Suppose that you find them to be satisfactory, but to assure yourself further, you decide to examine yet another five chips and find that all of them meet your specifications. Now, from one of the 10 boxes you have found one out of 14 chips to be defective.

But having found one defective chip, you are wary that there may be more. So you open all 10 boxes and at random select a dozen chips from each. You examine them all, and conclude that the proportion of defective chips is probably 3 out of every 120, or that 2.5 per cent of the chips fail to meet your specifications. More generally, you are able to conclude that the vast majority of the chips meet your specifications. In both cases, you are making a proportional generalization.

So generalization can take the form of universal, general, or proportional claims. What more can we say about what constitutes a good generalization? The key to a good generalization, no matter what type of claim, is a representative sampling of the members of the group in question, a sampling that fairly represents the group as a whole.

The first consideration in determining the suitability of the sample is obviously its size, for samples that are too small might be unreliable and are more likely to be affected by pure chance. In your initial sampling, you examined 16 of 1,000 microchips and concluded that they meet your specifications. Assuming that you have confidence in the firm that manufactured them—they have a good track record—and in the process by which the chips are produced—presumably by automated machinery that predictably turns out identical items—you have good reason to accept your conclusion despite the relatively small sample examined. In contrast, a sample size of one or two or three from one box would not be sufficient to support your conclusion, for it would be too susceptible to the luck of the draw. As more and more chips are examined, the chances that your results are mere coincidence continually diminish.

In the case of the proportional generalization, the discovery of a defective chip led you to enlarge your sample. Notwithstanding the good reputation of the firm, everyone knows that slip-ups can occur on production lines. To get a more accurate picture of the consequences of such a slip-up, you examined more chips. If you had settled for your first five chips, you would have concluded that 20 per cent of the chips were defective. As it turns out, a larger sample suggests that only 2.5 per cent are defective.

Other considerations have to do with *what* is being sampled. In the case of microchips, which are manufactured using sophisticated technology capable of producing identical items on a production line, we can assume a high level of consistency and predictability. But let's say that your business is selling fruit rather than computers, and the product you received is not microchips but perishable goods like bananas or strawberries. In this case there are different mitigating factors that make the general consistency of the product more difficult to assume: very simply, bananas are not 'produced' identically as are microchips, nor does their quality remain the same. Given that fruit is affected by many factors that produce imperfections, there is a greater chance that the quality will vary, and in that case you would probably want a larger sample than in the case of the microchips.

In everyday life we are prone to make many generalizations without sufficient evidence, and these hasty generalizations cause some people to conclude, as we mentioned at the outset, that you simply cannot generalize. But again, bad generalizations do not rule out the possibility of good generalizations, and using our critical faculties, as well as common sense, will help us to decide whether a generalization is reasonable. In particular, we should be on guard against anecdotal evidence, which consists of informal reports of incidents or circumstances that have not been made the subject of careful investigation. This can be unreliable and is used frequently in everyday generalizations to support conclusions about certain groups, such as the unemployed, welfare recipients, the very rich, particular ethnic groups, the homeless, and so on. We should be very cautious about such generalizations, which are often based on very few specific instances, in which case the minimal size of such samples usually means that they cannot provide a basis for reasonable conclusions. Given that the evidence is anecdotal, we may not even be in a position to verify its truth; it might be no more than hearsay, which does not usually constitute legitimate evidence. Finally, such evidence can originate in prejudiced or biased attitudes, which again means that it is very unreliable. This leads us to our second consideration about what constitutes a good generalization.

A sample must not only be sufficiently large, it must also avoid bias. Anecdotal evidence, since it is subjective, can exhibit bias. In a statistical context, bias is a way in which the individuals in the sample are different—in important ways—from others in the larger group. For example, if the microchips in your order had been made by two distinct processes and if your sample included only those made by one of the processes, then the sample would be biased. In other words, each process could have its own potential problems and we could not expect to account for this if we only look at chips made by one of the two processes. Another way of saying this would be that the necessary consistency in the sample is not present. In this case, a representative sample would have to include chips from both processes.

Bias is particularly problematic when we deal with groups of people. Different people are characterized by different economic situations, religious commitments, and political affiliations and by differences of gender, age, and ethnic background. As we saw in Chapter 10, all of these contribute to their belief systems, which affect their opinions and attitudes about virtually anything we may wish to investigate. Consequently, any attempt to generalize about people and their behaviour must carefully avoid a sample that is imblanced in any way, by taking account of relevant differences and variations in perspective.

For example, a common problem with many of our generalizations about people is that we tend to generalize from situations with which we are familiar, without asking whether our sample has a bias. When a social worker generalizes about single mothers, for instance, he must keep in mind that he is working in a specific geographic area with particular social, ethnic, economic, and political characteristics. He must therefore ask himself whether single mothers elsewhere share a similar situation. It is only when he has answered in the affirmative that he can use his experience as a basis for more comprehensive claims.

Bias can occasionally creep into a generalization in subtle ways. Information-gathering techniques, such as opinion polls or market surveys, can be subject to any number of problems having to do with bias or slant, both in the way the survey is set up and in the manner the data are interpreted. Any of these factors can seriously undermine the reliability of their conclusions. How samples of people might be biased can be illustrated by an incident that took place during the well-known and ongoing advertising war between Pepsi-Cola and Coca-Cola. In Pepsi surveys of customer preference, regular Coke drinkers were asked to choose between a glass of Coke, labelled 'Q', and a glass of Pepsi, labelled 'M'. Over half of those tested picked glass M, and Pepsi made a great deal of this statistic in its advertisements. We can diagram the implicit argument as:

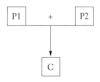

where

     Pl = Over half of the regular Coke drinkers preferred glass M over glass Q.
     P2 = Glass M contained Pepsi while glass Q contained Coke.
     C = Over half of the regular Coke drinkers prefer the taste of Pepsi.

Although this appears to be a reasonable generalization, Coke researchers detected a bias in the testing when they found that people asked to choose between any two glasses of cola marked 'M' and 'Q' generally preferred glass M. It appears that people, however unconsciously, may be choosing the letter, not the cola, or somehow making an association of letter and drink. Why people do so is an intriguing question. Is it because 'M' is familiar and associated with pleasant images or positive concepts, such as 'mother', 'magnificent', and 'marvellous', and that 'Q' is less familiar and tends to be associated with less positive concepts, such as 'questionable', 'quandary', and 'quack'? All we need to note is that the Coke researchers' discovery suggests that the preference is as much for a particular letter as for a particular taste, illustrating just how subtle biases can be (although we can also note that these findings came from Coke researchers, leaving open the possibility of a vested interest in their findings, which would be another type of bias).

More common biases have to do with the kinds of individuals canvassed in a particular poll or survey. Once again, it can be an issue of how representative the sample is, but the problem this time might have more to do with demographics, or with the sample being selected too specifically to the issue. If, for instance, a university alumni magazine publishes a survey of average earnings of those who graduated 10 years earlier and neglects to specify how the results were calculated, the claim is worth little. It might turn out, for example, that the majority of the respondents had been students in the business faculty, rather than from across the disciplines, and that these students had mostly gone on to careers in business. The results in this case would doubtless be weighted very differently from what would be obtained if former students in all professions, or former students from disciplines that traditionally lead into less lucrative professions, had been polled.

In addition, the problem faced by all surveys is the reliability of the information being provided. People may exaggerate or even lie on surveys if they want to present a certain image. Studies have shown, for instance, that the information people tend to give on questionnaires is often not the truth but what they think is socially desirable—what looks good. Given that much of this information can never be verified, we have to be cautious in accepting such results, and always must question the particulars and the structure of a survey.

One of the most famous biased samples is the one the *Literary Digest* used to predict the results of the 1936 US presidential election. It consisted of telephone interviews and written surveys by *Digest* subscribers. Some 10 million individuals registered their opinions and the pollsters predicted that the election would result in 370 electoral college votes for Alf Landon and 161 for Franklin Roosevelt. History showed the pollsters to be drastically mistaken; Roosevelt won hands down. You might wonder how a sample as large as the one the Digest used could be mistaken, but subsequent analysis revealed a fundamental bias. Not everyone could afford a telephone or a magazine subscription in 1936; in fact, only individuals of a certain privileged socio-economic background could. It turned out that the sample represented an economic class that was overwhelmingly predisposed to the Republican Party. The error cost the magazine its life.

To avoid such disasters, you must make every effort to keep biases out of the samples you use. The kind of sample you need for good generalizations should be sufficiently large, as neutral as possible, and 'random'—that is, one in which any individual in the group you are examining has an equal chance of being picked. This will make it more likely that various subgroups in the whole group will be represented in your sample.

Because truly random samples are difficult to obtain, polls and surveys conducted by professionals tend to use 'stratified random sampling'. Securing such a sample is not easy. It involves dividing the group of people to be polled or things to be examined into relevant categories and ensuring that a suitable number of individuals from each group is included in the sample. If 25 per cent of Americans have incomes under $20,000, then a study aiming to discover what percentage of Americans support their present government should attempt to have 25 per cent of its survey filled by Americans with incomes under $20,000. The sample must be selected in such a way as to ensure that all other significant classifications are considered.

In day-to-day affairs, you can approximate stratified random sampling by ensuring that the generalizations you make are founded on observations that do not exclude important subgroups. If you want to find out what people in society think about the extent to which the government subsidizes universities, you will want to make sure that your generalization fairly represents the feelings of those inside and outside the university system, for each group is likely to have a different perspective on the issue. In most day-to-day situations, common sense can serve as your guide to eliminating bias.

To summarize, we define a good generalization as:

A generalization based on a sampling of a group that is representative of the group as a whole in that it is (i) of reasonable size, and (ii) free of bias.

In controversial cases, an argument will have to include premises that establish both (i) and (ii). Often these premises must themselves be supported by arguments, which turns the inference into an extended argument.

Given these criteria for good generalizations, a good argument against a generalization must show that it is not based on a representative sample because conditions (i) or (ii) or both are not met. We must, of course, explain why we believe the sample to be inadequate and the conclusion skewed. In some cases, we may be able to show that it is impossible to back a generalization with a good argument and thereby dismiss the general claim.

Box 11.1 Generalizations

Generalization is the process of moving from specific observations about some individuals within a group to general claims about members of the group. The kinds of claims generalizations can make are called universal, general, and proportional claims. A good generalization is based on a representative sampling of the group as a whole that is (i) of reasonable size and (ii) free of bias.

EXERCISE 11A

1. For each of the following topics, state whether you are or are not in a position to make a reasonable generalization, and why. In each case, discuss the issues involved and the problems you may encounter in forming a generalization. Giving examples of possible generalizations, discuss how you could improve the sample to yield a more reliable generalization, and/or modify your generalization to fit your sample more accurately.
   a) students' work habits
   b) the policies of a particular political party
   c) bus service where you live
   d) the exams of a particular instructor
   e) psychology courses
   f) the attitudes of Americans
   g) the spending habits of tourists to California
   h) the colour of squirrels
   i) the price of automobiles
   j) the reliability of your make of car
2. Identify the generalizations contained in the following examples and assess their strength:
   a) [A letter to the *Toronto Star*, 17 Nov. 1987] Vit Wagner's review of the movie *Castaway* (Nov. 10) contains a paragraph that begins: 'From there, things just get worse. While Lucy frollicks (*sic*) around the island . . . .'
       One thing that keeps getting worse is the standard of spelling in Canadian newspapers.
   *b) A month-long poll conducted on people entering the Fitness First Health Club in Johnsonville found that people worked out on average twice and

sometimes three times a week. The study concluded that people in Johnsonville were very healthy.

c) Tony's first car was a Buick, and it was a very good car. His next car was also a Buick, and he had very few problems with it, so when his friend Kate needed a car, he recommended a Buick. Kate took Tony's advice and bought a Buick, which she is still driving seven years later, having had to take care of only minor repairs in the course of tune-ups. Tony has concluded that the Buick is a very good car indeed and has decided never to drive any other kind of car.

d) [Advertisement for Madame Zorina Zoltan, 'Tarot-reader for the rich and famous', *Weekly World News*, 24 Mar. 1992] Her record of accuracy for predicting the future is so incredible: She provided the solutions to unsolved Police Dept. crimes—Predicted to within one block, the whereabouts of kidnap victims.

e) [From the manifesto of the 'Unabomber', taken off the World Wide Web] It is said that we live in a free society because we have a certain number of constitutionally guaranteed rights. But these are not as important as they seem. The degree of personal freedom that exists in a society is determined more by the economic and technological structure of the society than by its laws or its form of government. Most of the Indian nations of New England were monarchies, and many of the cities of the Italian Renaissance were controlled by dictators. But in reading about these societies one gets the impression that they allowed far more personal freedom than our society does.

2. CAUSAL REASONING

Sometimes we use generalizations to establish cause-and-effect relationships. When Pepsi advertises that more than half of the regular Coke drinkers picked Pepsi in their taste test, it is suggesting that Pepsi's good taste caused them to do so. When a university tells you (or potential students) that graduates earn such-and-such an impressive average income, it is suggesting that a high income is, at least in part, a causal consequence of the stature of the institution and of the quality of education it provides. We usually attempt to establish more specific causal relationships by appealing to general causal claims, for example, that *you* have a promising future because you are attending your present college or university, whose graduates generally do well. Accordingly, we must examine ways of establishing both general and specific causal claims.

General Causal Reasoning
General causal arguments attempt to establish general or universal causal relationships. Scientists make such arguments when they attempt to show that a certain chemical will behave in a specific way under certain conditions, that smoking causes lung cancer, or that car emissions and other burning of fossil

fuels are causing acid rain. We make general causal claims when we say that students from a particular school are better prepared for university or that wearing seat-belts saves lives.

Some philosophers have argued that the structure of the world is a series of causal relationships; or conversely, that our minds are structured in such a way that we look at everything in the world in causal terms. That is, everything that happens and that we encounter is understandable as the effect of some given cause. It would certainly appear to be true that reliance on cause-effect explanations operates in a great many instances in everyday life. We would think that a mechanic or a telephone repair person had taken leave of her senses if she told us that there was simply no cause for our car not starting or for our telephone not working. In such cases, as in many others, we assume that there is a cause, even if it is not known at the time.

Many of the general causal claims we make are based on the knowledge we have accumulated about relations between events. In the course of growing up we learn to associate injuries with pain, broken glass with flat tires, concentrated study with good grades, and so forth. If, every now and then, we come up against a situation for which our accumulated knowledge cannot account, we are confident that there is still some cause for it, even if we do not presently know it.

Our assumption that events always do have a cause, even if it eludes us for the present, provides the framework for much scientific and medical research, especially when it takes the form of a kind of mystery-solving. Seeking to explain why certain natural species are in danger of extinction, scientists trace conditions and factors to determine the cause for the species' decline. In an effort to find a cure for cancer, medical researchers expend tremendous amounts of time, effort, and money to determine precisely what causes cancer, and thereby attempt to discover the appropriate cure.

Two kinds of causes play a role in general causal reasoning. A *constant condition* is a causal factor that is necessary for an event to occur. For example, the presence of oxygen is a constant condition for combustion. Without oxygen, there cannot be combustion. But under normal circumstances we would not say that oxygen causes combustion. We designate as the cause the *variable condition*, which is the condition that brings about the effect. Since dry foliage is a constant condition for a forest fire and oxygen for combustion, the carelessly tossed match—the variable condition—is what we would normally designate as the cause of a particular fire.

We call the set of constant and/or variable conditions that produce some event its *composite cause*. A full account of the composite cause of some event is very difficult to produce, given that most events are the result of a complex web of causal relationships and a number of constant and/or variable conditions. Sometimes it is important to specify the constant and variable conditions that produce an effect, but the variable condition is the most common focus of concern. When we ask what caused a forest fire, we are searching for the variable condition, such as lightning, a campfire left with glowing embers, or the like.

In the case of forest fires, the variable condition gets most of our attention because we want to prevent forest fires and the variable condition is easiest to control. That is why we take steps to ensure that campers carefully extinguish their fires. Trying to prevent such fires by eliminating constant conditions, like the presence of oxygen, is obviously impractical and would have other consequences we wish to avoid.

But there are circumstances when the only practical way to prevent some event is by reducing or eliminating the impact of the constant conditions. If we have excessively heavy rains in the spring, then we try to prevent floods, not by attempting to eliminate the rain, but by building dams to control the amount of water flowing in the rivers.

The key to a good argument for the general claim 'X causes Y' is a demonstration that X regularly leads to Y. If we find that this is the case, we say that there is a correlation between X and Y. The claim that gum disease is caused by the build-up of plaque is ultimately based on the work of scientists who have established a correlation between the build-up of plaque and gum disease.

Every causal relationship implies the existence of a correlation between two events, X and Y, but the existence of a correlation does not in itself guarantee a causal relationship; the assumption that this is the case is the most common error made in causal reasoning. The problem is that a correlation may be attributable to other factors. In particular, it may be the result of simple chance or of some third event, Z, which causes Y or both X and Y, and is referred to as a 'second' cause. We shall encounter correlations that are the result of luck or of second causes as our discussion proceeds. At this point let us define a good general causal argument as:

> An argument that establishes that X causes Y (where X is a variable condition or a composite cause) by showing (i) that there is a correlation between X and Y, (ii) that this correlation is not the result of mere coincidence, and (iii) that there is no second cause, Z, that is the cause of Y or of both X and Y.

In many cases, a good argument for the claim that X causes Y must include arguments for the claim that the correlation is not caused by chance. Such an argument should explain why it is plausible to see X and Y as causally connected.

Given our definition, good arguments *against* a causal claim or causal reasoning can be constructed by showing that conditions (i), (ii), and (iii) have not been met or, perhaps, cannot be met. In most controversial cases it is usually (iii), the problem of second causes, that demands the closest scrutiny.

The problem of second causes can be illustrated by the following article advocating school uniforms, adapted from an article that *The Globe and Mail* reprinted from the *New York Times* ('Making the case for school uniforms', *The Globe and Mail*, 13 Sept. 1993). One observation: when the author refers to dress codes, what he apparently has in mind are school uniforms in particular.

> In many countries where students outperform their American counterparts academically, school dress codes are observed as part of creating the proper learning environment. Their students tend to be neater, less disruptive in class and more disciplined, mainly because their minds are focused more on learning and less on materialism.
>
> Many students [in American schools] seem to pay more attention to what's on their bodies than in their minds. . . . The fiercest competition among students is often not over academic achievements, but over who dresses most expensively.
>
> It's time Americans realized that the benefits of safe and effective schools far outweigh any perceived curtailment of freedom of expression brought on by dress codes.

We have here the following causal argument:

P1 = In many countries where students outperform their American counterparts academically, school dress codes are observed as part of creating the proper learning environment.

P2 = Their students tend to be neater, less disruptive in class and more disciplined, mainly because their minds are focused more on learning and less on materialism.

P3 = Many students [in American schools] seem to pay more attention to what's on their bodies than in their minds.

P4 = The fiercest competition among students [in American schools] is often not over academic achievements, but over who dresses most expensively.

C1 = It's time Americans realized that the benefits of safe and effective schools far outweigh any perceived curtailment of freedom of expression brought on by dress codes.

HC(MC) = American schools should enact dress codes.

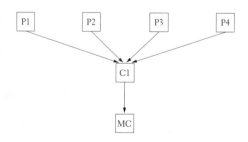

This argument hinges on the acceptance of several related correlations: students who wear school uniforms are focused more on learning and less on materialism; students who wear uniforms are also neater and more disciplined; students who do not wear uniforms are more preoccupied with appearance than with their academic achievements; and finally, that in countries where students outperform American students, their superior performance is related to the fact that those students wear school uniforms. These points can also be stated in the form of a causal chain, arguing that the wearing of uniforms instils better discipline in students, which in turn produces better academic performance.

There are a number of secondary correlations between uniforms and good behaviour, uniforms and focus on academic matters, which point to the larger correlations between school dress codes and the proper learning environment and school dress codes and superior academic performance. The main (and hidden) conclusion expresses, then, a causal relationship between the wearing of school uniforms and superior scholarly behaviour and performance.

However, along with the potential problems with some of the argument's generalizations (like those having to do with the behaviour and academic performance of some students, which seem largely anecdotal and would have to be supported by clear evidence), there is the problem with the argument's main causal relationship: it has not been shown that the allegedly superior performance of students who wear uniforms is caused by the wearing of uniforms, nor, conversely, that the allegedly inferior performance of American students is caused by the fact that they aren't usually required to wear uniforms. Nor is it shown that the wearing of uniforms instils better discipline in students, which in turn produces better academic performance. Any of these correlations would have to be supported much more extensively. In addition, the argument would have to show that these correlations are not the result of mere coincidence or of second causes. For example, if it is the case that some American students perform less well academically, we could point to other mitigating factors, such as certain poor social and economic conditions, that might play a greater role than their not wearing uniforms, or the possibility that American students are living in a culture that currently tends to undervalue academic achievement. We could argue that cultures where students wear school uniforms also tend to place an extremely high premium on the value and importance of education, with much more public and generalized promotion of educational standards and achievement—more so, perhaps, than in the United States. Conversely, it could be that such encouragement is in fact a form of intense pressure to excel academically, and the same culture that would mandate the wearing of uniforms could be putting a great deal of pressure on students to succeed. In both cases, the wearing of uniforms would be a secondary or related feature of a larger cultural phenomenon: in other words, both the wearing of uniforms and academic achievement could be features or even effects of a larger cause—the cultural context, in either positive or negative terms—rather than academic achievement being the effect caused by the wearing of uniforms.

We can construct a good argument *against* questionable causal reasoning by demonstrating how it fails to meet the requirements for good causal reasoning. In the present case, we can develop the points raised in the preceding paragraph. But we could further strengthen our argument against the author's claim by citing instances that would tend to undermine the author's overall claim, such as the presence of high academic (and competitive) achievement among American students who were not required to wear uniforms.

A more convincing case of general causal reasoning is provided by parents and educators who argue that violence on television, in the movies, and in popular video games is fostering violent behaviour in children. The evidence often cited involves incidents where children have engaged in violent behaviour that directly imitated violent action or events they had seen on television or in video games. That these children were acquainted with certain video games or watched certain television programs, and were directly taking on the names and imitating the behaviour of well-known characters in an effort to re-enact the character's actions, can establish the necessary correlation and discount the possibility of coincidence.

The possibility of a second cause of this particular violent behaviour is also minimized. The most plausible way to argue for one would be in terms of an aggressive tendency in certain children that would manifest itself in violent incidents, even if they did not watch television or play video games. That possibility, though, is discounted by the fact that the parents' observations are, implicitly, a response to a rash of incidents that represent an increase in violent behaviour, along with an increase in the popularity and frequency of the portrayal of violence in movies and television, and in many cases the direct imitation of the violent actions of well-known television or video characters. Although this needs to be given extra emphasis in the argument to counter the second-cause hypothesis, the parents' causal argument, while not necessarily conclusive, is initially a plausible one.

Box 11.2 General Causal Reasoning

General causal reasoning attempts to establish general causal principles that govern causes and effects. A good general causal argument is an argument that establishes that X causes Y (where X is a variable condition or a composite cause) by showing (i) that there is a correlation between X and Y, (ii) that this correlation is not the result of mere coincidence, and (iii) that there is no second cause, Z, that is the cause of Y or of both X and Y.

Particular Causal Reasoning

In Chapter 2, we distinguished between arguments and explanations. We saw that many of the words we use in constructing arguments are also used in explanations. One kind of explanation that plays a particularly important role in our lives is the kind that gives the cause of some particular state of affairs. Consider the following statements:

> The fire was the result of smoking in bed.
> He died of a massive coronary.
> You brewed the coffee too long. That's why it's so bitter.
> The reason the car wouldn't start was that the battery was dead.
> Motivated by greed, the banker embezzled the money.

Though none of the above statements uses the word 'cause', they all express causal relationships. Note once again that these are not arguments, but explanations; they seek to explain an event by pointing to the cause.

The causal arguments that we have discussed so far are arguments for general causal principles. When we make particular causal claims, we use these general principles to support the particular claims. In the most straightforward cases, such reasoning takes the form:

> X causes Y.
> Therefore, this y was caused by this x.

where x and y are instances of the general categories of X and Y. Thus, if 'X causes Y' means 'Carelessly discarded cigarette butts (can) cause forest fires', then 'This y was caused by this x' means 'This particular forest fire was caused by a (particular) carelessly discarded cigarette butt.' In more complex cases, we may not have obvious general causal principles that we can use to explain a particular causal claim and it may be necessary to investigate the situation further to determine what they might be. In either case, an explanation and defence of a particular causal claim depend on general causal principles.

Against the background of this discussion, we define a good argument for a particular causal claim as:

> An argument that establishes that some specific state of affairs, y, is caused by x, by showing that x is both consistent with general causal principles and provides the most plausible explanation of the state of affairs in question.

Similarly, an argument *against* a particular causal claim must show that it is inconsistent with general causal claims, or that the causal reasoning on which the claim is based does not satisfy the criteria for good arguments of this kind. We could argue, for instance, that the fire could not have been caused by smoking in bed because the owners who died in the blaze were lifelong non-smokers.

An example of particular causal reasoning is seen in the speculation that President Ronald Reagan would not survive his second term in office. The evidence given for this projection was the fact that every US president elected since 1840 in a year ending in zero died in office. The list begins with William Henry Harrison and includes Abraham Lincoln, James Garfield, Warren Harding, and Franklin Roosevelt, and ends with John Kennedy. (The proponents of the strange connection note other striking similarities between Lincoln and Kennedy: Lincoln was elected in 1860, Kennedy in 1960; both Lincoln and Kennedy had vice-presidents named Johnson; Lincoln had a secretary named Kennedy, Kennedy had a secretary named Lincoln; Lincoln's assassin shot him in a theatre and ran to a warehouse, Kennedy's alleged assailant shot from a warehouse and ran to a theatre; and finally, the names of both assailants have the same number of letters.)

The attempt to draw a correlation between the death of a president and the year in which he was elected is intriguing, but there are serious problems with the reasoning involved in it. The essence of this particular causal argument is the reasoning:

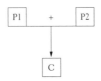

where P1 is the general causal principle 'Presidents elected since 1840 in years ending with a zero die in office', P2 is the claim that 'President Reagan was elected in a year ending in zero', and C is the conclusion 'President Reagan will die in office.'

Such reasoning is extremely dubious because it appeals to the causal principle we have included as P1. Given that it differs so radically from normal causes that determine the time of death, the theory would require very convincing evidence to justify it. But there is little for us to go on. Its proponents list seven presidents who were elected in the years specified and who died in office. That they died while holding office appears to be attributable to little more than coincidence. The reliability of the theory is weakened by several significant factors: (i) the presidents died in different ways, apparently due to different causal conditions; (ii) we know of no more sizeable correlation that can add weight to the theory, such as a correlation showing that every head of state elected since 1840 in a year ending in zero died in office; and (iii) the 'principle' is concocted specifically to exclude the two earlier presidents elected in years ending in zero (Thomas Jefferson and James Monroe), who did not die in office. To show that election in a year ending in zero is a causal factor in a president's demise, one would have to appeal to general causal principles that suggest that there is more than chance at work. It is difficult to imagine what such principles would state and how they could be defended.

> **Box 11.3 Particular Causal Reasoning**
> Particular causal reasoning attempts to establish the cause of some specific state of affairs. A good instance of particular causal reasoning shows that some state of affairs, y, is caused by x, by showing that x is both consistent with general causal principles and provides the most plausible explanation of the state of affairs in question.

3. SLIPPERY SLOPE ARGUMENTS

It often happens that causal arguments are used to show that certain actions should be performed or avoided because of their long-term consequences. Using upper-case letters to refer to actions, we can represent the form of such arguments as follows:

A causes B, B causes C, and so on to X.
X is undesirable (or X is desirable).
Therefore, A is undesirable (or desirable).

We call arguments of this form 'slippery slope' arguments because they reason that a given action commits us to something else, that performing some particular action initiates our sliding down a slippery slope of causal sequences to some inevitable consequence, a consequence that can be desirable or undesirable.

Slippery slope reasoning is used when it is argued that one should not smoke marijuana because doing so will lead to harder drugs and (eventually) to an unhappy life. Likewise, arguing that eliminating religious education in school will weaken the moral fibre of schoolchildren and ultimately result in increased unethical or criminal behaviour is an instance of slippery slope reasoning. Both of these examples illustrate undesirable consequences. But slippery slope reasoning can also point to desirable consequences, as in the argument that publicizing 'global warming' will result in such sensitivity to the problem that people will put pressure on politicians and scientists to take the actions necessary to alleviate the anticipated danger. That hard work in the early stages of your logic course will pay off on the final exam and in your final grade is another example of slippery slope reasoning toward a desirable consequence!

The issue in evaluating slippery slope arguments is whether the causal connections posited really hold and whether the final consequence has been properly judged to be desirable or undesirable. Accordingly, a good slippery slope argument can be defined as:

> An argument that shows either (i) that an action should not be performed or allowed because it will begin a causal chain leading to an undesirable consequence, or (ii) that an action should be performed or allowed because it will entail a chain of causes leading to a desirable end.

In both cases, the goal is to avoid or gain some consequence that is the end result of a causal chain.

A good argument *against* slippery slope reasoning must establish that the claimed causal chain does not exist, or that the value of its ultimate consequence has been misjudged. The causal chain can be challenged by questioning one of the causal links, by pointing out either that it lacks support or that it is supported by poor causal reasoning. To avoid such criticisms we may have to construct a good causal argument supporting every link in the chain.

Two examples can illustrate good and bad slippery slope reasoning. The following defence of exercise comes from John Hofsess (*Maclean's*, Oct. 1973) and is found in Johnson and Blair's *Logical Self-Defense*, 3rd Edition (Toronto: McGraw-Hill Ryerson, 1993), p. 182.

> If you don't get into the habit of exercising regularly when you're young, you are less likely to keep exercising during your later 20s and 30s when career, home, and family take up more and more time and interest. You'll then tend to become sedentary and physically unfit. That will set you up for various heart and lung diseases during middle age. No one wants to have a heart attack at 45 or 50, so to lessen that danger, you ought to get into the habit of exercising when you're young.

The claim is that failure to exercise while you are still young may put you on a slippery slope that begins with bad habits and ends with heart or lung disease. Therefore you should start to exercise regularly in your youth. Given the plausibility of the causal links, the argument is a good one.

Contrast this with the following attack on 'unseasonable' laughter by St John of Chrysostom.

> (T)o laugh, to speak jocosely, does not seem an acknowledged sin, but it leads to acknowledged sin. Thus laughter often gives birth to foul discourse, and foul discourse to actions still more foul. Often from words and laughter proceed railing and insult; and from railing and insult, blows and wounds; and from blows and wounds, slaughter and murder. If, then, thou wouldst take good

counsel for thyself, avoid not merely foul words, and foul deeds, or blows, and wounds, and murders, but unseasonable laughter itself. (*Post-Nicene Fathers*, v. IX, p. 442)

In representing St John's argument, it is useful to treat as separate premises the different causal links. We can represent the argument's components with the following legend:

P1 = Laughter often gives birth to foul discourse.
P2 = Foul discourse gives rise to actions still more foul.
P3 = Often from words and laughter proceed railing and insult.
P4 = From railing and insult proceed blows and wounds.
P5 = From blows and wounds proceed slaughter and murder.
C1 = To laugh, to speak jocosely, leads to acknowledged sins.
MC = If, then, thou wouldst take good counsel for thyself, avoid not merely foul words, and foul deeds, or blows, and wounds, and murders, but unseasonable laughter itself.

and by diagramming the argument as follows:

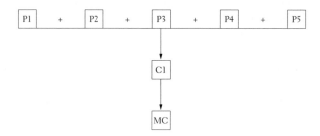

In certain cases the argument may be reasonable, but it is not convincing as a generalization about laughter in all contexts. There is no clear connection between unseasonable laughter and foul discourse, between foul discourse and railing and insult, between railing and insult and blows and wounds, and between blows and wounds and slaughter and murder. One could make the argument more plausible by restricting attention to certain kinds of laughter, such as derisive laughter in rough company, but even then the causal relationships would be rather tenuous.

Many other cases of slippery slope reasoning are more complex. In particular, moral and legal reasoning to the effect that we should treat certain cases in a similar way to avoid certain consequences entails a host of further questions. Moreover, moral and legal reasoning is also tied up with reasoning from analogy, to which we now turn.

> **Box 11.4 Slippery Slope Arguments**
> An argument that shows either (i) that an action should not be performed or allowed because it will begin a causal chain leading to an undesirable consequence, or (ii) that an action should be performed or allowed because it will entail a chain of causes leading to a desirable end. A good slippery slope argument must be founded on a plausible causal chain and an acceptable claim about what is or is not desirable.

Exercise 11B

1. In the following, identify the causal claim, then evaluate and discuss the reasoning.
   a) After his criminal record was disclosed, the local politician's standing dropped in the polls and he lost the election to his opponent.
   b) [Adapted from Vincent E. Barry, *The Critical Edge* (Fort Worth: Harcourt Brace Jovanovich, 1992)] News item: The jailed owner of a pit bulldog that fatally mauled a 2½-year-old boy has blamed the child's parents for leaving the boy unattended. 'If the parents had kept tabs on this kid, this never would have happened', said the owner. The child was savagely attacked when he walked past the two pit bulls, tied at the side of the owner's house, and across the front yard.
   *c) Whenever Bob plays poker, he wears his suspenders, because he has never lost at poker while wearing his suspenders.
   d) [From a letter to the *Toronto Star*, 5 Dec. 1984] Re, your picture of the truck that didn't quite make it under a bridge on the Niagara River Parkway (Nov. 27). Note that the bridge clearance sign reads '3.3 metres.'
      Now if it had read '11 feet . . .'
2. For the following topics, sketch slippery slope arguments concerning the resulting undesirable consequences. How could such arguments be countered or undermined?
   a) allowing stores to open on Sunday
   b) legislating mandatory bicycle helmet laws
   c) legalizing certain drugs, such as marijuana
3. Assess the slippery slope argument in the following. [Adapted from J. Gay-Williams, 'The Wrongfulness of Euthanasia', in Ronald Munson, ed., *Intervention and Reflection: Basic Issues and Medical Ethics* (Belmont, Calif.: Wadsworth, 1979)] Euthanasia as a policy is a slippery slope. A person apparently hopelessly ill may be allowed to take his own life. Should he no longer be able to act, he may be permitted to deputize others to do it for him; then the judgment of others becomes the ruling factor. At this point it becomes a matter of others acting 'on behalf of' the patient as they see fit, and this may incline them to act on behalf of other patients who have not authorized them to act on

their behalf. It is only a short step, then, from voluntary euthanasia (self-inflicted or authorized), to directed euthanasia administered to a patient who has given no authorization, to involuntary euthanasia conducted as part of a social policy. As social policy, it would give society or its representatives the authority to eliminate all those who might be considered too 'ill' to function normally any longer.

4. ARGUMENTS FROM ANALOGY

Analogies add richness to our language. Often they are used for poetic or picturesque purposes, but they are also used to clarify our claims or as a basis for conclusions. An analogy draws a partial similarity between two different things by identifying similar features they both possess. A neurosurgeon delivering a lecture on the structure of the human brain might introduce her lecture by saying that 'The brain is like a highly efficient and compact computer' and then organize her lecture around specific similarities.

As long as no conclusion is drawn from the comparison between the brain and a computer, we do not have an argument. It is an analogy, but one used simply for elucidation. When the comparison is used as a basis for some conclusion we then have an argument from analogy: the drawing of the conclusion that two things are analogous in a certain respect because they are analogous in one or more other ways. If on the basis of similarities that characterize both the human brain and the computer and from the fact that computers are machines, the neurosurgeon concluded that 'Humans are just complicated machines', we would then have an argument from analogy.

We call the two things compared in an analogy 'analogues'. For purposes of exhibiting the structure of and discussing analogical arguments, we can label the analogues X and Y. Those respects in which X and Y are said to be alike can be represented as p, q, r, and so on. Each of these letters represents a statement that is true of both X and Y. Since Y is like X in possessing the qualities p, q, r, . . . we conclude that it possesses some additional quality z that we know X possesses. Schematically, the argument can be depicted as follows:

$$X-p, q, r, . . . z.$$
$$Y-p, q, r, . . .$$
Therefore, $Y-z$.

The analogues do not have to be single entities. One or the other or both may be groups of things, in which case the form of the argument may look like this:

$$X, W, R, S-p, q, r, . . . z.$$
$$Y-p, q, r, . . .$$
Therefore, $Y-z$.

We analyse analogical reasoning in terms of the similarities between the analogues. In the extreme case, the analogues, X and Y, will be identical. In that event, the conclusion necessarily follows, for any property X has will be shared by Y. If X and Y are identical twins, for example, then finding out something about X's genetic make-up allows us to conclude the same of Y. Other instances where the conclusion of an argument from analogy is guaranteed by its premises are cases where the properties that X and Y share entail z. Two arguments, X and Y, let us say, have the same structure; hence if one is valid, the other one must also be valid. But the cases we usually consider are cases where X and Y are not identical and where the conclusion that X has property z is only probable, given the premises of the argument.

Such analogies are often used in science. Medical research provides ample examples in which discoveries about the effect that particular substances have on rats or other mammals are used as a basis for conclusions about the effects they will have on humans. Because there would be disadvantages to carrying out initial tests on humans, medical researchers use a species with a physiological system analogous to that of humans and conclude that humans would probably be similarly affected.

A convincing argument from analogy must enumerate real and not just apparent similarities between the analogues. Furthermore, the similarities must be relevant to the conclusion, and not incidental or irrelevant features. Often this will mean that particular aspects of an object are relevant in some contexts and not in others. If you want to buy a new car and decide to buy one similar to a friend's, then you must ask yourself what aspects of her car attract you. If it is style and appearance, then a comparable car will be one with similar shape, interior, and perhaps colour. If it is dependability that matters most to you, then you would focus instead on such things as engine design and size.

Considerations such as these lead us to define a good argument from analogy as:

> An argument that supports a conclusion about Y by pointing out (i) that it is true of X, and (ii) that Y is similar in sufficient relevant respects, and not relevantly dissimilar.

A good argument from analogy will have premises that establish that the conclusion does hold of the first analogue and that the analogues are similar in ways that are relevant to the conclusion, and it will not overlook any relevant dissimilarities.

Given these criteria, a good argument *against* an argument from analogy will show either that the purported conclusion does not hold of the first analogue or that the two things being compared are not analogous and should not be considered similarly. To construct a good argument along these lines, we must show that the criteria for a good argument from analogy cannot be met or are not met in a specific argument. If someone argues, for example, that human evil is like the thorns of a rose, and therefore necessary while not detracting from the overall beauty, we can reply that the comparison between humans and roses is simply too far-fetched and unsupported to provide evidence for the conclusion. In the process we construct an argument from disanalogy.

One of the best-known examples of an argument from analogy in the history of philosophy is the 'argument from design', which states that given that the universe exhibits a particular order, predictability, and design, it is reasonable to infer from this the existence of a designer. This designer is, of course, God, and the argument from design is one of the traditional proofs for the existence of God. David Hume, the eighteenth-century Scottish philosopher, provides an interesting discussion of this argument in his *Dialogues Concerning Natural Religion*. His argument takes place in the context of a dialogue between several participants, which allows Hume both to present the argument from analogy and then to criticize it.

> Look round the world . . . you will find it to be nothing but one great machine, subdivided into an infinite number of lesser machines, which again admit of subdivisions to a degree beyond what human sense and faculties can trace and explain. All these various machines, and even their most minute parts, are adjusted to each other with an accuracy which ravishes into admiration all men who have ever contemplated them. The curious adapting of means to ends, throughout all nature, resembles exactly, though it much exceeds, the productions of human contrivance—of human design, thought, wisdom, and intelligence. Since therefore the effects resemble each other, we are led to infer, by all the rules of analogy, that the causes also resemble, and that the Author of nature is somewhat similar to the mind of man, though possessed of much larger faculties, proportioned to the grandeur of the work which he has executed.

The world is compared to one large machine, made up of innumerable smaller machines, all of which are purposeful, ordered, and precise. The manner in which everything in nature appears to happen for a reason, to fulfil a particular purpose, suggests the product of a specific design, akin to human design but far superior. This resemblance in the origins or causes suggests that the Author of nature is analogous to the human mind, though on a much greater scale, appropriate to the larger scale of creation as a whole. Hume's particular modification here is to argue less for the existence of God as for the nature of God: we infer the nature and mind of God by analogy with our nature and mind, only extended to divine proportions.

Hume next proceeds to criticize the analogy, in the voice of another participant in the dialogue, Philo, who proclaims it to be a very weak analogy. Suggesting that analogies weaken the moment we shift the terms of reference,

Philo states that when we see a house, we conclude that it had an architect or builder, because this is the kind of effect we have observed to result from that kind of cause. However, he continues:

> Surely you will not affirm that the universe bears such a resemblance to a house that we can with the same certainty infer a similar cause, or that the analogy is here entire and perfect. The dissimilitude is so striking that the utmost you can here pretend to is a guess, a conjecture, a presumption concerning a similar cause.

Philo's point is that the dissimilarities between the universe and house are so great that they threaten to outweigh the similarities and the analogy breaks down; therefore the attempt to infer, on the basis of one thing, a similar cause in the other—or any cause at all in the case of a proof of God's existence—is fruitless. In fact, what we have is a guess, not a fully convincing argument.

Hume's discussion goes on to elaborate the ways in which the universe and a house differ, much of it rooted in the basic tenet of his philosophy, that nothing we do not know from experience can be proven or accepted, and while we know from experience where houses come from, we cannot say the same about the universe. Much more could be said about this discussion, but our purpose is to illustrate a basic and renowned philosophical example of an argument from analogy and its attempted counter-argument.

A more contemporary example of an argument from analogy comes from a letter to the *Toronto Star* (27 Apr. 1983) and centres on a definition argued from analogy:

> Whether or not a fetus is a human being is a matter of personal opinion but nobody can deny that forcing a woman to carry and give birth to a child against her will is an act of enslavement. Consider: someone approaches you and demands to be hooked up to your life support system for nine months, on the grounds that this is necessary for survival. It would be an unselfish gesture to comply, but you have every right to refuse. After all, it's your body—isn't it?

Using the method of diagramming we introduced in Chapter 2, we can diagram the argument as follows:

P1 = In forcing a woman to carry and give birth to a child and in forcing you to allow someone to be hooked up to your life support system, it is one's own body that is being used.

P2 = In both cases, the use of one's body is necessary to ensure survival of the person or the fetus.

C1 = Forcing a woman to carry and give birth to a child against a woman's will is like forcing you to allow someone to be hooked up to your life support system for nine months.

P3 = In the second case, you would have the right to refuse to comply (it would be an act of enslavement to force you to comply).

MC = A woman has every right to refuse to carry a child (it would be an act of enslavement to force her to carry it).

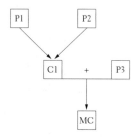

At first glance, this argument may strike you as plausible. One of the analogues appears somewhat fanciful, but there are grounds for comparing these two situations because, allowing that the fetus is a person, they both involve the dependence of one person on another. There are, however, at least two major dissimilarities that have been omitted, and once they have been introduced, MC, and therefore the whole argument, becomes completely unacceptable.

Should someone approach you and demand to be hooked to your life support system, it would be quite reasonable for you to point out that you are in no way responsible for that individual's predicament and to require some justification as to why that demand should be made specifically of you. In the case of a mother carrying a child, she usually bears some responsibility for her situation, and the justification for the demand implicitly made by the fetus is quite unlike that in the other analogue. There the person approaching you comes from the outside and, presumably, already has some autonomous existence. But in the case of a pregnancy, the fetus has developed from within and has had no antecedent existence. MC will not, therefore, be acceptable to any reasonable audience. If the two situations are to be analogous, these dissimilarities would have to be eradicated. If we can eradicate them (imagine, for the moment, that you are responsible for the predicament of the person who needs to be hooked up to your life support system), it is no longer obvious that it would be wrong to force you to support the sufferer in question.

This example illustrates the importance of being very clear about what counts as a relevant dissimilarity in any argument from analogy we construct.

Weaknesses in analogical arguments invariably arise because we overlook some relevant dissimilarity when drawing our conclusion. While the addition of relevant similarities strengthens an argument from analogy, the presence of major dissimilarities irretrievably weakens it.

> **Box 11.5 Arguments from Analogy**
> Arguments from analogy are founded on claims that individuals or states of affairs are analogous. A good argument from analogy supports a conclusion about Y by pointing out (i) that it is true of some X, and (ii) that Y is similar in sufficient relevant respects and not relevantly dissimilar.

5. APPEALS TO PRECEDENT

Morality and law require consistency. Similar cases must be dealt with in a similar way and, hence, we may appeal to precedents to establish that a particular situation should be treated in a particular way. If analogous cases were treated this way in the past, then justice demands that they be treated in the same way in the present and future. If two householders are allowed to add an addition to their house, this sets a precedent for other people in the neighbourhood to do likewise.

When we argue by appealing to a precedent we are arguing by analogy. The key question is whether the particular case that is said to be a precedent is analogous to the other cases with which we compare it. The underlying principle is one of justice. Consistency demands that a new situation, similar to a preceding one, be treated as the preceding one was treated. To resolve a dispute containing an appeal to precedent, we must decide whether the cases in question really are analogous. In particular, we must determine whether there are any relevant dissimilarities between the case at hand and the precedent with which it is compared.

Appeals to precedent can take a negative or a positive form. Sometimes we argue negatively that some action will set an undesirable precedent, allowing actions that are unacceptable. A professor may argue that it would be unfair to accept a late paper from one student because he or she must then accept late papers from other students in similar situations. In the present context, the important point is that this argument depends on the claim that the actions of other students will be analogous to those of the student in question and cannot morally or legally be separated.

We can also use appeals to precedent to argue that a given case should be treated in a particular way because it will establish a commendable precedent. We might argue, for instance, that we should prosecute a particular industrial polluter and not forgive a first offence since consistency would then demand that we forgive other first offenders.

In light of these considerations, we define a good appeal to precedent as:

An argument that some action X should be allowed (or disallowed) because some analogous case has been allowed (or disallowed); or because future analogous cases should be allowed (or disallowed).

Note that this definition allows us to appeal to precedents in the past and to establish them for the future. In both cases, the key question is the similarity to the precedent of cases said to be analogous.

A recent example of a negative precedent occurred when an Ontario court ordered that a man's extensive collection of old newspapers, magazines, and papers be seized and destroyed (*The Globe and Mail*, 25 Oct. 1995). It was argued that the collection, comprising numerous stacks of paper he had collected and stored in his basement for years, represented a fire hazard. Other collectors of old books and papers immediately saw this decision as setting an undesirable precedent, one that could be extended potentially to all collectors of old or antiquarian materials. In protesting the decision, booksellers argued that such a decision could prove a threat for antiquarian collectors and set a precedent for the suppression of private book collections. This kind of example highlights how an appeal to precedent is not only related to an argument by analogy but also bears some resemblance to slippery slope reasoning. Indeed, arguments from precedent can often be construed as slippery slope arguments. They often maintain that some action leads to an undesirable (or desirable) consequence because it sets a precedent for deciding future actions. Since the causal claims in arguments of this kind depend on an appeal to precedent, we must focus on that appeal. In constructing our own arguments and in assessing those of others, we must ensure that cases alleged to be analogous to the precedent cited are genuinely similar.

Another example of an appeal to precedent is found in what has become widely known as the 'Powell Doctrine', after General Colin Powell. Presented in the context of a discussion of the appropriate use of military force, the precedent being appealed to in this case is the Vietnam War. It is based on the perceived mistakes of the Vietnam War—in terms of both how it was undertaken and how it was carried out—with undesirable features and consequences that included lack of popular support and no clearly defined military objective. Consequently, the United States was trapped in an extended police action with heavy casualties and low morale. From this, many, including General Powell, have concluded that in the future the United States should never become involved in military action without having a clear and pre-established military objective, a high level of support from the public, and a clearly winnable position. (For more on this see *The New Republic*, 16 Oct. 1995.)

> **Box 11.6 Appeals to Precedent**
> Appeals to precedent establish whether some action should be allowed by appealing to analogous cases. A good appeal to precedent shows that some action X should be allowed (or disallowed) because some analogous case has been allowed (or disallowed); or because future analogous cases should be allowed (or disallowed).

Exercise 11C

1. Apply the criteria for assessing analogies to the following arguments. Be sure to provide full support for your decisions.
   a) [From Kathleen Gow, *Yes Virginia, There is Right and Wrong* (Toronto: John Wiley and Sons, 1980), p. 92. Background: In discussing various pedagogical techniques, Gow questions the use of exercises that put students in imaginary situations where they have to make difficult moral decisions.] Children may become so confused by all the qualifications and situational dilemma exercises—many of which are extreme and very far removed from everyday life—that they will decide that the world is totally without moral or social order. As one grade seven student asked, 'Isn't there anything you can count on?'

   When we are caring for babies, we do not give them a whole apple to eat. We know that their digestive systems are not sufficiently sophisticated to process the skin, the flesh, and the core. The risk that they will choke is very high. So instead of the whole apple, we give them applesauce—the essence of the apple. This does not mean that we are cheating them of their independence.
   b) [Adapted from a letter to the *Toronto Star*, 5 Nov. 1983] A man who drives his car into the rear of another is not guilty of careless driving if his brakes failed. Similarly, a man should not be found guilty of murder if his mind failed to perceive reality due to mental illness.
   *c) [From John Searle, *Minds, Brains and Science* (Cambridge, Mass.: Harvard University Press, 1984), pp.37–8] Why would anybody ever have thought that computers could think or have feelings and emotions and all the rest of it? . . . we can do a computer simulation of . . . the pattern of power distribution in the Labour party. We can do computer simulation of rain storms . . . or warehouse fires. . . . Now, in each of these cases, nobody supposes that the computer simulation is actually the real thing; no one supposes that a computer simulation of a storm will leave us all wet. . . . Why on earth would anyone in his right mind suppose a computer simulation of mental processes actually had mental processes?

2. In each case, comment on the appropriateness of arguing the stated claim by means of the analogies suggested.
    a) Claim: Marijuana should be legalized.
       Analogies:
          i) Legalizing marijuana is like legalizing cocaine.
          ii) Banning marijuana is like banning alcohol.
          iii) Making marijuana illegal is like banning novels, in that it entices more users.
          iv) Smoking marijuana is like giving people an easy fix rather than the opportunity to accomplish things by hard work.
    b) Claim: Rich nations should provide aid to poor ones.
       Analogies:
          i) Aid is like a handout people don't deserve.
          ii) Teaching a person to fish is like feeding him for the rest of his life.
          iii) Aiding poor nations is like putting too many people on an already overcrowded lifeboat.
          iv) Refusing aid is being like Scrooge, offering aid is being like Jesus Christ.
3. Take the following topics and sketch an appeal to precedent, first supporting and then criticizing this line of reasoning (positive and negative precedents).
    a) censorship of pornography (or particular kinds of pornography)
    b) medical procedures that transplant tissue from aborted fetuses to patients with Parkinson's disease
4. Evaluate the strengths of the following arguments by precedent.
    a) Several publishers who had been planning books about important people or companies have been threatened by lawsuits by their potential subjects. Once threatened, these publishers felt they had no choice but to cancel the plans to publish the controversial books. The situation, known as 'libel chill', will act to discourage writers, publishers, and commentators in the future from pursuing certain subjects. This situation represents undemocratic media control, censorship, and loss of freedom of expression.
    *b) [Adapted from a letter to the *Toronto Star*, 11 June 1983] If pro-choice doctors are allowed to go ahead and open abortion clinics under the banner of women's right to abortion on demand, then members of organized crime should be allowed to open gaming casinos because people have the right to gamble, and producers of pornographic movies to open theatres because people have the right to view what they wish. If pro-abortion groups can do it, so can other groups.

Major Exercise 11M

1. This assignment is intended to test your understanding of argument forms by using some of them in conjunction with specific normative issues.

a) Construct short arguments employing the following forms (one for each argument) in support of the claim 'Private ownership of assault rifles should be prohibited': slippery slope, analogy, appeal to precedent.

b) Employ the same argument forms in support of the opposite claim: 'Private ownership of assault rifles should be allowed.'

c) Construct arguments on the issue of euthanasia using an argument from analogy.

d) Using any of the argument forms of this chapter, construct a short argument on one of the following issues: animal rights; nuclear testing; pollution.

2. Decide whether each of the following passages contains an argument. If it does, assess the reasoning. For any specific argument forms dealt with in this chapter, explain whether the argument fulfils the conditions for good arguments of that form. Note that examples may involve more than one argument form.

*a) [From Vincent E. Barry, *The Critical Edge* (New York: Harcourt Brace Jovanovich, 1992)] Editorial comment on the colourization of classic black-and-white films, such as *Casablanca* and *Citizen Kane*: 'Let this sort of thing go on, and somebody will want to put a mustache on the *Mona Lisa*.'

b) Smokers are the most persecuted group on earth. First all the non-smokers decided that we should be segregated to separate parts of restaurants. Then they passed by-laws preventing us from smoking in most public places. Next they'll be storming our houses to arrest us for smoking in the privacy of our home, since even there 'we don't own the air.' This is a bad model for how to set social policy. Once a state begins overregulating its citizens, the door is opened to any number of infringements on personal liberty and freedom of expression.

c) [Adapted from a letter to *Omni* magazine, Sept. 1983] I am surprised that *Omni* continues to perpetuate the myth that bulls charge at a red cape because it is red. Bulls are colourblind and charge at a red cape because it moves. A matador does not face a bull until it has been enraged by picadors who run at it, shout at it, and jab it with swords. Any old farm-hand can, like me, attest to the fact that an enraged bull will charge at anything that moves.

*d) [From the *Windsor Star*, 24 Oct. 1995] Seven out of 10 women wear the wrong size bra, according to surveys by Playtex, a bra manufacturer . . . this statistic was based on women who came to Playtex bra-fitting clinics.

e) [From Francis Bacon, *Francis Bacon: A Selection of His Works* (Toronto: Macmillan, 1965), p. 17] There are seven windows given to animals in the domicile of the head, through which the air is admitted to the tabernacle of the body, to enlighten, to warm and to nourish it. What are these parts of the microcosmos: Two nostrils, two eyes, two ears and a mouth. So in the heavens, as in a macrocosmos, there are two favourable stars, two unpropitious, two luminaries, and Mercury undecided and indifferent. From this and from many other similarities in nature, such as the seven metals, etc., which it were tedious to enumerate, we gather that the number of planets is necessarily seven.

f) [Letter to the *Toronto Star*, 21 Nov. 1984] I was glad to see obscenity receive another great blow with the banning of December's *Penthouse* magazine. What shall we ban next? Libraries? We could stop a lot of book thefts by banning libraries.

*g) [*The Globe and Mail*, 6 Mar. 1987, from London (Reuters)] Farmer John Coombs claims his cow Primrose is curing his baldness—by licking his head.

Mr Coombs, 56, who farms near Salisbury, in southwestern England, says he made the discovery after Primrose licked some cattle food dust off his pate as he was bending down.

A few weeks later hair was growing in an area that had been bald for years.

The farmer has the whole herd working on the problem now, the *Daily Telegraph* reported yesterday.

Mr Coombs encourages his cows to lick his head every day and believes he will soon have a full head of hair.

h) [From Janet George, 'Saboteurs—the Real Animals', *Manchester Guardian Weekly*, 28 Feb. 1993, p. 24] People who believe that killing animals for sport is wrong might assume that banning field sports would solve the problem. They are wrong. Hunting is merely the first in a long list of targets. . . .

Already, butchers' shop windows are frequent targets for damage and incendiary devices have been used against department stores selling furs and leather goods. If another private member's bill is introduced successfully, and hunting is banned, animal rights extremists will see it as a vindication of their methods.

i) [From a cosmetics advertisement] Research among dermatologists reveals a lot of skepticism regarding anti-aging claims. Research also shows that 95% of the doctors surveyed recommended Overnight Success' active ingredient for the relief of dry to clinically dry skin.

The Overnight Success night strength formula dramatically helps diminish fine, dry lines and their aging appearance . . . And after just 3 nights' use, 98% of women tested showed measurable improvements.

Discover Overnight Success tonight. Wake up to softer, smoother, younger looking skin tomorrow.

*j) [From Deane Pollard, 'Regulating Violent Pornography', *Vanderbilt Law Review*, 43, 1 (1990)] [S]peeding is known to increase the likelihood of car collisions, and drivers are punished for this dangerous behaviour whether or not their particular sprees cause collisions. Violent pornography, like speeding, is intrinsically dangerous, and legislatures may regulate it on the basis of its known propensity for harm without a showing of particular harm.

k) [From a letter sent out by IIFAR—Incurably Ill For Animal Research, Mar. 1988] . . . what it all boils down to, after you eliminate all the hype, is that medical research is being conducted to alleviate human suffering, and testing on animals prior to testing on humans is essential. As long as society believes it is okay to kill cows for food, exterminate mice and rats that infect our homes, and kill more than 10 million cats and dogs each year in public pounds because they are nuisances, it surely must be okay to use animals to find cures for unfortunate human beings who suffer from incurable illnesses.

l) [From Gary E. Jones, 'On the Permissibility of Torture', *Journal of Medical Ethics*, 6 (1980), p. 12] Consider, for example, solar energy. It presently suffers from the same poor cost-benefit ratio as the use of torture allegedly does. However, the promise of future benefits from the use of solar energy, along with the assumption that the cost-benefit ratio will improve, are sufficient grounds for many to conclude that its use should be promoted. Analogously, it could be argued that technical improvements in the methods used to extract information in as humane a way as possible will improve the cost-benefit ratio of the use of torture.

m) [From Scott Piatkowski, 'Scorched earth tactics', *Waterloo Chronicle*, 3 Apr. 1996. Background: This is a column responding to the actions of a Conservative Ontario Premier, Mike Harris, who instituted major cuts to social, health, and education spending in an attempt to cut the Ontario government's sizeable deficit.] During the Second World War, Soviet leader Joseph Stalin used the strategy [of scorched earth tactics] as the invading Nazis overran much of the European part of his empire. His army burned fields and buildings as they retreated. . . . If the past nine months are any indication the current government of Ontario must have studied a lot of military history, with a particular focus on scorched earth tactics. While this analogy may seem a stretch at first the parallels are clear to those who care to look for them.

Mike Harris knows that he is going to lose the next election. He knows that there is little chance that he will be able to fool the electorate a second time around—not after they have seen the impact of his policies on their communities and their families. . . . When the next government . . . takes over the Premier's office, it is going to find the equivalent of scorched earth. . . . By 1999, Harris will have systematically devastated the tax base of the province. . . . He will not have reduced the deficit. . . . He will also have completely destroyed health care, education, affordable housing and child care infrastructures. . . . Harris will no doubt be sitting in a corporate boardroom somewhere, chortling as his successor attempts to deal with the destruction.

That is why it is so important to stop or soften Harris policies now, instead of waiting until the next election.

FURTHER

FORMS

Chapter 11 discussed a number of specific argument forms to add to your repertoire of arguments. This chapter continues the process by offering further forms,
particularly those involving arguments that in some way bear on the people who
stand behind arguments: those who argue, those who provide support for
premises through their character or expertise, and those who adjudicate reasoning. The forms discussed include:

- two-wrongs reasoning in both its forms;
- *pro homine* and *ad hominem* reasoning;
- appeals to authority;
- guilt by association; and
- appeals to ignorance.

Chapter 11 introduced us to some of the most frequently used argument
forms and showed how we can add these forms to our repertoire of logical
skills and employ them to effect. This chapter introduces further forms that
deal with two-wrongs reasoning and arguments that bear on the 'person'. In
our daily lives it is virtually impossible to escape the contexts in which these
argument forms are common currency.

1. Two-Wrongs Reasoning

The two-wrongs argument is used in defending or justifying a policy or action
undertaken by an individual or group on the grounds that it is necessary by

way of correcting or avoiding some actual or potential injustice. This argument is most frequently used by a person or group to respond to the criticism that their action or policy is wrong or that an action or policy with which they are in agreement is wrong. It takes either of two forms. In the first form, it is claimed that the action or policy is a response to another wrong it attempts to cancel or alleviate. This has the form:

> An action or policy X that is considered wrong cancels or alleviates some unfairness or injustice.
> Therefore, X is justified.

Here, the wrongness of the action or policy defended is explicitly or implicitly acknowledged, but reasons are given that show it is permissible or even necessary. In the second form, the action or policy is justified by indicating that other similar wrong actions have been allowed and, therefore, consistency justifies the current action. This second form will be discussed in detail in the next section. Since the second form is a subset of the first, the following comments apply to both.

If correctly argued, two-wrongs reasoning is quite acceptable. In fact, most justifications of self-defence or of civil disobedience are established through this form of reasoning. A government institutes a policy that seriously affects the rights of a group of people. Perhaps their right to vote or to assemble in public places is denied. We don't have to look far in the world for examples. In response to this perceived wrong people defy the government and congregate, and they justify this action by pointing to the wrongness of the policy that restricts them. In another context, the producers of a product may justify government subsidies to help them lower their prices by arguing that the same practice goes on in other countries and that, regrettably, they must also do so to be competitive on the international market. Such reasoning is two-wrongs reasoning. In our first example, the people apparently believed they had no better alternative. In our second example, a principle of fairness is at stake and some analogical reasoning is also involved.

Notice that in both the examples cited the two-wrongs argument does not deny that the action or policy defended is less than morally ideal. It admits this and tries to justify it as the lesser of two wrongs, thus arguing its acceptability to an impartial universal audience.

To be legitimate, two-wrongs arguments generally, and those of the first form specifically, must meet the following three conditions:

(i) The wrong that is said to be permissible is a response to another wrong, the unjust consequences of which it tries to cancel or alleviate;

(ii) The wrong that is said to be permissible is less wrong than any injustice it attempts to cancel or alleviate;

(iii) There is no morally preferable way to respond to the injustice in question.

A good argument against two-wrongs reasoning will have to demonstrate that one of these criteria has not been satisfied. To establish the claim that some wrong is not justified by another wrong, we must demonstrate that the criteria cannot be met.

Clearly, your judgement will play an important role in deciding when these conditions are and are not met. In particular, you will be called on to decide what is 'less' wrong in a specific situation and, with respect to the third condition, whether there is a morally preferable response. These are concerns to which you will have to pay particular attention when constructing your own two-wrongs arguments because, as always, the onus is on you to support adequately your argument on contentious points. Two-wrongs reasoning indicates that in the domain of moral argumentation we do not always find easy ways to grasp the right or wrong answer with which everyone will agree. Such argument forms shed light on the issue, tell us the kind of questions we should be asking, and facilitate our own reasoning on the issues as we strive to come to reasonable positions.

Let us briefly consider some examples where two-wrongs reasoning does not seem acceptable. The following comes from an editorial in the *Wall Street Journal* (Jan. 1984) and concerns the actions of Bernard Goetz, who shot four black youths he believed intended to rob him on a New York subway train:

If the 'state of nature' has returned to some big cities, can people fairly be blamed for modern vigilantism? Is it more 'civilized' to suffer threats to individual liberty from criminals, or is it an overdose of sophistication to say individuals can never resort to self-protection?

Since the reasoning is phrased in rhetorical questions intended as assertions and the conclusion is hidden, it is important to diagram this argument.

Pl = If the 'state of nature' has returned to some big cities, people cannot be blamed for modern vigilantism.
HP2 = The 'state of nature' has returned to some big cities.
P3 = It is not 'civilized' to have to suffer threats to individual liberty from criminals.
P4 = It is an overdose of sophistication to say individuals can never resort to self-protection.
HC = Self-protection in the form of modern vigilantism is justified.

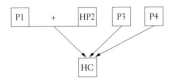

The thrust of this reasoning is quite evident, despite its awkward presentation. To justify the kind of self-protection in which Goetz engaged, the argument applies to the big cities the concept of the 'state of nature' understood as a survival-of-the-fittest struggle. It is important to acknowledge this context because, as a general statement about inner-city life, especially in the big cities of the United States, the argument may appeal to some people.

However, what is important about the Goetz case and what makes it difficult to justify on the basis of two-wrongs reasoning is the questionable existence of a first wrong. When we apply the first criterion for a good two-wrongs argument we find that it is not clear that Goetz was responding to an actual wrong since the youths didn't actually rob him but only asked him for five dollars. There are also doubts as to whether the second condition is satisfied. Was Goetz's act less wrong than the one he anticipated? The writer of the editorial clearly believes it was. But the writer also begs the question in an important sense. P3 already assumes the truth of the conclusion that the act was justified because it refers to 'criminals'. But there are no clear criminals in this case. To accept Goetz's labelling of people as criminals in a society where the law requires people to be assumed innocent until proven guilty is to grant Goetz status as both judge and executioner. Nor is the third condition satisfied. Because the sense of a first wrong is so weak, there are undoubtedly morally preferable ways in which Goetz could have responded.

As a further example, consider whether the execution of a convicted murderer constitutes a 'lesser' wrong legitimized by the wrong of the murder itself. Such a line of reasoning is used in arguing for capital punishment as a form of justice, rather than as a deterrent. As to the first condition, it is not clear how much an action, apparently motivated by revenge, cancels or alleviates the earlier wrong. Though it may be argued that the second condition is met, a strong case can be made that the third condition cannot be satisfied on the grounds that life imprisonment is a morally preferable course of action.

> **Box 12.1 Two-Wrongs Reasoning**
> Two-wrongs reasoning attempts to justify an action normally considered wrong by pointing out that it cancels or alleviates some worse wrong. A good two-wrongs argument establishes that (i) the wrong that is said to be permissible is a response to another wrong, the unjust consequences of which it tries to cancel or alleviate; (ii) the wrong that is said to be permissible is less wrong than any injustice it attempts to cancel or alleviate; (iii) there is no morally preferable way to respond to the injustice in question.

2. TWO-WRONGS REASONING BY ANALOGY

Two-wrongs by analogy is a more specific form of the kind of argument under discussion, and it merits separate treatment because it plays an important role in ordinary reasoning. We already encountered two-wrongs-by-analogy reasoning in the argument that subsidies for one country's industries are legitimate if similar subsidies are offered by other countries to their industries. Two-wrongs-by-analogy arguments arise because fairness demands that analogous situations be treated in a similar way. We have already noted the importance of this principle in our discussion of appeals to precedent. Two wrongs by analogy differs from the latter in admitting that the action it justifies is less than morally ideal.

Two-wrongs reasoning by analogy argues that some action or policy is justified by indicating that other similar 'wrong' actions have been generally accepted and, therefore, consistency justifies the current action. The form here is:

An action or policy X is similar to action or policy Y. (P1)
Y has been accepted/allowed. (P2)
X should be accepted/allowed. (C)

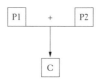

We can judge such arguments by appealing directly to the criteria for good two-wrongs reasoning. Thus, the wrong that is said to be alleviated is the inconsistent treatment of similar situations and a convincing argument must show that the remedy (allowing some new wrong) is not worse than the inconsistency (the wrong) that has been said to have been allowed, and that there is no preferable way to deal with the inconsistency in question.

The conditions for a good two-wrongs-by-analogy argument are similar to those for good two-wrongs reasoning, and may be expressed as follows:

(i) The wrong that is said to be permissible is analogous to other wrongs that have been permitted;
(ii) Fairness in the form of consistency is more important than preventing the wrong in question;
(iii) There is no morally preferable way to respond in the situation.

Both bad and good examples of two-wrongs-by-analogy arguments come readily to mind. If it is common practice not to ticket cars parked illegally on a city lot, it would be unfair to pick one car—a car owned, let us say, by a vocal critic of the municipal administration—and ticket it. Such an individual can reasonably propound the following two-wrongs-by-analogy argument:

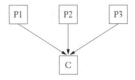

where P1 = Other people who park their cars in the lot are not ticketed, P2 = I am entitled to the same treatment as other people, especially for such a petty wrong, P3 = There is no other way of treating me fairly, and C = I should not have been ticketed. To refute this argument one would have to refute one or more of the premises. One might, for example, argue that the offence is not a petty one and that ticketing a few individuals is the morally best way to respond to the situation given that the city is short of parking officers.

Another scenario can provide a clear example of bad two-wrongs-by-analogy reasoning. It would be difficult to criticize a police crackdown on drunken driving by pointing out that they have been lax in prosecuting past offenders. Consistent treatment of future offenders would require that they go free, but such consistency is not as desirable a goal as the prevention of future carnage caused by drunken drivers. It follows that the proposed new wrong—turning a blind eye to new offenders—is not preferable to a crackdown.

The principle of consistency makes it wrong to treat differently individuals who commit the same offence. If one of them is not initially charged, a case can be made that none of them should be. But if the offence is a serious one, a preferable way to deal with the situation would be to charge all the offenders. In terms of the criteria for good two-wrongs-by-analogy reasoning, the argument that consistency demands that none be prosecuted fails to satisfy the third condition.

Box 12.2 Two-Wrongs Reasoning by Analogy

Two-wrongs reasoning by analogy is a specific form of two-wrongs reasoning that justifies an action normally considered wrong by pointing out that it is analogous to other actions that have been permitted. A good two-wrongs-by-analogy argument establishes that: (i) the wrong that is said to be permissible is analogous to other wrongs that have been permitted; (ii) fairness in the form of consistency is more important than preventing the wrong in question; (iii) there is no morally preferable way to respond in the situation.

EXERCISE 12A

1. In each of the following scenarios, explain whether the two-wrongs reasoning is legitimate or not. Give reasons for your decisions.

*a) In response to a law that restricts the immigration of South Americans, forcing many to be sent home to face possible torture and death, citizens hide in their homes people whom they believe to be genuine refugees. They argue that the law is morally wrong.

b) An elderly man kills his wife of 58 years. She is terminally ill and dying slowly in great pain. He defends himself by arguing that his was an act of euthanasia and that his wife's suffering was a greater wrong that his action terminated.

c) *In vitro* fertilization involves the surgical removal of an egg from a woman's ovary, fertilizing it by mixing it with semen in a dish, and then transferring this back to the uterus once it has started to divide. By means of drugs, 'superovulation' can produce several eggs in the same cycle. These can be collected in one surgical operation and then fertilized. Then, one or more of the embryos can be introduced into the uterus while the rest are frozen, either to be introduced into a uterus at a later date or to be used in research. Usually, embryos used in research would then be destroyed. The question arises about the morality of this last activity: producing human embryos for research with no intention of allowing them to develop. But if such research produces a cure for, say, cystic fibrosis—through the discovery of the defective gene, which can then be treated or replaced—then the initial moral wrong of using embryos in research would be justified.

d) [*Maclean's*, 21 Nov. 1983] I take exception to Bruce Colebank's letter castigating the United States for dropping two atomic bombs on Japan to shorten the Second World War (Balancing terror, Letters, Oct. 3). As a veteran, let me advise Colebank that both Germany and Japan were endeavouring to build atomic bombs at that time, and only last month a Japanese scientist confessed that he was working on such a weapon and that Japan would certainly have used it if they had completed theirs first.

e) [Are economic sanctions that result in suffering for those affected justifiable? The following concerns sanctions imposed on Iraq after the 1991 Gulf War.] Economic sanctions are always controversial because they inevitably result in the suffering of innocents whose only 'crime' is to live under a government that has attracted wide condemnation. In the case of children such suffering seems particularly unfair. And yet the responsibility for these innocents lies ultimately with their government and not with those who impose and enforce sanctions. When sanctions are imposed to bring into line a government that has flaunted the basic conventions of human rights or refused to abide by agreements to destroy materials and equipment of a military nature, then those sanctions are justified. The long-term desirability of defusing threats to global security most always outweigh the immediate welfare of a nation's citizens.

2. Imagine that you wish to be exempted from a final exam in some course you are taking. You know that in the past students have sometimes been exempted due to serious medical conditions. Explain why a two-wrongs-by-analogy argument could or could not be used to defend the claim that you should be exempted for the following reasons:

   *a) your father is very ill;
   b) you have just gone through an acrimonious divorce;
   c) you panic in test situations;
   d) you have to attend a funeral;
   e) you have been recovering from an accident for the last year.

3. Pro Homine and Ad Hominem Reasoning

So far, the kinds of arguments we have discussed focus on the issue an argument addresses. It remains for us to consider occasions when we do not have the time, the means, or the ability to investigate a question in sufficient detail to decide the proper answer to it. In these circumstances we often accept or reject particular views because they are offered and defended by individuals or groups we trust or do not trust, whom we do or do not deem competent to address the issue at hand. We label as 'pro homine' and 'ad hominem' arguments that defend or attack a claim or point of view by defending or attacking its proponent.

Pro Homine

In 1987, congressional hearings investigated allegations that the US administration acted improperly and illegally by selling arms to Iran and then diverting money from the sales to rebels trying to overthrow the Sandinista government in Nicaragua. One of the witnesses who testified at the hearings, Lieutenant Colonel Oliver North, became a special focus of media attention. His appearance in Marine uniform, his distinguished military record, and his patriotic fervour captured the imagination of many Americans. One New York Times columnist (6 July 1987) described North's appeal as the attraction of an 'underdog, true believer, one man against the crowd: there was a lot of Gary Cooper in him, the lonesome cowboy, a lot of Jimmy Stewart, too, the honest man facing down the politicians, and quite a bit of Huck finn.' Such a description is ironic, given that North admitted lying to Congress and the public, but this simply underscores the extent to which a person's projected image can influence us.

Many accepted what North said as true because they were impressed by him as a man. In the process, they relied on *pro homine* reasoning (reasoning 'for the man'). We engage in such reasoning whenever we defend or accept a conclusion because it is propounded by someone we trust to have the correct opinion. Such arguments have the general form:

Person X believes that y.
Therefore, y should be accepted.

A good *pro homine* argument is:

An argument that a claim should be accepted because it is held by some person, X, who is deemed to be (i) knowledgeable, (ii) trustworthy, and (iii) free of bias.

In proposing *pro homine* reasoning, we take our past experience of certain individuals as intelligent and honest as giving us good grounds for accepting their opinions now and in the future. The effectiveness of implicit reasoning of this sort is recognized by Aristotle, who says in his *Rhetoric* that one important means of persuasion depends on an appeal to a speaker's good character.

Although we concede that Colonel North is a knowledgeable person, there are problems with a *pro homine* appeal to his testimony on points (ii) and (iii). It is arguable that patriotism (or any other overriding motive) and obedience to authority—the very factors that make North appealing to some—may have blinded him to propriety and so cannot serve as plausible reasons for accepting his position. As to the question of bias, the fact that North himself is accused of wrongdoing makes it difficult for him to be objective and for us to know whether he is motivated by a desire to tell the truth.

Above and beyond the specific problems with a *pro homine* in North's case, more general concerns suggest that we should be cautious in any *pro homine* argument we undertake. Since we are naturally inclined to accept the opinions of individuals we respect in one way or another, it is easy to slip into an uncritical acceptance of their views. When all is said and done, an in-depth investigation of a position cannot be replaced by an appeal to the person who defends it. But an appropriate appeal to a person can contribute as evidence for a position.

> **Box 12.3 Pro Homine Reasoning**
> *Pro homine* reasoning argues for a claim by showing that it is held by some person X. A good *pro homine* argument maintains that it should be accepted because X is (i) knowledgeable, (ii) trustworthy, and (iii) free of bias.

Argument from Authority

We will focus here on the special kind of *pro homine* we call an 'argument from authority'. It defends a claim by appealing to the views of someone considered to be an expert on the subject encompassing that claim. Its general form is:

> Person X is an authority who believes and states y.
> Therefore, y should be accepted.

An authority is someone with special qualifications — a university degree, publications, and so on — that establish expertise in a specific field. It is this expertise that gives his or her opinions extra weight.

It is arguable that the vast proportion of the beliefs we hold are adopted because we accept the views of authorities who recommend them. Within all areas of study and research, progress in the acquisition of new insights is impossible without the transmission of old truths. In medieval times new generations were described as a pygmy standing on the shoulders of a giant. The giant symbolizes the accumulated wisdom of the centuries, the acceptance of which enables the pygmy to see a bit further and more clearly.

The frequency of appeals to authority is seen in practical affairs, where we depend on doctors, plumbers, electricians, and appliance and automobile mechanics as authorities with special competencies. To a very significant extent, education depends on students accepting the authority and the views of their teachers. Corporations hire consultants. In all such cases, we depend on others' views; indeed, it is difficult to see how we could get by without them. Our reliance on arguments from authority, and all *pro homine* appeals, must none the less be balanced by a consistent questioning of such appeals. We should keep in mind that the very best appeal to an authority is a secondary way of establishing a claim as true. The suggestion that we accept someone else's claims is predicated on the assumption that the person has good reasons for them, and these reasons, rather than the person's authority, are the ultimate determinant of the plausibility of such claims. A *pro homine* appeal is simply a promissory note assuring us that the experts — or simply 'people with good sense' — have good reasons for their views.

Other problems inherent in appeals to authorities arise when we ask whose judgement can be trusted. In dealing with authorities, we all know that there are good and bad doctors, lawyers, plumbers, electricians, and professors, but it is often difficult to sort out the competent from the incompetent. In fact, if we know virtually nothing about an issue, we may have little basis for judging who is genuinely knowledgeable and who is not.

One way to circumvent this problem is by appealing to 'big names' and paying particular attention to their views. There is obviously a place for such appeals, but even they are problematic. We tend to think of science as the place where authority is most easily established, but here there are great differences of opinion. It has been argued by well-known contemporary philosophers (among them, Thomas Kuhn and Paul Feyerabend) that science is structured in such a way that it suppresses views that go against accepted paradigms, even when they are logically persuasive. If we add to this the social factors that influence the making of 'big names' — where they studied and the respect accorded to them by their colleagues and by your instructors — we begin to see that appeals to scientific authority are open to many questions.

The problem of disagreement among authorities is magnified when we move outside the field of science. The ancient sceptics argued that discrepancies between different people and different authorities show that truth cannot be found. We still face that problem. The views of Kuhn and Feyerabend, as we noted earlier, conflict with those of other experts who take a less critical attitude to science. Numerous issues of immense significance to us, such as the best means for preventing nuclear war or motifs for understanding the human psyche, are characterized by disagreements among respected authorities. Such problems are not intended to dissuade you from using arguments from authority, but to alert you to their weaknesses and the importance of constructing them in a way that recognizes their provisional nature and makes them as convincing as possible. This requires that you keep in mind a number of considerations.

The basis of any argument from authority is the claim that we should accept others' views because they have special expertise that makes their claims persuasive. Their expertise is what we shall call their 'credentials', which are usually educational or professional qualifications. There are five factors you must incorporate in a good argument from authority.

(i) You must *state the credentials* of the person or group to whose opinion you appeal and identify that person or group. Anonymous experts rarely lend weight to a claim. And if you fail to state the credentials, a person who hears your argument has no reason to accept the views of the person or group you endorse.

Often what is required is relatively straightforward. If you want to establish some basic fact about chemical properties, then it makes sense to appeal to someone with a degree in chemistry. Perhaps it will be necessary to appeal to someone who specializes in a particular branch of chemistry. On other occasions, specifying credentials may be more complicated. If you are appealing to a panel that has been appointed to investigate a public scandal, you will not be able to say that they have degrees in 'public scandal investigation'. You would have to appeal to the general intelligence, character, and specific knowledge of the members of the panel.

(ii) You must make it clear that the stated credentials are *relevant* to the issue under discussion. This essential aspect of arguments from authority is often overlooked. Appeals to authority require specialized knowledge on the part of the experts to whom the appeal is made. It is for this reason that advertisements displaying the endorsement of movie stars, athletes, or other celebrities are usually cases of bad *pro homine* reasoning. Their expertise may be significant within their own areas of competence, but they are usually ill-qualified to judge whether a certain car is more dependable than another or whether this cereal is more nutritious than the next. If we really want an answer to such questions, we are better advised to consult a nutritionist or the head of a consumer group that tests cars.

(iii) You must ensure that the authorities to whom you appeal are *not biased*. The most obvious kind of bias arises when individuals have a vested interest, when they stand to gain from expressing some view or making some claim.

This is, of course, a further problem with the kinds of endorsements we see in advertisements. It is also evident in appeals to members of the nuclear industry over the question of whether food irradiation is safe. As the industry has a lot to gain with the approval of such technology, their assurances cannot carry the same weight as the views of independent authorities and researchers. Good *pro homine* appeals to authorities should rely on persons who have the capability to make an unbiased assessment of whatever is in question. We should take with the proverbial grain of salt recommendations from people who are paid for advertising or who have a vested interest to protect or promote.

(iv) You must ensure that the claim is one for which there is *wide agreement* among the relevant experts. The failure of members of an investigative panel to come to an agreement lessens the extent to which we can appeal to them to decide an issue. A selective appeal to an authority who takes a stand with which other authorities disagree is usually inappropriate. We may still say, 'My claim is supported by X but I must confess that no one else in the field agrees with her on this.' Such an appeal may provide some evidence for your view, but it is minimal and would have to be combined with other considerations if it were to be the basis of a convincing argument. Of course, lack of agreement is not necessarily a sign that a claim is false. Many revolutionary thinkers, such as Galileo and Darwin, whose claims eventually gained widespread acceptance, stood alone against other contemporary experts.

(v) You must ensure that the claim belongs to an area of knowledge where *consensus is in principle possible* because there are universally accepted criteria for making judgements. Many would insist that aesthetics is not a topic where appeals to authority are legitimate. Generally, in appealing to authorities, you must be prepared to argue that the issue at hand is one in which broad agreement is possible.

Though a good argument from authority requires that each of these criteria be established, there will be cases where some of them can be taken for granted because they can be assumed as part of the general knowledge of your audience. In the final analysis, all *pro homine* arguments, including appeals to authority, are implicit generalizations. An appeal to the claim that certain persons are trustworthy or have certain credentials is a way of saying that they are knowledgeable and have shown good judgement, or that they have acquired the appropriate education or certification and have demonstrated the requisite skills on past occasions. From this we infer that they deserve our trust and can exercise those skills in the case at hand.

> ### Box 12.4 Arguments from Authority
> Arguments from authority provide evidence for a claim by establishing that it is endorsed by authorities. A good argument from authority supports a claim on the basis that the person who endorses it is deemed to have (i) certain stated credentials; (ii) credentials that are relevant to the claim in question; and (iii) no biases that are likely to interfere with the assessment of the claim, provided that (iv) the claim in question concerns an area in which there is wide agreement among the relevant experts; and (v) the claim concerns an area of knowledge in which consensus is possible.

Ad Hominem

Just as arguments from disanalogy are the reverse side of arguments from analogy, so *ad hominem* arguments are arguments against the claim that we should accept someone's views or reasoning. *Ad hominems* give us reasons for not taking someone's position seriously or for dismissing it altogether by pointing out that the person is in some way unreliable. A general *ad hominem* criticizes the proponent of a position for some general reason. The *ad hominem*, which we call an 'argument against authority', argues that a person is not a reliable authority and need not, therefore, be taken seriously. The general form of an *ad hominem* argument is:

> Person X says y.
> But X is unreliable.
> Therefore we should reject y, or at least conclude that X's saying y does not provide support for y.

We use the *ad hominem* for the same reason we employ the *pro homine*. It is simply impossible to investigate every claim we come across. If we hear, for example, that Professor Obscurantus has just published another book on social psychology and decide not to read it because we have read her other six hefty tomes and found reading them a waste of time, we are employing *ad hominem* reasoning that can be diagrammed as:

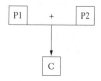

where P1 = Obscurantus's other work shows that she is not knowledgeable, P2 = she wrote this new book, and C = this new book is not worth reading. In reasoning in this way, we have decided that Obscurantus is not a good psychologist and it is on this basis, not on an assessment of the arguments in her book, that we have decided that it is not worth reading.

Like the *pro homine*, the *ad hominem* is always a second-best reason for rejecting a particular position. It, too, is only a promissory note we use, in this case to conclude that someone's endorsement of a position does not provide evidence for its truth. But that is not equivalent to saying that the position is mistaken. The ultimate determinant of the correctness or incorrectness of a claim must always be found in the reasoning that supports it. This does not mean that we should dispense with all *ad hominem* reasoning. But we must keep in mind the provisional nature of conclusions based on it and the possibility that they may have to be revised. If, for example, Obscurantus's new work gets fabulous reviews and all of our colleagues wholeheartedly endorse the theses it develops, then we should seriously reconsider our earlier decision not to read it.

The basis of a good *ad hominem* argument is a demonstration that someone has certain characteristics or specific biases that make his or her views unreliable. Thus, a good *ad hominem* is:

> An argument that a person's views should not be given credence or should be rejected outright because the person is deemed to be (i) not knowledgeable, or (ii) untrustworthy, or (iii) biased.

An *ad hominem* argument used as a basis for judging someone's views false (and not merely in need of further justification) must, of course, be particularly convincing.

Box 12.5 Ad Hominem Reasoning

Ad hominem reasoning can be considered the reverse of *pro homine* reasoning. A good *ad hominem* argument establishes that a person's views should not be given credence or should be rejected outright because the person is deemed to be (i) not knowledgeable, or (ii) untrustworthy, or (iii) biased.

Arguments against Authority

Just as an appeal to authority is a more specific form of the *pro homine*, so an argument against an authority is the more specific form of the *ad hominem*. Its general form is:

Person X is not an authority on y.
X's advocating some claim about y does not provide support for it.

The details of a good argument against authority are relatively straightforward. It casts doubt on the reliability of a person's views by showing that he or she fails to meet the criteria we have introduced for good arguments from authority. A good argument against authority is:

An argument that rejects an alleged authority by establishing that (i) the authority's credentials are questionable; or (ii) the credentials cited are irrelevant to the issue in question; or (iii) the alleged authority is biased; or (iv) the topic under scrutiny is one where there is significant disagreement among the relevant experts; or (v) it is one where expertise cannot be claimed.

All of these requirements can be understood in light of the considerations we introduced in connection with appeals to authority. If, for instance, someone does not have the credentials we would associate with authoritative standing in the mathematics field, this is a legitimate reason to take less seriously her views on such topics.

Serious shortcomings in any of the five prerequisites for good arguments from authority can be used to construct a good argument against authority. The strength of such an argument is a direct function of the extent to which the person criticized deviates from the criteria set out in our account of good authorities. One of the criteria was widespread agreement among authorities. Clearly, the value of an authority's opinion diminishes when the issue is one on which there is virtually no agreement among the experts. Likewise, our earlier criticism of commercial endorsements by celebrities as representing vested interests was an argument against authority.

The following example involves an *ad hominem* and also an appeal to authority. It concerns a disagreement among contemporary commentators over the authorship of an ancient text called the *Magna Moralia*. The passage is in a footnote in a work of one commentator, A.W. Price.

John Cooper attaches great weight to this passage. . . . It is consistent that he ascribes the *Magna Moralia* to Aristotle himself. . . . Others will find the author's treatment of 'goodwill' here . . . typical of his [the author of the *Magna Moralia*'s] 'constant botching', as Anthony Kenny has termed it. [A.W. Price, *Love and Friendship in Plato and Aristotle* (Oxford: Clarendon Press, 1989), pp. 122–3]

Both Cooper and Kenny can be considered 'experts' in the field by virtue of their published work and its reception. Price thinks that the *Magna Moralia* is not written by Aristotle and backs this claim by invoking Kenny's claim that the author of the *Magna Moralia* is a 'constant botcher' (thereby implying that it is not Aristotle's work). Here, then, one has an implicit argument from authority that can be diagrammed as follows.

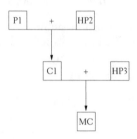

where P1 = Kenny claims that the author of the *Magna Moralia* is a constant botcher, HP2 = Kenny is a noted expert, C1 = the author of the *Magna Moralia* is a constant botcher, HP3 = Aristotle is not a constant botcher, MC = Aristotle is not the author of the *Magna Moralia*.

The passage in question contains an implicit argument *against* authority as well as an argument from authority, for the appeal to Kenny's authority is used to dismiss the views of another (Cooper). The argument against authority can be summarized as the claim that 'The author of the *Magna Moralia* is a constant botcher (C1), so Cooper is not a good judge of the passage in question and he is not a credible authority.' In essence, this implicit argument calls into question Cooper's credentials, by pointing to his alleged poor judgement.

This is, however, a case where appeals to authority are of limited value, for it is a case characterized by disagreements between authorities. Academia is renowned for its contentious debates and where disagreements arise it is always important to have both sides of the story. In this case, we have neither the grounds for Cooper's high opinion of the author of the *Magna Moralia* nor the grounds for Kenny's low opinion of the same author. In the face of their disagreement, the fourth condition of good appeals to authority cannot be met. Since the *ad hominem* critique of Cooper's credentials depends on the appeal to authority, it is also problematic. In this instance, Price can better make his point by showing how Cooper's interpretation of the passage could be considered a case of 'botching'. To his credit, he proceeds to attempt this next.

It is important to distinguish *ad hominem* attacks that discredit a person's position from attacks on the person alone. The latter is often called an *abusive ad hominem* because it does little more than hurl abuse.

Such a situation appeared to arise when actor Richard Harris wrote to London's *The Sunday Times* (8 June 1995) in response to a feature interview with the actor Michael Caine. The article discussed Caine's acting career as well as his successes as a businessman and art collector, and it applauded his return to England from self-imposed exile in Hollywood. In several direct quotations, Caine numbered himself among the premier English actors of his generation (including Harris) and implied that he had out-achieved these men in several respects — as an actor, a television star, and a businessman. Harris's letter was a study in abusive *ad hominem*.

> Any suggestion that he [Caine] has eclipsed the names of finney, O'Toole, Burton, Bates, Smith and Courtenay is tantamount to prophesying that Rin-Tin-Tin will be solemnised beyond the memory of Brando. . . .
> In truth, he is an over-fat, flatulent 62-year-old windbag, a master of inconsequence now masquerading as a guru, passing off his vast limitations as pious virtues.

Such remarks simply attack Caine and do not constitute an attempt to argue that Caine's remarks should be dismissed because of what he is rather than the substance of what he says. But buried in the rhetoric are indications of actual *ad hominem* reasoning.

For example, Harris insists that readers should dismiss what Caine is reported to have said about fellow actors because he is an overrated actor who has tried to achieve greatness by associating with great actors; that he is not in a position to criticize the low standard of British television because his own contributions to that medium are part of the problem; and that he should not pose as an expert on 'oenology and art' because he admits to buying things for their resale value and so recognizes only their price, not their worth.

In each case there is an element of Harris's general attack on Caine's person. But each case also constitutes a definite sub-argument whose premises could be evaluated.

In your own dealings with *ad hominem* reasoning, be sure to distinguish what is abusive from what is substantial. As always, we are looking to uncover a clear argument.

Box 12.6 *Arguments against Authority*

Arguments against authority can be considered the reverse of arguments from authority. A good argument against authority rejects an alleged authority by establishing that (i) the authority's credentials are questionable; or (ii) the credentials cited are irrelevant to the issue in question; or (iii) the alleged authority is biased; or (iv) the topic under scrutiny is one where there is significant disagreement among the relevant experts; or (v) it is one where expertise cannot be claimed.

4. GUILT BY ASSOCIATION

An argument form related to *ad hominem* is what is known as 'guilt by association'. As the name implies, this argument attributes guilt to a person or group on the basis of some association that is known or thought to exist between that person or group and some other person or group of dubious beliefs or behaviour. The argument has the form:

A person or group X is associated with another person or group Y.
Y has questionable beliefs or behaves in a questionable way.
Therefore, X's character and/or claims are questionable.

Sometimes, where the association does exist, guilt can be legitimately transferred or inferred in this way. But such arguments often serve as a vehicle for generalizations based on stereotyping, which should always be avoided because they inhibit fair moral assessments.

The conditions for good guilt-by-association arguments are:

(i) there is good reason to believe that the alleged association really does exist;
(ii) there is good reason to question the beliefs or the behaviour of the person or group with which X is associated;
(iii) there is no good reason to differentiate X from the person or group with which X is associated.

It must always be remembered that guilt-by-association reasoning cannot definitively dismiss the views or arguments of a person or group. This must be accomplished by critical examination of the views of the person or group in question. If someone offers social criticisms and we have reason to believe that he has close connections with American Nazis, perhaps even having acted as a spokesperson for them, then we have grounds for being sceptical about his analysis of social problems and even his moral character. In fact, if we have limited time and can only entertain the arguments of a few people or research a limited number of books, we have reasonable grounds for dismissing an argument where such questionable associations clearly exist.

More difficult and more interesting cases arise when there is some question about the relevance of a particular association. Consider the following, taken from Janet George's article on the English fox hunts, 'Saboteurs—the Real Animals' (*Manchester Guardian Weekly*, 28 Feb. 1993, p. 24):

. . . one can condemn . . . the dishonesty of the campaign against hunting. If the anti-hunt literature said 'We are against killing animals for any purpose: killing animals for food is morally as unacceptable as killing animals for sport but impossible to ban,' financial and political support for the campaign would be so greatly reduced as to make it unsustainable. Such an extreme view would be held by less than 2 per cent of the population, so a little misrepresentation is necessary to keep funds flowing.

Whatever claims are made by spokesmen of the anti-hunting campaigns, the truth is that more and more hunt saboteurs express their disapproval of legal activities with illegal acts. Anti-hunt organizations pay lip-service to peaceful protest, but by producing emotive and misleading propaganda . . . they must accept some responsibility for the actions of their supporters.

The point of the reasoning here is to shift some of the guilt of the hunt saboteurs, who have been guilty of increasing violence, onto the anti-hunt organizations who advocate peaceful protest, although, as we assess it, there might be some confusion over the identities of the associated parties. Set out as guilt-by-association reasoning it has the form:

P1 = The anti-hunt organizations are associated with the hunt saboteurs.
P2 = The hunt saboteurs behave in a questionable (violent) way.
C = The motives of the anti-hunt organizations are questionable.

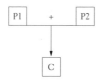

The first condition for appropriate arguments of this form requires that the alleged association really does exist. We will grant this for the time being. It seems charitable to grant that the anti-hunt organizations and the anti-hunt 'saboteurs' (allowing that this may be a loaded term and open to challenge) will share ideological views at least to the extent that they are working for the same end.

The second condition asks whether there is good reason to question the behaviour of the one group. There is less doubt here. Although we may shy from the term 'saboteurs', it is established (in the media) that the groups in question engage in violent acts against property and persons, including law enforcement officers.

The third condition focuses on the relevance of the association in this instance. Is there good reason to dissociate the two groups on this issue? Here we look to the evidence provided by the first paragraph. The link that establishes guilt in George's eyes is the dishonest literature. Although the anti-hunt organizations pay lip-service to peaceful protest, they must accept some responsibility for the violence because they produce misleading and emotive propaganda. Given that she grants that the groups pay lip-service to peaceful protest, we must believe that the propaganda does not incite violence. So it is difficult to see just how the propaganda establishes the relevant connection.

The misleading nature of the literature, according to the first paragraph, lies in it not telling the full extent of the group's position. But honesty here would, allegedly, lead to a loss of political and financial support. The people who would drop their support if the literature was honest are a different group altogether. No connection is established between the failure of the literature to be honest and the violence of the 'saboteurs'. In fact, the literature seems irrelevant to this group, since their actions do not appear to be a result of being misled by any *softer* expressed goal in the literature. At the very least, George has not established the association she requires between the violent offenders and the anti-hunt organizations.

Box 12.7 *Guilt by Association*

This is an argument form which attributes guilt to a person or group on the basis of some association that is known or thought to exist between that person or group and some other person or group. In a good guilt-by-association argument: (i) there is good reason to believe that the alleged association really does exist; (ii) there is good reason to question the beliefs or the behaviour of the person or group with which X is associated; and (iii) there is no good reason to differentiate X from the person or group with which X is associated.

EXERCISE 12B

1. Diagram and assess the following reasoning:
   a) [Letter to *The Globe and Mail*, 11 Mar. 1994] Crawford Kilian equates the specificity of recruiting a black person as head of the Johnston Chair for Black Canadian Studies at Dalhousie University to establishing segregated public toilets for blacks. The analogy is spurious.

   There is nothing black-related about a toilet; there is a great deal black-related about a Department of Black Canadian Studies.

   Does Mr Kilian, however painstaking and detailed his study of Canadian blacks, really believe that he, as a non-black, could successfully defend his credibility as head of such a department? Could he accurately communicate the total experience of being black? Indeed, would anyone listen?
   b) [Letter to the *Toronto Star*, 18 Oct. 1990] The letter by R.T. in the *Star* (Oct. 10) quotes liberal Catholic theologian Dr D. Maguire as stating that a fetus is 'a precious and beautiful form of life but it is not a person.'

   The key word is 'liberal'. Reasoning such as Maguire's is not accepted by the Magisterium of the Roman Catholic Church. When one reads the liberal views of Catholic theologian Maguire, one only needs to consider the source.

*c) [From a flyer advertising Astro-Guard security systems] You don't have to
be a statistic! The experts admit 'it's not IF you will be the victim of a
break-in . . . but WHEN.' Astro-Guard security systems stops burglars
BEFORE they get inside. ONE OUT OF FOUR! Those are the statistical
chances of you and your family being the victims of a break-in within the
next 12 months. . . . Psychiatrists, Psychologists, Criminologists, Security
Experts and Police Officials all agree: 'The earlier the intruder is discovered, the more effective the security system.'

2. Gary Hart, at one time the front runner in the 1988 Democratic presidential
primaries, was forced to withdraw his candidacy following a scandal that
involved an alleged extramarital affair with a woman in Miami. Many argued
that the alleged incident and his attempt to cover it up showed him to be
untrustworthy and lacking in political savvy. Could this incident be used as a
basis for a good *ad hominem* attacking Hart's views? Why or why not?
Discuss.

3. Assess the legitimacy of the following guilt-by-association arguments.

   a) [From a flyer announcing an October 1984 rally against apartheid in
   Peterborough, Ont.] The Canadian Imperial Bank of Commerce (CIBC)
   loans money to the minority White South African government. (Although
   80% of South Africa's population is Black, they are not allowed to vote.) If
   you invest your money at the CIBC, Bank of Montreal, Royal Bank, or
   Bank of Nova Scotia you also condone apartheid policies.

   b) [Letter to the *Toronto Sun*, 21 Nov. 1983] The article 'Hong Kong cash
   comes oh-so-quietly into Metro' (Nov. 7) is misleading because it does not
   mention the extensive nature of crime in the Orient. In Hong Kong, for
   example, organized crime wields tremendous power and influence.

   It has been estimated that one person in six in the colony is a member
   of the criminal Triad societies. These societies are major heroin
   traffickers. They have already completely corrupted the Hong Kong
   police force, and bribing of important officials is routine. Because drugs
   are so easily obtained, Hong Kong has a serious drug-addiction problem.
   Many Hong Kong residents, including businessmen, have become
   extremely wealthy through drug trafficking. If they are permitted to settle
   here, they would extend Hong Kong's problems to Canada.

   Allowing people into Canada solely on the basis of wealth is very fool-
   ish, and could result in the destruction of the moral fibre of our society.

   c) [From a letter to the *Peterborough Examiner*, 12 Nov. 1994] What people
   must understand is that if you support one aspect of the animal rights
   agenda you are supporting it all. You may not be against fur, but your support is helping animal rights groups in their anti-fur campaigns, and you
   may be against cosmetic testing, but that support also supports their stand
   against vital medical research which each and every one of us benefits
   from every day of our lives.

*d) [Letter to the *Toronto Star*, Sept. 1982. Background: The following concerned a suggestion that noted Canadian doctor Norman Bethune should be honoured for his service to humanity. Bethune died accidentally in 1939 while assisting Communist Chinese forces in their struggle against Japanese invaders.] Is it possible to honour Dr Norman Bethune as a humanitarian, despite the fact that he was a self-confessed Communist? Only a negative rejoinder is possible, for the morality of a person's acts must be judged by their consequences. Thus when Dr Bethune placed his medical skills and humanism at the service of international Communism, he unquestionably contributed to an evil ideology that has produced many mountains of corpses. When Canadians naïvely eulogize such a person as Dr Bethune, such praise unwittingly constitutes an endorsement of Communist ideology.

5. APPEALS TO IGNORANCE

The last form of argument we will consider arises when we have no evidence to use in supporting or rejecting a particular claim. In such contexts, arguments from ignorance (arguments *ad ignorantiam*) take our inability to establish the truth of a proposition as evidence for its falsity or, conversely, our inability to establish its falsity as evidence for its truth. The form of arguments from ignorance is:

We can find no evidence for the truth (or falsity) of x.
Therefore, x is false (or true).

To conclude that ghosts do not exist because it has not been proven that they do illustrates this kind of reasoning. Such arguments have traditionally been regarded as fallacious, but there are instances where they constitute good reasoning.

In our legal system, an accused person is presumed innocent until proven guilty. This is an implicit appeal to ignorance. We also use it in scientific reasoning by postulating hypotheses that may subsequently be rejected if no confirming evidence is found. The failure to find evidence of living dodos or of certain kinds of subatomic particles does contribute to the evidence against their (present) existence.

More commonplace examples of arguments from ignorance are found in everyday reasoning. 'I've looked everywhere for Lulu, my pet chicken, and can't find her, so she must have left the yard.' Here the failure to show that Lulu is in the yard prompts the conclusion that she is no longer there.

The criteria for good arguments from ignorance are implicit in these examples. The key to a good argument from ignorance is a responsible attempt to garner evidence that confirms or disconfirms the claim in question. Accordingly, we define a good argument from ignorance as:

> An argument that, after the failure of a responsible attempt to find evidence that some claim, x, is true (or false), concludes that x is false (or true).

Only after such an investigation is completed can we legitimately conclude the claim in question is mistaken. It would not be convincing to argue that Lulu is not in the yard on the basis of our not seeing her unless we have made some effort to locate her—by looking behind the mulberry bush that blocks our view, and elsewhere. It is the failure to establish a claim after a responsible attempt that makes appeals to ignorance plausible.

In cases where we argue to the conclusion that something does not exist, we can represent arguments from ignorance as:

where C = there are no Xs, P1 = there is no evidence for the existence of X, and P2 = we have taken reasonable steps to determine whether there are Xs. Note that this is a case where P1 and P2 are linked, for P2 would provide no support for conclusion C if P1 were not true as well (indeed, P2 can be true when there is good evidence for the existence of Xs).

We have an example of a bad argument from ignorance in the following letter criticizing comments made by the American lawyer Catharine MacKinnon in a speech on pornography (*The Globe and Mail*, 24 Mar. 1987).

> . . . I wonder if Ms MacKinnon has ever seen a snuff film, especially since no one else seems to have. In the absence of a genuine example, I continue to believe that snuff films are a fabrication of censorship crusaders, the purpose of which is obfuscation. . . .

Note that the author uses his *lack* of knowledge of a specific example as a basis for the conclusion that there are no examples. Had he investigated the matter further, he should have had no difficulty coming up with a number of examples.

One of the lessons to be learned from good arguments from ignorance is the importance of supporting our rejection of a claim with a responsible attempt to find evidence for it. Just how far such a search can take us may be seen in the research into the phenomenon of zombies recently carried out by

E. Wade Davis and described in his book *The Serpent and the Rainbow* (New York: Simon & Schuster, 1985). Before Davis undertook his research, there was little evidence for the existence of zombies other than stories found in Haitian culture. People who became zombies were said to have been killed and buried, only to reappear with the characteristic zomboid personality. Because of their inherent strangeness, such stories were given little credence. The implicit reasoning went like this: 'There is no substantial evidence for the existence of zombies, so they must not exist.' This is a clear example of an appeal to ignorance. But that appeal was not based on any significant search for evidence.

The shortcomings of such an appeal are highlighted by the research Davis carried out. After a lengthy investigation, he concluded that there are zombies and that people are transformed into zombies by being poisoned with a potent drug that slows the metabolism of the body to such an extent that the victim appears dead, but subsequently exhibits zomboid affectations. Davis's research provides evidence for the existence of zombies that undermines the argument from ignorance that many uncritically assumed to be a good argument.

We would probably not be willing to go as far as Davis did in quest of evidence for something unknown, but our failure to do so should temper what we profess to know. We should be prepared to admit it when we are not in a position to know much about certain issues. Above all, we must not yield to the all-too-human tendency to hold tenaciously to our prejudices and assumptions.

> **Box 12.8 Appeals to Ignorance**
> Appeals to ignorance attempt to establish the truth or falsity of some claim, x, by appealing to the lack of evidence for its truth or falsity. A good appeal to ignorance claims that x is true (or false) after the failure of a responsible attempt to find evidence for its falsity (or truth).

EXERCISE 12C

Describe specific circumstances in which you would or would not be in a position to construct a good argument from ignorance about each of the following topics.
*1. ghosts
 2. the alleged racism of a provincial or state ombudsman
 3. the hypothesis that there is a tenth planet
 4. the question whether someone is guilty of murder
 5. extrasensory perception
 6. the irradiation of food

6. Other Cases

In drawing to a close our discussion of specific forms of argument, we reiterate the point that some arguments do not fit neatly into the categories we have introduced. Sometimes no specific form of argument is used and sometimes the premises contain a mixture of specific forms. Where there is no specific form at all, we must depend on the general criteria of relevance and sufficiency and acceptability in assessing an argument. If an argument is a mixture of a variety of specific forms, we must appeal to a variety of specific criteria. To illustrate such complexities, consider the example of someone arguing that White is the killer the police are looking for on the basis of the following reasoning:

P1 = Green says White is the killer.
P2 = White is a mean and nasty person at the best of times.
P3 = Nobody has been able to provide any evidence to the contrary.
C = White is the killer.

Note that P1, P2, and P3 appeal to very different sorts of evidence. P1, implicitly appealing to Green as someone who should know who the killer is, is a *pro homine* argument. P3 is an argument from ignorance. P2 does not conform to any of our specific forms of argument. (Note that it is an attack on White, not an attack on White's views and, hence, not an *ad hominem* argument.)

We diagram the above argument as follows:

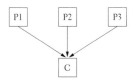

In assessing this argument, we must assess the weight each specific sub-argument lends to the conclusion. Then the overall strength of the argument must be evaluated by asking whether the conclusion is probably true, given the cumulative force of the different kinds of evidence introduced to justify it. Individually, each aspect of the total argument may be questionable and, therefore, only marginally convincing, but in conjunction with the others it can contribute to a strong argument, especially if there are no fundamental objections to the reasoning. The strength of the final conclusion is a result of the three separate kinds of considerations providing supporting evidence for it. Thus, although Green may not be the most trustworthy character, his claims must be taken seriously when they are corroborated by other evidence.

Other complications arise when different parts of the conclusion are established by different premises. We can add complexity to the example we have been considering by adding a fourth premise and rewriting the conclusion as a conjunction:

P1 = Green says White is the killer.
P2 = White is a mean and nasty person at the best of times.
P3 = Nobody has been able to provide any evidence to the contrary.
P4 = All those who have met him agree that Brown could not commit such a heinous crime.
C = White is the killer and Brown is innocent.

We can now represent the argument as consisting of four premises leading to conclusion C. The nature of the premises clearly shows that P1, P2, and P3 go to establish that White is the killer while P4 establishes that Brown is innocent. For purposes of assessing the argument, we can represent Brown's innocence as a hidden conclusion (HC2) following from P4 and the final conclusion as following from it and from the conclusion of the argument as we stated it earlier, which we now label HC1. Diagramming the argument, we get the following structure:

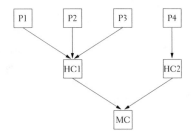

where:

HC1 = White is the killer.
HC2 = Brown is innocent.
MC = White is the killer and Brown is innocent.

Using this diagram, we can assess the argument in the normal way.

Because we need to assess the different premises in such arguments in different ways, we must separate premises that support a conclusion in different ways: by appealing to analogies, to causal reasoning, to *pro homine* considerations, and so on. If you keep in mind the goals of an honest and logically useful representation, then you should be able to deal effectively with whatever specific forms of argument you come across.

EXERCISE 12D

Take the above example and construct a scenario where the premises, taken together (but not separately), establish the probability of the conclusion.

Major Exercise 12M

1. This assignment is intended to help you test your understanding of argument forms by using some of them in conjunction with specific normative issues.

   a) Construct short arguments employing the following forms (one for each argument) in support of the claim 'Capital punishment should not be reinstated where it is currently disallowed': two-wrongs; *pro homine*; appeal to authority; guilt by association.

   b) Employ the same argument forms in support of the opposite claim: 'Capital punishment should be reinstated where it is currently disallowed.'

   c) Construct arguments on the issue of euthanasia using two-wrongs reasoning.

   d) Using any of the argument forms of this chapter, construct a short argument on one of the following issues.

      i) acid rain

      ii) the rights of indigenous peoples

      vi) insider trading

2. A current topic of discussion is the extent to which Western banks and nations should help Third World countries by forgiving the huge debts these countries have accumulated. Take each form of reasoning we have discussed and outline how you could use it in your deliberation on the issue. Write a 'Letter to the Editor' using the form of argument you regard as best suited to justify your position.

3. Construct an argument scrapbook by collecting from magazines and newspapers five examples of the forms of argument we have introduced. In each case, explain whether it is a good or bad argument. If it is a bad argument, explain how it could be strengthened or corrected.

4. Decide whether each of the following passages contains an argument. If it does, assess the reasoning. For any specific argument forms dealt with in this chapter, explain whether they fulfil the conditions for good arguments of that form. Note that examples may involve more than one argument form. It may also be necessary to diagram the arguments.

   *a) [Adapted from 'Smoking Benefits Amazing', a report on the effects of smoking on the economy: *Peterborough Examiner*, 10 Sept. 1994] According to economist Jean-Pierre Vidal in a study commissioned by Imperial Tobacco, while smoking kills, those deaths have economic benefits for society.

   A person who dies of lung cancer at age 70 will not be hospitalized later with another disease and the costs of hospitalization tend to increase substantially for people after the age of 70. Furthermore, wages forfeited by deceased former smokers are available for other, younger, workers.

   b) [From Daniel D. Polsby, 'The False Promise of Gun Control', *Atlantic Monthly*, Mar. 1994] If firearms increased violence and crime, then rates of spousal homicide would have skyrocketed, because the stock of privately owned handguns has increased rapidly since the mid-1960s. But according to an authoritative study of spousal homicide in the *American Journal of Public Health*, by James Mercey and Linda Saltzman, rates of spousal homicide in the years 1976 to 1985 fell. If firearms increase violence and crime, the crime rate should have increased throughout the 1980s, while the national stock of privately owned handguns increased by more than a million units every year of the decade. It did not.

c) [Letter to the *Toronto Star*, 14 Mar. 1988] If Nancy Reagan indeed did suggest that casual drug users were aiding in murder she's got things the wrong way around.

The economist Milton Friedman says the following in his book: 'The individual addict would clearly be far better off if drugs were legal. Today, drugs are both extremely expensive and highly uncertain in quality. Addicts are driven to associate with criminals to get the drugs, and they become criminals themselves to finance the habit. They risk constant danger of death and disease.'

Friedman goes on to say that it is estimated that from one-third to one-half of all violent and property crime in the United States is 'committed either by drug addicts engaged in crime to finance their habit, or by conflicts among competing groups of drug pushers, or in the course of the importation and distribution of illegal drugs. Legalize drugs, and street crime would drop dramatically and immediately.'

d) [From a letter to *The Globe and Mail*, 9 Nov. 1988] Dr Murphy suggests that, given our government's recent move to compensate Japanese Canadians for their internment during the Second World War, it is logical to ask the Japanese government to compensate Canadians it held as prisoners of war during the same period (letter—Oct. 24). The logic Dr Murphy invokes equates Canadians of Japanese origin interned by their own government with prisoners of war.

Dr Murphy should be reminded that the men, women and children he speaks of were citizens of his own country. They were not, as his parallel implies, prisoners of war, i.e., captured enemy soldiers.

e) [From a letter to *The Globe and Mail*, 23 June 1988] Re Tobacco Bills Could Pass Senate By Fall (June 2). William Neville, president of the Canadian Tobacco Manufacturers Association, is still waiting to see a single piece of bona fide evidence to suggest that advertising has anything to do with the total consumption of tobacco products.

I suggest that if the tobacco industry truly believed that it could commission a study to prove that advertising tobacco products does not affect consumption, it would have done so by now. It has the means and the funds to do so, but is aware that such a study would no doubt prove just the opposite.

*f) [From Geoffrey R. Stone, 'Repeating Past Mistakes', *Society*, 24, 5 (1987). Background: In the US in 1970 the President's Commission on Obscenity and Pornography found no causal connection between exposure to sexually explicit materials and criminal behaviour. In 1986 the Attorney-General's Commission contested that finding.]

The Attorney-General's Commission's contrary conclusion in 1986 is based more on preconception than on evidence. An issue that has long divided social scientists . . . can hardly be definitively resolved by a commission of non-experts, most of whom were appointed because of the pre-existing commitment to the suppression of obscene expression. . . . [E]ven those who claim a connection between exposure to obscene expression and unlawful conduct claim no more than an indirect and attenuated 'bad tendency'. Thus, although some individuals may on some occasions commit some unlawful acts 'because of' their exposure to obscene expression, the connection is indirect, speculative, and unpredictable.

h) [Letter to the *Kitchener-Waterloo Record*, Mar. 1985] Evolutionists claim that life progressed from one-celled organisms to its highest state, the human being, by means of a series of biological changes taking place over millions of years.

And they know full well that their claims directly contradict the Bible story of creation. They also state that anyone who puts a literal interpretation on the first two chapters of Genesis is out of touch with reality.

It's also been proven that most ministers believe the creation story is a fable.

The Christian belief in creation is not a theory. It is a fact and it doesn't need to be proven, no more than we need to prove that computers have a maker. The computers themselves are the proof.

There isn't one chance in a billion that a computer could evolve. It demands a maker, and so does our universe.

In spite of the claims of people such as CBC personality David Suzuki, the so-called missing link between man and beast has never been found. Each species was created with the programmed ability to evolve different types of its own species, but one kind cannot evolve into another. The basic teaching of evolution is based on assumption.

i) [Adapted from a letter to the *New York Times*, 7 Feb. 1987] In his Jan. 7 letter, Judge Bruce McM. Wright cites as historical fact the story of Thomas Jefferson's slave mistress, Sally Hemmings. It is simply ridiculous that this patent lie should still be seen in print. Its origin is almost as old as our Republic.

On July 14, 1798, the Federalist Congress passed the Sedition Act, which made publishing anything false or scandalous against the Government a crime. In May of 1800, James T. Callender, a Scottish immigrant and pamphleteer, went on trial in Richmond for violation of that act.

Callender was a pathetic creature, an alcoholic and hypochondriac, who never seemed able to extricate himself from debt. Jefferson had befriended him a few years earlier and had advanced him funds to enable him to continue his writing. At his trial, Callender was convicted and sentenced to nine months in prison and fined $200.

When Jefferson became President in 1801, he pardoned Callender. Since Callender had already completed his prison term the effect of this was to refund his fine and clear his name. When Callender received his money three months later, he had grown bitter against Jefferson and his party for the delay and the time he had spent in prison. He decided to chastise the President and succeeded beyond even his expectations.

In September 1802 in *The Richmond Recorder*, he published the story of Sally Hemmings, the slave mistress of the President. Callender cited no support for the story, saying merely that it was 'well known'. He subsequently changed elements of the story repeatedly to bring them into line with the facts of Jefferson's life. Several times he changed the version of how the affair began, and the number of children supposedly produced by it. To those who knew Jefferson's high moral standards and devotion to his dead wife's memory, the story was laughable.

I find it incredible that a story that all reputable historians, led by Jefferson's able biographer Dumas Malone, have discredited for years, should still find its way into print. Without the strictest accuracy, history is worthless.

j) [Adapted from a letter to the *New York Times*, Mar. 1982] As a true American, I wish to speak for what is near and dear to the hearts of Americans. I wish to speak against what is as foreign to these shores as communism, socialism, totalitarianism, and other foreign 'ism's', except of course Americanism. I speak of the Administration's 'medicare bill', better known as 'socialized medicine'.

Socialized medicine would commit us to the complete takeover by government of everything traditionally reserved for the individual. As the late Senator Robert A. Taft—a true American—warned, 'if we are going to give medical care free to all people, why not provide them with free transportation, free housing, free food and clothing, all at the expense of the taxpayer. . . . Socialization is just a question of degree, and we cannot move much further in that direction unless we do wish a completely socialist state.'

If medicare is sound, then a government-sponsored, -financed, and controlled program is sound for every aspect of our life. But this principle must be rejected. As Americans, freedom must be our watchword. And since freedom means no control, no regulation, no restraint, government programs like medicare are quite contrary to the American concept of freedom.

Unlike pseudo-Americans who want to socialize this country, I believe that socialized medicine would be an insult to true Americans. For true Americans don't want handouts. They want to stand on their own feet. They're willing to meet their obligations. They're willing to work and pay for their medical bills. As convincing proof of this, the AMA has advertised that it will give medical care to anyone who wants it, and practically no one responds to these ads.

We need only look at England to see what effects socialized medicine would have here — to see how it would lower the quality of medical care. For as Dr Lull of the AMA reminds us, the record in Great Britain shows that governmentally dominated medical systems burden doctors with red tape and paper work, thus robbing them of valuable time needed for careful diagnosis and treatment of patients. Not to mention all the freeloaders, hypochondriacs, and malingerers, who daily crowd the hospitals and doctors' offices and thus take away valuable beds and time from those who are really sick. In other words, socialized medicine is not only unnecessary but it would also be undesirable.

It should be obvious that it would not accomplish the utopia claimed for it. Indeed, what proof do we have that it would make everyone healthy overnight? Since there is no conclusive proof, we can only conclude that it would be a dismal failure.

*k) [Background: In May 1987, Klaus Barbie, the so-called 'Butcher of Lyon', was put on trial in France for crimes against humanity during the Second World War. With respect to the defence of Barbie, the following quote from Jacques Verges, Barbie's lawyer, was reported in *The Globe and Mail*, 2 May 1987.]: We will see during the course of this business that what Mr Barbie did as a loyal officer of his country was no different than what hundreds of loyal officers of this country did during the Algerian war. We will see that Mr Barbie operated under a legally accepted premise at the time and that he was assisted by citizens and officials of France. We will see that even French Jews and members of the Resistance assisted Mr Barbie in his work.

l) In response to significant changes to labour laws instituted by Bob Rae's left-leaning Ontario government of the early 1990s, groups opposed to the changes printed billboards like the following.

Source: Courtesy of the Mechanical Contractors' Association of Ontario.

ESSAYING

AN

ARGUMENT

The last important aspect of critical thinking is the writing of extended pieces of argumentation. We must be able to write critical responses to arguments we have analysed, incorporating the main features of our evaluation. Secondly, we will often be called on to construct our own argumentative essays. In this chapter we will:

- ◆ discuss the evaluative critique;
- ◆ discuss the argumentative essay;
- ◆ apply the techniques to a student essay; and
- ◆ offer our own revision of the essay.

In this text we have focused on the two arms of critical thinking, assessing others' reasoning and presenting our own. When we assess another person's argument, we evaluate the reasoning on its own terms and decide whether we are convinced by the claims on the grounds of that reasoning. Although we consider its context, we do not go beyond the reasoning in the sense of adding anything to it. However, *after* the evaluation, as we organize our critical remarks and *respond*, we do go beyond the original argument and bring in other considerations, emphasizing what the arguer has overlooked and perhaps providing reasoning that would remedy problems we have found. An *evaluative critique*, then, is an argumentative response that incorporates both the features of our evaluation and our own insights.

The other arm of critical thinking involves constructing our own arguments. The argumentative essay captures this activity in a more extensive form. Unlike the evaluative critique, the argumentative essay need not be based on any prior evaluation or response to another's reasoning. It is the form our writing takes when we are setting down the arguments for a position we hold, engaging in original research around a controversial issue, or conducting an inquiry to arrive at a position we will then hold, perhaps by testing a few hypotheses. In its clearest form it is the first of these, although the other two will often have gone into earlier drafts of the argumentative essay.

In this chapter, we will trace the details of both the evaluative critique and the argumentative essay before illustrating these activities by means of a critique of a student essay and then the writing of a revision of that essay.

1. THE GOOD EVALUATIVE CRITIQUE

There are seven steps to consider in preparing for and producing such a critique:

1. overview of the main claim and subclaims;
2. macro-structure and micro-structure;
3. language;
4. reasoning;
5. weighing strengths and weaknesses;
6. decision;
7. the body of the critique.

Overview

In a brief paragraph, set down the main claim that is being put forward and the sub-arguments that are offered in support of it. Also note any specific types of reasoning that have been employed. For example:

> In his article the author is opposing any form of gun control law because (a) such a law is essentially undemocratic and (b) it will mean innocent members of society receive criminal records. But the bulk of his argument is given to support the contention that (c) gun control is unnecessary because there is no clear connection between guns and crime. The author employs causal reasoning in support of (c). In particular, he attempts to show that any causal claim linking gun ownership to criminal activity is fallacious.

Macro-Structure and Micro-Structure

Depict the structure of the argument in a diagram, showing as much detail as is necessary. Minimally, this will involve a diagram of the macro-structure, that is, a diagram showing the sub-arguments and the main claim. To assist you in this, give a number or letter to each paragraph of the text with which you are working. A micro-structure diagram will be more detailed and show the supporting premises for each subclaim.

Language

Some consideration of language may have arisen in the overview if you had trouble with the meaning of the main claim or one or more subclaims. A complete analysis of the extended argument will include a review of its language, even if no problems may be evident.

Watch for vagueness, ambiguity, and heavily loaded language. And be especially alert to poor definitions or the failure to provide the definition of a term that is important to the outcome of the argument. The macro- and micro-structure diagrams will help you assess the importance of terms according to where they occur in the flow of the argument.

Reasoning

Here is the bulk of your analysis: a complete assessment of the reasoning employed according to the various criteria of good reasoning explained in earlier chapters of this text. This will include a general assessment of basic criteria of acceptability, relevance, and sufficiency, as well as the specific criteria associated with deductive and non-deductive argument forms. If a categorical syllogism has been employed, test it for validity. If the arguer employs an *ad hominem*, ensure that it meets the conditions for good instances of that argument form. With respect to the next stage in this procedure, it may be just as important that the arguer has employed arguments appropriately as it is that they have been employed fallaciously. When you assess the reasoning, you are not simply out to detect errors.

Weighing Strengths and Weaknesses

Now you have amassed all the information you require to make a decision about the argument and for responding to it. Stages 5 to 7 concern your reaction. You want to decide about the argument on the basis of a balanced appreciation of both its strengths and weaknesses. Set out two columns with the headings 'Strengths' and 'Weaknesses' and list under each heading the main discoveries of your analysis. Again, the diagrams will help you determine how detrimental or positive each discovery is. For example, the irrelevance to the main claim of an entire sub-argument is far more detrimental to the overall argument than the irrelevance of just one of many premises to a subclaim. With some arguments you may find all or most of your entries are in one column. Such cases make for an easy decision. But most ordinary arguments, when fairly assessed, have both strengths and weaknesses that have to be weighed against each other. The weighing should be done objectively. With the most difficult and balanced of arguments, you will appreciate that while you may decide one way, a co-evaluator might decide another way.

Decision

Having weighed the strengths and weaknesses, you must next decide both the degree to which you are persuaded by the argument and the manner of your response to it. Stage 5 allowed for a wide range of decisions about the evaluated argument. At the one extreme, the reasoning may be so weak that no reasonable person could be persuaded by it. If the argument happened to have been for a position that you were previously inclined to support, then to continue supporting it you will need to do so on the basis of quite different reasoning. At the other extreme, the reasoning may have such logical strength that if, in your response, you intend to challenge the position it advocates, you will have to counter those strengths with further, even more compelling, argumentation.

As will be clear from the above, this is the stage of evaluation (really post-evaluation) where your prior beliefs and attitudes come into play. You cannot dismiss a strong argument just because you do not like the conclusion (or the arguer!). The process of evaluation has shown you that there can often be quite good arguments advanced in support of positions that you do not support. Coming to such realizations is part of gaining maturity as a critical thinker.

You may agree with the reasoning but not the conclusion. Perhaps the reasoning, while strong, is not strong enough to override other reasons that you have for rejecting the conclusion. Those other reasons will form the core of your response. You may agree with the conclusion but find the argumentation for it to be weak. Strengthening that argumentation and perhaps adding to it will form the basis of your response. Again, you may accept some of the argumentation but not all of it, and respond accordingly. Or you may allow most of the argumentation but insist that it really supports a reworded claim. As you can see, there are many possible responses between the extremes of complete rejection or agreement. What is important is that your decision is fairly based on both the strengths and weaknesses and that you take account of these in your critique.

Critique

Criticism is simply the use of critical judgement. It does not have to be negative, although it often carries that connotation. Where a written critique is required, you should make use of the previous six steps. Acknowledge strengths and weaknesses. Use the weaknesses against the arguer where you disagree, and look to remedy or avoid them where you agree with the arguer's position. Promote the strengths and add to them where you agree, and look to counter them where you disagree. Your critique is where you develop your own extensive argument and so this is the stage at which the evaluative critique benefits from many of the pointers of the argumentative essay, to which we now turn.

EXERCISE 13A

Following the seven stages outlined in this section, write an evaluative critique for each of the following:

1. Since women and other visible minorities have been discriminated against by the system, it is appropriate to institute a policy that involves favouring these groups over others in employment decisions, those others being, for the most part, white males. Some harm is done to those not favoured by this policy, but nothing like the harm the system presently inflicts on the disadvantaged groups. And besides, white males have flourished in the system for so long that even under this policy they will still be fairly well off. The only alternative would be to change the attitudes of society, and thereby the system, at a fundamental level but this would take too long. Therefore, employment equity is currently justified.

2. [From A.J. Ayer, *Language, Truth and Logic* (New York: Dover, 1952)] If the conclusion that a god exists is to be demonstrably certain, then these premises [from which it follows] must be certain. . . . But we know that no empirical proposition can ever be anything more than probable. It is only 'a priori' propositions that are logically certain. But we cannot deduce the existence of god from an 'a priori' proposition. For we know that the reason why 'a priori' propositions are certain is that they are tautologies [statements that are necessarily true]. And from a set of tautologies nothing but a further tautology can be validly deduced. It follows that there is no possibility of demonstrating the existence of god.

3. [From the *Peterborough Examiner*, Mar. 1995. Background: During a recent debate on gun control, one gun owner reacted to a report that 'more guns means more suicide' with the following argument.] According to Dr Isaac Safinosky, who presented the Clarke Institute of Psychiatry paper to the American Association of Suicidology, in countries where the suicide rate is rising, control of inflation by the government is the main cause. This creates increased unemployment. As a consequence, he said, 'Society becomes demoralized, so even the employed start to worry, causing people to stop buying. In recent times, inflation has been seen as the major economic threat to society. Monetarist policies have deliberately raised interest rates to cool the economy and reduce inflationary growth; the resulting loss of jobs is seen as a necessary evil in order to bring down wages and prices. Suicide increase in young persons in such countries appears to be the unfortunate concomitant of these policies.'

    This study points the finger directly at those people who are blaming us. The economic policies of the government . . . [are] the major cause of the rising rate of suicide.

4. [Adapted from a brochure entitled 'Introducing—the flat Earth Society'] If the Earth were a gigantic globe, then half the world would be living upside-down! Why don't they fall off? Furthermore, one person's 'up' (in the 'southern hemisphere'), would be another person's 'down' (in the 'northern hemisphere'), which is obviously repugnant to Common Sense.

. . . The fantasy of a global Earth that spins (Gyroglobularism) contains even more preposterous absurdities. Thus, with the numbers dreamed up by the Globularists, a person standing at the 'equator' of this 'global' Earth would be whirled around at about 1,000 miles an hour and not know it! At this speed, why does not everything get spun off into space? Or at the very least, why do not all the oceans of the world accumulate at the 'equator' causing a giant tidal wave there?

The Globularists attempt to escape from all these obvious implications by resorting to one sacred word 'gravity'. . . . But this feeble attempt at an explanation is nothing more than a circular argument, as an extract from Ambrose Bierce's *The Devil's Dictionary* well explains: 'Gravitation, n. The tendency of all bodies to approach one another with a strength proportioned to the quantity of matter they contain—the quantity of matter they contained being ascertained by the strength of their tendency to approach one another. This is a lovely edifying illustration of how science, having made A the proof of B, makes B the proof of A.'

. . . When one surveys one's own environment with appropriate impartiality, there is an overwhelming *lack of evidence* for the above preposterous fantasies! One can only conclude that they are nothing more than the products of certain people's over-strained feverish imaginations.

5. [Letter to the University of Waterloo *Imprint*, 9 Mar. 1984] One question that should haunt the atheists as they scan these nicely packaged proofs against God's existence, is the question of whether or not man can trust his own reasoning. For if indeed man has evolved via the process of natural selection, then surely we have a rather shaky foundation to suppose that reasoning is trustworthy. For then our reasoning is no longer based on truth, but rather on its ultimate survival value. Consider the thoughts of Darwin when he wrote: 'The horrid doubt always rises whether the convictions of a man's mind, which has developed from the mind of lower animals, are of any value at all; would anyone trust the convictions of a monkey's mind, if there are any convictions in such a mind?'

Now, the second point that should disturb the atheist is the issues. It is often the case that the atheist likes to have the best of both worlds (Theistic and Atheistic) in this department. Let me illustrate. Man, who can be no more than merely a complex chemical machine, cries out against injustice, hatred, prejudice, etc., now, why is this so? Is there some sort of transcendent worth attached to a heap of chemical reactions contained in what we call the human body? Hitler seemed to believe in building a 'pure' race, one that would be stronger and one which would be white. He, in my mind, was simply following the natural selection rule to the realm of ethics. Yet, many atheists frown upon Hitler's morals and even go as far as to say that he was evil (with a capital 'E'). My point is this: few atheists are willing to accept the notion of relativism in ethics which MUST follow from their presuppositions. Good and evil are relative so how can you criticize Hitler, to whom is he accountable (for he was the law) and besides, he is supposed to be an autonomous free being.

So what if he reduced 6 million Jews to cinders. Tell me that you don't LIKE what he did or that his action were SOCIALLY unacceptable, but DON'T tell me that he was bad or evil (capital E). These terms do not belong in your world view . . . they went out with God (capital G).

Now, take careful note, this has not been a criticism of atheism as a world view, rather, an attempt to make atheists realize some of the nihilistic implications of that world view.

2. THE GOOD ARGUMENTATIVE ESSAY

Scope

Before you begin writing, you should have a clear idea of the thesis or claim you are advancing and the way you intend to defend it. Defining the scope of an argument is a matter of establishing manageable boundaries for your reasoning. Given the evidence that you have amassed for your subclaims, what is the main claim you might reasonably be able to defend? And how can you express that claim without promising too much or so little that the argument becomes trivial?

To answer these questions you need to have a clear idea of your intentions and your audience. You will have thought through the issue, looked at it from different perspectives (including the opposing viewpoint), and done as much research as your judgement tells you the situation requires.

Be clear about the context of your argument and its most important feature—your *audience*. Are you writing to reinforce the views of a *sympathetic* audience, as when you present an internal paper in a work situation? Are you writing for a neutral audience that is neither predisposed to agree or disagree but is open to be persuaded, as when you prepare a paper for an academic jury like a course instructor? Or are you writing for a *hostile* audience predisposed to the opposite position to your own, as in the case of a controversial public debate on a contentious social issue? Think carefully about the audience you will be addressing and decide what information you can assume they have (that is, what will count as shared knowledge for that audience) and how their beliefs and values will lead them to react to what you say.

Given that the hostile audience is the most demanding one to write for, it should be the default audience when you are unsure who you will be addressing, as when your argument is to appear in a public forum or in future contexts that you cannot control.

With your position clear in your own mind and your audience established, you can set down your main claim. State this in an opening paragraph in which you also outline the principal subclaims you will advance to support it. Some people like to hold their main point until the end of their argumentative essay, keeping the audience in suspense and building to a climax. This has rhetorical effectiveness and may work for an accomplished and experienced arguer. It would not work for our purposes because it is important for our audience to know our intentions from the outset so that they can appraise the support for our position as it develops. They can only appreciate the relevance of each point as it arises and admire our arguing technique if they are made aware from the outset of the claim for which we are arguing.

Given the essay form of the argumentative essay, there is a temptation to *discuss* the topic rather than argue a claim related to it. Avoid this by adopting the language of argumentation in your opening paragraph. For example: 'In the following I will argue . . .', 'my conclusion is . . .', 'The claim I intend to support is . . .'.

That said, the following are examples of introductory paragraphs that define the scope by presenting a clear claim and explaining how it will be supported.

> Advances in medical technology have given rise to new issues that concern society. One of these, perhaps the chief, is human-embryo experimentation. Critics insist this must not be permitted because the consequences may be too horrendous to handle. While I share such concerns, I will argue that, on balance, human-embryo experimentation should be permitted prior to the fourteenth day after fertilization. I will support this with the following subclaims: (a) prior to the fourteenth day the human embryo is not a person; (b) only persons are morally significant; and (c) the benefits of human-embryo experimentation far outweigh the negative aspects.

> In his *Civilization and Its Discontents* Sigmund Freud argues that humans are inherently aggressive. I wish to take issue with this viewpoint and will support the claim that humans are inherently good. To this end I will argue (a) that Freud's conclusion is an overgeneralization based on a selective sample of cases; and (b) that recent studies of children show that aggressive behaviour is learned, not innate.

Reading your introductory paragraph, no one should be in any doubt what it is you are arguing. You are also giving notice of how your argument is going to be structured, which will aid you in your writing as much as it helps your readers.

Clarity

The clear communication of our intentions will not flow automatically but will require that we think about how we are saying things as much as what it is we are saying. What may be clear to you may not be so clear to your readers and you should take time to consider this. In earlier chapters we have seen how vague or illegitimately emotional language can be counter-productive to our ends. With the argumentative essay we need to be particularly careful about the way we state claims. One common problem is the tendency to overstate a claim. That is, to claim more than we can support. Often, this can be avoided simply by qualifying our statements. Consider the following pairs of claims:

1 a)   There are a number of reasons why we should not manipulate the human gene pool.
1 b)   The human gene pool should never be manipulated.
2 a)   Freud's examples are rarely convincing.
2 b)   None of Freud's examples is convincing.
3 a)   It seems likely that the wearing of helmets while cycling will save lives.
3 b)   Clearly, the wearing of helmets while cycling will save lives.

In each case, statement (b) is much stronger than statement (a). But this is not a positive sense of 'stronger than' because in each case the onus placed on the arguer who would support statement (b) is much greater. It is more reasonable to expect that in each instance we can provide persuasive evidence for the qualified statements in (a). When you put down a claim ask yourself, 'Can I support this or should I modify it first?'

Also, consider whether you have adequately defined the key terms you are using. Central to the arguments of the introductory paragraphs on medical technology and Freud, above, are the terms 'human embryo' and 'aggressiveness'. You have the obligation to define such terms because it is likely that the entire extended argument will depend on how your audience understands them. Such definitions should come as early in the argument as possible, perhaps immediately after the introductory paragraph. It is possible for an otherwise clear argumentative essay to leave readers quite unsure about the central terms on which it depends.

Structure

A well-structured argumentative essay is an effective vehicle for the ideas it conveys. Develop your points in a logical order in terms of both strength and dependency. That is, (i) begin with your strongest point or sub-argument, and (ii) where points depend on one another, establish them in an order that shows that dependency and makes sense to the reader.

Beginning with your strongest and most plausible point will capture the reader's attention and, it is to be expected, conviction. If you create a basis for the acceptance of your position in this way, subsequent arguments can be built on it. Starting with your strongest point *for* your claim should not mean that your argument will weaken as it develops. Later arguments that deal with points *against* your claim, or that anticipate and meet objections to what you are saying, may be among the strongest points you will make overall, giving balance and completion to your reasoning.

For example, in claiming that circuses are undesirable because they mistreat animals, the following claim could be advanced:

C1 Circuses put animals in unnatural environments and require them to do unnatural things.

Such a claim could be supported by premises that indicate the natural habitats and behaviours of circus animals and further common-knowledge premises indicating the performance-focused circus environment of such animals. But this argument depends on the logically prior claim:

C2 What is natural is good and what is unnatural is bad/undesirable.

C2 and its supporting evidence should precede C1 or at least be conjoined with it. For C2 to be introduced a page or so later, with other sub-arguments intervening, would be a structural weaknesses since the flow of the argumentation would then not be sequential.

While no one would expect you to include a diagram even of the macro-structure, it is a good idea to plot this out for yourself and keep it by your side for reference while you are writing. Doing so allows you to take advantage of all the benefits of the diagramming technique. You will see how well your argument fits together, how easy (or hard) it is to detect the logical structure, and places where support is lacking or overly dependent on one idea. If you have difficulty diagramming your own argument, you can expect someone else to have trouble seeing the connections.

Argumentation

Our purpose in writing an argumentative essay is to convince an audience of our conclusion, or to reinforce the conviction they already hold. If we are to succeed in this, our argument must be strong.

The bulk of this text has dealt with assessing various types of argument. At this point, therefore, we shall simply restate some of the basic principles set forth elsewhere insofar as those principles apply to the writing of the argumentative essay:

(i) Reasons must be statements distinct and separate from your conclusion.
(ii) Each reason offered in support of a claim must, together with the other reasons, increase the probability of the acceptability of that claim.

(iii) Ensure that issues are correctly recognized and directly addressed, and that any version of an opposing argument has been fairly represented.

(iv) Back your claims with as many relevant reasons as necessary to convince your audience.

(v) Ensure that all your statements, including premises and conclusions, are consistent with each other.

(vi) Do not rely on hidden components. Make your assumptions explicit and defend them where necessary.

Objectivity

Besides communicating a sense of fairness and balanced judgement, objectivity in the argumentative essay covers two points. These seem connected, but involve distinct concerns.

(i) We have all seen overtly one-sided arguments, where all the attention is devoted to *directly* promoting the position held. After all, you might say, the whole point has been to argue for one's position. But in many, if not most, issues there is an opposing point of view with its own considerations. An *indirect* way to further support your case is to consider some of the *strongest* points of the opposing position and show how they can be dealt with or outweighed by your own points. This adds an atmosphere of objectivity to your argument because, if you do it fairly, it shows that you have thought about both sides of the issue and are prepared to recognize the stronger counter-claims.

Naturally, there is a danger of straw-man reasoning here. You must only attribute to the opposing viewpoint arguments that you know exist on that side, and you should support that knowledge in some way. It is also your judgement as to what arguments constitute the stronger ones of the opposition. If you choose those which are obviously weaker and respond to them, or if you attribute to the opposing viewpoint arguments that no one actually holds, then the whole process backfires. Rather than showing objectivity, your argument will appear to the discerning reader to lack it altogether and to be guilty of misrepresentation.

(ii) Another way to exhibit objectivity is to consider not only the known arguments of the opposing point of view, but what someone of that persuasion would respond to what you have specifically said. That is, anticipate objections to your own points. This demonstrates objectivity in that it shows you are prepared to consider criticisms of your own ideas and that you are able to look at your arguments from a different perspective. Quite often such a reading will enable you to detect flaws in your arguments and lead you to constructive revisions.

Even once you are satisfied with what you have argued, you will still see places where objections might be raised. Note these: 'Someone might respond to this point that . . . .' Then counter the objection with a reasonable response. Identifying likely objections, again without making false attributions, and answering those anticipated objections will add further indirect support to your position.

EXERCISE 13B

Think about one of the following topics. Diagram the structure of a macro argument that would express your position on the topic. Next, develop this argument by elaborating micro arguments.
a) Objectivity in politics.
b) The existence of intelligent life elsewhere in the universe.
c) The obligation of wealthier nations to help poorer nations.
d) Surrogate motherhood.
e) Prison reform.
f) Miracles.

3. A STUDENT'S PAPER

For easy reference in discussing the following paper, each sentence is labelled with a letter, signifying the paragraph, and a number, signifying the sentence within a given paragraph. Thus C identifies a particular paragraph and C3 the third sentence in that paragraph.

Assisted Suicide

(A1) Assisted suicide is an emotional and complex issue. (A2) You can get different views on it depending on who you talk to. (A3) But everyone agrees that when someone is suffering greatly they should be allowed to die. (A4) Society should help these people and not turn its back on them.

(B1) What is involved here is euthanasia where the person cannot bring about their own death but requires the assistance of someone else to do it, usually a physician. (B2) But they have decided that they want to die.

(C1) The main reason for this is that people should have the right to decide when they want to die. (C2) To force them to live in a state of pain is cruel and inhuman. (C3) When a pet is suffering badly we realize that the kindest thing to do is to 'put it down' in as painless a way as possible. (C4) But we treat each other much worse than our pets because society forces people to continue to suffer rather than letting them be put to sleep like their pets.

(D1) People have a fundamental right to decide what they want. (D2) This is the freedom to choose. (D3) And as long as we are not harming anyone else, no one has the right to prevent us from doing what we know is best for us. (D4) When people are not able to take care of matters for themselves then others should recognize that they have a right to this and that it is their duty to help them.

(E1) Many people are upset when they recognize what is at stake here. (E2) While it is frowned on, people do commit suicide all the time and that's okay. (E3) But when they are terminally ill it's not okay any more. (E4) What they could do when they were healthy they can't do when they are sick unless someone helps them, and the law doesn't allow anyone to help them.

(F1) Those who oppose assisted suicide do so for only one reason. (F2) They wrongly think it will lead to lots of abuses where people will be killed against their will. (F3) This is a Slippery Slope where attitudes will change and the taking of lives will be routine. (F4) This will not happen. (F5) Besides, physicians and others are already assisting people to die and in some cases, because of the law, this is leading to mistakes and suffering just like when abortions were performed in back alleys. (F6) Wouldn't bringing everything out into the light of day and regulating it more likely lessen abuses?

(G1) Health care costs have been steadily rising for decades now and as the babyboom generation moves into old age these costs will rise even further. (G2) No one should make a life-or-death decision solely on economic considerations. (G3) But where a terminally ill individual has expressed the desire to die and asked for assistance, then assisting them not only satisfies their request but saves society the cost of continued care for that person.

(H1) In conclusion, there are no good reasons not to allow assisted suicide. (H2) Most people want to have it and it's just a matter of time before they do.

4. CRITIQUE

Several positive things can be said about this paper. The main claim is relatively clear: assisted suicide should be permitted. Some attempt is made in paragraph B to define the key idea. Furthermore, the writer organizes the essay around several subpoints, devoting a brief paragraph to each. Also, an attempt is made in paragraph F to deal with the position of those who oppose assisted suicide. But there is room for improvement on each feature of the essay, as a detailed evaluation will indicate.

Overview

In this essay, the writer argues that there are no good reasons to oppose legal assisted suicide and society should permit it. To this end, it is claimed (a) that people have a fundamental right to decide when they will die and (b) that others have some sort of duty to assist the terminally ill to die. Also, (c) legalized assisted suicide will not lead to abuses and will prevent the kinds of abuses that currently arise. finally, (d) there are economic benefits to consider.

The arguer uses analogical reasoning in paragraphs C and F. In comparing terminally ill humans to terminally ill pets, the writer judges society to have inconsistent attitudes. And the current unregulated state of assisted suicide is compared to the time when illegal abortions were performed in 'back alleys'.

Structure

We can provide both macro- and micro-structure diagrams for this argument. Doing so reveals which statements and paragraphs contribute directly to the argument and which do not. We will take this paragraph by paragraph.

Paragraph A *should* have the main claim in it. If so, A4 is the only clear candidate. The first two statements report in a general way facts about the issue. A3, if correct, undermines the need for real argumentation since, if everyone did agree, the matter would not be so controversial. A4, on the other hand, is a claim that could, and should, be argued. We will come back to it when we look at paragraph H.

Paragraph B is definitional. It attempts to clarify the key term. We will consider this under 'language'.

Paragraph C is the first clear sub-argument. C1 gives the main reason for 'this', presumably the main claim. People should have the right to decide when they die because this avoids the cruelty of being forced to live in a state of pain (C2). That such a thing is cruel and inhuman is supported by the analogy in C3 and C4. So a diagram of paragraph C would be:

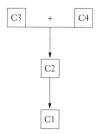

There are two things to note about paragraph D. first, it contains three unsupported independent assertions of 'rights': D1, D3, and D4. (D2 provides clarification of D1.) These are crucial claims to the outcome of the argument, especially D4. Secondly, D1 has been presupposed by C1. D1 asserts the *general* right of an individual to make decisions on the basis of his or her desires. C1 asserts the *specific* right of an individual to decide about his or her death. If D1 is accepted, then it serves as support for C1. So, in terms of the argument's structure, D1 is logically prior to C1 and should have been presented (and an attempt made to establish it) before C1. The structure of paragraph D simply consists of three unrelated claims, with D1 leading in the direction of C1 and D3 and D4 giving separate support to the main claim.

The four statements of paragraph E report states of affairs about the issue. But none of them asserts a claim or contributes support to the claims in other paragraphs. It is unclear how the student intends this paragraph. But a charitable reading would judge it as background rather than argumentation.

Paragraph F deals with the question of abuse, particularly the opposing concern that legalized assisted suicide will lead to abuses. F4 asserts the author's denial of such an outcome. The reason for this lies apparently in the opposing viewpoint depending on a bad slippery slope argument (F2 and F3). F5 shifts attention to the abuses currently arising from the status quo and supports the claim in F6 that legalizing the practice will probably lessen abuses. A diagram of paragraph F reads:

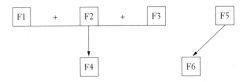

Paragraph G introduces the consideration of the cost to society of the current situation. G3 expresses the author's claim, while G1 and G2 combine as support for it.

In paragraph H we are brought back to the question of the main claim. H1 expresses a very strong claim that there are no good reasons not to allow assisted suicide. From reading through the whole argument it seems wise to understand the main claim as a hidden one, to the effect that 'assisted suicide should be legalized'. There is no question that the student is arguing for this, although nowhere is it expressly stated. Such a hidden main claim captures the sentiment of both A4 and H1. It also weakens the effect of H1. If we take H1 as the main claim, much of the reasoning will not support it. In fact, we will invoke the principle of charity again here and see H1 as the conclusion only to the first argument in paragraph F. This is because H1 asserts there are, in conclusion, no good arguments *against* assisted suicide, and paragraph F had allowed only one reason for people opposing it.

On the other hand, H2 relates to the earlier statement in A3 in that the writer sees popular support for the change being proposed. H2, unlike A3, is expressed like a reason intended as support for the main claim: 'most people want to have it'.

Understanding paragraph H this way, we arrive at the macro-structure of the argument:

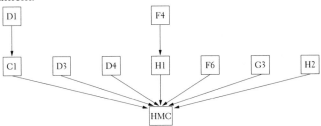

Language

You should have already noted several problems with the language in this argument. We had difficulty in deciding on the main claim. We also decided against treating the statements in paragraph E as part of the argumentation. The vagueness contained in E2 and E3 contributed to this charitable decision.

Generally, the language is neutral in its tone, which is a strength. The definition in paragraph B, while awkward, is adequate to the student's purpose. It assigns the question of assisted suicide to the euthanasia debate and identifies the main characteristic as helping someone to take his or her own life. It would clarify things further to add that the practice is illegal and that it usually arises in cases of terminal illness.

We had to interpret C1 as referring to the main claim, as presenting the arguer's main reason for the overall position. Here we used the context to resolve the question of vagueness surrounding 'this' and its referent.

Two other things worth mentioning concern F3 and F6. The charge of slippery slope reasoning is unclear. We understand the arguer to be attributing a bad slippery slope argument to the opposing viewpoint, where the practice is seen to lead to routine acts of euthanasia. But we had to make this interpretation ourselves using what we know of slippery slope arguments. The onus was on the arguer to be clearer. F6 is a rhetorical question that masks an assertion. Including F6 as a subconclusion involved recognizing that assertion. As a practice, the use of rhetorical questions is to be discouraged because the audience may miss entirely the statement that is being made.

Reasoning

We will look first at the macro-structure of the argument and consider the sub-arguments as the need arises.

We have taken the hidden main claim to be that assisted suicide should be legal. Most of the claims given in support of this are relevant to it. If people should have the right to decide when they die and what is best for them, then C1 and D3 increase our reasons for holding the HMC. Likewise, if members of society have some sort of duty to give such assistance, then D4 is relevant. H1 certainly increases the case for the HMC if there are no good reasons for not legalizing assisted suicide. Again, F6, G3, and H2 all provide relevant considerations for the HMC, if those claims are deemed acceptable. Thus the argument exhibits the general strength of internal relevance of its subclaims to the HMC.

Serious concerns arise, however, when we start to consider whether those claims are acceptable in themselves or adequately supported. Some of these are difficult to decide about. Many audiences would accept C1 as expressing a common value, and added to this is the relevant support of D1, which also forms part of the shared values of many audiences. But if we assume a hostile

ESSAYING AN ARGUMENT |

audience for this argument, then both C1 and D1 could be questioned, at least to the extent of requiring further reasons for accepting them. Someone who believes that human lives are governed by divine authority may not accept C1, or even D1, and such beliefs can fairly be attributed to the hostile audience for this argument. Given this, it would be wise for the arguer to address this feature of the opposing viewpoint.

D3 suffers from the same weakness and D4 even more so. D4 is a crucial claim since it covers not the right of an individual to be assisted, but the duty of others to assist. No such duty is obvious and the claim is very controversial. Even a sympathetic audience might be bothered by it. Undefended, we have no reason to accept D4. And since it was crucial to the HMC, its questionable status is a serious blow to the sufficiency of the argument.

The sub-argument leading to H1 is also a concern. H1 claims there are no good reasons not to allow assisted suicide. If correct, it provides very strong evidence for the HMC. But only one reason against assisted suicide has been considered. While F4 is relevant to H1, it is not sufficient for it, in part because H1 is worded so strongly. The acceptability of F1 becomes important to this sub-argument. We have no reason to accept that there is only one reason against assisted suicide. In fact, in our consideration of C1 and D1 we have already recognized one other. So F1 is contradicted by what we know, and thus is unacceptable. The one reason given is the slippery slope argument suggested by F2 and F3. Why the arguer believes the abuse envisioned at the end of this slope will not happen is unclear. The arguer has failed to give any evaluation of the suggested slippery slope. F2 and F3, while relevant to F4, do not provide sufficient support for it and so F4 cannot be accepted. This renders ineffective an important sub-argument and reveals the arguer's appearance of objectivity to be quite the opposite.

The author believes in F6 that legalizing assisted suicide may decrease the number of abuses. F5 provides relevant support for this. But again, F5 itself lacks adequate support. The implied analogy with back-alley abortions seems plausible. But we cannot evaluate it unless we have reason to believe that the one analogue exists: that is, that there are current cases of botched assisted suicides. Such evidence may exist, but the arguer has not provided any of it, and the acceptability of F5 requires that it be given.

G3, while a very controversial reason, does stand up to scrutiny. G1 reports a common state of affairs and G2 expresses a value that even a hostile audience is likely to share. Together they provide adequate support for G3. But G3 will be subject to serious counter-argument just because it is controversial to weigh such costs against human lives.

H2, on the other hand, stands alone. Like A3, it purports to express a general sentiment. But the claim that 'most people' want to have assisted suicide requires the backing of a recognized poll or survey before we will have reason to accept it.

The only remaining aspect of the reasoning to be evaluated is the argument from analogy provided in C3 and C4 as support for C2. This is an often-used comparison and it carries some force. In both cases we have beings we love (animals or humans) and who are suffering. In the one case (animals) we painlessly end that suffering. So we should do the same in the other case. Of course, what is at issue is the difference between analogues. Animals have no say in the decision to provide euthanasia. But this difference *adds* to the strength of the argument from analogy in cases where the patient has asked to die (the cases of concern to the arguer). The remaining key difference is the value assigned to human and animal lives. People generally, including those who invoke divine authority, would assign greater value to humans than animals. Many audiences would be persuaded by this argument from analogy, seeing the greater value assigned to humans as a further reason to avoid human suffering. This makes for quite a strong argument from analogy. We should note, however, that the hostile audience envisioned above would also assign greater value to human life (because of a special relationship to the divine), but not see this as inconsistent with their stand against assisted suicide.

Strengths and Weaknesses

Strengths	Weaknesses
– good internal relevance of subclaims to HMC	– a number of points of vagueness
– reasonable argument from analogy (C3-C4)	– key claims D1, D3, and D4 are questionable
– Acceptable sub-argument G3	– sub-argument F4 for H1 is unacceptable
	– sub-argument to F6 is questionable
	– H2 requires statistical support
	– insufficient evidence for HMC

On balance this argument as it stands must be rejected. This is not due to the longer list of weaknesses but to the more detrimental nature of some of those weaknesses. In spite of being characterized by strong internal relevance, the argument has too many claims that cannot be accepted or whose acceptability cannot be determined. D4 is crucial here since it deals with the important matter of whether people should assist others to die. D4 is the only statement that deals with this aspect of the issue, but we are not given information to accept it. The appearance of objectivity is lost due to the inadequacy of the sub-argument to H1. On examination, we see that the arguer has not really considered what is at stake in the opposing viewpoint. The problematic nature of these claims, together with that of F6, means that there is not sufficient evidence for the HMC and the argument is unpersuasive.

Many of these flaws, however, are of a kind that might be remedied. While the sub-argument H1 rests on the misconception in F1 and would have to be replaced or substantially rewritten, the sub-arguments to C1 (and D1), F6, and H2 could all conceivably be strengthened.

In the light of this critique, the student's draft clearly needs a good deal of polishing. Taking note of our comments, we will rework the argumentative essay we have been analysing. We are not suggesting that what follows is how the student would rewrite the essay. This is our rewriting of the argument, and in many respects it is more than would be expected after a first critical thinking course. But we also have an obligation to discharge: having critiqued the paper, we submit our own, which we invite you to critique. Usually, a rewrite like this would pass through a number of drafts. In this case, you will only see the final draft, but in your own revisions you should be aware that rewriting is a progressive job that may require a number of revisions. In proposing the following revision, we must also emphasize that other possible revisions could successfully amend the draft with which we began.

5. REVISION

The Case for Assisted Suicide

In the 1990s one issue that has caused public controversy and attracted media attention is assisted suicide, seen as a form of active euthanasia. As progress in medical technology allows people with terminal illnesses to live longer, and with similar advances in pain control, the question arises whether people have the right to say 'No' and, if they are unable to end their own lives, have others assist them in dying. A number of high-profile cases in the United States and Canada have brought home the human drama involved in this issue.[1]

We hold that assisted suicide should be available for those terminally ill patients who request it, either at a crucial stage in their illness or in an advance directive, and that legislation should be enacted to accommodate such requests. We will argue that (a) the fear of unnecessarily drawn out and distressing death is an evil that society should strive to avoid; (b) just as people have a right to life, so they have a right to give up that life if no one else is directly harmed; and (c) that legislation to allow assisted suicide will permit the regulation of the practice and so prevent current and future abuses.

In this essay, 'euthanasia' will be understood to mean the act or practice of painlessly putting to death persons suffering from incurable and distressing diseases,[2] and 'assisted suicide' will be understood as the provision of advice or the means for someone in such a condition to commit suicide. We will treat assisted suicide as one aspect of the practice of euthanasia, without going into the details of the relationship between the two.

(a)

As a society we have an obligation to eliminate evil wherever we recognize it and are able to do so. This conforms to our common set of values. Where we disagree is in our identification of what is evil. Pain and suffering, however, can be thought of as evil where it leads to no valuable outcome and diminishes the quality of life of those suffering. In the case of people dying from advanced distressing illnesses, with no hope of recovery, their continued suffering should be counted an evil and, consequently, something that society is obliged to eliminate.

(b)

This does not mean that society's duty to eliminate suffering outweighs all other values. The principle of respect for autonomy[3] recognizes that people have a right to live their lives as they wish and have their decisions respected. Thus a society must respect an individual's choice to live with his or her suffering. But by the same principle, where someone decides, free from interference and pressure, to end his or her life, and requires assistance to do so, then respect for the individual's autonomy should lead us to abide by that person's wishes.

The right that people have to life, widely respected in civilized societies, carries with it the right of a rational individual to give up that right, to choose to die. There is little point in having fundamental rights if we do not also have control over the exercising of those rights, and this involves giving up those rights when they conflict with our values and desires.

It will be objected that humans do not have ultimate control over their lives, that they are subject to divine authority and it is God who will decide how and when they die. There are a number of reasons not to be persuaded by this. firstly, this argument loses its force in a pluralistic society such as we see throughout North America. As society becomes more and more secularized, the theistic view becomes one perspective competing with others. Secondly, even where divine authority is recognized, human agency can still be seen as the expression of divine desire. God, on these terms, has favoured humans with Reason, and Reason judges that undue suffering is bad and should be ended. Medical interventions constantly subvert the natural course of events through things like vaccinations and surgeries. Thus humans have a significant role in the control and maintenance of human life. finally, it is part of the historical record that parts of the Christian church have recognized the justification of killing—in war, in self-defence, in cases of capital punishment. If justification can be shown for assisted suicide, then there are precedents for religious acceptance of it.

(c)

A major point against our position is that it will lead to cases of abuse. Critics point to the Netherlands, where controlled physician-assisted suicide is permitted, as a situation where relaxed legislation has led to people being killed *against* their will.[4] That a practice can be abused is not necessarily a reason to prohibit the practice itself. Clearly, any legislation permitting assisted suicide would have to be carefully worded and include provision for strict regulation. Should abuses be identified elsewhere, those cases will be instructive in avoiding cases here. But even allowing that some abuses may arise from the practice of assisted suicide, we would argue that they, as future and therefore avoidable abuses, are outweighed by current abuses that result from the absence of regulation.

There is ample evidence of 'botched' suicides comparable to the cases of 'botched' abortions prior to legislation to permit that practice. In his study *Euthanasia, Assisted Suicide and* AIDS, social worker Russel Ogden interviewed 17 people who had assisted in suicides.[5] Some of these suicides were botched due to outdated drugs or improper information. They resulted in prolonged deaths and additional suffering for those who died. Ogden himself has compared the current situation to the equivalent of back-alley abortions. The practice goes on in secrecy, shrouded with fears of criminal proceedings if caught, and the results are often painful and emotionally distressing for those involved. This is a situation that legislation could address.

In conclusion, there are strong reasons supporting the legalization of assisted suicide under strictly controlled circumstances. Polls indicate wide public sympathy for such a cause and juries have shown an unwillingness to convict those who assist in suicides.[6] The time has come to change the law and respect the wishes of those who choose to die but need assistance if they are to have a good death.

Notes
1. In the United States Dr Jack Kevorkian and his suicide machine have received wide media exposure due to a number of suicides. In Canada, the case of Sue Rodriguez, who was denied the right to assisted suicide by the Canadian Supreme Court, received enormous national sympathy.
2. H.C. Black, *Black's Law Dictionary*, 6th edn (St Paul, Minn: West Publishing Co., 1990).
3. See Peter Singer, *Practical Ethics*, 2nd edn (Cambridge: Cambridge University Press, 1993), p. 195.
4. According to the Report of the Remmelink Committee established by the Dutch government, there are about 2,300 cases of euthanasia each year, 400 cases of physician-assisted suicide, and 1,000 cases of involuntary euthanasia. In virtually all involuntary cases, doctors issued false certificates of 'natural' death.
5. Russel Ogden, *Euthanasia, Assisted Suicide and* AIDs (New Westminster, B.C.: Peroglyphics Publishing, 1994).
6. See Anne Mullens, 'Euthanasia: Dying for leadership', *Toronto Star*, 15 Oct. 1994. After Michigan legislators wrote a law specifically to prevent Jack Kevorkian from continuing to assist suicides, a jury refused to convict him.

6. CONCLUSION

Assisted suicide is a highly controversial and often divisive issue, but it is just the kind of issue that demands clear, critical thinking. The benefits of the skills we have discussed throughout this text should be recognized when you work on issues such as this. Since it is such a controversial issue, we have no doubts that impressive argumentation can be constructed for the opposite point of view from that which has been advocated in our rewrite.

Good reasoning is not limited to our thinking about difficult issues, however. It permeates all corners of our lives, clarifying our ideas and enriching our experiences. We wish you all the best in your dealings with arguments, with those you construct and those you evaluate. We hope you will continue to build on the skills discussed here and value your development as a critical thinker. Good reasoning is often difficult, but it always matters!

MAJOR EXERCISE 13M

1. Diagram the revised essay and write an evaluative critique of it.
2. Research and write an evaluative essay that supports the opposite position to that argued in the revision.
3. Select a topic from the list below or propose a controversial topic for approval by your instructor. Research it and reflect on it, and then write an argumentative essay (about four double-spaced typewritten pages in length, or 1,000 words). Assume a universal audience.
   a) gun control
   b) human embryo experimentation
   c) homeopathy
   d) the morality of zoos
   e) United Nations peacekeeping
   f) affirmative action
   g) gene manipulation
   h) DNA testing in criminal cases
   i) universal medicare
   j) workfare vs. welfare

EXERCISE

ANSWERS

CHAPTER 1

Exercise 1M

1. The following is excerpted from an article by Laurier Sarkadi that originally appeared in the *Edmonton Journal* (20 Dec. 1990).

Sex assaults in North are often less violent, judge says

A Northwest Territories judge says sexual assault among Northern natives is sometimes less violent and cannot always be judged in the same light as southern Canadian cases.

. . . Bourassa incensed native women's groups in April 1984 when he sentenced three Inuit men convicted of having sexual intercourse with a consenting, mentally deficient 13-year-old girl to one week in prison and eight months probation.

Bourassa's sentence was based on the belief Inuit culture accepted that 'when a girl begins to menstruate she is considered ready to engage in sexual relations.'

The territorial Court of Appeal increased the sentence to four months without probation.

In a very strongly worded editorial the newspaper accused Judge Bourassa of racism and sexism and called for his dismissal from the bench. In response to a public outcry this sparked, the Judicial Council of the Northwest Territories appointed Madam Justice Conrad to head an inquiry into Bourassa's alleged comments and judicial conduct. In her report she writes that 'I found it difficult to come to any conclusion other than that the article [above] was slanted against Judge Bourassa, and that it did not present a balanced view of him.' Her more specific findings illustrate the kinds of slanting discussed in Chapter 1. The following are particular instances.

Distortion
1. The charges of racism stem from the suggestion that Judge Bourassa said that there was a difference between native and non-native cases of rape. On investigation it turned out that the judge never used the word 'native', a point admitted by the reporter. Rather he distinguished between 'northern' and 'southern' cases of rape. The reporter incorrectly treated 'northern' as equivalent to 'native'. Though the majority of northern cases involve natives, many of them don't and it was wrong to construe the judge's remarks as remarks about racial differences.

Omission
1. In discussing the 1984 case, the article creates the impression that the territorial Court of Appeal was decidedly critical of Bourassa by mentioning only that it increased the sentence. It neglects to mention that Chief Justice W.A. McGillivray, speaking for the Court of Appeal, stated that 'We are all of the view that [Bourassa's] judgment as a whole is thoughtful and careful and that the learned trial judge has considered all the matters that should have been present to his mind, including deterrence, not only to these accused, but to others.'
2. In discussing the 1984 case, the article suggests that Bourassa's sentence was based on the belief Inuit culture accepted that 'when a girl begins to menstruate she is considered ready to engage in sexual relations.' This was only one of a number of considerations in the case, and this is a partial quotation. The point made in the full quotation is not that Inuit culture makes it permissible to violate Canadian laws on rape, but the claim that because of this it was likely that 'the offenders grew up with this attitude and did not consider the act as illegal.' If this is so, then the offenders did not have the *mens rea* necessary to fully commit the accused offence. It follows that this is a case of adhering to, not violating, normal legal standards.

CHAPTER 2

Exercise 2C
12. Indirect arguments, also called implicit arguments, are chains of reasoning attributed to other reasoners without the use of quotes. If I write 'John says he won't take logic because it is not applicable to real life situations', then I attribute to John the implicit argument:

1. P1 = Logic is not applicable to real life situations.
    C = Logic is not worth taking.

Exercise 2D

1. The word 'since' functions as a premise indicator in this passage.

    P1 = We have defined an argument as a unit of discourse that contains a conclusion and supporting statements or premises.

    P2 = Many groups of sentences do not satisfy this definition, and cannot be classified as arguments.

    C = We must begin learning about arguments in this sense by learning to differentiate between arguments and non-arguments.

4. No logical indicator.

    P1 = Money is not an issue for people who have chosen to eat in this restaurant.

    C = You don't need to worry about our recent increase in prices.

5. 'Therefore' functions as a conclusion indicator.

    P1 = In logic, we have an argument whenever we have reasons suggested as premises for a conclusion.

    P2 = Explanations can contain reasoning in this sense.

    C = Explanations can be classified as arguments.

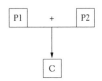

7. 'Because' acts as a premise indicator.

    P1 = Sun Tzu's famous book on *The Art of War* tells us that a success-
           ful military force must act swiftly and cannot sustain a military
           operation for a protracted period of time.
    P2 = Hitler's decision to attack Russia inevitably committed him to a
           long war.
    C = Once Hitler decided to attack Russia, he was bound to fail.

15. In this passage, the word 'deduce' and the question 'Why?' act as logical
indicators. The word 'deduce' tells us that an inference is being made and 'Why?'
is a request for reasons (premises), which are then provided.

    P1 = The claim that the crime was committed by someone strong does
           not support the conclusion that George cannot be the culprit
           until we combine it with the second premise, which tells us that
           George is weak.
    C = These premises are 'linked'.

Major Exercise 2M

1.   P1 = Historians of religion agree that it had its beginnings in magic
           and witchcraft.
    P2 = Today's religious belief is just an extension of this.
    C = Religion is nothing but superstition.

2. This passage contains no logical indicators. It does address a controversial
issue. It is written as a report of a personal reaction rather than as an argument
justifying some conclusion. So we would judge it not to be an argument.

    If we were to treat the passage as an argument, the argument would be:

P1 = Sealing is a Canadian industry that involves cruelty to animals and callous brutalization of men for profit.

C = The seal hunt is sickening.

But this would be a very weak argument (P1 makes very strong claims but they are completely unsupported). The principle of charity thus confirms our decision not to treat the passage as an argument.

10. This is a contribution to a debate—a clearly argumentative context—and offers a clear reason for believing the Bosnian Serbs are justified, so we should treat it as an argument.

P1 = We didn't stand in the way when the Slovenes and Croats—as well as the Bosnian Muslims—sought independence from the then very viable state of Yugoslavia.

C = We don't have a right to deny the Bosnian Serbs their wish to form a separate state of their own in Bosnia.

12. This passage is merely a description, not an argument.

13. Given that this is a remark made in defence of a commitment to the coverage of New Age issues, it is most plausibly interpreted as the following argument.

P1 = When I was going through a recent bout with depression, I sought comfort in Artemis, built an altar to her in my room, burned incense, and meditated, and I found comfort in these ritualistic practices.

C = This type of paganism can be an important tool for women to discover their inner strengths.

CHAPTER 3

Exercise 3A

1. b) The word 'wealthy' is vague. Its meaning needs to be made more precise.
   e) The sentence is ambiguous. It may mean that 'Vitamin E is good for elderly people' or that 'Vitamin E is good for making people older.'
   f) The sentence is vague. It needs to be made clearer what 'by the people' means. It needs to be made clear whether 'democracy' means 'by elected representatives', 'in the people's interests', 'by consensus', 'by 51 per cent majority', 'with regard to minority interests', and so on.
   j) The sentence is ambiguous. It could imply one $100 prize (for both you and your husband) or two (i.e., one each).
2. a) 1. Convicted criminals must compensate their victims for their crimes. 2. Convicted criminals must be dealt with harshly.
   c) 1. The lives of other beings continue after our deaths. 2. One's soul survives after bodily death.
   e) 1. Enabling legislation should be introduced to make passive euthanasia permissible. 2. Enabling legislation should be introduced to make active euthanasia permissible.

Exercise 3B

1. b) An intensional definition of 'cat', by genus (cat) and differentia (immature).
   f) An intensional definition of 'mammal', by genus (four-legged creature) and differentia (suckles its young).
   g) An extensional definition.
   h) A contextual definition.
2. d) The rule of neutrality.
   e) The rule of clarity (few people will know what a 'proximal eructation' is).
   f) The rule of equivalence (other countries—Iceland and Greenland, for example—lie north of the 49th parallel).
   j) The rule of essential characteristics (distance need not be measured by the yard).
   k) The rule of equivalence (other languages—Spanish and Italian, for example—are also Romance languages).
3. c) Liberalism is a political perspective that emphasizes individual liberty (freedom) over state regulation and individual choice over social control. Examples of liberalism are found in the writings of John Stuart Mill, Adam Smith, and F.A. Hayek.

Major Exercise 3M

1. a)   P1 = If people are affected by their environments, by the circumstances of their lives, then they certainly are affected by pornography.

     P2 = Even a fool has the sense to see that someone who wallows in filth is going to get dirty.

C1 = Pornography must necessarily effect evil.

MC = People who spend millions of dollars to try and prove otherwise are malicious or misguided, or both.

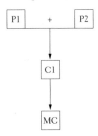

This clearly is a biased argument. The words 'evil', 'fool', 'wallows', 'filth', and 'malicious' show that the author is emotionally committed to his/her viewpoint and may not have considered seriously the views of commentators who argue that pornography does not corrupt, either because it is a healthy extension of sexual desires and needs, or because individuals can rise above its influence.

The passage is particularly problematic because some key terms — 'common sense', 'intuitive', and 'pornography' — are not defined. If 'common sense' means 'views common to everyone', then it is not true that common sense dictates that pornography corrupts, for many people think otherwise. The claim that [knowledge of] the evil effect of pornography is intuitive has not been substantiated and, being subjective, is inaccessible to debate. A better argument would have to make clearer what is meant by pornography, for many would argue that we must distinguish between hard- and soft-core pornography — or 'pornography' and 'erotica' — although what is meant by these terms may itself be a subject for debate.

CHAPTER 4

Exercise 4A

5.   P1 = If his bus was on schedule and he could get a cab straightaway, he'd be here by now.

HP2 = Bill's not here.

C = Either Bill's bus didn't get in on time or there was no cab available.

8.   P1 = Moyers makes virtually no attempt to place the poet in a larger social context—to view poetry as a profession (or, perhaps more to the point, to analyse what it means that ours is a culture where it's all but impossible to be a professional poet).

        P2 = But as Ezra Pound once pointed out in regard to history, we cannot understand poetry without economics—without some sense of the ebb and flow of the megamercantile society surrounding the poet.

     HC = Moyers's program fails to understand poetry.

11.   P1 = You are mortal.

     HP2 = Mortals should not cherish immortal anger.

      C = You should not cherish immortal anger.

Exercise 4C

1. Society is morally obliged to respect a right, but society is not obliged to provide a college education, so a college education is not a right.

     P1 = Society is morally obliged to respect a right.
     P2 = Society is not obliged to provide a college education.
      C = A college education is not a right.

2. Though television beer advertisements encourage sexual stereotypes many do not approve of, they should not be banned, for such action would violate advertisers' freedom of expression.

     P1 = Television beer advertisements encourage sexual stereotypes many do not approve of, but banning them would violate advertisers' freedom of expression.
      C = Television beer advertisements should not be banned.

3. However careful we are, it is always possible that the legal system will convict an innocent person. But killing an innocent person is wrong, so capital punishment is wrong.

P1 = However careful we are, it is always possible that the legal system will convict an innocent person.

P2 = Killing an innocent person is wrong.

C = Capital punishment is wrong.

Major Exercise 4M

2. P1 = Motorists will only obey the speed limits that they perceive as reasonable.

HP2 = Motorists will not perceive a speed limit of 30 kilometres per hour as reasonable.

P3 = Such a low speed limit . . . could have the detrimental effect of increasing fuel consumption and exhaust pollution.

C = Reducing the speed to 30 kilometres per hour on city streets would be unreasonable and unenforceable.

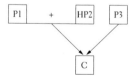

Argument against the conclusion: Pat Curran and the CAA are mistaken when they say that a speed limit of 30 kilometres per hour is unenforceable on city streets. We can reconstruct city streets so that they contain speed bumps and curves that can't be managed at more than 30 kilometres per hour. And if we do so, the 30-kilometre limit will be respected.

P1 = We can reconstruct city streets so that they contain speed bumps and curves that can't be managed at more than 30 kilometres per hour.

P2 = If we do so, a 30-kilometre speed limit will be respected.

C = Pat Curran and the CAA are mistaken when they say that a speed limit of 30 kilometres per hour is unenforceable on city streets.

4. A causal explanation, but not an argument.

5.   P1 = A long time ago, I had a health problem that wasn't solved by a doctor who was a nice guy.

P2 = Finally, I gave up and went to see a doctor who was a jerk but cured me.

HC = When it comes to your health and other important matters, you can usually count on a jerk and not on a nice guy.

(Note that we have designated the conclusion as a hidden conclusion because it contrasts jerks and nice guys. This is not an explicit aspect of the argument, but it is implicit from the premises, which are based on a comparison. The implication is not just that you can count on jerks, but that you can count on them in a way that you can't count on nice guys.)

Argument against HC: I have gone to many doctors, including many jerks. The jerks were no better than the pleasant doctors, and what's more they were a pain to visit. So when it comes to your health and other important matters, you can't tell me that you can rely on jerks more than nice guys.

P1 = I have gone to many doctors, including many jerks.

P2 = The jerks were no better than the pleasant doctors.

P3 = What's more, the jerks were a pain to visit.

C = When it comes to your health and other important matters, you can't rely on jerks more than nice guys.

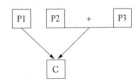

7.　P1 = Politics ordains which of the sciences should be studied in a state.

P2 = Politics ordains which of the sciences each class of citizens should learn and up to what point they should learn them.

P3 = Even the most highly esteemed of capacities fall under this, e.g., strategy, economics, and rhetoric.

C = Politics appears to be the master art.

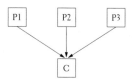

Argument against the conclusion: Modern thinkers on the right and left have recognized that economic interests determine how people act. So economics, not politics, is the master art.

P1 = Modern thinkers on the right and left have recognized that economic interests determine how people act.

C = Economics, not politics, is the master art.

17.　P1 = The nobility want only to oppress.

P2 = The people desire only to avoid being oppressed.

C = The nobles cannot be satisfied if a ruler acts honourably, without injuring others, but the people can be thus satisfied.

Argument for P2: People who are oppressed desire only to avoid oppression. The people are oppressed, hence they desire merely to avoid oppression.

P1 = People who are oppressed desire only to avoid oppression.

P2 = The people are oppressed.

C = The people desire merely to avoid oppression.

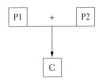

20.   P1 = The pigs in the Media Pig Race weren't racing, they were terrified animals running in a panic from the noise of the crowd.
       P2 = We kill pigs for food, we should not torment them first.
       C = This is a display of cruelty that the *Sun* should not condone by endorsing one of the unfortunate participants.

Argument for P2: Mistreating animals encourages a callousness that is easily extended to mistreatment of humans. So though we kill pigs for food, we should not torment them first.

       P1 = Mistreating animals encourages a callousness that is easily extended to mistreatment of humans.
       C = Though we kill pigs for food, we should not torment them first.

Chapter 5

Major Exercise 5M

1. a) P1 = There is pleasure knowing that events and not an expiring clock will decide when the evening's entertainment is done.
        C = Major League Baseball shouldn't institute new rules designed to speed up the game.

This is a poor argument, primarily because P1 is questionable. In basket-ball, hockey, football, and other sports it is often the race against an expiring clock that adds excitement and pleasure to 'the evening's entertainment'. And if ignoring the clock allows any kind of game to drag on and on, we tend to become bored and exasperated. It follows that the first criterion of good arguments—acceptable premises—is not satisfied in this case.

2. b)   P1 = Strikeouts are a trademark of power pitching.
    P2 = Games are averaging 12.7 strikeouts this season, more than the game has seen in the past.
    C = Pitching is better than in the past.

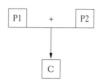

This is a valid argument, for if strikeouts are up (P2 is true) and pitching is worse than in the past (C is false), then it is false that strikeouts are the 'trademark' of power pitching (P1 is false). That is, C cannot be false and both P1 and P2 be true.

e)   P1 = The objective of an argument is to convince an audience.
    P2 = If the objective of an argument is to convince an audience, then it is sufficient for our purposes that the premises of a good argu-ment be accepted as true by both us and our audience (i.e., if P1 then C).
    C = It is sufficient for our purposes that the premises of a good argument be accepted as true by both us and our audience.

This is a valid argument of the form 'P1; if P1 then C; therefore C.' In any such argument, it is impossible for the premises to be true and the conclusion to be false, as that would imply that C is false and that P1 is true, and (because of premise 2) that C is simultaneously true.

3. c) This is an invalid argument, for the X that are Y and the X that are Z may be different. There is nothing that requires that they be the same X. So both premises can be true while the conclusion is false. The following are three examples of arguments of this form:

(i) Let X = dogs, Y = dogs with tails, and Z = dogs with no tails; then the following argument is an instance of the stated form: 'Some dogs have tails. Some dogs do not have tails. So some dogs do and do not have tails.'

(ii) Let X = doctors, Y = rich doctors, and Z = charitable doctors; then the following argument is an instance of the stated form: 'Some doctors are rich. Some doctors are charitable. So some doctors are rich and charitable.'

(iii) Let X = philosophers, Y = intelligent people, and Z = boring people; then the following argument is an instance of the stated form: 'Some philosophers are intelligent. Some philosophers are boring. So some philosophers are intelligent but boring.'

4. a) The law of identity. The statement says that 'the man in the big hat' is equivalent to 'the cowboy' so a song about the former can be said to be a song about the latter.

   d) The law of non-contradiction. The claim is that Sparky Anderson is inconsistent because he both refuses to manage replacement players and manages replacement players (i.e., Mike Christopher).

CHAPTER 6

Exercise 6A

a) *Some* dentists are those who have six-digit incomes. PA
b) *All* dinosaurs are extinct dinosaurs. UA
c) *Some* people *are not* people prepared to pay higher taxes. PN
g) *All* people who know the way I feel tonight *are* lonely people. UA
m) *All* things that are New York (city) *are* things that are in New York (state). UA
n) *All* survivors are courageous people. UA
u) No circumstances *are* circumstances in which the courts should deal leniently with people who drive vehicles while inebriated. UN
w) *All* cars parked on the street whose permits have expired *are* cars that will be towed away. UA

EXERCISE 6B

a) All people who will be admitted are ticket holders.
   It is false that some ticket holders are not people who will be admitted.
   No people who will be admitted are non-ticket holders.
b) Some New Yorkers are people who vacation in Florida.
   Some people who vacation in Florida are New Yorkers.
   It is false that no New Yorkers are people who vacation in Florida.
g) Some donors to the club are non-users.
   Some donors to the club are not users.
   Some non-users are donors to the club.

Exercise 6C

c) All vegetables harvested within the last 48 hours are vegetables that should be considered fresh.

All of these beans are vegetables harvested within the last 48 hours.

All of these beans are vegetables that should be considered fresh.

S = these beans
P = vegetables that should be considered fresh
M = vegetables harvested within the last 48 hours

All M are P
All S are M

All S are P

Major Exercise 6M

1. a) Some cats aren't pests but all cats are pets, so no pets are pests.

Legend:
S = pets
P = pests

M = cats

Form:
Some cats are not pests
All cats are pets

No pets are pests

P1

Some M are not P

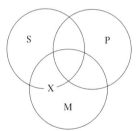

P2

All M are S

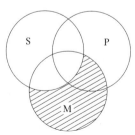

C

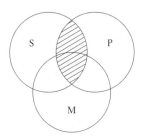

No S are P

We put P1 and P2 together in a Venn diagram:

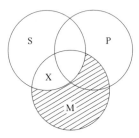

The conclusion is not contained within the premises. Therefore, this argument is invalid.

    b) All buildings over 50 tall are in violation of the new city by-law and the bank building is over 50 tall. Therefore, it is in violation of the by-law.

Legend:	*Form:*
S = bank building	All buildings over 50 feet are buildings in violation of the by-law.
P = buildings in violation of the by-law	All of the bank building is a building over 50 feet.
M = buildings over 50 feet tall	All of the bank building is a building in violation of the by-law

P1

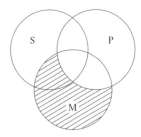

All M are P

P2

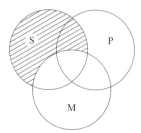

All S are M

C

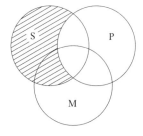

All S are P

We put P1 and P2 together in a Venn diagram:

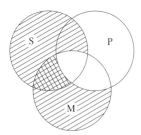

Here we see that the premises shade all of S outside of P, which is what the conclusion requires. Therefore, this argument is valid.

   i) To make love is to engage in battle! This must be true because it takes two to stage a fight and it also takes two to make love.

Legend:	*Form:*
S = acts of lovemaking	All acts of engaging in battle are acts that take two people.
P = acts of engaging in battle	All acts of lovemaking are acts that take two people.
M = acts that take two people	All acts of lovemaking are acts of engaging in battle.

[Note that P2 is not 'All acts that take two people are acts of lovemaking', since the experience of most people contradicts it.]

P1

All P are M

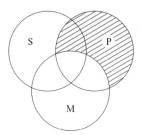

P2

All S are M

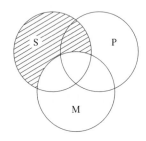

C

All S are P

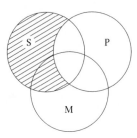

We put P1 and P2 together in a Venn diagram:

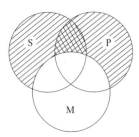

The conclusion requires that the section of S be shaded that overlaps with M and is outside of P. But the premises leave that section of S unshaded. Therefore, this argument is invalid.

2. a) No person who values integrity will go into politics because the realities of political life force people to compromise their principles.
   All people who will go into politics are people whose principles are compromised.

   ───

   No people who value integrity are people who will go into politics.

   Legend: *Form:*
   S = people who value integrity   [   ]
   P = people who will go into politics   All P are M
                                                          ─────────
   M = people whose principles are compromised   No S are P

P

All P are M

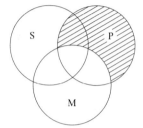

C

No S are P

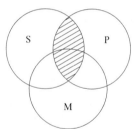

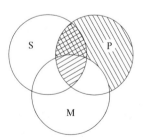

For the conclusion to be contained in the diagram (indicating validity), the hidden premise must relate S and M so as to leave shaded the area shared by S, P, and M. The hidden premise must therefore be: No S are M.

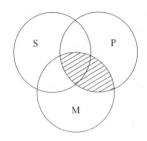

3. a) This syllogism is valid.

     S = this syllogism   All P are M

     P = valid syllogisms   All S are M

     M = syllogisms with three terms   All S are P

   c) No one does wrong voluntarily.

     S = people   All P are M

     P = those who do wrong voluntarily   No S are M

     M = those who are consciously evil   No S are P

Chapter 7

Major Exercise 7M

a) Some valid syllogisms are not syllogisms with a false conclusion. (A is false)
Some valid syllogisms are not syllogisms with acceptable premises. (A is false)

C: No syllogisms with acceptable premises are syllogisms with false conclusions.

Legend: *Form:*

S = syllogisms with acceptable premises   Md O Pu

P = syllogisms with false conclusions   Md O Su

M = valid syllogisms   Sd E Pd

Test:

Rule 1: *Okay:* The middle term is distributed in both premises.

Rule 2: *Violated:* S and P are distributed in the conclusion but not in the premises.

Rule 3: *Violated:* There are two negative premises.

Argument is invalid.

f) All beasts are creatures that know some pity.
    No Richard III is a creature that knows some pity.

    No Richard III is a beast.

S = Richard III	Pd A Mu
P = beasts	Sd E Md
M = creatures that know some pity	Sd E Pd

Test:

Rule 1: *Okay:* The middle term is distributed in the first premise.
Rule 2: *Okay:* Both terms are distributed in the conclusion, but also in the premises.
Rule 3: *Okay:* There is a negative premise, but also a negative conclusion.

Argument is valid.

(j) The writer is arguing that some acts of violence are acceptable because they are a form of self-defence.

Premise: Violence in defence of self or family is usually acceptable. 'Usually' denotes that this is not a universal statement.
              P: Most acts of violence in defence of self or family are acceptable acts.
Conclusion: [No acts of violence are acts that can ever be condoned] is incorrect.
              = Some acts of violence are acts that can ever be condoned.

    S = acts of violence
    P = acts that are acceptable (can ever be condoned)
    M = acts of violence in self-defence

[   ]
Most acts of violence in defence of self or family are acceptable acts.

Some acts of violence are acceptable acts.

[   ]
Mu I Pu

Su I Pu

Test:

Rule 1: To be valid the M term must be distributed in the hidden premise. So it is an A, E, or O.
Rule 2: Not applicable.
Rule 3: To be valid the hidden premise cannot be an E or an O, since there is no other negative statement.

Thus, the hidden premise must be an A statement with the M term distributed:

Md A Su

1) The following syllogism can be extracted:

All killings are uncivilized and barbaric acts.
___
All judicially ordered executions are uncivilized and barbaric acts.

S = judicially ordered executions
P = uncivilized and barbaric acts
M = killings

[   ]
Md A Pu
___
Sd A Pu

Test:
Rule 1: The middle term is already distributed: *Okay.*
Rule 2: S must be distributed in the hidden premise, so it cannot be an I statement.
Rule 3: The hidden premise can be neither an E nor an O, since there is no other negative statement.

Thus, the hidden premise must be an A statement with the S term distributed:

Sd A Mu

CHAPTER 8

Exercise 8A
1. a) Pluto is the planet we should explore.
   d) Pluto or Venus is the planet we should explore. (Or, alternatively, Pluto is the planet we should explore or Venus is the planet we should explore.)
   g) If space is the final frontier and there are humanoids on Venus that eat human beings, then Venus is not the planet we should explore.
   l) Space is the final frontier. If space is the final frontier, then Venus is the planet we should explore. Therefore Venus is the planet we should explore.

2. b) l = We let c = I am a crook.
      r = -c represents Richard Nixon's famous statement 'I am not a crook.'
         l → r
   c) c = Lee Mun Wah produced the film *The Color of Fear*.
         c

(Note that this is a negation of a negation: the first negation is implied by the phrase 'You're wrong . . .', the second by the word 'didn't'.)

    f) v = An argument is valid.
        n = Its conclusion follows necessarily from the premises.
        $v \rightarrow n$

    h) c = You should try Shredded Wheat with cold milk.
        h = You should try Shredded Wheat with hot milk.
        c or h

    k) s = A neighbourhood is safe.
        o = A neighbourhood is organized.
        $s \rightarrow o$

Exercise 8B

1. c) m = You make a mistake.
        d = You say it with a deep enough voice.
        g = You can get away with it.
        $m \rightarrow (d \rightarrow g)$

    f) m = You have multimedia skills.
        v = You have worked on video.
        a = You can apply for the job.
        $(m \text{ or } v) \rightarrow a$

    j) p = I'm paranoid.
        y = You are out to get me.
        $(p \text{ or } y) \& \text{-}(p \& y)$

(Note that this is an exclusive disjunction, for if you *are* out to get me, then I am not paranoid, but see things as they are.)

    k) t = They were there.
        t

(Note that this is a negation of a negation. The first negation is implied by the word 'lying', the second by the word 'weren't'.)

    m) s = You can stand a lot of pain.
        p = You can get a PhD.
        $p \rightarrow s$

(Note that $s \rightarrow p$ is incorrect, for this does not imply that you can get a PhD if you can stand a lot of pain: there are many other requirements as well.)

    r) i = I'm interested in that car.
        m = It's in mint condition.
        $i \rightarrow m$

    v) t = The temperature is constant.
        p = The pressure of a gas varies.

v = The volume of the gas varies.
t → ((p → v) & (v → p))

2. a) a = A person is alive.
s = A person's EEG records brain signals.
(a → s) & (s → a)

d) e = Metal expands.
h = It is heated.
e → h

e) m = Abortion is murder.
p = The fertilized ovum is a person.
(m → p) & (p → m)

3. c) o = The objective of an argument is to convince an audience.
s = It is sufficient for our purposes that the premises of a good argument be accepted as true by our audience.
o → s; o; therefore s

e) w = The Conservatives will win the election.
d = Liberal support will decline in urban ridings.
d → w, -d

Major Exercise 8M

1. a) 1. a → b   P
2. a   P
3. b   1, 2, AA

c) 1. (e or d) & f   P
2. -d   P
3. e or d   1, &E
4. e   3, 2, orE
5. f   1, &E
6. e & f   4, 5, &I

f) 1. a → d   P
2. d → e   P
3. a & b   P
4. a   3, &E
5. d   1, 4, AA
6. e   2, 5, AA
7. a & e   4, 6, &E

2. a) h = The planetary system is heliocentric.
v = Venus will show phases.
p → v; v; therefore p
A case of the fallacy affirming the consequent.

f) h = The government minister is not honest.
t = She can be trusted.

g = She holds a government post.
r = She should return to her law firm.
   1. (-h → -t) & (-t → (-g & r))   P
   2. -h   P
   3. -h → -t   1, &E
   4. -t → (-g & r)   1, &E
   5. -t   3, 2, AA
   6. -g & r   4, 5, AA
   7. r   6, &E

(Note that one could also do this proof by applying the rule CS to lines 3 and 4.)

  g) l = You love our great nation.
     g = You leave it.
     1. l or g   P (what the speaker thinks should be the case)
     2. -l   P
     3. g   1, 2, orE (what the speaker thinks should be the case)

As this proof shows, this is a valid argument. But it is also a case of the fallacy false dilemma, for l and g are not the only two alternatives—if you don't love the nation you might try and change it instead of leaving.

  4. a) l = You should listen to the Zen master's teaching without trying to make it conform to your own self-centred viewpoint.
       a = You will be able to understand what he is saying.
       1. -l → -a   P
       2. a   P (what you want)
       3. l   1, 2, DC
    d) o = The objective of an argument is to convince an audience.
       s = It is sufficient for our purposes that the premises of a good argument be accepted as true by our audience.
       1. o → s   P
       2. o   P
       3. s   1, 2, AA
    f) l = The Liberals will win the election.
       c = Conservative support declines in the rural ridings.
       1. (l → c) & (c → l)   P
       2. -c   P
       3. l → c   1, &E
       4. -l   3, 2, DC
    i) a = Americans will win the most medals at next year's Olympics.
       g = Germans will win the most medals at next year's Olympics.
       r = Russians will win the most medals at next year's Olympics.
       1. a or g or r   P
       2. -r & -g   P

3. -r	2, &E
4. -g	2, &E
5. a or g	1, 3, orE
6. a	5, 4, orE

5. a) a = There is anarchy.
    c = Criminals are punished.
    b = Corporations break the law.

1. -c → a	P
2. b → a	P
3. -a	P (i.e., we don't *want* anarchy)
4. c	1, 3, DC
5. -b	2, 3, DC
6. c & -b	4, 5, &I

   c) The implicit argument has the form: If you were so smart, you would be rich. You're not rich. So you're not so smart. It can be proven valid as follows:

    s = You're so smart.
    r = You're rich.

1. s → r	P
2. -r	P
3. -s	1, 2, DC

   g) z = Zsa Zsa Gabor is 54.
    f = She was only five when she entered and won the Miss Hungary beauty title in 1933.

1. z → f	P
2. -f	P (a hidden premise)
3. -z	1, 2, DC

7. b)
1. b → c	P
2. a → b	P
3. d → a	P
4. -c	P
5. -b	1, 4, DC
6. -a	2, 5, DC
7. -d	3, 6, DC

   e)
1. a → (b & c)	P
2. c → d	P
3. a	P
4. b & c	1, 3, AA
5. c	4, &E
6. d	2, 5, AA
7. a & d	3, 6, &I

CHAPTER 9

Major Exercise 9M

1. c) j = You can join the Air Force.
   e = You're eighteen.

1. j → e		P
2. -e		P/CR
3. -j		1, 2, DC
4. -e → -j		2-3, CR

2. b) Religion fulfils some deep human need. For suppose it didn't. Then it wouldn't be found in virtually every human society. But it is found in virtually every human society. So religion must fulfil some deep human need.

   r = Religion fulfils some deep human need.
   f = It is found in virtually every human society.

1. f		P
2. -r → -f		P
3. -r		P/RAA
4. -f		2, 3, AA
5. f & -f		1, 4, &I
6. r		3-5, RAA

3. a) y = You answer yes to the question 'If I die, would you marry again?'
   n = You answer no to the question 'If I die, would you marry again?'
   w = You will be taken to mean that you are waiting for your spouse to die.
   u = You will be taken to mean that your marriage is unhappy.

1. y or n		P
2. y → w		P
3. n → u		P
4. w or u		1, 2, 3, Dor

   One might try to escape through the horns of the dilemma, though this does not seem promising (the most obvious alternative to y and n is 'I don't know', but it might also be given a negative interpretation, probably by suggesting that it implies that one does not know that one is happily married and may be waiting for one's spouse to die). The best way to answer the dilemma is, therefore, by taking the dilemma by the horns and denying that y → w and/or that n → u. One may, for example, point out that a 'no' answer to the question may mean the opposite of u, for one may not want to marry again because one believes that a new marriage could not match the happiness of the present one.

4. d) j = Jacinth is well.
   f = Francis is well.
   k = Kirstin is well.
   f = Fred is well.

p = Paul is well.
    1. j & -f & -k & (-f or -p)   P
    2. -f or -p   1, &E
    3. f & p   2, DeM

5. c) 1. -(a & b)   P
    2. a   P
    3. -a or -b   1, DeM
    4. -b   3, 2, orE
  d) 1. a & b & c & d   P
    2. -(c or e)   P/RAA
    3. -c & -e   2, DeM
    4. c   1, &E
    5. -c   3, &E
    6. c & -c   4, 5, &I
    7. c or e   2-6, RAA

6. b) h = You do your homework assignments.
  l = You learn informal logic.
  g = You'll be a good reasoner.
  s = You succeed in your chosen field.
    1. (h → l) & (l → g) P
    2. g → s   P
    3. h → l   1, &E
    4. l → g   1, &E
    5. h → g   3, 4, CS
    6. h → s   5, 2, CS
  d) s = You're a great singer.
  y = You're Shakespeare.
  m = The moon is made out of green cheese.
    1. s → (y & m)   P
    2. -(y & m)   P (a hidden premise)
    3. -s   1, 2, DC
  h) d = The court decides for me.
  e = Euthalus must pay.
  w = Euthalus has won his first case in court.
    1. d or -d   P
    2. d → e   P
    3. -d → w   P
    4. w → e   P
    5. -d → e   3, 4, CS
    6. e   1, 3, 5, D
  m) s = The universe stretches forever.
  i = The universe contains an infinite number of stars.
  w = Whichever way you looked, you would see a star.
  l = The sky would be all light.

1. $(s \& i) \to w$ P
2. $w \to l$ P
3. $-l$ P
4. $(s \& i) \to l$ 1, 2, CS
5. $-(s \& l)$ 4, 3, DC
6. $-s$ or $-l$ 5, DeM

7. b) Like the sky in this example, your predicament is dark. You are unlikely to survive, as the following proof shows.

s = You survive.
r = You run to a lifeboat.
l = You will be lost at sea.
c = The storm continues.
d = The sky is dark.

1. r or $-r$ P
2. $r \to l$ P
3. $l \to -s$ P (a hidden premise)
4. $-r \to (-s \to c)$ P
5. $c \to (s \to r)$ P
6. $d \to c$ P
7. d   P
8. $-r$ P/CR
9. c   6, 7, AA
10. $s \to r$ 5, 9, AA
11. $-s$ 10, 11, DC
12. $-r \to -s$ 8-11, CR
13. r   P/CR
14. l   2, 13, AA
15. $-s$ 3, 15, AA
16. $r \to -s$ 13-15, CR
17. $-s$ 1, 12, 16, D

8. a) 1. (p or q) $\& -(p \& q)$ P
     2. p   P
     3. $-(p \& q)$ 1, &E
     4. $-p$ or $-q$ 3, DeM
     5. $-q$ 2, 4, orE

Sample argument: He can spend his money on a present (p) or on a video (q). He'll spend it on a present, so he won't buy a video.

c) 1. $p \to q$ P
     2. $-q$ P/CR
     3. $-p$ 1, 2, DC
     4. $-q \to -p$ 1-3, CR

Sample argument. If he had climbed out the back window (p), there would be footsteps in the flower-bed (q), so if we don't find any, then he didn't climb out the back window.

g) 1. p & -p   P/RAA
   2. -(p & -p)   1-1, RAA

Sample argument: She can't be honest and a liar.

9. The Case of the Missing Brother:
Day 2.   Louis wasn't working the day of his disappearance.
Day 3.   Louis went running when he left the house on Thursday morning.
Day 4.   Louis is not in Montreal.
Day 5.   The note is from the real kidnappers, and they and Louis are in Quebec City.
Day 6.   If Mary had a hand in it she hired her brother Ted.
Day 7.   The anonymous phone call is wrong. (Louis is not held by some strange cult called Cabala.)
Day 8.   Mugsy is a culprit.
Day 9.   The case is a 'SP_____.'
Day 10. You must try the right door.
Day 10½. The police were wrong. (It's not true that Louis is in one of these two rooms.)
Day 11. Louis must be in the third room.
Day 12. This is not a serious kidnapping, but a SPOOF.
Day 13. Louis paid Mary and Mugsy to fool me.
Day 14. You charge me the full rate.
Day 15. . . . send the bill to Louis.

CHAPTER 10

Exercise 10A
1. a) Audience profile: university students:
   Likely above-average intelligence; general basic knowledge; interest in issues affecting education; likely in late teens to early twenties, but demographic is changing; likely to have strong social conscience with an interest in changing things for the better; interest in popular culture.
4. a) Acceptable by definition. According to the meanings of the terms 'cause' and 'effect', we know this statement to be true.
   b) Unacceptable according to common knowledge. However much the vestiges of the old structure remain, it is generally known that the Soviet Union has changed politically, economically, and even geographically.
   g) The first statement is supported by reasonable premises and is acceptable on that basis.
5. b) The premise (second statement) begs the question in relation to the claim (first statement). It expresses the same idea in different language without producing support for an argument.

Exercise 10B

1. a) and b) together connect the ideas of suffering, animals, and the experiencing of pain. Thus, they increase our reasons for holding the claim and are relevant to it. c) is irrelevant to the claim. Although it may be acceptable, it does not support the wrongness of inflicting suffering. d) provides negative relevance for the claim. It weakens the belief that the infliction of suffering is wrong. Being stewards of Nature (e) in no way entails not inflicting suffering on animals. This statement is irrelevant to supporting the claim.

Exercise 10C

1. The claim is not qualified in any way. It advocates boxing without conditions. People who support prohibiting the sport argue that it is dangerous (professional boxers die in the ring), aggressive, and demeaning as a 'sport' (watching grown men hurt each other). Arguably, the five reasons offered respond to these concerns.

    The premises provide balance in that they acknowledge the charge of dangerousness [(b) and (d)] and respond to it. Premise (c) can be seen to respond to the charge of aggressiveness, and (e) meets the objection that this is not a 'sport'. Both (a) and (c) offer positive reasons for the claim.

    Still, the support here is contentious and the statements may not be acceptable. We may also doubt that the charges have been adequately met rather than just recognized.

Major Exercise 10M

1. 1 [Elementary school teachers should be better paid than university professors]. The reasons for this are as follows. 2 [The complex material dealt with at university requires that students be well-grounded in basic skills of reading and writing]. 3 [And according to many educators] 4 [elementary school teachers teach students in their most formative years when basic skills are best taught]. Therefore, 5 [the job of elementary school teachers is more important than that of university professors].

    Furthermore, 6 [people should be paid according to the importance of their jobs to society]. And lastly, 7 [university professors are already overpaid].

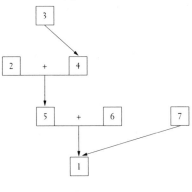

Together, the subconclusion 5 and statement 6 are relevant to the MC (1). If one job is more important than another and more important jobs should be better paid, then elementary school teachers should be better paid.

Again, statements 2 and 4 provide relevant support for 5, increasing its strength. Although the authority for 4 provided by statement 3 is weak ('many educators' is vague and unspecified), statement 4 would seem largely a matter of common sense and to share the common acceptability of 2. However, 2 and 3 are not sufficient support for 5. They show the importance of the job done by elementary school teachers, but not that it is more important than that done by university professors because they are not balanced with an assessment of university professors' contributions.

Statement 6 is important to the support 5 provides for the MC. But 6 itself is unsupported. It is evaluative and certainly does not report a state of affairs. Thus it remains questionable until supported. Statement 7 is an interpretation and one that is irrelevant to the MC.

On balance, the argument has merit but lacks enough support for the subconclusion. An assessment of what professors contribute (showing it to be less important) and support of statement 6 would be needed to make the argument a strong one.

2. 1 [Astronomy, however, is accessible to everyone]. 2 [For only a modest investment, anyone can purchase or build a telescope and begin viewing the sky. . .]. 3 [Magazines such as *Sky & Telescope* and *Astronomy* are written for amateurs and help them keep up with the latest research results]. 4 [In addition, many books for the nonscientists have been written on a variety of astronomical subjects, from the origin of the solar system to the future of the universe].

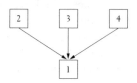

'Accessible' in the conclusion is ambiguous. Does it mean everyone can afford astronomy as a hobby, or that everyone can understand the principles of the science? Statement 2 supports the first of these meanings; statements 3 and 4 the second. So we will charitably understand it to involve both senses of 'accessible'.

This understanding allows for the relevance of all three premises to the conclusion. Statement 2, though, is questionable since 'modest investment' is unclear. Given the strong wording of the conclusion — 'accessible to everyone', we cannot judge 2 sufficient for the monetary sense of 'accessible' in the conclusion without clarification of what 'modest' means.

Statement 3 appears to report a statement of fact that could be checked, and so is acceptable. Common knowledge allows the acceptability of statement 4. But again, the 'everyone' of the conclusion suggests that the support of 3 and 4 is insufficient. A large segment of the adult population of North America has poor literacy skills, and the premises also exclude most children.

The premises (even statement 2) would support a qualified conclusion like 'Astronomy is accessible to most (many) people.' But the support is insufficient for the conclusion given.

8. 1 [The noisy demonstrations against First Choice television are a blatant display of malicious selfishness]. 2 [The hormonal chemistry of the sexes is such that women do not derive pleasure from watching semi-nude buxom blondes]. 3 [Women derive analogous sexual titillation from soap operas and romance novels]. Therefore, 4 [women objecting to male enjoyment of the female form are like deaf people demanding prohibition of music because they are incapable of enjoying it themselves].

We judge this argument contextually irrelevant. Were women objecting to the programming because they could not enjoy it? The background suggests otherwise, and this argument does not address the real issue.

Internally, the statements exhibit relevant support. If people demand that something be prohibited because they cannot enjoy it, then that supports a charge of selfishness. And if women are incapable of enjoying this material, then that increases support for the analogy in 4.

When we examine the acceptability of the premises, however, further weaknesses arise. Besides the fact that deaf people can enjoy music, the subconclusion 4 still needs the support of 2 and 3 to have any chance of being acceptable. As we saw in our earlier discussion of unacceptability versus questionability, statement 2 is unacceptable—it lacks the support of scientific study and is contradicted by the existence of women who do derive pleasure this way. Statement 3 is unacceptable because we cannot conceive of any plausible study that would provide adequate support for it.

Therefore, this is a very weak argument (contextual irrelevance, unacceptable premises) with few merits.

10. Whether or not [William of Sherwood] was a student at the University of Paris, we have several reasons for believing that 1[he was a master there]. In the first place, 2[he lived at a time when 'scholars were, indeed, to a degree which is hardly intelligible in modern times, citizens of the world' and when 'almost all the great schoolmen . . . taught at Paris at one period or other of their lives']. Secondly, 3[in each of his two main works Sherwood uses an example with a Parisian

setting: in one case the Seine, and in another the university]. Finally, 4[all the philosophers who show signs of having been influenced directly by Sherwood or his writings were in Paris at some time during a span of years when he certainly could have been lecturing there].

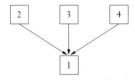

This historical argument requires that we accept the authority of the scholar who produced it. Since each of the reported facts (and statements 2, 3, and 4 all report facts) can be verified, we can accept the premises on the grounds of the reasonableness of the authority.

Each premise provides relevant support for the conclusion. The presence of most great schoolmen in Paris (2) increases the probability that Sherwood was there. Likewise, Parisian settings (3) suggest an acquaintance with the city. Finally, Paris seems a common ground for Sherwood and those he influenced (4).

However, the relevance provided for 1 is not that strong in the case of 2 and 3, and they do not directly support the hypothesis that Sherwood was a master at the University of Paris. Only statement 4 provides direct support for that. So on balance, much more evidence is required to strengthen the argument.

CHAPTER 11

Exercise 11A

2. b) There are a number of things wrong with this generalization. First of all, a month isn't a really long time for a survey. Secondly, chances are this is quite possibly a private health club; at any rate, it probably is not completely representative of the general population but only of those who belong to the club or who can afford to belong. Thirdly, this survey is not representative of people in Johnsonville as such, but only of those people who work out—a smaller and selected group. And finally, just because these people may work out twice a week doesn't mean they're healthy—or at least, we don't have the evidence to claim that. There are often any number of factors that would differentiate working out or even being fit from being healthy.

Exercise 11B

1. c) There is no evidence that there is any causal connection between Bob wearing his suspenders and winning at poker. It cannot be demonstrated that it is anything more than mere chance or superstition.

Exercise 11C

1. c) This is an argument from analogy.
   Analogues: We can do a computer simulation of (C1) the pattern of power distribution in the Labour party, (C2) rain storms, or (C3) warehouse fires.

   Premise: nobody supposes that the computer simulation is actually the real thing (that a computer simulation of a storm will leave us all wet).
   MC: There is no reason to suppose a computer simulation of mental processes actually has mental processes.
   Simplified:
   P1: Computer simulations of the pattern of power distribution in the Labour party, rain storms, warehouse fires, and mental processes are all similar in that they can be given a formal description.
   P2: Simulations of power distribution, rain storms, or warehouse fires are not real.
   C: Simulations of mental processes are not real.

   Assessment: The difficulty lay in organizing the argument more than in analysing it. The premises do not seem grounded on questionable claims. Searle's claim is that while computers can simulate mental processes, they cannot have them. We could look for dissimilarities in the differences between fires and rain and mental processes. But that would be to miss the point. It is not those things that are involved, but simulations of them. From this point of view, Searle offers a reasonable analogy.

4. b) This appeal from precedent also bears a resemblance to an argument by analogy and a slippery slope argument. The idea is that opening abortion clinics, as a legal activity, implies social sanction (for the percentage that agreed to legalize abortion clinics). It is argued that this sets a precedent for the opening of other venues, such as casinos and pornographic theatres. Moreover, it compares the doctors or social workers who open clinics to members of organized crime and porn movie producers—in other words, the doctors are engaged in immoral and criminal activity, even if it is presently legal under current law. This would appear to be a problematic argument, even if one is pro-life. While you may be against abortion, and may even feel that the doctors performing it are immoral, it is extreme to liken it to organized crime or porn movie producers. Furthermore, although casinos and porn movies are legal, as is abortion in many places, it is difficult to compare the reasons for frequenting or taking advantage of the services of the former, with the reasons for going to the latter. And for the same reason, those individuals taking part in the different activities—gamblers, porn movie viewers, and women seeking abortions—would not seem comparable in ways that support the claim that a bad precedent is being set.

Major Exercise 11M

2. a) This could be seen as an appeal to precedent, and even a slippery slope. In the first instance, it's saying that once we allow ourselves to tamper with and change someone else's artistic product, there is a precedent for modifying and changing any work of art, no matter how famous or revered. There is plausibility to this, if we consider that the artist's product is unique and autonomous, and once we have breached that autonomy, there is presumably no difference between changing a movie and changing the *Mona Lisa*. And to the extent that we could read that last formulation as going from a first-instance case to the extreme, this would be the slippery slope aspect.

By the same token, it could be argued that there are significant dissimilarities between the case of a movie, which most often is a more collaborative effort, and a painting, which is more the work of a solo artist (although in Leonardo's time, many paintings were the result of collaborative efforts of several studio artists); colourizing a movie could be read as merely the most recent modification or 'improvement' made to the product. Also, movie-making is a more commercial, some might say less highbrow, art than the paintings of the Old Masters, and as such, it is arguably less sacred when it comes to outside changes.

In sum, depending on how you argue, and what your presuppositions about art and art forms are, this argument could be construed as an acceptable appeal to precedent or as one that has some problems.

d) The survey is undertaken by Playtex, which is one of the leading manufacturer's of lady's lingerie and therefore presumably in a position to make judgements about sizing and fitting. Their survey is based on women who came to bra-fitting clinics, which would be an indication that these women were unsure about the size they wore, and indeed may have been wearing the wrong size, thus lending credence to the relatively high finding of seven out of 10 women. Such high findings have been reported elsewhere also. Whether the sample is too selected is difficult to say—it wouldn't really be possible to poll women outside of such a clinic or to conduct telephone questionnaires on such a topic: most people don't knowingly wear the wrong size of something, so it would seem that polling women at such a sizing clinic is one of the better locations. Where there might be a problem is that we don't really know the size (so to speak) of the sample—how many women were surveyed to arrive at the result? There is also a possible bias, since Playtex could be concluding that women were wearing the wrong size in order to sell them new merchandise. So while this is mostly a plausible generalization, we would need additional information about the size of the sample, the manner in which the survey was conducted, and so forth, before we could judge it a strong generalization.

g) It would be quite reasonable to judge this a report and not an argument. But if we look further, we find some interesting causal reasoning on the part of Farmer Coombs. Despite the initial absurdity of the example, it remains the case that, if he is reliable witness, something caused the phenomenon of hair growth. The reasoning structure is quite simple.

P1 = Primrose licked his pate.
P2 = Hair grew in that spot.
C = Primrose is curing his baldness.

It bears noting that, as a farmer, Mr Coombs would lead a life of fixed routines. Thus, he is likely to notice irregularities in his life. This adds credence to his choice of Primrose licking his head as the key antecedent event prior to the new growth. While there is no correlation to support the causal claim, that is exactly what Mr Coombs is in the process of establishing (or not). So it's too early, perhaps, for a definitive conclusion. Of course, the key factor may be the cattle food dust and not Primrose's licking. The report does not tell us if Farmer Coombs is including this in his experiment.

j) P1 (1): [S]peeding is known to increase the likelihood of car collisions, and drivers are punished for this dangerous behaviour whether or not their particular sprees cause collisions.

P2 (2): Violent pornography, like speeding, is intrinsically dangerous.

C (3): Legislatures may regulate it on the basis of its known propensity for harm without a showing of particular harm.

Recast as the argument from analogy that it is:

P1: Violent pornography (analogue) is like speeding (analogue) in that both are intrinsically dangerous (similarity).

P2: Speeding drivers are punished whether or not their sprees cause collisions.

C: Violent pornography should be punished whether or not particular harm can be shown.

Assessment: This argument from analogy is not strong. It is not clear that the claim made in P1 is the case. This may be challenged and needs support. The intrinsic dangerousness of speeding is acknowledged by mention of its known likelihood to increase collisions; no comparable attempt is made to show something like this to be the case with violent pornography. So the similarity is not established. Moreover, speeding is prohibited, not 'regulated': the conclusion suffers from vagueness here. These concerns point to a problem of dissimilarity. Violent pornography is not like speeding exactly because its harmfulness is less direct and not easy to establish. While both analogues are serious societal problems, the difference in types of harm involved are too great for the argument to be strong.

CHAPTER 12

Exercise 12A

1. a) This is the kind of two-wrongs argument that indicates the usefulness of this kind of reasoning when handling difficult moral dilemmas. It gives us a way to think about the issue. This argument satisfies all three conditions. There is a genuine belief on the part of the citizens who hide these people that they are trying to cancel another wrong: the torture and death of those deported. So the first condition is met. Breaking the law by harbouring illegal aliens is a civic wrong, but one that has to be seen as permissible if the alternative involves the deaths of those refugees. This meets the second condition. The third condition is always the hardest. Here we might imagine morally preferable alternatives like convincing the government to allow these people to stay or urging the United Nations to put pressure on South Amercian governments to change their behaviour. But are these alternatives practical? Many would argue that they are not.

2. a) For a two-wrongs-by-analogy argument to work in this case, you would have to show that the two circumstances are relevantly similar and/or have no relevant dissimilarities. That would be difficult here. The two analogues are 'exemption due to a serious medical condition' and 'exemption due to a sick father'. They are similar in that a sickness is involved, but not to the relevant person. Unless the sickness of the father is expected to be prolonged (which would change the circumstances), the best that might be fairly expected is a postponement of the exam. A serious medical condition in the examinee, however, warrants exemption rather than postponement. Under the circumstances, allowing the one and not the other would not be inconsistent.

Exercise 12B

1. c) P1: The experts admit it's not if you will be the victim of a break-in, but when.
    HC1: You will be the victim of a break-in.
    P2: Psychiatrists, Psychologists, Criminologists, Security Experts and Police Officials all agree: 'The earlier the intruder is discovered, the more effective the security system.'
    HC2: You need a security system that detects the intruder earlier.
    HP: The Astro-Guard Security System detects the intruder earlier.
    HMC: You should buy an Astro-Guard Security System.

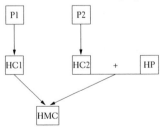

Assessment: The context indicates we are dealing with argumentation, but the key claims are hidden, allowing readers to draw the conclusions for themselves. But are these conclusions warranted? Both sub-arguments depend on weak appeals to authorities. P1 is too vague to play any meaningful role as support. Experts must be identified, and here they are not. P2 tells us about the groups being appealed to, but not their specific identities. We do not know whether all members of the groups would agree with the statement. But such seems unlikely. Thus, we cannot even determine whether there is likely to be agreement among the experts.

3. d) Diagrammed, the argument appears this way:

PI = Dr Bethune was a self-confessed Communist.

P2 = The morality of a person's acts must be judged by their consequences.

C1 = When Bethune placed his medical skills and humanism at the service of international Communism, he unquestionably contributed to an evil ideology that produced many mountains of corpses.

HC = This involvement in evil shows him to have been immoral.

C2 = It is not possible to honour Dr Bethune as a humanitarian.

MC = When Canadians naïvely eulogize Dr Bethune they unwittingly endorse Communist ideology.

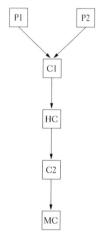

There is a double charge of guilt here, one against Bethune and the other against Canadians who eulogize him. Both are weak. We can accept P1 as common knowledge or at least knowledge that is readily accessible. Bethune was a Communist. The question is whether his association with a rather large and often segmented political ideology implicates him in any of the crimes that are alleged to have been committed by adherents of that ideology.

Following our diagram, we can see that if HC is the case, there is good reason to accept C2. But problems lie with the terms of the association that support HC. In C1 it is claimed that Bethune 'unquestionably' contributed to an ideology that produced many mountains of corpses. As it stands, this is quite unacceptable. We are not told the extent of that unquestionable contribution, nor are we given any evidence for the 'many mountains of corpses'. There is a further problem with P2 in that it is too limiting, because the morality of a person's acts are often judged not by the consequences, but in light of the motives behind them. The writer does not even consider this.

The guilt-by-association argument fails here because it is not shown either that the Chinese Communists were immoral or that he was associated with them in an immoral way. In consequence, the further claim that Canadians who praise Bethune become associated with Communism is also unsupported.

Exercise 12C

1. To be in a position to construct a good argument from ignorance about ghosts you would need to have conducted, or have access to the results of, a detailed investigation of the phenomenon. This might involve the study of relevant literature, looking at alleged cases of hauntings, and evaluating the results. Or it could also involve searching out alleged cases and investigating them firsthand. Then you would be in a position to construct a reasonable argument. If someone had made a concerted effort to demonstrate the existence of ghosts and failed to come up with any evidence, then that would count against the hypothesis.

Simply postulating the non-existence of ghosts on the speculative grounds that no one appears to have proven otherwise would not constitute a good argument from ignorance.

Major Exercise 12M

4. a) The first statement is background.

MC (2): While smoking kills, those deaths have economic benefits for society.

P1 (3): A person who dies of lung cancer at age 70 will not be hospitalized later with another disease.

P2 (4): The costs of hospitalization tend to increase substantially for people after the age of 70.

P3 (5): Wages forfeited by deceased former smokers are available for other, younger, workers.

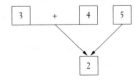

Assessment: This is principally an appeal to authority. The reasoning rests on the authority of Vidal. He is the right kind of authority (economist) for the subject matter, but his authority is weakened by potential bias. Since the report was commissioned (and paid for) by Imperial Tobacco, he might have been inclined to produce a report they would find favourable.

Otherwise, the reasoning is strong on the criterion of relevance. Statement 3 is self-evident. But we have only Vidal's authority to accept statements 4 and 5. Overall, the poor appeal to authority makes this a weak argument.

f)　C: The Attorney-General's Commission's contrary conclusion in 1986 is based more on preconception than on evidence.

P1: An issue that has long divided social scientists . . . can hardly be definitively resolved by a commission of non-experts.

P2: Most of the committee members were appointed because of their pre-existing commitment to the suppression of obscene expression.

P3: [E]ven those who claim a connection between exposure to obscene expression and unlawful conduct claim no more than an indirect and attenuated 'bad tendency'.

MC: Although some individuals may on some occasions commit some unlawful acts because of their exposure to obscene expression, the connection is indirect, speculative, and unpredictable.

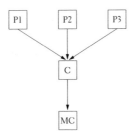

Assessment: Although MC is a causal claim, there is no evidence of a causal nature to support it. Instead, Stone attacks the membership of the commission, charging that they are non-experts (P1) and biased (P2). This amounts to an *ad hominem* attack on the commission members: two features of the members' characters make them unreliable.

But the *ad hominem* is itself not adequately supported. The burden of proof is on Stone to support accusations in P1 and P2, since they are not obvious. Of course, even if adequate, the *ad hominem* would not support the causal claim in MC. Poor argument.

k)　This is a report. But it is a report that contains reasoning: that of Barbie's lawyer. Verges uses two-wrongs reasoning by analogy to justify Barbie's actions during the Second World War. Accordingly, we can set the justification out in the following way:

P1: Mr. Barbie's behaviour was 'no different than' that of loyal French officers during the Algerian war; citizens and officials of France; and even French Jews and members of the Resistance.

P2: The behaviour of those other three groups has been accepted/allowed.

C: Barbie's behaviour should be accepted/allowed.

Assessment: This appeal for similar treatment falls short of meeting all three of the conditions for assessing such reasoning. It is not clear that Barbie's actions, in sending thousands to death camps and allegedly being involved in executions, were analogous to the comparison cases. The numbers involved, the motive of genocide, and his position in authority over those who may have 'assisted' him all weaken the analogy.

On the question of consistent treatment (condition 2), it's not clear that it would be more important given the general attitude toward trying those involved in what is seen as the key act of inhumanity in the twentieth century.

To meet the third condition, Verges would have to argue that there was no morally preferable course of action at the time. In the circumstances, this seems a non-starter. So, on balance, there is nothing to recommend this instance of two-wrongs reasoning by analogy.

INDEX

Abbreviated arguments, 62–3
Acceptability; and belief systems, 197–9;
  of premises 84–9, 195–205; universal
  conditions of, 201–5
Ad hominem, 275–6
Affirming the antecedent (AA), 157–61
Agreements, verbal , 48
Ambiguity, 45–6, 148–9
Analogy: argument from, 216, 250–5; by
  precedent, 255–7
Appeals: to/against authority, 205, 272–9;
  to ignorance, 284–6; to precedent,
  255–7
Argument: abbreviated, 62–3;
  constructing, 19, 74–8; definition of,
  19–20; diagramming, 33–8, 75–6;
  extended, 20–1, 33–4, 38, 75; from
  analogy, 216; indirect, 26–7; simple,
  20–1, 36–8; strength of, 304–5;
  translating, 73, 150; valid and invalid,
  89–93; visual, 72–3
Arguments; Good, 74–8, 84–9
Argument forms, 93–5; *ad hominem*,
  275–6; analogical, 250–7; appeals

to/against authority, 205, 272–9;
  appeals to ignorance, 284–6; appeals
  to precedent, 255–7; biconditional,
  162–3; categorical syllogism, 111–15;
  causal, 238–49; conditional (AA, DC),
  157–61; conditional reasoning (CR),
  174–6; conditional series (CS), 163–4;
  conjunctive (&E, &I), 153–5; De
  Morgan's laws (DeM), 183–4;
  dilemma (D, Dor), 179–83;
  disjunctive (orE), 155–7;
  generalizations, 230–7; guilt by
  association, 280–2; *pro homine*, 270–1;
  propositional, 140–65; *reductio ad
  absurdum* (RAA), 176–9; slippery
  slope, 246–9; two wrongs, 263–8; two
  wrongs by analogy, 267–8
Assumptions, 67–71, 76–8
Audience, 2, 19–20, 51–5, 74, 76–7,
  197–201, 301–2; belief systems of, 19,
  199–201; hostile, 19, 301–2;
  sympathetic, 301; universal audience
  (definition), 77; and specific, 197
Authority, appeals to/against, 205, 272–9

Bad Reasoning, 86–7
Begging the question, 206–7
Beliefs, and claims, 2
Belief systems, 57; and acceptability, 197–9; and audience, 19, 199–201
Bias, 4–16, 144, 233–6, 271, 276, 277; and vested interest, 4–9, 274
Biconditionals, 149, 162–3

Categorical statements, 102–6; A, E, I, O, 130–2; common variations, 104–5; pure forms, 103–4, 106; UA, UN, PA, PN, 103
Categorical syllogisms, 111–5; schematizing, 130–2; testing validity of, 112–14, 115–26
Causal reasoning, 238–49; general, 238–43; particular, 244–6; slippery slope, 246–9
Charity, principle of, 29–30, 58–9
Circular reasoning, 206–7
Claim kinds: descriptive, 202–3; evaluative, 202–3
Claims, and beliefs, 2
Clarity, 48–54, 74–5, 303
Cognitive environments, 203
Common Knowledge, 202–3
Common Variations, 104
Complex propositions, 140–6
Conditional arguments, 157–61, 174–6; rules (AA, DC), 157–61
Conditional fallacies, 161
Conditional reasoning (CR), 174–6
Conditional series (CS), 163–4
Conditional statements, 144–6
Conjunction elimination (&E), 153–5
Conjunction introduction (&I), 153–5
Conjunctions, 142–3, 177–9
Consistency, 177, 255, 267–8
Constant condition, 239–40
Context, 27–30, 44–57, 77
Contextual: definitions, 51–2; relevance, 213–16
Contradiction, 2, 97–8, 108
Contraposition, 110
Conversion, 109–10
Correlations, 240–3, 245

Deductive/inductive distinction, xvi
Definitions, 49–57, 201–2; by genus and differentia, 50–5; contextual, 51–2; conventional and stipulative, 51–2; extensional, 50–5; intensional, 50–5
De Morgan's laws (DeM), 183–4
Denying the consequent (DC), 157–61
Descriptive claims, 202–3
Diagramming arguments, 33–8, 75–6
Digressions, 38
Dilemma, 179–81; answering a, 181–3; rules (D, Dor), 179–83; false, 156–7
Disjunction elimination (orE), 155
Disjunctions, 143–4
Disjunctive arguments, 155–7; rule (orE), 155
Disputes, verbal, 46–8
Distortion, and omission; 9–13
Distribution, 131–2

Equivalence, 53, 96–7, 142, 149
Equivocation, 46–8
Euphemisms, 44–5
Evaluative claims, 202–3
Evaluative critique, 295–9
Existential Interpretation (syllogisms), 135
Explanations, 23–6, 244
Extended arguments, 20–1, 33–4, 38, 75; definition of, 20
Extension, 45, 50–5
Extensional definitions, 50–5

Fallacies: conditional, 161; syllogistic, 132–3
Forms of argument. *See* Argument forms

Generalizations, 230–7; general, 231–2; hasty, 219, 230, 233; proportional, 232–3; universal, 231–2
Guilt by association, 280–2

Hidden conclusions, 63–6
Hidden premises, 66–71, 212–13
Hypotheses, 219
Hypothetical Interpretations (syllogisms), 134

Identity, principles of. *See* Laws of
thought: identity
Ignorance, appeals to, 284–6
Immediate inferences, 107–10; contra-
diction, 108; contraposition, 110;
conversion, 109–10; obversion, 108–9
Immediate perception, 202
Indicators, logical, 21–4, 27–30, 74–5
Inference, rules of, 153–65, 174–85
Informative discourse; 1–3, 14, 46, 50–1;
directly informative; 2–4, 46;
indirectly informative; 2–4
Intended meaning; 3, 38, 44, 48, 53,
57–9
Intension, 45, 50–5
Intensional definitions, 50–5
Invalidity, 89–93; definition of; 93

Justifying good reasoning, 78

Language, 297: functions of, 1–4;
informative, 1–3, 14, 46, 50–1;
mythopoetic, 2; and rhetoric, 74
Laws of thought, 95–8; excluded middle,
97–8; identity, 95–7, 148; non-
contradiction, 97
Logical indicators, 21–4, 27–30, 74–5

Mythopoetic language, 2

Noise, 33–5

Objectivity, 220, 305–6
Obversion, 108–9
Omission, and distortion, 9–13

Particular affirmative statements: PA,
103–6; I, 130–2
Particular negative statements: PN,
103–6; O, 130–2
Precedent, appeals to, 255–7
Premises: acceptable, 84–9, 195–205;
hidden, 66–71, 212–13; linked and
convergent, 35–8; relevant, 88–9,
209–16; sufficient, 88–9, 217–20;
unacceptable, 206–8
Principle of charity; 29–30; 58–9

Principles of identity. *See* Laws of
thought: identity
Probability, 193–5; criteria for assessing,
195
Pro homine, 270–1
Propaganda; 13–15
Propositional arguments, 140–65
Propositions: complex, 140–6; simple,
140–6

Reasoning: causal, 238–49; circular,
206–7; conditional (CR), 174–6; two-
wrongs, 263–8
Red herring, 215–16
Reductio ad absurdum (RAA), 176–9
Reflecting, 77–8
Relevance, of premises, 88–9, 209–16;
contextual, 213–16; internal, 210–13
Rhetoric, 74
Rhetorical questions, 29, 34
Rules of inference, 153–65, 174–85; of
validity, 132–7

Schematization, 130–2
Scope (of project), 301–2
Simple arguments 20–1, 36–8; definition
of, 20
Simple propositions, 140–6
Slanting; 9–13
Slippery slope arguments, 246–9
Square of opposition, 107–8
Statements: categorical, 102–6;
conditional, 144–6; particular
affirmative: PA, 103–5; I, 130–2;
particular negative: PN, 103–5; O,
130–2; universal affirmative: UA,
103–4; A, 130–2; universal negative:
UN, 103–5; E, 130–2
Straw-man, 213–15
Strength (of arguments), 304–5;
acceptable premises, 84–9, 195–205;
relevant premises, 88–9, 209–16;
sufficient premises, 88–9, 217–20;
unacceptable, 206–8
Structure (of essay), 303–4
Sufficiency, of premises, 88–9, 217–20

Syllogisms, categorical: circle diagrams 116–26; definition of, 111–15; schematization, 130–2; testing validity of, 112–14, 115–26

Tone (of words), 45, 50, 54
Translation, 73, 147–50
Two-wrongs reasoning, 263–8; by analogy, 267–8

Unacceptability: of premises, 206–8; universal conditions of, 206–8
Universal affirmative statements: UA, 103–6; A, 130–2

Universal negative statements: UN, 103–6; E, 130–2

Vagueness, 45–6
Validity, 89–93, 112–14; definition of, 93; testing by diagram, 115–26; rules of, 132–7
Variable condition, 239–40
Venn diagrams, 115–26
Verbal: agreements, 48; disputes, 46–8
Vested interest, 4–9, 274

Writing, 48, 49–50, 52, 58, 301–6; clarity, 48–54, 74–5, 303; scope, 301–2; structure, 303–4